"Gene Steuerle is one of the wisest and most generous public policy thinkers at work today. *Contemporary U.S. Tax Policy* is a volume every budget reporter and tax analyst in America will want to keep close at hand."
—Peter G. Gosselin, National Economics Correspondent, *Los Angeles Times*

"I am a long-time fan of Gene Steuerle and his work, most importantly his ability to bring clarity and balance to a debate that is often dominated by partisanship and bias. *Contemporary U.S. Tax Policy* provides a compelling examination of how theoretical arguments have blended with powerful constituencies to shape and reshape tax policy over the past 50 years. Academics as well as tax lawyers should read this concise history."
—Daniel Halperin, Stanley S. Surrey Professor, Harvard Law School

"Gene Steuerle's command of history, combined with his practical experience and savvy economic analysis, make him—and this book—unique. Steuerle is in a class by himself by being able to sort out how idealistic principles, economic ideas, crass self-interest, and unpredictable events have all shaped taxation in America since World War II. His vivid, well-written book is a must read for historians of public policy, and for anyone who wants to understand the complicated and conflicted history of modern tax policy."
—W. Elliott Brownlee, Professor Emeritus of History, University of California, Santa Barbara

"Anyone wondering why the U.S. tax code is the mammoth, miasmic mess that it is need look no further for an answer than Eugene Steuerle's new study of contemporary U.S. tax policymaking. In America, as Steuerle lucidly explains, the tax code has been the great engine of compromise, offering (usually disguised) rewards to virtually every political faction from tax cutters to spending boosters, social engineers and economic stimulators alike. Even if readers do not all agree with Steuerle's 'bittersweet' conclusions, in arriving at that point they will surely have learned enough about the 'tax-policy ropes' to participate knowledgeably in the ongoing debate."
—Jodie Allen, Managing Editor, *U.S. News & World Report*

"I cannot put Gene's new book down. He has done it again. His history of our tax policy over the last 30 years is thoughtful, incisive, stimulating, and quite readable. Whether your interest in the tax area is as an academic, an economist, a journalist, a policymaker, a practitioner, or a regulator, this is a must read."
—The Honorable Larry Gibbs, former Commissioner of Internal Revenue

"The preeminent writer on public finance today brings us a succinct and thorough guide to the exigent yet contested social issue of tax policy. In his clear and compelling prose, Gene Steuerle masterfully reviews the history of endless 'reform' and offers prescriptions for the future. In unpacking the

legislative and administrative process, he identifies the major players, their principles and ideologies, and the winners and losers. This practical volume is essential reading for policymakers as well as practitioners and students of economics, law, accounting, policy studies, and political science."
—Evelyn Brody, Professor of Law, Chicago-Kent College of Law

"This book demonstrates why Gene Steuerle is the country's foremost analyst of tax legislation. It lucidly explains why Congress continually tinkers with the tax code, and how their efforts rob the government of revenue and taxpayers of fairness. Steuerle is truly remarkable in bringing understanding and insight to this complicated area of public policy."
—Allen Schick, School of Public Affairs, University of Maryland

"Gene Steuerle's clear, concise analysis and ability to put tax law changes in historical perspective makes this book an essential part of any tax course with a policy component."
—Richard Sansing, Associate Professor of Business Administration, Tuck School of Business at Dartmouth

"This is an accessible and engrossing analysis of recent tax policy by an important participant in the process, full of useful facts and plenty of interesting anecdotes. The U.S. tax system's current state may be difficult to justify, but it will be easier to understand after one reads Steuerle's account of how & why things happened."
—Alan J. Auerbach, Robert D. Burch Professor of Economics and Law, Director, Burch Center for Tax Policy and Public Finance, University of California, Berkeley

"I think it fair to say that Treasury I [the treasury proposal leading to the tax reform act of 1986] would not have moved forward had it not been for [Gene's] early leadership."
—Ronald A. Pearlman, former Assistant Secretary of The Treasury for Tax Policy and former Staff Director, Joint Committee on Taxation

"Had I not read [Gene's] work . . . there never would have been a presidential decision to double the personal exemption . . . the tax exemption portion [of the 1986 tax bill] is all due to [his] insightful analysis."
—Bruce Chapman, Director of the White House Office of Planning and Evaluation under President Reagan

"Gene Steuerle combines both well-written historical narrative and insightful economic analysis in providing a thoughtful description of current U.S. tax policy. Whether one is a tax-and-spend redistributionist, a tax-cutting supply-sider, or something in between, Steuerle's book presents a balanced perspective that is useful and informative regardless of one's prior beliefs about how tax policy should be changed."
—Eric M. Engen, Economist and Resident Scholar, American Enterprise Institute

CONTEMPORARY
U.S. TAX POLICY

C. EUGENE STEUERLE

C. Eugene Steuerle

Also of interest from the Urban Institute Press:

CONTEMPORARY
U.S. TAX POLICY

THE URBAN INSTITUTE PRESS
WASHINGTON, DC

THE URBAN INSTITUTE PRESS
2100 M Street, N.W.
Washington, D.C. 20037

Library of Congress Cataloging in Publication Data

Steuerle, C. Eugene, 1946–
    Contemporary U.S. tax policy / C. Eugene Steuerle.
        p. cm.
    Includes bibliographical references and index.
    ISBN 0-87766-720-9 (pbk. : alk. paper)
    1.   Taxation–United States–History–20th century. 2.   Fiscal policy–United States–History–20th century.   I. Title: Contemporary United States tax policy. II. Title.
    HJ2381.S737 2004
    336'.00973–dc22

                                                            2004006717

ISBN 0-87766-720-9 (paper, alk. paper)

Printed in the United States of America
10 09 08 07 06 05 04   1 2 3 4 5

THE URBAN INSTITUTE is a nonprofit, nonpartisan policy research and educational organization established in Washington, D.C., in 1968. Its staff investigates the social, economic, and governance problems confronting the nation and evaluates the public and private means to alleviate them. The Institute disseminates its research findings through publications, its Web site, the media, seminars, and forums.

Through work that ranges from broad conceptual studies to administrative and technical assistance, Institute researchers contribute to the stock of knowledge available to guide decisionmaking in the public interest.

Conclusions or opinions expressed in Institute publications are those of the authors and do not necessarily reflect the views of officers or trustees of the Institute, advisory groups, or any organizations that provide financial support to the Institute.

This book is dedicated to all those who have propped me up when I could barely stand—loved ones, friends, and so many whom I have never even met. It is in people like you that I put my hope.

Contents

Preface

Nearly every day a tax policy debate makes the front page of newspapers—a debate surrounding tax proposals designed to spur the economy or to reduce budget deficits; new tax incentives to build low-income housing, increase charitable giving, reduce the cost of purchasing equipment, or establish tax-favored enterprise zones; and tax boosts to support child care, help low-income taxpayers, or finance school construction. Who can be against improving the economy, helping families, or promoting good social programs? Yet from another perspective—who can be for higher tax rates or raising the cost of government?

Many of these debates cannot be understood without some background on the history, economics, and politics of modern tax policymaking. After working almost 30 years in budget and tax policy, I rediscovered the eternal verity that our history and experience must be passed on to each succeeding generation. Countless courses on taxation and public finance teach a particular discipline and a set of skills. But this academic knowledge does not impart the driving forces behind tax changes. We cannot assume the young have learned the lessons that this history offers. This fact struck me during a recent talk at Swarthmore College when I likened the early tax policy of President Reagan with that of President Kennedy. All the professors in the audience nodded to acknowledge the connection I was making. The students wore blank stares. I suddenly realized that those students were in diapers when Reagan was president! The analogy didn't work for them because they weren't familiar with *either* event being compared. Yet, without some understanding of Reagan tax policy and its precedents, students will have trouble understanding later developments. They may not understand that an expansion of the child care credit in the first part of the 21st century came about partly because social conservatives suddenly discovered family tax policy in the Reagan era. Or that what might seem revolutionary, such as tax breaks for education, has its roots in a decades-old policy trend toward putting provisions in the tax code that are unlikely to be enacted as direct expenditures.

I published *The Tax Decade* in 1990 to emphasize the development of tax policy from 1981 to 1990, a period of significant turbulence and reform. U.S. tax policy obviously has not stopped evolving since 1990, nor did it start there. Accordingly, *Contemporary U.S. Tax Policy* reengages and updates the story of recent tax policy developments—an exciting, if not always pretty, tale of democratic decisionmaking.

A warning is required. Those looking for a simple story of triumph and defeat will be disappointed. A better analogy is chaos theory's explanation of the weather: new and unexpected events often occur—but usually within fixed boundaries and with some degree of correlation from one time period to the next. As you will read, congresses and presidents usually act with an amazing herd instinct—moving one more step forward or backward on a familiar path rather than shifting paths altogether. Rather than move onward toward new societal issues with forged political agreement on the old ones, our tax policy history is normally filled with attempts and reattempts to fight on familiar battlegrounds. Yet in the midst of what appears as repetitive clamor, evolution (even revolution) does occur.

The American tax system, despite its many reforms and notable efficiencies at collecting revenues, is also broken. Reforms may not be more necessary than in the past, but policymaking processes today seem incapable of the broad and comprehensive trade-offs required to make 21st century government effective. My hope is that this book will impart some ideas about how to interpret the past in ways that increase the probability that future governmental reforms can be comprehensive enough to make the tax system significantly fairer, simpler, and more efficient.

My perspective transcends that of researcher and writer. Over the course of nearly three decades, I have spent about half of my time at the

Treasury Department in various roles, including deputy assistant secretary of the Treasury for Tax Analysis,[1] 1987 to 1989, and economic tax coordinator of the Treasury Department's 1984 to 1986 Project for Fundamental Tax Reform, a project that led to the Tax Reform Act of 1986. I spent the other half of my time as a researcher at the Urban Institute, the American Enterprise Institute, and the Brookings Institution, analyzing budget and social policy issues while writing regular columns for such publications as *Tax Notes* magazine and the *Financial Times*. I also served as president (2001–2002) and board member of the National Tax Association for many years and as an editorial adviser to the *Journal of Economic Perspectives* for its *Policy Watch* series. I had the privilege of learning from the best minds devoted to tax and budget issues and became well acquainted with those officials and staffers of all political stripes who "made" tax and budget policy for more than a quarter-century.

Parts of this book were first published in or presented before the American Bar Association, the American Enterprise Institute, the American Tax Policy Institute, the American Law Institute, the Brookings Institution, the Internal Revenue Service, the John F. Kennedy School of Public Policy at Harvard University, *The National Tax Journal, Tax Notes*, the Urban Institute and, where relevant, are reprinted with permission. Two sources, in particular, are used: my earlier book, *The Tax Decade*, and a chapter in *American Economic Policy in the 1990s* (MIT Press) entitled "Tax Policy from 1990 to 2001."[2]

Other books cover some of the politics behind the events discussed here—especially within a given president's stay in office.[3] This book covers a much longer period. It emphasizes how the various events fit together across recent decades, the role of economic factors in the shift in the nation's fiscal and tax structure, how reform is organized, and where various forces are leading tax policy. My aim is to provide enough information to allow readers to judge the trends and form conclusions, even when they differ from my own. In the end, their votes, more than anything else, will determine whether good tax policy can prevail.

NOTES

1. The Office of Tax Analysis is the government's principal office for analyzing the economics of tax issue. It works closely with tax lawyers in the Offices of Tax Legislative Counsel, International Tax Counsel, and Benefits Tax Counsel. Together, they form the Office of Tax Policy within the Treasury Department.

2. See Steuerle 1983b, 1985a, 1985b, 1986a, 1986b, 1987a, 1987b, 1988, 1990c, 1991, 1992b, 2001a, 2002e, 2002g; Brownlee and Steuerle 2003; Steuerle and Hartzmark 1981.

3. For some political perspectives on particular events, see Regan (1988) and Stockman (1986); on 1986 tax reform, see books by Birnbaum and Murray (1987) and Conlan, Wrightson, and Beam (1990) and articles by Haskel (1987), Verdier (1988), McLure (1988), Minarik (1987), and Witte (1985). Some tax events of the Clinton period are covered in Waldman (2000) and Woodward (1994). A special issue of the *Journal of Economic Perspectives* in 1987 included work by such stalwarts as Richard Musgrave, Charles McLure, and George Zodrow.

Acknowledgments

N o one can write a book of this breadth without much dependence upon others. Alan Auerbach, Jon Bakija, Thomas Barthold, Evelyn Brody, Elliott Brownlee, Leonard Burman, Adam Carasso, Joseph Cordes, Martin David, William Gale, Daniel Halperin, Peter Orszag, Rudolph Penner, Joseph Thorndike, Eric Toder, and two anonymous referees provided an extraordinary array of helpful and insightful comments. Adam Carasso, along with Meghan Bishop, generously did much work on pulling together data and charts and finding sources. Anya Arax performed her usual wizardry in coordinating draft after draft. Kathy Courrier provided invaluable insights on an early draft. My editor, Susan Kellam, was amazing in her ability to make mishmash into prose, while making clear the most obscure technical points. William Bradbury copyedited with distinction, while Scott Forrey managed the production process in the most professional and timely manner. Glenn Popson has made extraordinary efforts to market the book. None of these acknowledgments sufficiently conveys the delight I had in working with these friends and colleagues and how much I learned from them.

All errors, omissions, confusions, and other transgressions are, of course, the author's, but they are the natural consequence of tilling so long in the tax field, with fill of what might be called both productive harvest and decaying material.

1
Introduction

The Income Tax has made more liars out of the American people than Golf has: Even when you make one out on the level, you don't know when it's through if you are a Crook or a Martyr.
— Will Rogers, The Illiterate Digest

No area of policymaking "taxes" the brain more than taxation. Although the nuances of tax reporting and accounting are mind-boggling, they reflect the implementation of a much wider, sometimes disenchanting, but ever engaging policy process. Sound tax policy and administration—like a trustworthy judiciary and reliable financial accounting system—is one of the pillars of modern governance. In examining those nations that aspire to be republics but have not yet firmed up this pillar, you will find crumbling or barely viable government.

When policymakers decide to change the economy or society's behavior, the tax code is usually their tool of choice.[1] Most fundamentally, taxes are collected to support the activities of government agencies. Oliver Wendell Holmes, Jr., was referring to this basic function when he stated that taxes are the "price we pay for a civilized society."[2] Today, however, raising revenues to support government's direct-expenditure programs and operations in society is only the tip of the iceberg.

There are tax breaks for homeownership that by themselves provide more subsidies than the entire budget of the Department of Housing and Urban Development (HUD). The Earned Income Tax Credit (EITC)[3] is now larger than any other welfare program, such as Food Stamps or Temporary Assistance to Needy Families (TANF). The tax break for employer-provided health insurance, which costs more than $150 billion per year, represents the largest health subsidy granted to the nonelderly anywhere in the federal budget and is growing faster than almost all other domestic programs. Meanwhile, every recent U.S. president has proposed expanding the use of tax subsidies for health. Tax breaks abound as a favored mechanism to "provide energy independence," subsidize energy producers, and promote energy conservation—even when extra production works at cross purposes to conservation. In other words, to understand housing, welfare, health, energy, or almost any government policy, you have to look at what is going on in the tax code.

Today, tax breaks rather than direct expenditures account for one-fourth to one-third of the benefits and subsidies granted to the public. As if that situation weren't enough to overburden the tax agenda, in recent decades politicians have decided that taxes are a primary instrument for dealing with growth and recession and implementing macroeconomic policy. Further, presidents and Congresses constantly try to use taxes to change the distribution of income and affect behavior among farmers, research firms, energy suppliers, the poor, or hundreds of other groups that benefit from various tax grants and subsidies. Finally, taxes powerfully influence how we all consume, work, save, and invest.

Various U.S. agencies, such as the Treasury Department, sometimes formally assess these non-revenue functions of the tax system, in part through an accounting system known as the tax expenditure budget. This controversial budget attempts to calculate the size of tax provisions that operate essentially like direct expenditures even though they are put forward as tax breaks. Because such a large chunk of government subsidies or expenditures are in the form of tax breaks, elected officials often turn to the Treasury and the congressional tax-writing committees to resolve budget and deficit problems.

The Budgetary Myths Surrounding Tax Policy

Everyone is an expert on three subjects—medicine, education, and taxes. After all, each of us has firsthand, sometimes harrowing, experiences dealing with doctors, teachers, and tax officials. But just as there are "quack" medical practices and bad educational theories, so too are there pieces of conventional wisdom about taxes that are highly questionable or downright wrong. Those closely associated with one political party can develop a mythical view about what the other party has done wrongly in the past. These myths need to be dispelled, or at least put in perspective, as they have been pervasive throughout the recent history of tax policy.

Of course, tax cuts and increases often influence the magnitude of government. But a lot of other factors also have to be weighed. For instance, tax cuts can actually expand (or tax increases reduce) the government's size. If additional debt is incurred to finance a tax cut, then future taxpayers have to pay more to pay off that additional debt. Consider, for example, a new tax cut to dairy producers that might provide a tax credit of 5 cents for every gallon of milk delivered, yielding a total subsidy of $100 million. There is little difference between this tax cut and a direct spending program giving 5 cents per gallon to dairy producers and also costing $100 million. In effect, an expenditure increase to dairy producers can be designed or disguised as a tax cut. But the end result is the same—even if the dairy subsidy shows up as a negative tax rather than a positive expenditure in the budget. Either way, this expenditure must also be paid for through higher tax rates

Disguised expenditures such as this hypothetical dairy subsidy are a political favorite. Since our elected officials prefer to be characterized as increasing expenditures and reducing taxes, it is not surprising that they like to talk about the benefit and not the cost side of their actions.

Tax-rate cuts for both individuals and corporations may also reduce government's size, depending upon what happens to expenditures. Higher deficits from a reduced revenues might discourage future Congresses from increasing expenditures. Although this "starve the beast" strategy can add to deficits, there is evidence that Congress tends to increase spending when taxes are higher and to restrain spending when they are lower. While empirical evidence on how tax changes drive expenditure changes is inconclusive, the accounting truth is undeniable: the nation's fiscal system is a balance sheet, and the tax or expenditure side can be looked at separately only by closing one eye.

Budget myths about tax policy have prevailed throughout the history covered in this book, and we should begin by dispelling some of their various manifestations.

The Reagan Budget Myth: Reagan's 1981 tax cuts created the deficits in the 1980s. As you will see, the large revenue cutbacks of the early 1980s added significantly to deficits at that time. But broader factors also contributed to the budget deficit. A temporary and significant increase in the defense budget as a percentage of Gross Domestic Product (GDP) coincided with the early 1980s tax cuts. Also in that time period, the inexorable growth in health and retirement programs absorbed larger and larger amounts of national income. In fact, the extraordinary surge in so-called entitlement spending has become the dominant budget force in the past few decades. Essentially, the budget numbers didn't add up in the early 1980s, and there wasn't enough money around to pay for the tax cuts of 1981, the defense increases, and the automatic increases in entitlement spending. For example, if several cars play "chicken" and all crash together, it is less useful to blame one car—in this case, Reagan's tax cuts—than to address the broader process that led to the game in the first place.

The Clinton Budget Myth: Clinton's 1993 tax increases were responsible for the elimination of the deficit by the late 1990s. Despite the tendency of Republicans to attack the Clinton tax increases for being historically large and Democrats to praise them for leading to extraordinary deficit reduction, the increases were moderate. Indeed, the deficit-reduction package under George H. W. Bush was larger in magnitude as a percentage of GDP than was the one President Clinton pushed through.

Again, a broader perspective is required. The 1990 budget enforcement rules helped maintain enough discipline in the mid-1990s so that few large expenditures or tax cuts were added to the budget even as the economy grew. This constraint—along with a pleasant economic upturn—helped to temporarily reduce the deficits.

The George W. Bush Budget Myth: Bush's tax cuts recreated large deficits in the first years of the 21st century. Once again, talking about taxes in isolation does not make sense. The 2001, 2002, and 2003 tax cuts, especially if eventually made permanent, were large. But spending increases from 1997 through 2004 were quite large, too—not only for defense or national security, but also for discretionary and entitlement spending as well. In fact, Congress and the president went on a wild legislative "spending" spree, authorizing both tax cuts and increases in expenditures while adding to, rather than containing, the large, automatic, growth in retirement and health spending already scheduled. Meanwhile, independent from the tax cuts, revenues fell dramatically with changes in the economy as the unusual revenue gains of the 1990s failed to continue. Yet, with the retirement of the baby boomers a few years away, the long-term budget issue was ignored.

And Some Realities in Tax Policy

Some factors or trends have long played important and continual roles in tax policy evolution:

Fact 1: Reliance on principles seems to go up when times are tough. Almost all changes to the tax law seem to be called "reform" by their sponsors, but true reform is based on principles. Many believe that principled reform requires budget surpluses. The "good times" rationale is that unwarranted tax breaks can be eliminated only when those people formerly benefiting from the breaks can be compensated some other way. For instance, suppose Tom unjustly pays less tax than Harry when in principle they should pay the same. With a surplus, Tom's tax break can be eliminated and tax rates lowered for both Tom and Harry. In that way, Harry's taxes can be reduced to the level of Tom's, but Tom won't pay any more because the rate reduction will roughly offset his loss of a special tax break.

The history of modern tax policy belies the notion that such easy exchanges are possible. Instead, when Congress has to show directly how it is taking something from someone—i.e., when it is reducing the deficit—it is more likely to appeal to the public on grounds of equal justice or some other principle. When there is no budgetary pressure, Congress is less compelled to remove anyone's tax break. Indeed, when Congress is engaged in additional give-aways, it is often indiscriminate— not worrying whether Tom gets more than Harry or Harry more than Tom as long as neither is hurt and perhaps campaign contributions go up.[4] Of course, it is hard to adhere to all principles at the same time. For example, an attempt to create equity or parity can at the same time cause complexity. Nonetheless, though the coming chapters highlight important exceptions, concern for principles in general seems to wane when Congress's or the president's feet are not held to the fire.

Fact 2: Both political parties like to provide subsidies and expenditures through the tax system. Providing subsidies and expenditures in the form of tax breaks gives the appearance of reducing government's size since the measure of net taxes goes down even as government interference in the economy increases. For this reason, tax subsidies have strong political appeal.

Many tax subsidies in the 1960s and 1970s were delivered as business tax breaks and deductions that higher-income taxpayers found more valuable. In that earlier period Republicans tended to embrace such breaks more than Democrats (although, as in the case of the investment credit, they were often proposed first by Democrats). But even as some of these business preferences were cut back, social tax expenditures increased and credits expanded even for those with no tax liability. Eventually, support for using the tax code to accomplish social and economic policy, not simply to raise revenues, became increasingly bipartisan.

Fact 3: The Internal Revenue Service doesn't just collect revenues; it administers social policy and children's programs. A corollary to the bipartisan embrace of tax subsidies and expenditures has been the expanded use of the earned income tax credit, child tax credits, and other tax benefits targeted toward lower-income families, especially those with children. Because Republicans embraced helping families with children as a family issue and Democrats embraced family as an issue of progressivity, there has been bipartisan movement on this front.

Fact 4: The investment and business tax policy debate evolves toward ever more complex issues. Although tax policy is crucial for investment and saving policy, rules are neither always steadfast nor adhered to. Broad-based incentives, such as investment tax credits, eventually got abandoned in favor of lower rates, but selective incentives for such items as research and energy remained or expanded. One heated and unresolved debate concerns the ways that taxpayers "arbitrage" differences in the treatment of different assets, income sources, or taxpayers. Government seems to have limited ability to prevent new "tax shelters" born of complex forms of arbitrage, forcing Congress constantly to rewrite the law or the Treasury Department and the Internal Revenue Service (IRS) to reinterpret the regulations. Such shelter opportunities arise from many sources, including variations in tax rates by country, limitations on loss deductions that may be avoided when companies merge, the tax exemption for charitable activity, and the differential taxation of equity and debt. Tax professionals' growing skillfulness in exploiting every differential in the tax system, the computerization of tax accounting, and the emergence of split-second electronic transfers of billions of dollars all perpetuate the tax shelter crisis.

Fact 5: The real postwar growth in taxes occurred at the state, not the federal, level. Although most tax policy fights are over federal taxes—federal income taxes in particular—state taxes took larger and larger shares of national income over the post–World War II era. The state and local share grew relative to the national, while the states themselves took over much larger shares of the combined state/local budgets.

Fact 6: The tax code must change with the times. Among tax lawyers, accountants, and practitioners, this is heresy. They are right that change is complex, and that there is an administrative, as well as efficiency, cost to constantly retooling (Feldstein 1976). Many of the changes of the past few decades have also made the tax laws permanently more complex—increasing the time and transaction costs of dealing with tax preparers and tax professionals, filling out tax forms, and adjusting portfolios and other parts of our lives to minimize taxes.[5]

Nonetheless, the tax code is a major instrument of U.S. policy. No one argues that expenditure policy should be left alone. As an evolving society develops new needs and new information sources, institutions must change, and government must spend its money differently. The same holds true for collecting taxes. Certainly, some aspects of the tax code should be changed only gradually, especially those that involve complex accounting matters. But an equal claim for a modest pace of reform can be made for many expenditures, such as deposit insurance. Other expenditure provisions, such as size of the armed forces, must evolve more rapidly. Thus, the tax code will evolve not just because politicians can't keep their hands off of it, but also because they should not.

Fact 7: Controlling the budget plays an increasingly dominant role in the evolution of tax policy. In terms of causal direction, tax policy has always been a handmaiden to budget policy. A nation raises taxes to pay for government functions. Read almost any history of the United States that covers financial matters, and it will become clear how much of the nation's success—and at times, its survival—was made possible by coming up with the necessary money at the right time.[6] Taxes have been raised to meet such budget policy goals as reducing debt obligations arising from the Revolution, building roads and other infrastructure for westward expansion, paying for wars, and restraining the growth in national debt; they have been lowered to reduce distortions and the drain of government on the economy.

Compared to most of the nation's history, it is only in the contemporary period covered here that deficit reduction or surplus spending has largely defined policy. During this period, Congress has paid limited attention to the underlying purposes of tax or expenditure programs, which is unfortunate, since a government doesn't exist to reduce deficit or spend surplus. In any case, tax bills have played a vital role in both deficit and surplus—with success often defined politically by the simple standard of whether enough money was raised or spent.

The name of the game in Washington in recent decades has been to "spend" or use up money before someone else does. On the expenditure side, entitlement programs like those for retirement and health are precommitted to absorb ever-larger shares of revenue in an automatic fashion—that is, even in the absence of legislation. Not to be outdone, those who favor lower taxes have legislated tax cuts into the future. The net result is gridlock. Never in the nation's history have dead and retired officials been able to exert such control over current and future budgets, as you will read.

NOTES

1. One former deputy assistant secretary for tax analysis at the U.S. Treasury claimed that "tax policy is an extraordinarily poor instrument for rapid reaction to short-term policy problems" (Burman 2002).

2. This quotation stands at the entrance to the IRS Main Building in Washington, D.C.

3. That portion of the EITC that is paid to households without tax liability is technically treated in the budget as a direct expenditure. However, the EITC is passed as part of tax legislation, and the IRS administers it.

4. Note that I am not suggesting that this set of tendencies always *must* apply, simply that it does apply to modern tax policymaking.

5. New tax software, of course, has reduced the amount of increased cost. In fact, some change might not even have been tolerated were it not for the new software.

6. See, for instance, Brownlee (2004), who also stresses that most major changes in the tax system have come in times of emergency. World War II stands out in this regard (see chapter 3). Joseph Thorndike (2004) suggests such changes "were orchestrated by political leaders wielding cogent arguments about social justice."

2

Tax Policy's Principles and Principals

The United States should have a tax system which looks like someone designed it on purpose.

—Former Secretary of the Treasury William E. Simon,
Blueprints for Tax Reform

Despite its seemingly random application to almost every sphere of human activity, tax policymaking is far from random. Many forces drive taxes, but principles do matter. Part of being human is "justifying" our actions according to some principle or standard. Some attribute this deep-seated impulse to a natural law.[1] When it comes to tax policy, this fascinating call of conscience to justify action might be manipulated, but it cannot be ignored. Even the narrowest special-interest pleader in the tax policy arena couches arguments in terms of principles or theories, however illogically.

John Maynard Keynes's famous quip that "ideas of economists and political philosophers, both when they are right and when they are wrong, are more powerful than is commonly understood"[2] is even truer in the age of mass media and celebrity. Scholars today can spark new policy developments, but, just as often, they "defend the faith" of politicians by giving them academic cover for their biases and legislative actions already taken.

The important principles and theories applied to tax policy by influential principals in the tax arena are defined in this chapter. As you will see, principles sometimes conflict. A common battleground is the debate

9

between progressivity and the belief that individuals are entitled to the product of their own labor. Nonetheless, principles are useful guides for policymaking. Many proposals and tax provisions unduly violate one principle without any further adherence to another. Sometimes tax legislation is aimed at removing such violations. For instance, some efforts to broaden the tax base and simultaneously lower tax rates seek to improve efficiency and horizontal equity without changing progressivity or revenue capacity. More often, "reform" aims to advance one principle with less regard for the others (e.g., more progressivity or more efficiency regardless of horizontal equity). In chapter 12, we shall reprise which of these theories in recent decades might have triumphed in the never-ending tax debate.

Basic Principles of Public Finance

Horizontal Equity

In the tax laws, horizontal equity—often called equal justice—asserts that those with equal ability to pay should pay equal taxes. No principle seems to permeate debates over policy—and not just tax policy—more than this one. Yet while there is almost universal agreement on the principle, the rub is the frequent lack of agreement on exactly who are equals. Those with equal incomes? Those with equal incomes, less such extraordinary expenses as chronic medical care? Those with equal potential to earn income, whether realized or not? Or, moving beyond income, those who consume or absorb equal amounts of societal resources? Of course, how one measures equals and equal treatment is yet another complication.[3]

Horizontal equity is perhaps the queen of all principles affecting government policy, or at least the one to which people pay the most homage.[4] Many tax breaks for one type of household or tax penalties for one type of business are often opposed (or favored) on the grounds that they unfairly distinguish between two types of taxpayers who should be treated equally. Politicians, of course, may skirt this principle, but seldom do they deny its existence. Even when a class of investors or consumers is favored, the principle usually applies internally to that group. For example, the subsidy allowed for charitable contributions favors those who give, but then all taxpayers who give to charity can claim roughly equal rights to the subsidy.

Vertical Equity

Horizontal equity is almost universally accepted as a principle. Other principles, however, are more likely to produce conflict. Vertical equity, known in tax circles as progressivity, suggests that those with greater needs should receive more from government and those with greater "ability to pay" should pay more to government. Many revile this notion. One attack on progressivity, in fact, claims that it prompts class warfare. While some progressivity arguments may indeed invite that risk, any general attack on the progressivity principle, in my view, is almost tantamount to an attack on natural law theory.[5] That is, some progressivity—greater contributions to the community by those who are more capable of contributing—is apparent in nature when the stronger or older of a species support the weaker or younger. And so must it be, at least at some level, with the human species. As a practical matter, for instance, those with little or no resources can hardly pay an equal share of government costs. Once on this redistributive track, the issue is not whether government will redistribute, but *how* progressive it can or should be.

Even tax experts can lose their way in tax policy discussions of progressivity because the term is usually defined narrowly as rising average tax rates with increasing income. On the expenditure side of the budget, however, most public discussions tend to define progressivity as greater absolute benefits for those with lesser incomes or other means. As an example, a $100,000 educational benefit for a millionaire and a $1,000 benefit for someone with a $9,000 annual income does not tend to be defined as progressive, even though the latter benefit is a higher share of income for the poorer person. This inconsistency invites all sorts of confusion in the public debate, and self-defined liberals and conservatives fail to deal with progressivity consistently across tax cuts, tax increases, expenditure cuts, expenditure increases, and budget policy in general (Steuerle 2002a, 267–70). For example, pure flat rate taxes with no exemption for even poverty-level income are not progressive by the typical tax definition, but if those flat-rate taxes support programs with roughly equal benefits per person, then a substantial net progressive redistribution from the well-off to the less-well off will result.[6]

Think about a two-person society with a 20 percent tax rate on both incomes where one person earns $100 and the other earns $10. If the tax is redistributed equally to each of them, then the richer person on net pays $9 ($20 paid minus $11 received) and the poorer person receives

$9 ($2 paid minus $11 received). In another more real-life example, Social Security provides greater absolute benefits to the rich even though middle-income people pay a higher proportion of their wages and salaries into the system than upper-income individuals do. By either definition cited above, this program is regressive if the usual inconsistent measures are used, even though the Social Security expenditure and tax system as a whole is meant to redistribute resources.[7]

In this book, we will try to keep clear this confusing distinction between progressive policy that results in net redistribution and "progressive tax systems" with tax rates that rise with income (whose ultimate effect on redistribution still depends upon what happens to expenditures).

Efficiency

The efficiency principle—a favorite of economists—suggests that programs should never operate in a way that makes someone better off at the expense of making someone else worse off. Rare are situations where such pure tax trades are possible. In tax reform, that ideal would require creating a situation in which there are no losers and at least some households are better off after the reform. Unhindered by the pure constraint, however, many tax policy reforms tend to produce clear gains in overall economic output even if there are losses to some individuals—for instance, when for no obvious or stated reason the unreformed tax arbitrarily favors one particular form of work, investment, or consumption.

Taxes by their very nature distort behavior. They usually lead people to avoid the taxed activity, whether it is work, saving, or some particular form of consumption or investment. It is this change in behavior—for example, doing less or more of something than we would otherwise do—that causes the efficiency loss. Generally speaking, tax policy cannot eliminate but only reduce efficiency loss.

Even when distortions are minimized for some level of tax collection, those taxes, because of their remaining effect on behavior, must be justified by gains from the programs they support.[8] Even taxes collected to support income-transfer programs depend upon the notion that progressive transfers add to the good of society—a variant of an efficiency construct. In theory, that gain—however hard to measure—should be greater in value than the losses due to the economic distortions of the taxes (and expenditures) imposed.[9]

There are many applications of the efficiency principle, but in taxation the primary applications are to choices among what is consumed or produced, between work and leisure, and between consumption today and saving for tomorrow. If a tax discourages people from working, for instance, then they will produce less than they would in absence of the taxes and contribute less to national output. Using taxes to push growth (as opposed to removing distortions or barriers to growth) is another matter, and there is a legitimate debate over whether it is "fair" or "efficient" for one generation to enhance growth even further if the benefits go mainly to future generations who are likely to be richer anyway. Put another way, higher growth does not necessarily imply greater efficiency. Many economists suggest that the efficient part of the pro-growth reform agenda involves removing disincentives to saving rather than adding new incentives (or biases).

Individual Equity

The individual equity principle holds that individuals are entitled to the product of their own labor and to a fair return on their own saving.[10] The principle is closely associated with the right to individual liberty. At an extreme, individual equity is violated *prima facie* by almost all government taxes, rules, or regulations that force individuals to do something they do not want to do and for which they have not voted. More practically, the principle suggests that government taxes essentially confiscate private property if the individual doesn't get government services or benefits of at least equal worth in return. The government should provide a *quid pro quo* if the tax is mandatory; if voluntary, the taxpayer can act as one would in any market where the price is unfavorable—by refusing to buy.

Individual equity considerations come up in many situations. For instance, although Social Security tries to be progressive by design, its architects also gave some weight to the individual equity principle and granted greater (though still not proportional) benefits to taxpayers who pay more in tax. Proponents of individual accounts in Social Security often suggest that depositing an individual's Social Security taxes into his or her own account better serves the individual equity principle.

A common application of this principle is the adoption of "benefit" taxes—taxes where individuals pay what it costs government to deliver a service. Fees, such as those charged by national parks and toll roads, are classic forms of benefit taxes that subscribe closely to individual equity norms. Benefit taxation is sometimes contrasted with taxation according to ability to pay, as per the progressivity principle.[11] Efficiency, as well as equity considerations, comes into play with benefit taxation, since its application implies that the marginal cost of any benefit received is charged to each recipient at the margin. In practice, however, exact assessment according to benefits received is difficult (e.g., using tolls to charge exactly the right amount to each vehicle-weight class).

The argument for greater "choice" among individuals is another variant on this theme of paying heed to both individual equity and efficiency considerations. Here, a taxpayer would always be better off if allowed to decide between equal-costing A and B than if forced to accept A. For instance, a credit for higher education would usually leave the taxpayer a choice of what school to attend, rather than specifying the specific school. Using vouchers or voucher-like tax credits for college education, food stamps, training programs, or health is often viewed as improving individual equity and efficiency by providing greater choice for the same level of expenditure or credit. In some cases, however, these programs of choice can cause distortions or inequities relative to a more universal provision of a good or service. For instance, unless designed well, vouchers for health insurance can lead those who are relatively healthy to seek health plans that exclude those who are less healthy, thus leaving the latter in a high-cost insurance pool.[12]

Simplicity

All things being equal, who opposes simplicity? Since government doesn't exist to simplify itself, the issue is not whether simplicity should be given priority so much as whether it is given adequate weight or consideration in the legislative process and administration of the law.

Complexity arises for a variety of reasons, including pursuit of other worthy principles. For instance, the attempt to tax all income equally— following efficiency and horizontal equity criteria—can work against simplicity when some forms of income are hard to measure. Whenever Congress or the president wants to appear to do something symbolically important but doesn't want to spend the required revenues (or raise tax rates commensurately), taxes get more complex. Similarly, legislative logrolling leads to complex rules when small benefits are granted to many constituent groups. Complexity also arises from cobbling together programs as monies become available rather than implementing a comprehensive approach.

Usually the easiest way to simplify tax preferences or subsidies is to get rid of them. On the other hand, merely paring them—say, on some horizontal equity or efficiency ground—might actually add to complexity and recordkeeping when the basic provision remains intact and taxpayers have to go through elaborate calculations to figure out whether they qualify.

Closely associated with the goal of simplification is that of *transparency*. Transparency demands that the purpose of a tax policy, including who pays and who doesn't, be presented in an open manner. Following the principle requires administrators to provide statistics and data on government programs, and it requires legislators to try to make clear what they are doing. Transparency is often the bane of special interests or those who want to hide their special status. Even those who advocate on behalf of particular principles at times prefer to be opaque.

Revenue Raising

Revenue raising is probably more a goal than a principle, but its primacy can't be overstated. With a few small exceptions, such as a pollution tax, tax systems don't exist to increase progressivity, tax equals equally, or remove economic distortions. They are created to pay for government's activities. Revenue raising is related to efficiency in the broad sense that government must pay for what society needs and avoid the economic costs of unsustainable deficits. At stake is nothing less than government's ability to achieve its purposes and run its functions. Maximizing revenues, however, is not a principle or goal and generally violates efficiency. Still, the tax system must provide the revenues sooner or (with borrowing) later to pay for the costs of government.

The Government Principals

Many parts of government have some responsibility for tax policy. The executive branch departments—in the case of taxes, the Treasury Department—often develop proposals to be vetted through policy councils or departmental meetings and perhaps ultimately leading to decisions by the president. The proposals are sent to Congress, which examines and amends or rejects the proposals in committees, with the

House Ways and Means Committee and the Senate Finance Committee designated for tax matters. Special interests, as well as nonpartisan private individuals and groups, have the opportunity to testify on matters important to them. The committees then amend bills and report them to Congress as a whole. First the House, and then the Senate, vote them up or down, sometimes with amendments.[13] A conference committee rewrites the different versions and presents a compromise measure to both houses for approval. The president accepts or vetoes the legislation

Alas, legislation seldom follows this neat path and division of labor. Many of those promoting different ideas—in particular, on tax cuts they want—enter the process at different stages and skip steps they consider to be obstacles. Furthermore, certain tax policies are developed internally by the Treasury rather than by other offices or departments of the executive branch—offices which typically have much less knowledge of or concern for broader tax principles. Nonpartisan staffs both in the executive branch and in the Congress are frequently left on the sideline. Their analysis, for instance, will often make it only as far as an assistant secretary or director, but never be made public or even reach the ears of the president or members of Congress. The process often fails to give principles of taxation their due. For example, Treasury staff is called upon mainly to justify past political promises rather than to offer options to the president, Congress does not always ask its own nonpartisan staff to analyze the pros and cons and what might best serve the public interest, and testimony may not be taken before important provisions are added to bills.

One very difficult period for a rational reform process is the first year after an election, when political appointees in the White House typically direct the Treasury to put together packages incorporating campaign promises. The overwhelming temptation is to ignore the almost inevitable administrative, implementation, or other problems with campaign promises that are developed with limited analysis and that tend to promise maximum benefits at minimal cost to the public. Treasury staff may not even be asked to suggest alternative options aimed at achieving roughly the same end, yet more realistically deal with the impact of the promises on the budget.

In recent decades, much of what the president ends up promoting comes out of the Executive Office of the President and, in particular, from White House special assistants to the president and other appointees. Only in the last part of the 20th century have so many political appointees been put in the White House, creating an enormous amount of information filtering between civil servants and the president.

The head of the president's National Economic Council (NEC)—as well as the economic coordinating council in the White House that preceded this position— has become increasingly powerful because he or she coordinates economic policy coming out of all parts of the executive branch. For instance, Lawrence Lindsay headed this council in the early years of the George W. Bush presidency, and he was largely responsible for developing the administration's early tax policy proposals in the campaign and for putting them forward in 2001. Two other recent heads of this office (James Baker and Robert Rubin) found it to be a stepping-stone to Secretary of the Treasury. Other offices with substantial influence include the Office of Management and Budget (OMB), which must put together the budget and see how expenditures and taxes add up, and the Council of Economic Advisers, which mainly advises the president on economic matters.[14] These last two offices still perform significant amounts of analysis, but they have often seen their influence dissipated, both because of rising expertise in many of the agencies of government and because of the growing influence and number of pollsters and political advisers within the White House.

The Secretary of Treasury is considered the president's lead person on implementing tax policy, partly because the Internal Revenue Service (IRS), which administers the law, falls under Treasury's wing. In theory, if not always in practice, the Treasury has substantial say over the development of the president's economic and tax policies. As the White House staff has grown, however, the Treasury's role is often reduced to trying to figure out how to make workable a rough idea emanating from a political conversation in the White House.

The largest group of nonpolitical appointees devoted to tax policy anywhere in government resides in the Treasury's Office of Tax Policy (OTP)—largely composed of economists, lawyers, and a few accountants. Generally speaking, its role is to try to represent the public interest in the development of tax policy by analyzing options using the principles outlined above. Along with the IRS, it also writes regulations to implement laws already passed. Among their many analytical functions, the economists estimate the revenue cost of tax bills—often causing hand wringing among politicians who want lower costs assessed on their tax cuts.[15] The Treasury's Office of Economic Policy, in turn, provides useful analysis of broad tax and budgetary matters and tends to handle the secretary's role as lead trustee of the Social Security and Medicare trust funds. Despite its highly competent staff, at times it has been extremely politicized and used mainly to provide an economic justification for whatever policy the administration has proposed.

Usually, tax bills must be forwarded to Congress only after being approved by the House Ways and Means and Senate Finance committees. These committees tend to control the details of what goes into the bills, often deviating substantially from what a president might initially want or suggest, and taking many actions without his backing. These tax-writing committees also have responsibility for much of the expenditure side of the budget, including Social Security, Medicare, and some welfare programs. This combination of responsibilities gives these tax-writing committees extraordinary power that extends beyond tax legislation. Throughout the period examined in this book, almost all major expenditure and budget legislation—not just tax legislation—went through these committees.

While House Ways and Means and Senate Finance committees divide into majority and minority staffs, they often work together in a bipartisan manner and tend to be highly professional and well regarded.[16] The staff of the nonpartisan and distinguished Joint Committee on Taxation (JCT), established by the Revenue Act of 1926 and comprised nominally of members of each house of Congress, mainly support the tax-writing committees—in particular, their chairpersons—by providing analysis somewhat similar to that made available in the executive branch by the Office of Tax Policy.

Another nonpartisan congressional agency, the Congressional Budget Office (CBO), was established (along with the House and Senate Budget Committees) by the Congressional Budget and Impoundment Control Act of 1974 to provide nonpartisan analysis for economic and budget decisions. Like the OMB, its counterpart in the executive branch, the CBO tries to determine how well the budget numbers add up. Unlike the OMB, the CBO is especially recognized for its ability to publish and analyze budget options—including tax options—for consideration. The General Accounting Office (GAO) and the Congressional Research Service (CRS) also provide occasional tax analysis for Congress upon request; the GAO often investigates administrative and enforcement problems, and the CRS sometimes provides background material on tax issues.

Although nonpartisan staffs try to figure out what is in the public interest, they are not always right, and they often disagree on how to weigh sometimes-conflicting principles. Nonetheless, the Office of Tax Policy, the Joint Committee on Taxation, the Congressional Budget Office, the General Accounting Office, and the Congressional Research Service are national treasures that need to be valued and respected. These staffs often work closely together, exchanging information and views, as well as methods of estimation and model building.

Advocates and Their Theories

Each policymaker and adviser impacting tax policy is influenced by various theories. Unlike principles, theories tend to be more personal and tied to particular advocates for their purposes, whether disinterested or self-interested. For the record, these theories are subtler than the following summaries suggest, but in political debate they are far more crudely represented.

Taxes as a Means of Financing Government

Throughout most of history, tax policy has been viewed mainly as a mechanism for financing government. If the state wanted to collect revenue, tax policy was the means by which it was done. Traditional tax reformers are those who accept this basic function, then ask how it can be done in the most effective way.

A traditional tax reform position taught by both conservative and liberal economists in most public finance courses has stressed horizontal equity and efficiency—mainly by trying to remove provisions that favor particular forms of income or consumption. Inevitably under such differential taxation, some taxpayers pay more than others who have equal levels of income or consumption since, by design, the system favors those who hold more tax-preferred assets (e.g., tax-exempt bonds) or tax-favored consumption goods (nontaxable fringe benefits).

Traditional tax reform is neither a strictly liberal nor conservative notion, and it has a long lineage of distinguished economic promoters ranging from Richard Musgrave, writing mainly at Harvard, to Henry C. Simons at the University of Chicago. One problem for some liberals not steeped in traditional reform is that, strictly speaking, traditional tax reform tends to be neutral about issues such as progressivity and the size of government. Hence, not every progressive tax enactment passes muster on the basis of principles like horizontal equity and efficiency. On the other hand, an efficient system can often attain the same level of progressivity and sometimes larger direct expenditures at lower tax rates.

One problem for some conservatives not steeped in traditional reform is that, until recently, many tax preferences favored businesses and capital owners, while most personal preferences were in the form of deductions and exclusions of greater value to higher-income individuals (because of their higher tax rates) and were of little or no value to those who did not pay taxes. Eliminating these preferences, therefore, might simply make additional money available for other activities that progressives favor. Still, conservatives generally embrace efficiency, and there is no reason why savings from removing differentials and preferences needs to finance larger spending elsewhere. The money raised this way can just as easily be returned to taxpayers in the form of lower rates, which enhance the efficiency gains. When the removal of a preference finances a reduction in tax rates, there is an added benefit: any remaining preferences in the form of deductions are simply worth less because lower rates are applied to those deductions.[17]

Income Tax Reformers. Traditional tax reformers today can be divided into two camps with many similar, although not identical, goals. Almost since the creation of the modern income tax, traditional income tax reformers have concerned themselves with the question of whether the income tax complies with principles of horizontal equity and efficiency. Do those with equal incomes pay equal tax? Does a deduction really reflect a difference in ability to pay, or does it merely tend to favor one form of income or consumption over another? Many of the reforms reviewed in this book were adopted with these concerns in mind.

Many income tax reformers believe that capital income should be subject to tax, just as labor income is. Indeed, in the early decades of the income tax, government mainly taxed capital through the corporate tax, and individual taxes on labor income were much lighter. However, since those with higher incomes earn the most capital income, the underlying concern for income tax reformers seems to be progressivity. One overlapping subgroup of traditional reformers—usually but not always from the income tax camp—is composed of tax expenditure theorists enamored with the idea of trying to measure preferences in the income tax that tend to serve expenditure-like functions (e.g., see Surrey and McDaniel 1985).

Consumption Tax Reformers. A long-standing debate in economics centers on whether people should be taxed on what they earn for society (an income tax) or what they take out of society (a consumption tax). Many of the arguments for consumption taxes are efficiency arguments—basically, that lowering taxes would distort saving decisions less, possibly leading to higher growth. Much research also suggests that taxes on capital, compared with taxes on labor, may reduce output (or otherwise distort productive behavior) more, although there is another body of research that asserts that such evidence is weak since we don't accurately estimate people's reactions to taxes.[18]

Many consumption tax theorists believe that one can assess a progressive tax rate schedule on total consumption that would approximate the progressivity of the income tax (U.S. Department of the Treasury 1977). This position differs from that of some business and capital owner groups that simply favor consumption taxes as a way of lowering their own taxes. These theorists say a consumption tax would be fairer on net because it would better meet horizontal equity criteria (U.S. Department of Treasury 1997). That said, whether or not equal progressivity can be obtained at the very top depends on the perspective used. For individuals who consume only a tiny fraction of their income—and this occurs frequently among those with substantial income—one has to accept that the tax will be collected down the road when income is finally consumed by taxpayers or their heirs. If the same amount has to be collected on an annual basis, the consumption tax rate might have to be well over 100 percent to collect as much revenue on an annual basis as a 35 percent income tax rate.[19]

One of the stronger arguments for a consumption tax is based on horizontal equity concerns. Consider the case of two people, both currently earning the same amount; one saves and the other doesn't. Under an income tax, the saver would pay the same tax up front on the earnings, and then pay an additional tax later on any interest or other income earned on the saving, while the non-saver would pay no later tax. Since both taxpayers are initially in the same situation, the income tax tends to discriminate against the saver and the consumption tax doesn't. This equity argument gets trickier when there is inherited wealth.[20] Some consumption tax theorists, therefore, are quite willing to levy an estate tax.[21] However, this position appears to be more of an academic than a political compromise because much of the money pushing for consumption taxation comes from wealthy families. Since they are more concerned with the estate tax than with income taxes, the compromise is unacceptable to them.[22]

Among the many important debates surrounding consumption tax theory, three especially bear mention here. First, capital formation lobbyists use the consumption arguments to favor the immediate write-off of expenses for capital investment, but unwavering adherence to consumption tax theory would also deny deductions for interest paid on borrowing or require that any measure of net saving take into account additional borrowing and not just asset purchases. Second, theory suggests that a consumption tax can be designed to tax windfalls or returns to risk, yet exclude from tax the equivalent of the interest rate on an asset with zero risk. Third, many small business interests adamantly oppose the adoption of a value-added tax (VAT)—the most common form of consumption tax prevalent in many countries around the world—in exchange for lower income tax rates. Some abhor the additional complexity, and some simply fear that the VAT is too good a tax and will too easily generate revenues to finance big government.

Taxes as an Instrument of Economic Policy

Keynesians. One of the most powerful figures among 20th century economists, British economist John Maynard Keynes, suggested that government could increase expenditures or reduce taxes to help an underemployed or depressed economy, even if higher deficits result. Often referred to as pump priming or demand stimulus, Keynesian policy seemed to prove effective in the United States when World War II wartime spending—despite large deficits—helped end the Great Depression. By the 1960s, the followers of Keynes turned to the tax system (and wage withholding) as the fastest and simplest way to disburse money. President Kennedy, a Democrat, explicitly promoted Keynesian policies in his early 1960s tax proposals, while in 1971 the Republican President Nixon declared, "Now I am a Keynesian."[23]

A popular political version of Keynesian theory began to hold that almost all deficit spending was acceptable as long as the economy was headed toward a recession, in a recession, emerging from a recession, or had high levels of unemployment—which, politically, meant almost any time. The theory's popularity began to wane, especially in the 1970s, when inflation and stagnation came along hand-in-hand, and reasserted the importance of monetary policy.

Nonetheless, Keynesian policy lives on. In virtually every recession, Congress and the president have invoked the language of "stimulus" to prove they were "doing something" with tax cuts and expenditure increases to get the economy moving again. In this regard, modern conservative presidents have been little different from liberal ones. Both sides feel it necessary to tell the public they are doing something to deal with a downturn.

Supply-Side Theorists. Like the political Keynesians, supply-side theorists support tax cuts—and, as with the Keynesians, the level of support sometimes seems indifferent to the state of the economy, the size of the deficit, or the level of the current tax rates. Their emphasis is on lowering marginal tax rates to spur saving and work by people seeking greater after-tax rewards. Marginal income tax rates are the rates paid on the last or "next" dollars of income received—the rates that would apply, say, if one worked or saved more.

Supply-side theory was espoused strongly from the late 1970s to at least the early 21st century by a few political columnists and by the editorial page of the *Wall Street Journal,* where its more populist versions would appear. These pages would also attack civil servants who would not "score" feedback effects from the higher revenues from the economic expansion supposedly resulting from the tax cuts (regardless of whether expenditures were reduced).[24] Irving Kristol (2003b, 10), a contributor to the *Wall Street Journal* editorial pages, credits the long-time editor of those pages, Robert Bartley, with converting the Republican Party to this "new economics." Bartley had helped convince some Republicans—in particular, Congressman Jack Kemp of New York and, through him, Ronald Reagan—to move away from the "self-defeating" strategy of "cutting spending . . . while leaving the programmatic initiatives in the hands of Democrats."

Supply-side supporters like Kemp frequently used the tax cuts backed by the Keynesians in the early 1960s as an example of supply-side economics, even though its original Keynesian adherents might have been appalled by the apostasy. Still, there is an important distinction in that the Keynesian notion of spurring demand is met by getting money to people to spend, whereas supply stimulus increases the incentive to work and save through lower tax rates. Although both camps often revile each other, both like to claim that the economic rebound would generate new taxes to offset some of the static cost of the stimulus. The political appeal of this idea—called "dynamic scoring"—is self-evident: politicians can make proposals whose costs are only partially held against them. Economists may claim there is no such thing as a "free lunch" but they understand its appeal.

In the end, supply siders are right that a leaner, sleeker government with lower tax rates may enhance economic growth and increase revenues.[25] However, the "feedback" effect's size depends upon far more than tax cuts. If financed merely by increased deficits, these cuts may lead to higher taxes in the future. Much depends upon monetary policy and other choices. Taxes with broad bases will often distort less than equal-revenue taxes with narrow tax bases.[26] Finally, one must figure out whether expenditures financed by taxes are doing good or bad things for the economy.

Capital Formation Reformers. Like supply-siders, the capital formation reformers pay special attention to trying to lower the tax rates on capital income, but they are much less concerned with the rates on labor. The basic argument used by most in this group is that growth is good and capital formation is the way to achieve it.

Many interests fall under the capital formation banner. Some of these interests represent capital-intensive industries, such as the American Council for Capital Formation. The physical capital interests tend to support almost any reduction in the tax on capital income, but their pet issue is usually incentives for depreciable capital through accelerated depreciation, cost-recovery allowances, or investment credits. Businesses more dependent on human capital, such as medical supply or software firms, instead emphasize lowering tax rates and providing research credits, and they often break ranks with the physical capital formation proponents. The capital formation advocates often support converting the income tax to a consumption tax (which would remove much of the tax on capital income), but many would not be adverse to a negative tax rate on capital either, if enough subsidies could be found.[27]

Capital income taxation is an exceedingly dense subject. Some capital formation reformers are intent on removing all taxes on capital income, while others simply want to eliminate multiple taxation. Opposing them are some progressives who will accept almost any type of additional tax on capital, including estate taxes, property taxes, real estate taxes, franchise taxes, and corporate taxes, while other progressives simply want to insure capital income is taxed at least once.[28]

Anti–estate tax and anti–capital gains tax advocates, such as the American Council on Capital Formation, represent some of society's economic elite. They also include farm and small business interests, whose owners tend to save substantial amounts of their personal income in their business or land. For many of the richest people in society, income has largely been accrued as capital gains and will not be subject to personal income tax unless the underlying assets are sold and the income "recognized." Indeed, accrued capital gains are forgiven any tax liability at death.[29] But the threat of the estate tax looms large even if little income tax is paid. Bill Gates, Sr., the father of one of the richest people in the world, claimed that much of the opposition to the estate tax is financed by a tiny group of other extremely wealthy individuals (see chapter 11).

Although some rich taxpayers' income is double- or triple-taxed by estate taxes and capital income taxes, other income may escape the tax altogether. As an example of multiple taxation, consider labor income that goes to purchase corporate stock directly (not through a retirement plan). The earnings of the purchased companies, in turn, are subject to corporate tax. Meanwhile, the retained earnings of the corporation will add to the value of stock held by individuals, which will be taxed again if the stock is sold. Any remaining assets held by the individual may be subject to estate tax. As an example of low taxation, some individuals achieve very large capital gains on their successful investments far in excess of any retained earnings on which corporate tax may have been paid. This income may never be taxed if it is not recognized as gains and if estate planning is successful. If they borrowed to buy the stock, taxpayers may even declare zero or negative income by taking interest deductions while recognizing few or no capital gains.[30]

Taxes as an Instrument of Social Policy

Our final category includes theorists and advocates who view taxes as a means to achieve some social policy goal. Although liberals have historically dominated this group, this is no longer the case. Many conservatives now view taxation as a means to enact "pro-family" or "market-based" reforms of social policy.

The Progressives. Progressivity is more than a goal: it is a principle and follows from the natural order that only those with the ability to pay can pay. Still, progressivity becomes a goal when we determine that more progressivity is required to form a just society. Progressives tend to favor higher taxes at the top of the income distribution, while at the bottom they favor tax cuts or refunds, even for those who pay little or no tax. Antipoverty advocates particularly worry about the impact of taxes on the poor or on recipients of other government assistance programs. Progressives scrutinize the distributional tables that the Office of Tax Policy and the Joint Committee on Taxation develop for the government or that are produced by nonprofit organizations such as the Urban-Brookings Tax Policy Center or Citizens for Tax Justice.

From its inception, the income tax has been the main instrument for promoting progressivity—higher incomes are taxed at higher rates.[31] The estate tax is much more progressive but applies only to a few people. Debate exists on whether the property tax might also impose higher rates on those with more resources. In general, however, those concerned with progressivity focus their attention on the income tax.

Many progressives also tend to favor larger government, but big government and progressive taxation (as defined by tax rates rising with income) are not as compatible as they first appear. True, when the income tax was created in 1913 and when the Sixteenth Amendment to the Constitution was ratified, the tax was often linked to questions about the size of government. Those who favored larger income taxes often favored more government expenditures, and vice versa. Early "reforms" reflected the exigencies of government's early growth.

What is generally ignored is that income tax is also inherently a conservative instrument of taxation. The flip side of a higher tax rate on the rich is a lower or zero tax rate on those with lower incomes, and a moderate amount of income exempted from tax for all taxpayers (who also benefit from the zero rates that apply at the beginning of a progressive tax rate schedule). One consequence, generally forgotten by both proponents and opponents of progressive taxes—is that lower taxes on lower and middle-income classes (and the corresponding low initial tax rates on the first dollars earned by all taxpayers) limit the amount of revenues collected and the expenditures that those taxes would support.[32] The types of personal exemptions and credits that make the income tax progressive are generally less available for other taxes, such as sales taxes or taxes on earnings.[33] Thus, as the income tax began to mature by the middle of the 20th century, all developed nations began to finance further expansion of government mainly through growth in Social Security and flatter-rate sales and consumption taxes—not through the income tax. The upshot is an anomaly: liberals favoring progressive taxes often cannot raise the money for the larger government they may want, whereas conservatives favoring flat-rate taxes often get the larger government these taxes support.[34] Unwittingly, antiprogressive proponents of flat taxes may support larger government, while pro-progressive opponents of flat taxes may help the cause of small government.

Table 2.1 shows the overall levels of taxation in numerous developed countries, as well as the reliance of each upon different types of taxes. Compared with the European Economic Community (EEC), the United States collects a similar percentage of gross domestic product (GDP) through progressive income taxes. On the other hand, the average EEC country collects almost 8 percentage points more of GDP in the form of flat or regressive (as defined by rates) consumption taxes on goods and services than the United States. Although exceptions abound, stricter U.S. reliance on progressive-rate income taxation, and the corresponding failure to adopt a more regressive national tax on goods and services, correlates with its smaller size government.

Tax policy, of course, can be used to support all sorts of social goals, such as charitable contributions or purchases of health insurance by taxpayers. While liberals have concerned themselves with the poor, conservatives have often worried about marriage penalties or high levels of taxation on families with children when little adjustment is made for the effect of those children on the taxpayers' ability to pay.

Other Influences

The following discussion of other influential groups and their disparate tax positions rounds out the inner workings of the tax policy arena.

The practitioner community—tax lawyers, accountants, and professional tax preparers—often complain about complexity. They mostly align themselves with traditional tax reformers, and maintaining a viable tax system depends in no small part on the extent to which they take their profession seriously. Their professional associations often lobby for simplification, partly because they see too many inequities arising from a complex system and partly because they are trained to account accurately and are threatened by a system under which that goal is hard to achieve. For some practitioners, simplification is a mixed blessing since less complexity can mean less business. Of course, some lawyers and accountants will lobby for special interests and find ways to skirt the edges of tax laws. There is also a debate over the consequences for the tax system as greater numbers have abandoned professional goals, such as transparent and accurate reporting in favor of becoming salespeople for tax shelters.

Budget balance hawks can be either liberal or conservative in their view of overall levels of taxation. If conservative, like former senator

Table 2.1 *Tax Receipts in Various Countries as a Percentage of GDP, 2000*

	Total tax receipts	Personal income tax	Corporate income tax	Social Security contributions		Taxes on goods and services	Other taxes
				Employees	Employers		
Japan	27.1	5.6	3.6	3.8	5.0	5.1	4.0
United States	**29.6**	**12.6**	**2.5**	**3.0**	**3.5**	**4.7**	**3.3**
Ireland	31.1	9.6	3.8	1.3	2.7	11.6	2.1
Australia	31.5	11.6	6.5	0.0	0.0	8.7	4.7
Switzerland	35.7	10.9	2.8	3.9	3.9	7.0	7.2
Canada	35.8	13.2	4.0	2.0	2.9	8.7	5.0
United Kingdom	37.4	10.9	3.7	2.5	3.5	12.1	4.7
Germany	37.9	9.6	1.8	6.5	7.3	10.6	2.1
Netherlands	41.4	6.2	4.2	8.1	4.7	12.0	6.2
France	45.3	8.2	3.2	4.0	11.3	11.7	6.9
Sweden	54.2	19.3	4.1	3.0	11.9	11.2	4.7
EEC average[a]	41.6	10.9	3.8	3.9	6.5	12.3	4.2
OECD average[a]	**37.4**	**10.0**	**3.6**	**3.0**	**5.7**	**11.6**	**3.5**

Source: OECD Revenue Statistics 1965–2001, 2002.

Note: EEC = European Economic Union; OECD = Organization for Economic Cooperation and Development; GDP = gross domestic product.

a. Unweighted.

and former presidential nominee Robert Dole, they are more likely than radical supply-siders to support higher taxes to pay for expenditures already promised. If liberal, like former President Clinton, they might still be more willing than other liberals to accept some slowdown in the rate of expenditure growth.

Another group hard to define along any traditional conservative-liberal continuum is the employee benefit community. Tax preferences for pensions and for employer-provided health benefits have been around since the birth of the income tax (Acs and Steuerle 1996), reinforcing the government's tendency to use taxes as an instrument of social policy.[35] The pension community often lobbies to expand these benefits, but not remove all taxes on capital since the latter would eliminate the net incentive to save for retirement. Meanwhile, many progressives object that most taxpayers do not accrue much in the way of retirement benefits, while related tax subsidies accrue mainly to the well-off. The health benefit community faces a number of problems, among them that the tax benefits due to the preference for employer-provided health insurance accrue mainly to higher-income people who are in higher tax brackets and tend to have better insurance policies; the tax benefits are not available for health insurance other than that offered by an employer; and the tax benefits are open-ended, rising with the generosity of the health insurance package.[36] To the extent this last feature increases health costs, individuals become more reluctant to buy insurance, employers are less likely to offer it, and the number of uninsured rise.

Whatever the inequities and inefficiencies of today's system, some employer involvement in health and pensions tends to help people buy health insurance and save for retirement. Many people do not buy health insurance or retirement assets on their own, but sign on when the employer contributes directly or encourages participation. At the same time, confining many tax incentives to those offered through employers excludes many individuals and makes agreement on reform options difficult.

Democratic and Republican labels seem to mean very little when elected state and local officials lobby on tax issues. Most of these officials favor increased revenue sharing from the federal government to the states and oppose any cutbacks on their ability to float federal tax-exempt bonds. In recent years, they have become extremely adept at eviscerating state balanced budget rules by borrowing against future tax collections, while taking advantage of federal tax preferences for this borrowing. In sum, they will take what they can get, and political party doesn't seem to matter a great deal.

Many states piggyback their own state income tax systems on federal definitions of income—whether it is adjusted gross income, taxable income, or some similar measure reported on federal returns. State receipts, therefore, are partially subject to the whims of federal legislation. For instance, state income tax revenues fall when Congress grants a more generous depreciation allowance or when it generates fewer realizations of capital gains through higher federal rates. States cannot stray too far from basic federal definitions of taxable income without further complicating life for taxpayers. Think, in particular, of a multistate business having to allocate income among various states. States also audit mainly by following the IRS lead on whom and what to audit.

Finally, as a matter of both activist social and economic policy, corrective taxes are sometimes proposed to deal with problems, such as pollution and smoking.[37]

NOTES

1. "It looks, in fact, very much as if both parties had in mind some kind of Law or Rule of *fair* play" (Lewis 1943, 17).

2. The rest of the quote reads, "Indeed, the world is ruled by little else. Practical men, who believe themselves to be quite exempt from any intellectual influences, are usually the slaves of some defunct economist." (Keynes 1936).

3. For a more elaborate treatment of two equity principles—horizontal and vertical equity—see Steuerle (2002a, 253–84). We have given little attention here to some of the more complex issues, such as how one tries to measure who are equals and what compromises are required to deal with nonmarket transactions, such the returns from equity ownership of one's own home.

4. "Horizontal equity is the command that equals be treated equally" (Kaplow 1989, 139).

5. On the subject of vertical equity, economist Harley Lutz (1945, 70, 82) states, "There is no just or progressive tax rates scale. Every such scale is the product of guesswork and of political and fiscal expediency. And where expediency is the basis of policy, it is easy to lapse into injustice" (Steuerle 2002a, 259).

6. Steuerle (2003a) takes up the issue of integrating taxes and expenditures in determining overall progressivity.

7. See Cohen, Steuerle, and Carasso (2002) for a detailed analysis of just how progressive Social Security may be once it also accounts for such issues as differential mortality rates among groups of recipients. As it turns out, Social Security would redistribute little without disability insurance, as higher mortality rates among lower-income groups tend to offset a progressive schedule for paying benefits relative to lifetime taxes paid.

8. Altruism may be required if taxpayers incur net losses to themselves to support some broader gain to society, as when defense expenses paid for by one generation of taxpayers are valuable mainly to the next generation.

9. Note that the aggregate net income in society may be unchanged when one person loses a dollar and another gains a dollar in a tax/transfer scheme.

10. For a much broader discussion of the individual equity principle, see Steuerle (2002a). I find it useful to discuss individual equity separately from efficiency and the efficiency implications of benefit taxation because the equity argument lays underneath some of the rationale for "choice" programs, vouchers, and for those aspects of social insurance programs that try to relate benefits to taxes.

11. This split can be traced back to Adam Smith, who argued that "individuals ought to contribute to the support of the government, as nearly as possible, according to their respective abilities [to pay taxes]; that is, in proportion to the revenue which they respectively enjoy under the protection of the state [benefit taxation]" (Smith 1904, 310, brackets mine).

12. Note that this issue, often called "adverse selection," comes up mainly in areas like health and primary and secondary education. For a further discussion of the many pluses and minuses of vouchers that provide choice, see Peterson et al. (2000).

13. See, for instance, Pechman (1971, chapter 3).

14. The CEA's role has waned with the increased number of economists in the departments of government and with the strengthening of the Economic Policy Council. While the Office of Tax Analysis has the greatest number of public finance economists assembled anywhere in the executive branch, the CEA still maintains a strong connection with academia, and its three "advisers" usually come from there. The Congressional Budget Office, however, now has more public finance economists than any agency in the executive branch, which reflects the shifting of power between the two branches of government.

15. As noted below, the Joint Committee on Taxation handles the revenue-estimating responsibility for changes in the law in Congress, while the Congressional Budget Office is in charge of estimating long-run receipts under current law.

16. Reviewers of this book have noted that the Ways and Means staff has become more partisan over the last 15 years or so.

17. As more preferences began to be granted to lower-income individuals, moreover, the political dynamic between liberals and conservatives began to change as well.

18. This condition is among those examined to determine if a switch to consumption tax enhances efficiency.

19. For example, if a person earning $10 million and consuming $1 million were to pay $2 million in income tax (assuming much income escapes tax), the consumption tax rate would have to be 200 percent of the $1 million of consumption to generate equal revenues. Again, if government is willing to live with promises of future revenues when the taxpayer or her heirs finally consume the income, then it can forego the initial collection, assess a lower rate, and count on getting its money down the road.

20. If the saver saves because her discount rate is less than the rate of return on the investment, then she also has access to some additional "income" even on a present-value basis.

21. When an estate tax is attached to a tax on earnings, it is equivalent to a tax on lifetime income. In a sense, it is an income tax with an accounting period of a lifetime rather than a year. See Steuerle (1980).

22. Much of their income may already avoid income taxation if it comes in the form of unrealized capital gains on their assets.

23. As Herb Stein (1988, 135–36) explains, President Nixon was not advocating an activist policy, but simply that it would be folly to raise taxes in a recession.

24. Elliot Brownlee suggests in a note to me that arguably some progressives (e.g., Roosevelt, Brandeis, and Morgenthau) were also supply-siders (see also Brownlee 2004). They believed that progressive redistribution would stimulate competition, economic growth, and tax revenues.

25. I suppose I should take the scoring issue more personally. In January 2003, while I was a candidate for the position of director of the Congressional Budget Office, a lead *Wall Street Journal* editorial attacked me as "not an agent for change" on the grounds that I would not adequately "score" feedback effects that made tax cuts less expensive than their initial costs. To be fair, it is the tendency of some extreme supply-siders to engage in personal attacks, as well as argue that tax cuts wouldn't cost anything at all, that gives the theory its bad reputation.

26. A sanguine but well-articulated view of the supply-side revolution and its various historical claims can be found in Bartlett (2003).

27. A very good summary of different approaches to consumption taxation, as well as some of the pluses and minuses, can be found in Rosen (1999, chapter 20).

28. Two taxes are not necessarily more distorting than one. The resolution depends upon both the combined tax rate achieved and how the two tax bases are related. For instance, the existing corporate income tax creates a bias in favor of debt, an issue separate from whether it leads to a higher rate on corporate capital.

29. The basis value of the underlying assets are "stepped up" to market value at death, so that an heir immediately selling an inherited $100 asset that originally cost $10 would calculate gains as $100 minus $100, or $0.

30. The law attempts to limit this game-playing to prevent net negative declarations of income, but there are ways around these limitations. For instance, one can borrow against one's house and take mortgage interest deductions while never recognizing any investment income, or one can at least use negative investment income from one set of transactions at least to offset positive income from others.

31. The estate tax is more progressive in taxing top wealth holders, but it collects only a small fraction of what is raised by the income tax.

32. Early supporters of the income tax argued that their tax would "not touch the wages and salaries of ordinary people, but would instead attack the unearned profits and rents of monopolists. Thus they firmly believed that the income tax could itself contribute to an assault on monopoly power . . . Democratic party leaders such as [William Jennings] Bryan . . . added income taxation to tariff reform as a central party cause." (Brownlee 1989, 1616).

33. Sales taxes do attempt to restore some progressivity by exempting food or other items, but the method is crude and still taxes the poor on other items of consumption. Exemptions may be easier to administer with income taxes.

34. As we will see, advocates of a pure flat tax generally want to displace the progressive income tax with a flat tax that raises no more revenue. But whether they would be able to hold the line keeps even some conservatives in check as to whether they will join the flat rate parade. For instance, a progressive tax with rates up to 35 percent or 40 percent may be harder to increase than an equal-revenue flat rate tax with a rate like 18 percent.

35. At first it was not codified, and IRS regulations or rules sometimes provided the effective exclusions from tax.

36. Of course, the net impact on progressivity of any expenditure provision cannot be examined in isolation. The higher rates necessary to support the exclusion may still leave the overall system progressive.

37. Cordes (2002) makes the case for "corrective taxes" as an instrument of social policy. On a different tack, Cavanaugh (2003) goes so far as to argue that "political equality" requires shifting the tax burden onto the wealthy.

3

A Summary of Contemporary Tax Changes

A democratic government is the only one in which those who vote for a tax can escape the obligation to pay for it.

—Alexis de Tocqueville, *Democracy in America*

This book presents contemporary tax policy developments in chronological fashion, period by period. To place these events within a broader context, this chapter precedes the fuller tale with a brief but thorough data-oriented history of changes in the tax system. The extent to which one action relates to another becomes clearer in this longer-term analysis. Many stories about the evolution of the tax system, such as the influence of rising and falling inflation rates on taxes, are also easier to visualize with graphs and tables covering long segments of time rather than in filaments of legislative cycles. Details on the developments and ramifications of specific tax policies follow in succeeding chapters.

Levels of Taxation

"From a class tax to a mass tax" is how many describe the postwar explosion in coverage and collections. No crisis affected the expansion of the modern income tax more than the need to finance participation in World War II (Brownlee 2004). Before the war, the federal individual income tax applied only to a sliver of the population, and it wasn't until the war that wage withholding was applied to a large portion of the middle class. In the 1930s, federal individual income taxes never exceeded 1.4 percent of gross domestic product (GDP) and federal corporate taxes never more than 1.6 percent of GDP (see figure 3.1 or, for more complete data, appendix table A.1). By 1943, these taxes had risen, respectively, to 8.0 and 6.9 percent of GDP.

Policymakers opted to maintain the withholding of taxes on wages— the principal administrative mechanism adopted to implement higher taxes during the war. As the United States entered peacetime, income taxes were reduced moderately, but to nowhere near prewar levels. For the individual income tax, a postwar low of 5.8 percent of GDP in 1949 was still more than four times greater than the highest percentage before World War II. By the 1950s, even the small tax reductions of the late 1940s were largely offset by tax increases used to finance the Korean conflict. From that time on, federal individual income taxes remained a fairly constant percentage of total GDP, with cyclical low points in 1964 and 2004, and cyclical high points in 1969, 1981, and 2000.

Figure 3.1 *Total Tax Receipts as a Percentage of GDP, 1929–2002*

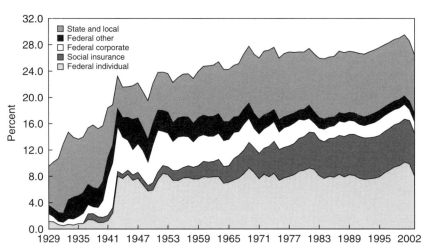

Source: Bureau of Economic Analysis, National Income and Product Accounts, Annual Tables 1.1, 3.2, 3.3, 3.6, and 8.29.
Note: "Federal other" includes federal estate taxes, gift taxes, and custom duties plus employer contributions for federal unemployment tax, railroad unemployment insurance, and federal worker's compensation; it excludes federal nontaxes.

After the Korean conflict, total federal, state, and local tax receipts increased gradually. In 1954, government at all levels received 22 percent of GDP. Receipts then rose gradually to a high of 27.4 percent of GDP in 1969, when a surtax was put into effect to help pay for the Vietnam War. From 1969 to the early 1990s, total tax receipts zigzagged slightly, but there was little change overall. Total taxes as a percentage of GDP dipped below 26 percent in the early 1970s and early 1980s, but not again until 2003 and 2004.[1]

In the mid- to late 1990s, federal and state revenues began to rise again. At both levels of government, stricter fiscal regimes were adopted just before economic growth picked up more quickly than expected. Higher growth rates not only boosted revenues, but also pushed people into higher income tax brackets faster than government made tax cuts. Unusual levels of capital gains realizations and stock options in a bubble stock market especially added to income tax receipts. Both total federal taxes and total government taxes reached all-time highs by 2000 (see figure 3.1) before dropping significantly as the economy slowed and new tax laws took hold. By the same token, the subsequent fall in total taxes after 2000 ranks among the most dramatic in contemporary tax history. These revenues are expected to rebound somewhat as capital gains return to more normal levels and more taxpayers are swept into a federal alternative minimum tax (AMT), which denies filers the use of dependent exemptions, deductions for state and local taxes, and other tax provisions that can reduce regular income taxes only.

State and Local Taxes: The Main Source of Growth

State and local taxes were the main source of growth in the post–World War II era, rising from 6.1 percent of GDP in 1954 to a postwar high of 9.7 percent in 1972.[2] This was an increase of 3.6 percentage points compared with a total increase in all taxes (including federal taxes) of 4.5 percentage points over the same period. From 1947 to 1972, state and local taxes almost doubled as a percentage of GDP. From a longer-term perspective, state and local taxes might be viewed as simply recovering from their dramatic drop in importance as the federal government role expanded during the Great Depression and especially World War II. In the mid- to late 1970s, a tax revolt led to a modest decline in state and local tax collections relative to GDP. Tax levels remained relatively steady for more than a decade before climbing in the 1990s, and then falling off in the 2001 to 2002 economic slowdown. In 2003 and 2004, they began to rise again because of the recovery and, in contrast to the late 1990s, states legislated tax increases rather than decreases. The stock market bubble affected states with the same boom-and-bust cycle as it did the federal government.

These postwar increases in state and local tax collections came through various sources: higher tax rates on sales and income and the adoption of new taxes in many states. State and local income taxes, in particular, grew steadily more important over the entire postwar period, rising from only 0.18 percent of GDP in 1946 to 2.2 percent by 2000 before falling off to 1.9 percent by 2002. Not only did many more states adopt an individual income tax, but growth in the economy forced taxpayers into higher tax rate brackets over time. By the mid-1970s, combined federal, state, and local income taxes had risen to a new high as a percentage of income because of state and local, not federal, tax increases. After that point, state and local taxes remained much steadier as a percentage of GDP.

Individuals were not the only ones affected by increases in state and local taxes. Cline et al. (2004) estimated that businesses paid substantial taxes in fiscal year 2003, of which $156 billion came from property taxes, $35 billion came from state and local corporate income taxes, and $16 billion came from corporation and business license fees. Businesses also paid sales taxes on goods and services sold to other businesses, not just to consumers.[3]

The Rise of Social Security Taxes and Fall of Corporate and Excise Taxes

Social Security taxes stand out for their large and consistent growth up until the early 1990s. In fact, the pattern of Social Security taxation was so consistent that it can be traced by a rule of thumb: Social Security tax rates rose by roughly 3 percentage points per decade from 1950 to 1990, regardless of economic and political cycles. The combined employer and employee tax rate equaled 3.0 percent in 1950, 6.0 percent in 1960, 9.6 percent in 1970, 12.26 percent in 1980, and 15.3 percent in 1990— where it has remained. These rate increases, as well as expansions of the Social Security tax base, resulted in Social Security taxes rising from less than 1 percent of GDP before 1950 to close to 7 percent by 1990 and thereafter.

Since Social Security and state and local taxes went up far more than total taxes, something must have gone down. First, corporate income taxes declined significantly, thanks to a combination of overlapping causes. From the 1950s through the 1970s, corporate profits became a smaller share of national income, partly because the large increase in interest payments after World War II meant that a smaller share of the nominal returns to capital (that is, a smaller proportion of the total income to both bondholders and stockholders from firms) was subject to corporate income taxation. This growth was especially prevalent in the inflationary period from 1973 to the late 1980s, but even after interest rates fell with the end of that inflationary period, corporate debt remained high, at least by historical comparison, relative to corporate equity. In addition, corporate taxes fell as more tax reductions were legislated—first, tax preferences for business investment, then lower tax rates. The relative growth in foreign income deferred or excluded from domestic tax also contributed to the decline in corporate income taxes. By the early 21st century, a new wave of tax shelters for business seemed to reduce corporate tax payments significantly, but the amounts were hard to estimate (Manzon and Plesko 2002; Steuerle 2002c; Sullivan 1999, 2002a, 2002b, 2003; Yin 2001, 2002).

Second, other federal taxes, mainly excise taxes, also shrank. A conscious decision to rely less upon excise taxes (as witnessed in 1965 legislation[4]), the erosion in value of fixed nominal excise taxes because of inflation, and the rising importance of services untaxed by excises (such as the burgeoning health care sector) account for this decline.

Because states and localities rely heavily on excise and sales taxes, the eroding sales tax base is much more important to them than to the federal government. Services have been especially hard to tax. For a while, states overcame these obstacles by increasing sales tax rates. Also, because many specific excise taxes are stated in terms of cents per carton or per gallon, many excise tax payments only rose with numbers of purchases, not at the much faster rate of increases in prices and incomes. Even legislated tax increases driven by spurts in excise tax charges per carton or per gallon were handily outpaced by the rise in personal incomes.

Tax Preferences and the Declining Value of Personal Exemption

Complaints about levels of taxation are often bandied about in political campaigns ("no new taxes"), but they give a misleading picture of the government's use of resources. Even if levels of taxation or average tax rates stay constant, changes in exclusions, deductions, and credits—that is, various tax preferences—can affect the size of the tax base.

Exclusions, which grew from 13 to 25 percent of personal income from 1948 to 1982, and then gradually declined to 15 percent in 2000, are the least understood source of preference because they are not counted in income subject to tax, nor are they reported on tax returns. Instead, total income, adjusted gross income (AGI), and taxable income—those income measures reported on individual income tax returns—exclude income derived from certain sources or used in certain ways.

Many of these exclusions apply to a large percentage of the population, including much of the middle class. Employer contributions to (and earnings from) health, pension, and other retirement vehicles like 401(k) plans are one example.[5] From 1948 to 2000, the net exclusion applying to health and pension plans alone increased from 0.5 to 1.1 percent of personal income (see appendix table A.2). The 2000 figure is misleadingly low since many employers avoided making excludable deposits to pension plans when a booming stock market made it appear that no new saving was required, at least temporarily, to meet promises of future benefit payments. The health exclusion knows no such cycle and has moved inexorably upward as a percentage of personal income.

Such nontaxable public transfers as Social Security and Medicare also grew considerably in the second half of the 1900s, as did other nontaxable labor compensation, including employer-provided life insurance. The expansion and growth in home ownership, which the tax system favors, was another important source of exclusion.[6]

Deductions reported on tax returns also generally increased, except during a few brief periods. Itemized deductions are allowed for state and local taxes, interest on home mortgages, contributions to charity, extraordinary health expenses, and other miscellaneous items. As a percentage of personal income, these deductions grew from 3.3 percent in 1948 to 10.0 percent in 1970 and have hovered around there since then, hitting 9.1 percent in 2000. On occasion, declines in overall deductions reflected legislated increases in the standard deduction (an allowance for a minimum amount of deductions that may be taken in lieu of itemizing or detailing deductions on a tax return). All in all, the standard deduction grew from a postwar low of 2.2 percent of income in 1970 to 6.9 percent in 1977 and was back down to 3.7 percent in 2000.

The most dramatic change in the individual income tax base over the postwar era, however, was not in the expanded use of exclusions, deductions, and credits. Rather, it was in the declining value of the personal exemption allowed to each taxpayer and dependent. On taxable returns, that exemption had eroded from more than 24 percent to just 6.4 percent of personal income between 1947 and 1978. This decline moved many formerly nontaxable individuals into the tax system, expanding the tax base further.

The decline in relative value of the dependent exemption for households with children eventually prompted attempts by both Republicans and Democrats to make the tax code more "family friendly," especially as evidence showed that moderate- and low-income households were hit hard (Steuerle 1983a). Press coverage of this issue began in the early to mid-1980s, and the ensuing debate launched a continual wave of reforms aimed at helping the family. These reforms included increases in the personal exemption in the late 1980s and, more important, in credits granted to working households with children.

The growth in tax credits has been quite large since 1986. The total value of credits hit an all-time high at the beginning of the 21st century, due almost entirely to earned income tax credits (EITC) and child credits. For low- to moderate-income households—but not for middle- to upper-income households—these credit expansions have now far more than offset the long postwar decline in the value of the dependent exemption.[7]

Changes in the Tax Base

Table 3.1 summarizes how the tax base has changed since 1948. Note not only the overall expansion of the base relative to personal income (due mainly to erosion in importance of the personal exemption), but also the extent to which taxpayers reduce the tax base through their behavior. In effect, the increased use of exclusions, deductions, and credits reflects greater differentiation in tax burdens by source or type and use of income. These preferences generally affect behavior, as taxpayers shift toward preferred forms of income or consumption. On the other hand, the erosion of the personal exemption reduced the percentage of income that could effectively be taxed at a zero rate, and many individuals with only modest incomes (relative to the average in the economy) began to pay income tax.[8] For a long time, these reductions in importance of the personal exemption more than covered losses from all additional exclusions, deductions, and credits eroding the tax base. For a typical taxpayer, in other words, a larger portion of income would be subject to tax unless

Table 3.1 *Aggregate Change in the Tax Base as a Percentage of Personal Income*

	1948–1961	1961–1979	1979–1988	1988–1999	1948–1999
Increases in the tax base due to declining importance of:					
Personal exemptions	8.2	10.5	1.2	1.2	21.1
AGI of nontaxable individuals, nonreported AGI and reconciliation	4.6	1.0	0.9	–1.8	4.8
Decreases in the tax base due to further use of:					
Net exclusions from AGI	–2.1	–5.3	0.3	4.3	–2.8
Itemized deductions	–5.0	–0.2	–0.3	–0.1	–5.6
Standard deductions	1.8	–3.4	1.1	1.0	0.5
Income offset by credits[a]	–0.2	–1.1	0.7	–1.7	–2.3
Net change in the tax base	7.3	1.5	3.8	3.0	15.6

Source: Author's calculations based on historical tax data from the Internal Revenue Service.
Note: AGI = adjusted gross income.
a. Uses 1954 for 1948.

the taxpayer sought out more tax preferences by, for example, paying more in deductible mortgage interest or shifting saving into tax-favored retirement plans. Even the personal credits more recently put into the law—which have made many low- to moderate-income households non-taxable once again—can affect behavior since they are tied to earnings and income in a variety of ways that induce more work for some individuals and less for others.

Most exclusions, deductions, exemptions, and credits can be defined as "tax expenditures"—items similar to those in spending programs. The tax expenditure budget is highly controversial, as we shall see in later chapters, partly because it is incomplete and sometimes tends to be used incorrectly to judge various preferences as "bad" simply because they are on the list. Still, it is one of the few accounting systems we have for such items, and it can gauge historic changes. In particular, economists and budget watchers sometimes categorize tax expenditures by those that benefit business and those that benefit individuals other than through businesses they own. Figure 3.2 tracks tax expenditures over the period from 1980 to 1999, dividing these into "social" and "business" tax expenditures. Total tax expenditures, over 40 percent of which favored business, peaked in 1985 at 8.1 percent of GDP, whereas social expenditures have been on the rise since 1990 and now dominate the tax expenditure

Figure 3.2 *Trends in Tax Expenditures, 1980–2003*
(Expressed as a Percentage of GDP)

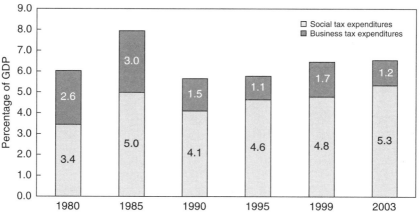

Source: Toder (1998). Updated to 2003 by author.

budget. In 2003, social tax expenditures comprised almost five-sixths of the total tax expenditures of 6.5 percent of GDP or $645 billion.[9]

In sum, though the extent to which personal income falls into the tax base varies over time, a general rule is that the size of the base is increasingly influenced by individuals' behavior, especially social behavior. Exceptions exist. A few reforms removed preferences, mainly for businesses, while lowered tax rates reduced the gains from engaging in many types of tax-preferred behavior. But the general legislative trend toward adding new preferences has dominated the postwar period, except for the few years from 1982 to 1986.

Tax-Exempt Levels of Income and Personal Tax Credits

Minimum tax-exempt levels of income—those levels below which no income tax is due—are determined mainly by the personal exemption, the standard deduction, and, for eligible taxpayers, personal credits.[10] Figure 3.3 presents data on tax-exempt levels of income—both before and after the EITC and the child credit are taken into consideration— from 1948 onward and compares these figures with per capita personal income (see appendix table A.3 for details). As can be seen, the tax-exempt

Figure 3.3 *Tax-Exempt Threshold by Household Size, Excluding Tax Credits, 1948–2000*

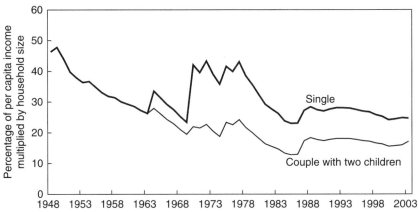

Source: Author's calculations and data from U.S. House of Representatives, Committee on Ways and Means (1996, 2000) and the Bureau of Economic Analysis.

level of income (per person in the household) in 1948 neared one-half of per capita personal income, but by 1986 had declined sharply. In effect, more and more people were pulled into the tax system throughout the first decades after World War II.

More recently, however, the expansion of personal tax credits has substantially offset the tax burden for moderate-income individuals. Even without these credits, by 2001, those filing a joint return with two children and income only from earnings would not begin to pay regular taxes until their joint income exceeded $21,700—approximately 17 percent of per capita personal income multiplied by family size (appendix table A.3). However, personal credits increasingly dominate this story.

Figure 3.4 shows the real "spending"[11] growth over time for the two largest tax credits that affect lower-income families—the EITC and child credit.[12] The EITC is available to low- and moderate-income working families with earnings above zero, while the child credit is not available until income reaches $10,500 (in 2003) and is largely available to those with middle to moderately high income. Together, these two credits can push the tax-exempt income threshold for a family of four to nearly

Figure 3.4 *Real Federal Spending on the EITC, Child Credit, and Welfare (AFDC/TANF), 1976–2009*

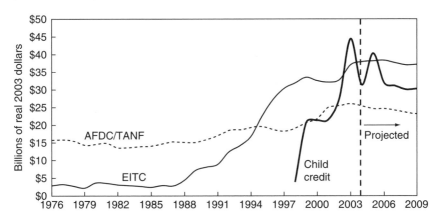

Source: FY 2000–2005 U.S. budgets and IRS statistics on income data.
Notes: The child credit curve after 2004 is driven by both scheduled credit increases and expirations in 2001 and 2003 tax legislation. AFDC = Aid to Families with Dependent Children; TANF = Temporary Assistance to Needy Families; EITC = Earned Income Tax Credit. EITC and child credit aggregate amounts include both outlays and receipts.

$40,000.[13] The figure compares the growth in outlays for these credits against the growth in what is sometimes defined as welfare, or Aid to Families with Dependent Children (later called Temporary Assistance to Needy Families) (OMB 2004). In 2003, the federal government spent $35.5 billion on families through the EITC and $27.3 billion through the child tax credit, compared with $26.0 billion on welfare.[14]

Beginning with the *Economic Report of the President* in 1964, the government began publishing statistics on the number of persons living in "poverty"—defined as having incomes below the federal poverty level. Since then, poverty-level income thresholds have been adjusted yearly for inflation only. With the inflation rate lower than the rate of growth in income, over decades the poverty level has fallen considerably relative to such measures as per capita or average personal income.[15]

Poverty statistics have had an enormous impact on tax policy development over time, as various tax acts attempted to raise the tax-exempt levels of income to reflect changes in these published poverty levels. Excluding tax credits, joint-return filers with two children—the prototypical example presented in congressional tax debates—would be exempt from paying taxes on income roughly equivalent to the poverty level. In the mid-1980s, provisions affecting tax-exempt levels were adjusted automatically over time for inflation by the same index used to determine poverty levels. Of course, real economic growth still gradually eroded the value of the exemptions and tax-exempt portion of income relative to per capita personal income.

Note that the tax-exempt level discussed here reflects the minimum amount set by the personal exemption, standard deduction, and certain personal credits. For groups with sizable exclusions, including those receiving significant Social Security checks or other nontaxable transfers (e.g., food stamps), the tax-exempt level has generally been higher.

Since the mid- to late 1980s, however, the growth in personal credits has also raised the tax-exempt level well beyond poverty thresholds for working households with children. For the most part, these credits are not available to households without children. By way of contrast, in the earlier postwar period Congress paid much less attention to children in determining tax liability. When it came to other low-income provisions, it applied the personal exemption to both taxpayers and dependents, while it granted no increase in the standard deduction to any household with more than one dependent.

Changes in Tax Rates

Changes in tax rates derive mainly from two sources. Either Congress changes the rates by statute or income growth gradually pushes people into higher brackets. When tax brackets are "indexed" for inflation, real growth is the sole cause of "bracket creep." The term was originally applied merely to inflation's effect on average tax rates, but people will also creep through brackets and see their average tax rates rise when their taxable income increases because of an expanding economy.[16] One way or the other, the federal income tax and state income taxes now in 43 states (Tax Foundation 2003) have automatically and almost inexorably increased tax rates through bracket creep. This real and inflationary bracket creep helps explain how federal and state governments can enact multiple tax cuts over time even while people still see their average tax rates remaining the same or even rising.

Economists are particularly concerned with the tax bracket into which the taxpayer's last or next dollar of income falls. This tax bracket reflects the marginal tax rate—the rate paid on any additional dollar of income. To the extent that taxes influence behavior—whether encouraging people to substitute work for leisure or saving for consumption—marginal tax rates are often considered the main lever.[17] However, economists still dispute evidence on the scope of the behavioral response to marginal tax rates. The main exception is for items like capital gains or portfolio adjustments, where almost everyone recognizes significant behavioral shifts (Slemrod 1994).

Figure 3.5 shows how the top rate—always a prime focus of congressional attention—has changed over time. When the income tax was first introduced in 1913, it boasted a top rate of a mere 7 percent of those earning above $500,000 (close to $9 million in 2003 dollars). However, the nation's entrance into World War I prompted an explosion in the top rate to 67 percent by 1917 (the threshold for the top rate jumped fourfold to $2 million). The top rate would remain around 70 percent until 1925, when it fell to 25 percent.

The reprieve was temporary. The top rate was revived to 63 percent in 1931, in the midst of the Depression, and jumped into the 70, 80, and 90 percentile ranges, with a peak in 1945 at 94 percent for incomes of $200,000 or more (a historically low threshold, although still about $2 million in 2003 dollars). High rates persisted through the 1950s—especially during the Korean conflict.

Figure 3.5 *Top Tax Rate on Individual Income, 1913–2004*

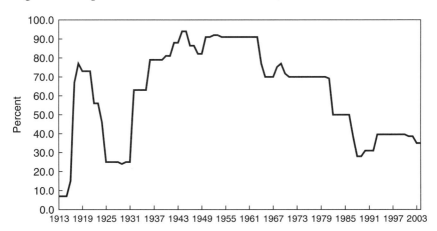

Source: Eugene Steuerle, The Urban Institute; Joint Committee on Taxation; Pechman (1987).

Note: This figure contains a number of simplifications and ignores a number of factors, such as a maximum tax on earned income of 50 percent when the top rate was 70 percent and the current increase in rates due to income-related reductions in the value of itemized deductions. Perhaps most importantly, it ignores the large increase in the percentage of returns that were subject to this top rate.

The Kennedy round of tax cuts in 1964 reduced the top rate to 70 percent for incomes over $200,000 (about $1 million in 2003 dollars). Outside of some very temporary surcharges for the Vietnam War, the top rate remained at 70 percent until Reagan-sponsored legislation in 1981 lowered it to 50 percent (although there already was a maximum tax on "earned" income of 50 percent). Tax reform in 1986 further dropped the 50 percent rate to 28 percent by 1988—the lowest since 1931—although the meaning of "top rate" was confused by an intermediate or "bubble" rate of 33 percent that applied to some below the "top."

The 1990 budget agreement under President George H. W. Bush raised the top rate to 31 percent, while the 1993 budget agreement under President Clinton pushed the top rate to 39.6 percent (on incomes over $250,000 or about $300,000 in 2003 dollars). The rate was cut through 2001 legislation to 38.6 percent in 2002, with scheduled drops in successive years. However, this schedule was superseded by the 2003 tax cut that dropped the top rate immediately down to 35 percent in 2003—although with the caveat that the top rate would climb back to 37.6 percent in 2005 unless the 2003 tax cut was extended. Interestingly, the 35 percent rate is the same as originally proposed in the Treasury's 1984 landmark study that led to the Tax Reform Act of 1986.

The distribution of returns by marginal tax rate in 1961, 1979, 1988, and 2000 are shown in figure 3.6. Although most discussions of the tax system's progressivity focus on the very top rate paid only by the wealthiest taxpayers—such a myopic view was to dominate the debates over taxes in 1981, 1986, and 2001—few taxpayers pay the top rate. The year 1961 is one of those years remembered by some as the pinnacle of postwar progressive taxation because the top rate was still 90 percent even though the war had been over for 15 years. In fact, the tax rate structure then was mainly a flat rate for the vast majority of those filing taxable returns. Only

Figure 3.6 *Cumulative Percentage of Federal Income Tax Returns Taxed at or below Each Successive Marginal Rate of Tax*

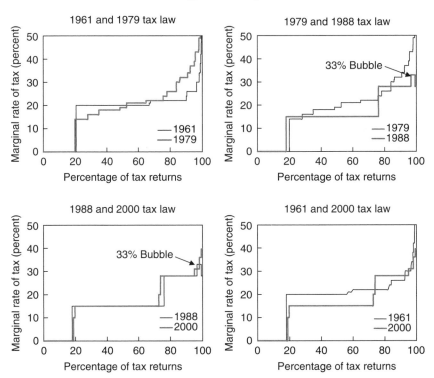

Source: IRS statistics on income, various years.

about 10 percent of filers paid any positive marginal tax rate other than the flat rates of 20 to 22 percent (see upper-left-hand graph in figure 3.6). Over the next two decades, the effective or average tax rate structure grew much more sloped or progressive, with roughly half of all those filing returns paying higher marginal tax rates in 1979 than in 1961, and three-tenths paying lower rates (two-tenths remained nontaxable).[18, 19] Some of the greatest changes affected filers with the highest marginal rate of tax. For instance, for returns at the 95th percentile (the richest 5 percent of all taxpayers), the marginal tax rate increased from 26 percent in 1961 to 38 percent in 1979.

After this long rise in tax rates, especially for upper-middle-income taxpayers, tax rates were cut and partially restored on several occasions. Top rates fell to 50 percent in 1982 and then to a variety of rates between 28 and 40 percent over the following years. Taxpayers in the 95th percentile saw marginal rates vary up and down between 26 and 37 percent over the period from 1961 to 2000.

Figure 3.7 shows effective or average tax rates on households by income class at four points in time. The first chart shows effective total federal tax rates for all federal taxes, including income and Social Security taxes, exemptions, and credits. The second chart shows just the effective income tax rate.

The comparison years are 1979, 1989, 1993, and 2001 (prior to the 2001 tax cut). Despite all the economic and legislative changes over this time frame, there are few major changes in the basic progressivity of the federal tax structure—with two exceptions. The top 1 percent fares better, as does the lowest income or first quintile ("Q1"): its rates become increasingly negative as tax credits grow increasingly generous. A similar, more permanent gain at the very top and in the first two quintiles will result if 2001 and 2003 legislation is extended.

Tax Rates at Half the Median, the Median, and Twice the Median Income

For lower-income individuals at one-half median income, the average combined income and Social Security tax rate tended to increase over time until 1977 (when a tax bill temporarily reduced rates) and again following tax acts passed in 1990 and 1993. As shown in figures 3.8 and 3.9 (with detailed data in appendix table A.4), the average tax rate then fell steadily throughout the 1990s. Their marginal rate increased more dra-

Figure 3.7 *Effective Tax Rates for All Households by Income Class and Select Year*

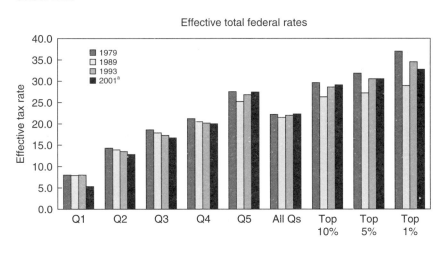

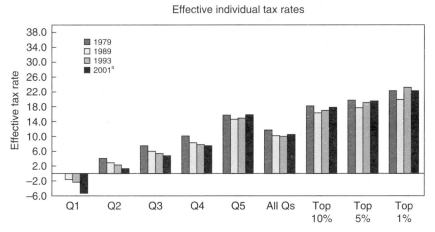

Source: Congressional Budget Office (2003, table B1-A).

a. April 2001 tax law applied to 1997 income distribution; does not include effects of 2001 or 2003 tax legislation.

Figure 3.8 *Marginal Income and Employee Social Security Tax Rates for a Family of Four at Various Income Levels, 1955–2003*

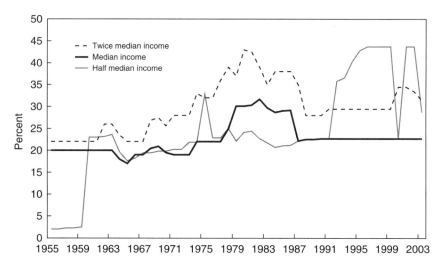

Figure 3.9 *Average Tax Rates for a Family of Four at Various Income Levels, 1955–2003*

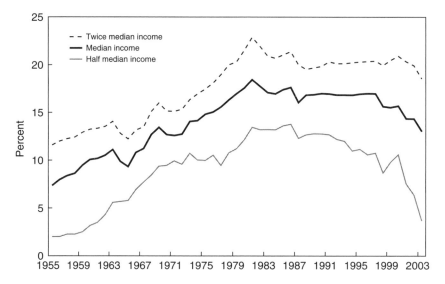

Source: Median incomes from U.S. Census Bureau, "Current Population Reports, Series P-60," various issues. Average and marginal tax rates from Treasury Department (Allen Lerman) calculations. Years 1997–2001 updated by Elaine Maag, the Urban Institute.

matically for a while. By 1960, lower-income households had moved from being nontaxable in the income tax to being taxable, and their marginal income tax rate rose from 0 to 20 percent. Their Social Security tax rate, however, was still only 2 percent. Over the 1990s, the combined marginal rate at one-half median increased significantly, from about 23 to 44 percent with successive expansions of the EITC and its imposition of a high phase-out rate (usually 21.06 percent). The credit itself does not phase out completely until income levels become higher than one-half median income, so loss of that credit creates an add-on effect. After the 2001 and 2003 tax cuts, this marginal rate fell 15 percentage points to 31 percent.[20]

For a long time after World War II, median-income households also watched their average combined income and Social Security tax rate rise. Personal exemptions or standard deductions became less and less valuable relative to income and so a higher percentage of income became taxable. And Social Security tax rates continued to rise. Since 1981, however, the average combined rate has fallen, despite yet another increase in the Social Security tax rate. Marginal rates, on the other hand, have been relatively constant at around 19 to 23 percent of income, with peaks just above 30 percent in 1978 and 1982. They have remained at about 23 percent since 1987.

For households with twice the median income, the change in marginal tax rate has been the most dramatic. From 1967 through 1980, it almost doubled from 22 to 43 percent. After that all-time peak, it fell significantly in the late 1980s to about 28 percent, but crept upward again in the 1990s to 34.5 percent. After the 2001 and 2003 tax cuts, it fell to 31 percent. These households also saw their average rate of tax peak in 1981, but tax cuts in the 1980s for the most part have been sustained.

In all these comparisons, it must be noted that average and marginal rates would be much higher for all types of taxpayers if we attributed the employer portion of the Social Security tax to the individual, which many economists suggest as appropriate. In that case, both average and marginal rates at all income levels would rise significantly, as the employer portion of the Social Security tax (just like the employee portion) rose from 2.0 percent of taxable earnings in 1955 to 7.65 percent in 2003.[21]

Some Issues of Capital Income Taxation

No tax issues are more complicated and vexing than the taxation of capital income, which are proceeds from assets rather than from labor. Here, we merely note some historical changes in the forces that drive how that income is taxed.

Double and Triple Taxation of Income

Legislators often attack capital income through various doors, thus leading potentially to double and triple taxation. In particular, income can be taxed when earned by the corporation and again when paid out to individuals as dividends. More recently, the extra tax on capital gains already taxed as retained earnings of corporations was recognized as a double tax. Other cases of multiple taxation can arise because of an estate tax, denial of legitimate business deductions, extra layers of state and local business transactions and franchise taxes, or, as discussed below, disallowance of some real depreciation allowances in a period of inflation.

If all income were double or triple taxed equally, then the main issues would be whether the combined tax rate was appropriate or not and why the system lacked transparency. On the other hand, when only some income faces such double taxes, all sorts of portfolio and financial decisions are affected. Again, the classical case presented is the influence of a corporate tax on the issuance of new stock, where a double tax might be paid, or bonds, where only one level of tax is paid. On the flip side, as we shall see, some capital income is not even taxed once.

Inflation and Interest Payments

The tax system does not operate in a vacuum. Taxes influence and are strongly influenced by the larger economic world. Changes in inflation and associated changes in interest payments have a powerful impact, in particular, on measures of income and income distribution among taxpayers. They can also drive taxpayers' attitudes toward the tax system.

Roughly speaking, after averaging a rate of below 2 percent for a decade after the Korean conflict ended, the nation (and most of the developed world) went through an extended cycle of rising and then falling inflation rates. As measured by the consumer price index, which the public watches, inflation reached a high of 13.3 percent in 1979 (see figure 3.10) before falling to below 2 percent again by the beginning of the 21st century.

Besides bracket creep on tax rates, inflation wreaked havoc with the financial systems. Depreciation statements, as well as accounts of interest

Figure 3.10 *Percentage Change in Price Level, 1955–2003*

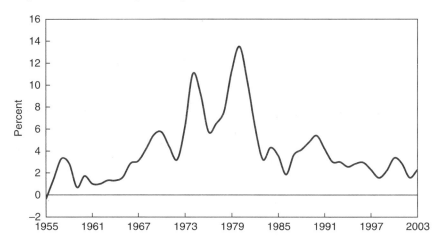

Source: U.S. Department of Labor, Bureau of Labor Statistics.
Note: Seasonably adjusted consumer price index for all urban consumers (CPI-U).

paid and received, became misleading. As inflation accelerated, individuals with prior investments in many pensions and interest-bearing assets with fixed nominal payments saw the value of their assets decline significantly, while borrowers often made large gains. Sometimes borrowers even found themselves facing financial incentives to borrow and "dissave." As an example, a household borrowing at an 8 percent interest rate in 1976 found that when inflation rose to 10 percent, it was paying a negative real rate of interest on the old debt. On the flip side, as inflation fell, the effective real rate of interest often turned out to be very high. Those who borrowed on long-term mortgages paying 12 percent or more at the height of the inflationary era found their real rate of payment would increase substantially as inflation fell toward 6 percent or less.

With changes in inflation, however, also came changes in the tax advantages and disadvantages of borrowing or lending. Meanwhile, the nation had become addicted to debt. Total private debt held by households and businesses rose from 71 percent of GDP in 1948 to 144 percent of GDP by 1978 and to 203 percent of GDP by 2001.

For various reasons, the amount of interest deductions on tax returns is far in excess of the amount of interest received. This gulf reflects payments to pension and insurance plans, other tax preferences, tax cheating, and tax arbitrage (see below).[22]

Total Returns to Corporate Capital

Figure 3.11 illustrates that owners of corporate capital tend to survive periods of declining corporate profits by receiving capital income in other forms or paying lower taxes. Most output of the U.S. economy is produced by corporations, so most income is generated within corporations and paid to or earned by labor, shareholders, bondholders, and, of course, the government. That mix changed significantly over the past six decades. Despite all these changes, the after-corporate-tax share of net national product received by all owners of corporate capital—shareholders and bondholders alike—did not change nearly as dramatically as total profits. Instead, it remained amazingly steady at about 5.9 percent of GDP throughout this period.

Corporate profits (as measured by the Bureau of Economic Analysis) fell significantly from their 1940s and 1950s level of about 10 percent of GDP on average to 7 percent for the 1970s and 6 percent for the 1980s and 1990s, falling off a bit in the modest recession of 2001. At the same time that corporate profits fell, so did taxes on corporate profits and the retained earnings of corporations.[23]

How could corporate capital owners hold their own during the long declines in corporate profits? Two breaks nearly offset these losses: (1) a decrease in corporate taxes and (2) an increase in the net amount of interest paid to bondholders (both measured as a percentage of GDP). Of course, there are cycles: when corporate profits picked up again in the late 1990s, there was not so large a decline in interest payments or increase in tax payments. As a consequence, after-tax payments to corporate capital owners temporarily rose again, only to fall again around the 2001 recession. Confusing the turn-of-century data may also reflect how accurate accounting has been in the midst of such scandals as those involving Enron, Arthur Andersen, WorldCom, and others.

Once again, inflation plays havoc with these measures. In the case of bondholders, the return for expected inflation leads to nominal interest statements in excess of the real amount received. Inflation also forces corporate shareholders to receive financial statements that understate the corporation's earnings. These two errors net to zero: bondholders receive interest deducted by the corporation on behalf of its shareholders. For instance, if $1,000 is paid out—$500 of which represents nothing more than a return for inflation—the corporation understates real earnings (of stockholders) by $500, while the corporations' bondholders overstate real

Figure 3.11 *Profits, Returns to Capital Owners, Taxes, and Interest Income of Nonfinancial Corporations, 1940–2002*

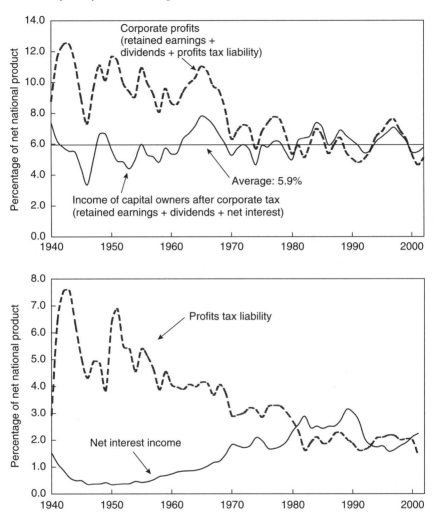

Source: Author's calculations. Based on data from U.S. Department of Commerce, Bureau of Economic Analysis (2003, tables 1.9 and 1.16).

interest received by $500. When the statements of total returns of stock and bondholders of corporate capital are added together, the errors wash out. These measurement problems prevail when inflation is high, but they continue to be important even at quite moderate inflation rates.

The bottom line is that after walking through all these accounts, on net, corporate capital owners suffer neither the losses nor garner the gains that are conveyed in anecdotal press stories about corporate profit cycles.[24]

Depreciable Assets and Corporate Returns

Inflation also has a substantial impact on the value of depreciation allowances that business can take. Depreciation allowances have never been directly adjusted for inflation. When a company deducts, say, $20 of its initial purchase cost of $100 each year for five years, each successive year after the first year is worth less and less because the real value of each $20 erodes with inflation. In effect, businesses have never been allowed to deduct all of the real cost of their asset purchases in periods of inflation.

Congress reacted to this predicament indirectly several times in the postwar period—not by making adjustments for inflation, but by shortening the period over which assets could be depreciated and, for a while, providing investment tax credits. Only sometimes was the goal stated as compensating for inflation; more frequently Congress simply said it wanted to provide investment "incentives" or spur the economy. Sometimes the value of the tax break exceeded that of the tax penalty because of additional inflation. As inflation rates fell in spurts after the 1970s, the real value of existing depreciation allowances rose again and reduced the inflation penalty. After 1986, Congress did not reduce incentives for most assets as inflation and the related tax penalty continued to fall.

Corporate tax is assessed on all equity returns from the corporate sector, not just on returns from depreciable plant and equipment. Corporations profit from ideas, inventions, new techniques, good marketing practices, and innovation. A company moving to a new region or country may "invest" heavily in learning about the laws and customs in that location. Some companies have also been able to garner profits as monopolies or oligopolies. Service industries, which have employed increasingly larger portions of the population fairly steadily throughout the past century, generate profits from their activities without much investment in plant and equipment. These other types of investments often did not benefit, at least directly, from the tax reductions offered to physical capital. However, it can be argued that that these other firms already get to deduct many of their investments in training of labor or human capital development immediately and don't have to amortize or depreciate them over time.

Marginal Effective Tax Rates on Capital Income

Another way to assess taxes on capital is to estimate their impact over time on investments that produce a stream of income for the future. A summary of the marginal effective tax rates on capital income from 1953 to 2003 (Gravelle 2004) is graphed in figure 3.12 (details in appendix table A.5). Owner-occupied housing was never subject to very high rates (it briefly rose to over 10 percent in the inflationary late-1970s), while noncorporate capital, subject only to individual-level tax, has paid a marginal effective tax rate between 13 and 37 percent in this period. For long periods, the tax on noncorporate capital has been in the low 20s.

Corporate capital has been subject to rates as high as 70 percent in 1953 and rates between 42 and 60 percent up to year 1980. After 1980, the trend has been downward due to a variety of factors, including the adoption of an accelerated system of cost recovery in 1981, the replacement of investment credits and accelerated cost recovery with lower corporate and individual rates in 1986, and the steady drop in inflation (which, as explained

Figure 3.12 *Marginal Effective Tax Rates on Capital Income*

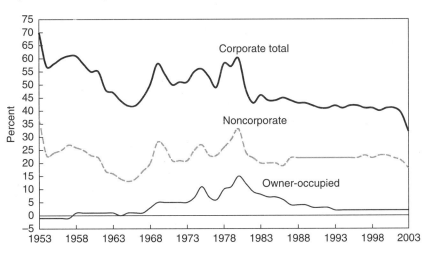

Source: Gravelle (2004).

above, increases the value of depreciation allowances). At the beginning of the 21st century, several changes again lowered the effective tax rate: a reduction in the statutory rates of tax paid by individuals, a temporary "bonus" depreciation scheme adopted in 2002 and expanded in 2003, and lower rates of tax on dividends and capital gains adopted in 2003.

These calculations assume that investments are made at the margin by individuals who have already fully used pensions and retirement accounts. If the figures were adjusted to reflect the share of investment returns essentially not taxed at the individual level because of tax preferences for retirement plans, effective marginal tax rates would fall by about 6 to 8 percentage points in recent years.

Tax Arbitrage and Tax Shelters

A key development in taxation throughout the postwar period is the rise of "tax shelters" and "tax arbitrage." To understand the relationship between taxes and the economy, this somewhat dense subject must be tackled. Stagflation—persistent inflation combined with stagnant consumer demand and high unemployment—is also due to inaccurate accounting and its effect on investment decisions, as influenced by tax arbitrage opportunities.[25] Such stagflation hit the U.S. economy hard in the 1970s. In other periods as well, tax sheltering is an issue of far more consequence than simple tax avoidance; it often leads to investment in less productive assets than otherwise would occur, thus reducing the growth rate of the economy.

The most common form of arbitrage is borrowing to buy preferred assets. For instance, if one can borrow at 7 percent to purchase assets that increase in value by 7 percent a year, the tax system can be arbitraged if the 7 percent interest payment is deductible but the 7 percent return (in the form of capital gains) is not recognized for tax purposes. In this example, net saving and net income from capital is zero in each case, but positive tax savings are generated as though one had saved and invested. Other forms of arbitrage are much more sophisticated and complicated.[26]

Relative to taxable interest income, almost 80 percent of the individual returns from assets benefit from one tax preference or another (Steuerle 1985b). Assets are seldom subject to individual tax on both their cash yield and their change in value. For instance, houses and stocks may provide rental and dividend streams that may not be fully subject to tax, but, just as important, the gains in value are not subject to tax until sale, if ever. Even depreciable assets at times benefit from allowances that accelerate the amount of deduction taken, basically giving their holders an interest-free loan from the government.

When individuals and corporations engage in tax arbitrage, it shows up in the world economy partly as an increase in the number of financial transactions. Usually, taxpayers sell or "sell short" one type of asset and "buy long" another—transactions they might have avoided were it not for the tax incentives.[27] The easiest and most common way of selling short is to borrow—that is, to promise to deliver the number of borrowed dollars plus a return rate equal to the interest rate in some future year. Commercial real estate purchases, for instance, are commonly bought with borrowed dollars even when the company has enough money to buy the real estate outright. But there are various other common short sales, too—as in the stock market, where the effective rate of payment is the increase in the value of the stock that must be delivered in the future.

When a taxpayer pays interest or sells one type of asset short, the payments made are all usually recognized by the end of the sale year. In that way, the taxpayer gets to deduct those payments or losses on the tax return immediately. Thus, in the case of interest, the entire income stream, including both real interest and inflation, are deducted. On the other side of the balance sheet, the returns on many purchased assets are not recognized right away. With such assets as common stock, for instance, increases in value are not taxed until the stock is sold, or not taxed at all if left to heirs at death.

Inflation actually adds a subsidy because the taxpayer is allowed to write off more than the full cost of the asset. For instance, suppose the real interest rate and the real rate of capital gain increase on non-dividend-paying stock is 5 percent, and inflation of 5 percent increases the nominal rate of interest and the expected rate of capital gain to 10 percent. Then the taxpayer may end up deducting 10 percent each year instead of 5 percent, while still avoiding any tax on the gains as long as they are not recognized or avoiding most tax because of a capital gains tax exclusion for recognized gains.

Of course, some other person or business somewhere owns the right to those interest payments and could be forced to pay a penalty in the same way that the borrower is subsidized. However, many of these penalties are routinely avoided. In the case of interest, pensions and life insurance companies garner many receipts while accrued individual income is tax deferred. Also, parts of the tax system are discretionary. In the stock market, there are also gains and losses, so one person can avoid declaring capital gains earned even while another person makes sure to declare all capital losses. Over time, the law has attempted to restrict loss write-offs to constrain such tax avoidance through arbitrage, but not always effectively.

Individuals and businesses don't even have to know they are engaging in arbitrage as long as they follow incentives. Thus, more and more individuals maintain higher mortgages even as they hold more assets in individual retirement or 401(k)-style retirement accounts. Essentially, the individual borrows from himself, taking deductions for the interest paid and then deferring tax on the interest received. An obvious example under current law would be someone who put money into a Roth individual retirement account (Roth IRA), which excludes interest payments from tax. Suppose that after depositing the money, he pays less on his mortgage (or he increases its size) by an amount equal to the deposit. If the Roth IRA pays 7 percent and the mortgage interest rate is 7 percent, his before-tax net income from the two transactions is exactly zero. Yet he will declare an interest deduction on the mortgage each year, but never declare the interest received as income subject to tax. He is subsidized as if he saved, but no net saving has occurred; he merely is arbitraging the tax system.

Note that the arbitrager is often playing tax games that decrease the total productivity of the economy. Tax-motivated borrowing and investing involve transaction costs that must be paid, even though net saving may be zero when an investment is financed through borrowing or negative saving.

Tax arbitrage is pervasive, affecting the lives and habits of almost every individual and business in society. Examples include using tax-deductible borrowing (e.g., by use of a primary or secondary mortgage) to purchase housing, consumer durables, pension assets, IRAs, state and local bonds, and real estate and corporate stock for which special treatment or exclusions are provided for capital gains.[28] Businesses often engage in tax arbitrage when they borrow to buy stock, create a merger, or engage in a leveraged buyout of another company. Within a business, borrowing to purchase equipment may involve some tax arbitrage, as can borrowing to buy inventory that is favorably treated through "creative" though quite legal accounting methods.[29] Some corporations purchase other companies' stock and are allowed to deduct dividends from income even when the interest costs of financing the purchase are also deducted. Other corporations use partnerships as tax arbitrage vehicles—perhaps because the corporation does not want the debt to show up on the books of the corporation when it is hidden in net value of the partnership.[30]

These developments have serious consequences for tax administration. Some deductions and credits are illegitimately claimed, but the IRS has generally had to play a game of catch-up with new developments. Moreover, many types of shelters are hidden in the books in ways that make them hard to detect, so that if a taxpayer is skirting on the edge of what is legal, the IRS may have a hard time finding the item, much less contesting it.

The Treasury Department over time has put forward proposals for getting better reporting by businesses on transactions that might be shelter-like, but this is a complex matter since businesses not only buy shelters that have lawyers' or accounting firms' imprimaturs, among others, but can engage in arbitrage almost inadvertently. Some argue that it is impossible to catch most of these transactions, and one should simply throw in the towel by abandoning any attempt to tax capital income. Regardless, the sale of hidden shelters by accounting firms has raised ethical questions, since perhaps the major social purpose of accounting as a profession is to conduct transparent and accurate financial reporting.

Summary

For most of the post–World War II era, federal taxes have remained generally constant relative to the economy's size. Still, after hitting an all-time high in 2000, taxes have quickly plummeted to their lowest level since 1950. Where they end up depends upon a great many factors, including the direction of tax legislation and whether provisions with sunsets are really allowed to sunset. Most growth in tax payments in the post–World War II period came about through state and local, not federal, tax increases. Among the major shifts in federal taxes were increases in Social Security taxes (except for the late 1990s) and reductions in corporate tax payments.

With one major exception in the early to mid-1980s, exclusions, deductions, and credits have generally risen in importance, although for many years they were offset by the decline in the personal exemption. More recently, lower- and moderate-income individuals have been helped by a one-time increase in that exemption and by the great expansion in the availability of tax credits available even for those who owe no tax. Tax rates have risen because of bracket creep, but Congress has legislated lowered rates as well. Capital income taxation has been ever vexing. Among the many issues involved have been inaccurate measurement of net income during periods of inflation, double and triple taxation of some income while other income is not taxed at all, and the pervasive creation of tax shelters to exploit differences in tax rates and tax regimes in different countries, depending upon how and where income is earned or accrued. However vexing, tax rates on capital income fell significantly between 1980 and the first years of the 21st century.

NOTES

1. The Bureau of Economic Analysis (BEA) numbers cited here are available only for prior years. However, it is possible to make statements about future federal taxes under current law by making use of estimates provided by the federal government on its own receipts (OMB 2004). If state and local tax collections do not change greatly as a percentage of GDP, then total tax collections would follow the trends in federal tax collections.

2. Note that state and local taxes had actually reached slightly higher levels during 1932 and 1933. They were then eclipsed by federal tax increases, especially during World War II and its immediate aftermath.

3. Most economists consider taxes on inputs to other businesses (turnover taxes) to be inefficient since, among other problems, they penalize firms that are not vertically integrated enough to handle various stages of a production process (and, hence, must buy inputs from outside the firm, thus generating an additional tax).

4. The Excise Tax Reduction Act of 1965, Public Law 89-44.

5. With retirement plans, the exclusion from current income actually operates as a deferral of both the wage income put aside and the earnings on the retirement plan deposits. Employer contributions and most employee contributions and the earnings on those deposits are taxed only when finally withdrawn. The value of exclusion is equivalent to the non-taxation of the normal return to the plan assets if the taxpayer is in the same tax bracket at the time of withdrawal as at the time of deposit. Newer Roth individual retirement accounts and 401(k) plans, still relatively small in size, operate differently: they do not allow the investor an up-front deduction or exclusion but, in return, the earnings on these plans are not taxed.

6. The value of home-ownership is enhanced because the homeowner effectively gets nontaxable income by owning rather than renting. Consider the tax that is saved by owning rather than investing that equity money in the bank, paying tax on the interest, and then renting a similar home. Thus, compare a taxpayer who owns a house worth $100,000 and one who rents and keeps $100,000 in a bank earning interest. The latter has higher taxable income because of the taxable interest payments on the bank deposits.

7. For taxable returns, the credit-equivalent amount rose. For all returns, credits rose from $6.8 billion in 1975 to $7.02 billion in 1986, to $8.4 billion in 1997, and to $34 billion in 1999.

8. In table 3.1, the income of nontaxable individuals cannot be separated from nonreported income and certain reconciliation items, including possible changes in compliance, and error terms. Hence, they are reported as one number.

9. In theory, one cannot add up tax expenditures exactly. Each is estimated as if all other tax provisions are unchanged. A simple example shows the type of problem that can arise with addition. If a taxpayer with $10,000 in income has $10,000 in deductible charitable contributions and $10,000 in deductible mortgage payments, then each set of deductions alone might suffice to make her nontaxable. Each deduction estimated separately would have a positive value, but if one were stacked on top of the other, the second would entail no benefit at all to this taxpayer and no cost to the government.

10. As always, there are exceptions. General tax credits of a modest amount were available only briefly from 1975 through 1978. Also, as discussed, those who have additional sources of nontaxable income such as Social Security may exceed minimum tax-exempt levels of income.

11. These credits have both refundable and non-refundable components. The refundable component is treating as a federal outlay because it goes to an eligible family in the form of a refund regardless of whether that family owes tax or not. The non-refundable component is treated as a tax expenditure because it only gets counted against actual tax liability, if any. However, the net effect is very similar to a federal outlay and makes the credits comparable to other federal programs for lower-income families.

12. The crazy quilt pattern for the child credit in the chart reflects the temporary nature of some increases, as well as how these increases were reflected in withholding and other adjustments during each year.

13. This calculation takes into account the 2001 and 2003 tax cuts that increased the standard deduction for joint filers in 2003.

14. Technically, reductions in tax are counted in the budget as tax reductions, and only the amount of credit paid that does not offset taxes (the refundable portion) is counted as spending.

15. For a discussion of the many problems associated with adjusting poverty measures for inflation, see Ruggles (1990) and Burtless et al. (2000). Among the many issues are in-kind benefits and taxes that are not taken into account when measuring the number of those below the poverty line.

16. We will use the term to apply to both phenomena. There are some who believe that inflation should not be allowed to raise tax rates, since individuals' real circumstances have not changed, but that a tax system over time should impose ever-higher tax rates as people become richer in real terms. Applying the term "bracket creep" to average rates rising with average real income does not mean I am making a judgment as to whether tax rates should change in this manner. I am simply asserting as a factual matter that a population can "creep" up in "brackets" with real, as well as inflationary, growth in income.

17. Of course, tax rates also affect behavior by changing the amount of after-tax income left to the taxpayer. A taxpayer, for instance, may work more to cover the shortfall. However, other "income" effects derive from what the government does with the money. For instance, it can make transfers to others by collecting the tax, and those who get the additional transfers may decide they can now consume what they want without working as hard.

18. Filers include some (but not all) nontaxable returns—for instance, those who file for refund of all withheld taxes. For more details on the distribution and progressivity of the tax burden, see chapter 2 in Slemrod (1994).

19. Fullerton and Rogers (1993) develop a very interesting analysis of the distribution of lifetime, rather than annual, taxes. They find that the distributional effects of taxes are likely to be muted over the long term. Unfortunately, there is no long-run data set on lifetime incomes and tax regimes by which to compare generations as fully as one might like.

20. The drop in 2000 is mainly the result of a half-median family falling just below the start of the EITC phase-out rate.

21. Separate income and Social Security tax calculations can be found at http://www.taxpolicycenter.org.

22. In 1981, when inflation was still at a peak, the value of tax deductions for private interest paid was $61 billion or 2 percent of GNP more than tax payments made on private interest received. Technically, interest paid equals interest received on a worldwide, not domestic, basis. See Steuerle (1985b, 52, 56) for details of this calculation.

23. See Jorgenson and Yun (2001) for a time series of effective tax rates on business assets from 1970 to 1996.

24. One explanation may be that labor bears some or much of the corporate tax burden—an issue we do not pursue further.

25. See Steuerle (1985b). A few paragraphs here obviously cannot substitute for what is conveyed in that book. Tax arbitrage was not the only problem created by inaccurate accounting for income in an inflationary era. As discussed in later chapters, I was privileged to serve as the economic coordinator of the Tax Reform Project that led to the Tax Reform Act of 1986. I like to believe that that reform, along with monetary policy, was significantly responsible for moving investment to more productive assets and allowing for the two long growth intervals of the 1980s and 1990s. While stagflation is less of an issue in most developed nations at the time of this writing, the problem can arise again, and it still affects many middle-income nations.

26. Again, for a thorough review of tax arbitrage, theory, and practice, see Steuerle (1985b).

27. The rate of payment on the short sale is essentially the increase in value of the asset that must be delivered down the road. The rate of return on the long purchase is simply the return on the owned asset.

28. Not all interest on borrowed assets is deductible. For instance, for years after 1986, Congress placed limits on borrowing to purchase consumer durables and on secondary mortgages in excess of $100,000. A taxpayer can usually figure out a way, within limits, to borrow against the right type of asset to finance tax arbitrage activities.

29. For instance, under the LIFO (last-in, first-out) method of accounting, a firm is allowed to deduct first the cost of items purchased last. This provides a form of adjustment for inflation, but no inflation adjustment is made to reduce the amount of interest paid.

30. This was the case in the Enron collapse in 2001, though the tax enticement was not the only factor at play. See Gravelle (2003).

4

The Postwar Period
through 1980

The Government that robs Peter to pay Paul can always depend upon the support of Paul.
—George Bernard Shaw

It gradually dawned on the nation by the mid-1950s that a larger government was not just a temporary wartime phenomenon. Nor was government, as in the Depression, going to be composed mainly of programs to deal with unemployment. The federal government took on new activist roles building a national highway system, expanding civil rights, and gradually increasing its social policy. Defense spending was still high after the Korean conflict, although it was to begin a gradual decline as a sizeable portion of the economy that, with some exceptions, would continue throughout the rest of the century.

When the Republican President Dwight D. Eisenhower supported a significant expansion of the Social Security system in 1954, he essentially ended a debate over its survival that had been held in abeyance while the nation was at war. Eisenhower further solidified acceptance by both political parties of a modern welfare state in which the federal government took on significant responsibility for its citizens' well-being through transfer programs.

The large and significant growth in taxes brought about during World War II and the Korean conflict was essentially maintained, initially reinforced by the government's need to support a large defense establishment. In the first few years after the Korean conflict, over half of all taxes were spent on defense. But as these defense expenditures gradually fell relative to total expenses and national income, increases in domestic spending, not large tax cuts, were to take over defense's declining share of the national income "pie."

The Easy Financing Period

In hindsight, the postwar period up until the mid-1970s can be defined as the Era of Easy Finance (Steuerle 1996). The nation's expenditure programs were mainly discretionary—that is, they required annual appropriations. As the economy expanded, uncommitted revenues grew, and only a small portion of revenue growth was committed to such entitlement programs as Social Security, which does not require annual appropriations. Still modest in size, Social Security also had fewer sources of automatic growth than it would by the mid-1970s. Thus, the increase in revenues made possible by economic growth left congresses considerable room to increase discretionary expenditures and cut taxes, at least nominally. The economic growth rate, as defined by real gross domestic product (GDP) was also significant, averaging about 3.3 percent from 1946 to 1974—adding further to potential future revenues relative to existing levels of expenditure.

But economic growth and its associated revenue growth was only one source of easy financing for domestic programs. The defense budget started out at about 14 percent of GDP at the end of the Korean conflict, and its gradual decline toward 3 percent by 2000 (back to about 4 percent in 2004) made it possible to spend far more on domestic programs without increasing taxes. When measured in dollars at the beginning of the 21st century, 10 or 11 percentage points of GDP translates to well more than $1 trillion extra per year that could be spent on domestic programs without increasing average tax rates.

In addition, substantial bracket creep afflicted the income tax system, as documented in chapter 3. Besides inflation, the gradual but continual increase in the number of two-earner couples fueled bracket creep as increasing numbers of women entered the workforce.

With so much money available for spending, policymakers entered a world where their primary legislative goal was to give something back to the people while seldom, if ever, suggesting cutbacks in expenditures or increases in taxes. In reality, government can never avoid the constraints of double-entry bookkeeping: someone always pays for what someone else gets. Still, in politics, it helps if payers are not identified and if their tax obligations to government can be blamed on the actions of past presidents and congresses or passed onto future ones. In short, as long as the money appeared to grow on trees, politicians only had to decide what to do with it, not how to raise it. Even when the budget got tight in some brief periods during this easy finance period, there was plenty of room to maneuver. Some people may remember that President Lyndon B. Johnson proposed a modest and very temporary surtax to help pay for the Vietnam War, but they are less likely to note that even that surtax was packaged as part of a permanent, long-run tax cut.

There was one major exception. The system of old age support had been set up back in the 1930s so that its special Social Security tax was deposited to a trust fund that was supposed to cover the cost of directed Social Security programs. Gradually, this rule would be eroded. From its inception, Medicare insurance was to be financed only partly through the Social Security tax; non-hospital payments would be met through general revenues. Later, Social Security benefits were made subject to income taxation, and the revenues from those additional taxes were transferred to both the Social Security and Medicare trust funds. Still, the partial "fiscal discipline" in administering the trust fund rule added yet another source of funds for the easy financing era. Congress passed benefit increases that would be paid for through tax-rate increases in the future as more and more of these obligations became due. When the program was young in the 1940s and 1950s, the elderly had lower average levels of income and consumption than the nonelderly. Moreover, life spans earlier on were shorter and health care less advanced and costly. On balance, the system then was more truly an "old age" system. Tax increases did not make political waves, partly because future congresses were often left to implement them and future generations had to pay them.

The continually rising inflation rates indirectly added a fourth source of easy finance: the value of old debt was continually eroding. The person who bought a government bond at a 3 percent interest rate lost out substantially when interest rates rose to 6 percent, largely because of inflation. But that person's loss was the government's gain and only added to the sense that financing the future was indeed easy.

Codification and the Turn toward Macroeconomic Policy

If there was money to be spent, it is not surprising that elected officials figured out ways to spend it. And much of the "spending" came through tax legislation. The higher level of taxation born of war created many new ways of doing tax business, and the higher rates significantly increased the value of existing deductions and exclusions. By the early 1950s, Congress decided to codify and give greater permanence to many practices established through regulation or standard practices of the public. The result was the Internal Revenue Code of 1954, a major achievement of legislative drafting at the time. The top individual tax rate was kept about where it had been—at 90 percent, but without additional surtaxes. Exclusions that had been allowed through administrative practice or regulations were put into the law.

One other change is worthy of note: the 1954 code allowed taxpayers to accelerate depreciation allowances, writing off a greater portion of asset cost sooner rather than later. Perhaps this change can be justified as reflecting the faster economic depreciation in those early years of asset ownership—and, thus, lead to a more accurate measure of income for tax purposes. From another perspective, such a depreciation allowance can also be viewed as the first of many investment incentives whose goal by 1981 was totally unrelated to the correct measurement of economic income. The 1954 code carved out this path by allowing methods known as "double-declining balance" and "sum-of-the-years digits." The wartime tax had clearly evolved into a peacetime tax.

The major economic fear, more prevalent in the 1950s than the 1960s, was that the nation would somehow return to depression. War yanked the nation out of the Depression, but what would allow economic growth to continue? And wouldn't defense cutbacks depress the economy? This combination of fears led both to conservatism in spending money before it came into Treasury and to liberalism in thinking about an activist fiscal policy.

Keynesian Heyday

In the latter part of this easy finance period, especially the 1960s to early 1970s, that Keynesian tax policy hit its political heyday. The simplified version of this theory—which some Keynesian experts claim does not represent Keynes—called for tax cuts to spur the economy as long as there were underemployed resources, a situation which, we have noted, was politically interpreted to mean whenever the mood struck. A less-tilted version of Keynesian policy suggests that active fiscal policy is fine as long as it is balanced out by raising surpluses in good years, or at least by having zero deficits under conditions of full employment (Stein 1994). Many economists would argue that such a balanced approach to fiscal policy had long preceded Keynes. Regardless, tax legislation had now taken on a new and major role as a macroeconomic tool, not simply as a revenue producer—to the chagrin of some who believed that it could dangerous for the evolution of sound tax policy.[1] Furthermore, fiscal stimulus through tax cuts began to be stressed more than expenditure increases by the 1960s. (By way of contrast, during World War II, the expansion in wartime expenditures not fully covered by new taxes provided the major spur to demand.) Tax cuts held greater appeal to some conservatives even though, according to Keynesian theory, they had less stimulative effect than direct expenditures.

Even with tax cuts, throughout most of the late 1940s to the early 1970s, the nation's debt-to-GDP ratio fell significantly. Thus, even when nominal deficits were modest, income was growing much faster than debt. Nominal income growth, moreover, was enhanced by higher rates of inflation. The rise in the inflation rate often caught bondholders off guard so that the federal government was paying low and sometimes even negative interest rates on some of its public debt. At times nominal federal debt to the public would rise even though the real value of the debt would fall.

This raises the question of whether the net fiscal posture of the federal government was expansionary at all, if something like change in debt-to-GDP, rather than simple size of the deficit, is the measure. Tax cuts weren't so expensive, after all, in an easy financing era when automatic tax increases due to bracket creep more than covered the costs of tax cuts. The two forces more or less hung in balance—witness the relative constancy of revenues to GDP (see figure 3.2).

Looking back at the literature of the day, that overall dynamic seems to have gone largely unnoticed. True, economists recognized that bracket creep produced a "fiscal dividend." Some worried it would slow down growth unnecessarily, while others suggested that it would slow down growth appropriately when the economy began to grow too fast. But much less attention was paid in those days to debt-to-GDP ratios or the problems caused by inaccurately measuring government's real interest payments by failing to take inflation into account. The focus—business as usual in politics—was on whether the next proposed discretionary tax cut was needed to expand the economy. Even opponents of stimulus policy often measured impact by whether or not there was any nominal deficit, as evidenced by their fights over raising the nominal debt ceiling.

In the early 1960s, President John F. Kennedy became sold on Keynesian policy. Kennedy prided himself on his connections to academics, especially those from Boston, such as John Kenneth Galbraith. Based partly on the evidence provided by deficit spending during World War II, Keynesian policy almost became accepted as politically correct within economics. Remember, too, that the nation had endured three recessions in the mid- to late 1950s. Nixon had blamed his defeat to Kennedy on the last of these, and Kennedy made a campaign pledge to get the economy moving again.[2] Finally, it didn't hurt that a Democratic president was promoting tax cuts heavily focused on investment incentives and on reducing the top rate from 70 to 50 percent—often against the opposition of Republicans who viewed it as fiscally imprudent. Fascinatingly, Republicans in the early 1980s and early 2000s looked back nostalgically on the 1960s tax cuts, and the political lesson—that arguing for fiscal prudence might not be very popular—survives to this day.

In 1963, President Kennedy sent a tax message to Congress. His opening salvo consisted of an appeal "to step up the growth and vigor of our national economy" and a complaint that "our present income tax rate structure holds back consumer demand." The president did note, but only later, that, "in addition, the present tax code contains special preferences and provisions, all of which narrow the tax base" (Executive Office of the U.S. President 1963). Thus, Kennedy's proposals contained numerous features of traditional tax reform, but they shouldn't be exaggerated. Taking into account new investment incentives, his net base broadening would have increased revenues by only $3.4 billion on an annual basis (Executive Office of the U.S. President 1963, iii, 3, 19), or only 0.6 percent of GDP.

This tax cut proposal excited debate over the demand-creating thesis. Amid the clamor, members of Congress asked the administration point blank which it preferred: tax "reform" as tax reduction or traditional tax reform. The latter was said to be impeding the former, so Kennedy decided to abandon horizontal equity and efficiency goals in favor of the deliberate use of tax cuts as a fiscal policy tool—all in the name of Keynesian and macroeconomic theory.[3]

The Evolving Meaning of "Tax Reform"

Another interesting irony should be noted: investment tax credits were first put into the tax code in 1962 as part of the effort to spur the economy. At the time, macroeconomic objectives held such sway over narrower concepts of tax reform or hopes for ideal tax bases that these investment incentives were viewed as progressive reform, even though they effectively narrowed the tax base. These investment tax credits were new and exciting. Economists were especially enamored of applying the incentives only to new investments, thus keeping whatever taxes could be collected on the income from already existing capital that was ineligible for the credit.

The notion of incremental incentives—essentially granting the full benefit of incentives for new capital but zapping old capital (which didn't get the incentives and would become less valuable due to competition from subsidized new capital)—was another legacy that was to carry over from past changes in depreciation allowances to many future tax cuts.[4] Almost totally neglected were such problems as the potential inequity to existing capital owners, the inability to constantly surprise the next set of "old" capital owners with changes that made their capital less valuable, the difficulty of defining what is really marginal versus what would have taken place anyway, the complexity of different tax regimes applying to different vintages of capital (depending upon age), and, in the early 1960s, a lack of recognition that the form of investment incentive chosen unduly favored shorter-lived capital.[5]

The U.S. Treasury in the 1960s was heavily engaged in justifying its traditional tax reform agenda with analysis, though it often lost the battles to Congress and other parts of the executive branch when it came to actual legislation. The same Stanley Surrey (the assistant secretary for tax policy) who led the charge in the executive branch for a tax expenditure budget believed strongly in rooting out negative deviations from a purer form of income taxation. However, while the Treasury continually opposed special tax preferences, it put less emphasis on the ways in which some income would be taxed more than once, as in the case of corporate income. The concept of "negative" tax expenditures, where more than income was counted in the tax base, was given little attention.

In the late 1960s, the Treasury began work on another set of traditional tax reform studies. In this case, the lens focused on charitable foundations. The target was some fairly rich people who seemed to be using foundations to maintain control of their corporations. A number of foundations were making grants that represented only a tiny percentage of their total endowment.

In January 1969, outgoing Treasury Secretary Joseph W. Barr also reported to Congress that 155 individual taxpayers with incomes above $200,000 ($1.1 million in real 2001 dollars) paid no federal income tax on their 1967 tax returns. This announcement catalyzed the development of various alternative minimum taxes that would affect far more people in later decades than ever dreamed at the time (Burman et al. 2002). Congress seemed especially taken with the story of Mrs. Dodge, of the automobile family, who had earned $1 million in tax-exempt interest income and had paid no tax (Graetz 1997, 190).

The Tax Reform Acts of 1969, 1975, and 1976

The Tax Reform Act of 1969 demonstrated the power of traditional tax reform concerns to transcend political parties. Hardly a beat was missed when the mantle passed from President Johnson, a Democrat, to President Richard M. Nixon, a Republican. In many ways, this seamless transfer demonstrated the type of professionalism that was applied to tax policy development at the time. It also reflected the limited number of political appointees in the White House who tried to gain control over tax policy. Those days were numbered.

Although the act covered only a modest number of issues, the reforms were generally well designed and well accepted. John Nolan, a deputy assistant secretary at the time (who later helped to found the American College of Tax Counsel and the American Tax Policy Institute) viewed it as among the most important achievements of that decade and the next.[6] In many ways, it was the process rather than the size of change that was appealing. The 1969 act clearly represented a classic textbook-style reform: problems were identified, staff came up with options and solutions for elected officials to consider, and both political parties accepted the initial agenda. Legislative compromises were reached without sacrificing the basic objectives underlying the executive's proposal.

In the early 1970s, inflation accelerated, leading President Nixon to temporarily promote wage and price controls that quickly became impossible to administer. The Vietnam War was also winding down. With help from both bracket creep and a substantial peace dividend,

Nixon presided over the largest increase in total domestic spending as a percentage of GDP under any president in history—and by a wide margin (Gramlich et al. 1998, 62).[7]

Tax cuts also remained possible, and the speed of legislation picked up, including passage of the Revenue Adjustment Act of 1975 and the Tax Reform Act of 1976, both of which contained numerous important provisions. The 1975 act included a tax cut, a tax rebate, and increased expenditures totaling $23 billion. The 1976 act extended the one-year 1975 tax cuts, making some $4 billion of tax reduction permanent and extending the rest until 1977 (Joint Committee on Taxation 1975, 1976).

Because of high rates of inflation, the 1970s produced more bracket creep relative to GDP than other decades. The 1970s were also a decade of continual tax cutting that, despite the revenues available, usually left out traditional tax reform. Constantly expanding revenues, especially at high rates of inflation, allowed policymakers to do more than offset reductions in rates or increase the standard deduction. Tax preferences and favors to various interest groups were fixtures in those bills.

The 1976 act became one of many tax reductions that made traditional reform so difficult. As John Witte (1985, 194) noted:

> The final Senate bill . . . was unsatisfactory to both the reform liberals and such conservatives as James Buckley [I-NY], who lamented the revenue loss and the structure of the bill as the "worst possible collection of tax preferences for lobbied interests." The liberals, in a last ditch act of defiance, proposed the word 'reform' be dropped from the title of the act. . . . The bill accounted for a greater cut in taxes than any bill to that time. . . . The reduction was estimated at $15.7 billion for fiscal year 1977 and $11.6 billion for 1978.

Again, despite its size, the bill did not fully offset bracket creep from previous years.

Carter as Thwarted Tax Reformer

President Jimmy Carter was elected in 1977 as a reformer. Whether his target was flood insurance, Social Security, or tax reform, he wanted to do the "right" thing—often ignoring the interest groups affected. Unfortunately, legislative politics bested this idealism, and Carter had trouble mustering even the Democratic votes that he needed. Although some blame his administration's failures on his outsider status, the greater complication was that the easy financing era had led to a legislative process that tended only to identify winners through tax cuts and expenditure increases. Whenever Carter tried to identify who would pay—whether his motivation was trying to do right or simple budgetary arithmetic—he got into trouble.

After his election, Carter put the Treasury to work designing a tax reform package. Once again, however, tax reduction was to win out over reform. The final 1978 proposals by President Carter contained only $9 billion of revenue-raising reforms, but $25 billion in net tax reduction for the first year. By the time the proposals saw daylight, Congress had already convinced the White House to soft-pedal reform. The first part of Carter's program was launched as a trial balloon—a spur to the economy would be granted in 1977 in the form of a quick rebate. Some other reforms were enacted, such as unification of estate and gift taxation (formerly gifts to heirs were treated independently from assets passed to them at death). In 1978, Congress took up the broader package. As time passed, however, it became clearer and clearer that the support for many suggested reforms was not there. Lack of momentum was not just a question of finding common ground within Democratic Party or between Democrats and Republicans. Inflation continued to accelerate and a second energy crisis and spike in gasoline prices (the first having reared up under President Gerald Ford) made the nation feel more vulnerable. Also, the postwar economy's capacity to constantly exceed people's expectations was shrinking. As the percentage of adults who had lived through the Depression decreased, the productivity growth that had continued until about 1974 began to slow, dashing heightened expectations.

By the time that Congress finished the 1978 legislative year, President Carter's proposals had been transformed. Most base-broadening reforms were dropped, and capital gains relief was provided, partly to counter the large percentage of capital gains due to inflation. The legislation increased the personal exemption and the standard deduction. These measures cut taxes at the bottom and pared back the number of taxpayers needing to itemize deductions (a number which otherwise grew steadily because of inflation and real income growth). The 1978 act also condensed the number of tax brackets from 25 to 15.

President Carter and Congress also later agreed on The Crude Oil Windfall Profit Tax Act of 1980 (Joint Committee on Taxation 1981). The OPEC-led restriction on oil exports had dramatically raised oil prices—a benefit to domestic as well as foreign producers. Of course, while Congress was willing to tax away these windfall gains when prices rose, it had no intention of balancing the tax with extra benefits whenever there was a windfall loss due to falling prices.

The 1980 act also retroactively repealed "carryover of basis"—a reform enacted in 1976 that no longer allowed heirs to "step up" the basis of their inherited assets to market value at time of death. In effect, capital gains that the deceased person had accrued but not yet realized for tax purposes would once again not be taxable to the heirs if they ever sold the assets. One of the major complications with the 1976 reform was that many estate lawyers complained they could not find the original basis for assets held by decedents, either because the decedents did not keep accurate records or because the assets involved multiple purchases, multiple sales, or changes in basis due to depreciation or additional capital purchases.

Repeal of carryover of basis also demonstrated the power of the anecdote to drive tax policy. As discussed by Graetz (1997, 190), Congress was moved by the story of a pig farmer who discussed the difficulty of determining the cost of pigs inherited from his father. "Shortly thereafter, Erwin N. Griswold, former dean of the Harvard Law School and solicitor general of the United States, told . . . of the heartaches [carryover of basis] would cause his heirs in determining their tax liability, when they sold his extensive stamp collection, which he had acquired over many years."

Beyond the always powerful impact of the anecdote, many political and economic developments influenced Americans' attitudes toward tax policy during the last part of the 1970s: the ending of the easy-financing era, the continued slowdown in productivity, an energy crisis dramatized by American hostages in Iran, the beginning of a tight money era (at the hand of Paul Volcker, chairman of the Board of Governors of the Federal Reserve System, in the late 1970s), the beginning of a military build-up and higher budgetary costs in reaction to Soviet aggression, and a very high rate of inflation driving bracket creep in the income tax. The American public decided it was ready to try something different, and that difference would become embodied in the presidency of Ronald Reagan.

NOTES

1. The economist E. Cary Brown was one who sounded this alarm.

2. In retrospect, the 1950s look to be a period of substantial overall growth, despite the recessions in July 1953 to May 1954 and August 1957 to April 1958. Recessionary periods are recorded by the National Bureau of Economic Research (2003).

3. Herbert Stein provides further explanation for the neglect of equity principles in the Kennedy tax cut: "The only possibility of holding the net tax cut to the neighborhood of $3 billion was to accompany the rate reduction with major revenue-raising 'reforms' or 'loophole-closings.' Indeed, this was the Treasury's intention. But each of these

reforms would be unpopular with someone. The loopholes were not in the tax law by accident; someone had wanted them there and the Congress agreed. Once the President had proposed and promised rate reduction, and described it as terribly important, where would be the compulsion on Congress to enact the reforms? It could only be in the sentiment for balancing the budget. But this sentiment was not strong enough for the task. Therefore, the administration, having opened the door, was led unavoidably to large net tax reduction" (Stein 1969, 411).

4. In many economic models, the new incentive would lower the price required for output, thus hitting old capital with a reduced valuation in the market.

5. One reason was that shorter-lived capital could receive multiple investment incentives over the period of time that longer-lived capital would receive only one investment credit.

6. Personal statement to author.

7. The measure of total domestic spending is total government outlays less spending on defense, international affairs, and interest on the debt.

5

The Early Reagan Era: 1981

Like mothers, taxes are often misunderstood but seldom forgotten.

—Lord Bramwell

In 1980, candidate Ronald Reagan campaigned against big government. True to form, he would embrace proposals to reduce taxes—the most obvious and visible costs associated with government. Early in 1981, President Reagan proposed two fairly simple but substantial tax reductions. Each proposal took partial advantage of a reaction against the impact of inflation on individual tax rates and on the taxation of depreciable capital income.

First, he proposed to reduce individual income tax rates by 10 percent per year for three years. This so-called "10-10-10" reduction in tax rates, the more expensive of the two proposals, would apply to all individual income, including wages.[1] Second, he proposed an accelerated cost recovery system (ACRS) to make the deductions allowed for depreciable assets available in earlier years. Under this simplified scheme, the cost of any piece of machinery or equipment, even if it might last for 8, 12, or 20 years, would be written off over 5 years rather than over the life of the asset. ACRS was also referred to as the "10-5-3" depreciation method, after the number of years of life assigned to plants and buildings (10 years) and various forms of equipment (5 years and 3 years).

Development of the 1981 Tax Proposals

The nicknames "10-10-10" and "10-5-3" had a certain flair and gave the illusion that tax law could be described simply. Both were ideal campaign proposals. Unfortunately, presidents are often reluctant to change campaign proposals immediately after election, and in 1981 some of those who backed these proposals in the campaign were made political appointees to the Treasury. Despite inflation's influence on the tax system, President Reagan's proposals were barely adjusted to offset inflation's adverse effects. The 10-10-10 reduction in individual tax rates had originally been propounded within Congress by Representative (and later vice-presidential nominee) Jack Kemp (R-NY) and Senator William Roth (R-DE), while the 10-5-3 proposal was developed by a business coalition led partially by the American Council for Capital Formation, a Washington-based lobbying group.

Both proposals took advantage of a simmering tax revolt in the late 1970s—a revolt largely influenced by inflation's impact on tax rates and asset values. At the state level, real estate values had skyrocketed at rates even faster than the high rates of inflation, and individuals objected to the large nominal increases in taxes that typically accompanied these higher valuations. This revolt against property taxes, symbolized by California's Proposition 13—a constitutional amendment limiting tax increases for existing homeowners—served as a catalyst for a revolt against federal income taxes.[2] Inflation moved individuals into higher-income tax rate brackets while businesses suffered from lower-valued depreciation allowances as inflation eroded the real value of future deductions. Neither proposal, however, adjusted for inflation directly. By sticking with simple campaign promises and avoiding give and take, the president set the stage for later corrections. Had redesign been allowed, some major and enduring problems, such as the inflation-induced taxation of the poor, a spurt in the growth of tax shelters, and some of the rising deficit problem, might have been avoided. Then again, mid-1980s tax reform also might never have occurred.

Tax rates mattered greatly to President Reagan, who remembered paying the top income tax rate of 90 percent in place from World War II to the early 1960s.[3] Supply-side economists also were concerned about tax rates—witness their emphasis on the marginal rate on the last dollar of income earned. Some enthusiasts, however, failed to recognize this philosophy's full implication. Supply-side economics is closely related to the theory that ultimately a head or a poll tax (the same amount of tax collected from each individual) is the most efficient, although not necessarily the most equitable, form of taxation. That is, to distort choices the least, government should impose the highest tax rates on the first dollars of income—in the extreme, it should make taxes equal for all persons regardless of income—so that each additional dollar of income from work or saving should go untaxed. Another way of saying this is that a "lump sum" tax on people, if it were possible to impose, would be most efficient because it would eliminate any additional tax as a consequence of behavior, such as working or saving more to generate higher income.

Despite this inherent logic, supply-side economists in America never proposed anything nearly so drastic as a head or poll tax. Great Britain's Prime Minister Margaret Thatcher did get a small poll tax enacted in the late 1980s—an event that some have cited as a phyrric victory since it was followed quickly by her downfall and the demise of the tax, though the two are probably at best only loosely correlated. In 1981, supply-siders' main role was to provide the apologetics needed by President Reagan to justify the tax-rate reductions he so fervently favored but would never be able to finance by expenditure reductions.

One distinction between President Reagan and some of his supply-side supporters may not have been fully appreciated at the time. President Reagan opposed all taxes, those paid at both the bottom of the income distribution and the top. Consistent with that view, he wanted to reduce tax rates throughout the income distribution—a costlier proposition than simply reducing the top rate of tax. Later in his administration, he would take a further stand in favor of increasing the personal exemption. Many Reagan advisers balked at these higher-cost approaches. These two moves in particular, they contended, would have at best a modest effect on marginal tax rates and, hence, on the "supply" of labor and capital.

Because supply-side economics emphasizes the last rate of tax paid by individuals, it tends to care most about the top or last rate of tax in the rate schedule and less about rates at the bottom or about exemptions and personal credits. In a system with progressively higher rates, the last or top rate of tax is one that applies at the margin to all who have income sufficient to reach that bracket. Personal exemptions and the other rates of tax, however, will be "infra-marginal" to many taxpayers. For instance, consider a tax system with a simple exemption amount of $5,000, a 20 percent tax rate on the next $10,000 of income, and a tax rate of 40 percent on income above $15,000. Then, for taxpayers with incomes above $15,000, lowering the 20 percent tax rate or, in most cases, increasing the exemption will still leave them with a 40 percent tax rate at the margin.[4]

The Not-So-Hidden Cost

When President Reagan first pushed campaign proposals, no one clamored for analyses. The Treasury Department, nonetheless, had to do its job and estimate the costs of the 1981 proposals. From the beginning, the Treasury provided accurate estimates of the large costs involved. One published estimate, for instance, showed that when fully implemented by 1986, the individual rate reductions would cost $162 billion (3.7 percent of the gross domestic product [GDP]) and the accelerated cost recovery system $59 billion (1.3 percent of GDP) or, together, about 5 percent of GDP (OMB 1981, 16). Despite pressure to lower these cost estimates (see discussion below), and the administration's adoption of some optimistic economic assumptions, the costs could not be hidden.[5]

As the public got wind of the program's large costs, many Democrats and Republicans in Congress tried to cut back on the proposals. In particular, they envisioned limiting individual rate reductions to one year while keeping the drop in the top rate to 50 percent. This change would allow Republicans pro-business tax relief and allow Democrats the revenues needed to more easily support social programs. Many in both parties would have been happy with this compromise, even though additional tax preferences in a world of higher tax rates would have further exacerbated the tax-shelter problem.[6]

Yet a popular new president was going to get his way and a much larger tax package. The country was tired of very high inflation rates and of recent tax rises. The changing of the political guard in the White House and the final release of the hostages from Iran signaled that it was time to try something new. President Reagan had also recovered from an assassination attempt, showing character and wit by joking to the masked surgical team about to operate on him, "Please tell me you're Republicans." Soon after his recovery he boldly approached Congress to persuade them to enact his program while appealing directly to the American people, who were ready to sign on to a new initiative.

Congress eventually abandoned its cautious approach to President Reagan's proposals. A bidding war started. Many new provisions were added to the original Reagan tax proposals, including an extension of individual retirement accounts (IRAs) to taxpayers already covered by employer-provided pension plans, a new deduction for some earnings when both spouses in a family worked (a "second-earner deduction" designed to relieve marriage penalties or higher rates of combined tax that resulted when two earners married), an exclusion of interest from qualified tax-exempt savings certificates ("all-savers" certificates) from taxable income, a charitable-contributions deduction for individuals who did not normally itemize expenses, a credit for increasing research activities within a business, the elimination of estate taxes for a significant number of moderately wealthy taxpayers, and a number of other special preferences.

To partly pay for these changes, the individual rate reductions were made slightly less valuable: the first rate reduction would be 5 percent— not 10 percent as originally proposed—followed by two 10-percent reductions in later years ("10-10-10" had become "5-10-10"). The net reduction in tax rates turned out to be about 23 percent, and inflation was to further offset some of this reduction.[7] Perhaps the most important addition of all was little noted at first: Congress required that tax brackets, the personal exemption, and the standard deduction be indexed or adjusted for inflation—effective after 1984. Meanwhile, the accelerated cost-recovery system of depreciation was adopted for assets purchased between 1981 and 1984, and cost recovery deductions would be even more generous for certain assets purchased after 1984.

The Economic Recovery Tax Act of 1981 (ERTA) passed with all these bells and whistles. To give some idea of its long-term impact, the cost of the 1981 tax act was estimated for fiscal year 1990 at about $323 billion, or close to 6 percent of the gross national product (GNP) (see table 12.1).

Reassessing the Individual Changes

Many opponents of President Reagan claimed that the 1981 tax act was the chief cause of the budget deficits of the 1980s. To many of his supporters, the tax reductions represented the outstanding legislative success of his tenure. The story, however, is much more complex than either of these views allows.

Looking first at individual taxation, the cost of the rate reductions appears quite high compared with what would have happened under the 1980 law then in force. However, under the older unindexed system, individuals would move into higher-tax brackets and see their tax rates increase significantly. Much of the 1981 rate reduction did nothing more than offset past and future increases in tax rates stemming from inflation (as well as real economic growth).

One way of seeing how these factors combined is to examine federal individual income tax receipts, which never fell below 8.05 percent of GNP during the Reagan era. In contrast, these receipts were 7.94 percent of GNP in 1976. Thus, Reagan's seemingly radical reductions did not even bring tax rates down to the level of only a few years earlier. In 1984, after reaching the lowest point they would hit under Reagan, average individual rates began increasing gradually. As in periods before indexation, individuals continued to move (albeit more slowly with indexation for inflation) into higher-tax brackets, owing to increases in real income.

Indexing for Inflation

The major individual reform instituted in 1981 was not the direct reduction in tax rates, but the indexing of tax brackets, including (after 1984) what might be viewed as a zero-rate bracket that personal exemptions and standard deductions created for all Americans. As noted, this indexing provision was not part of the original Reagan proposals, but it has dramatically altered tax legislation ever since. No longer could Congress follow the pattern of providing tax reductions that merely offset tax increases driven by inflation. By 1990, the inflation adjustment reduced receipts by an estimated $57 billion relative to an unindexed tax code. Eventually compounded over years and decades, of course, indexing would outweigh all other provisions of the 1981 act.

An alternative way of looking at the 1981 rate reduction is to compare it with the amount of receipts that would have been collected under an indexed tax system starting right at the beginning, rather than delayed until after 1984. According to estimates made by Sally Wallace of Georgia State University and formerly of the Treasury's Office of Tax Analysis, if the individual tax base had simply been indexed for inflation in the years after 1981, by 1990 receipts would have been almost $180 billion lower.[8] In contrast, individual receipts due to all provisions of the 1981 act were reduced by about $260 billion. Indexing since 1981, therefore, would have cost over two-thirds as much as all of the changes in individual receipts, including the indexing that went into effect after 1984.

The 1981 tax act, however, also embodied a reaction to the significant bracket creep of the high-inflation years before 1981. Strikingly, the entire revenue loss from provisions for individuals in 1981 could have been achieved simply by indexing the tax code for inflation from about 1979 onward.

In retrospect, it's hard to imagine that the 1980s could have passed without either an indexed tax code or, in its stead, further tax cuts. The 1981 act still reduced revenues more than indexing alone could have, but, of course, any comparison over time requires some strong assumption about how much the 1981 cut deterred Congress from enacting cuts later. The national debt also went up faster than it would have had the cuts been implemented more gradually—especially since the defense build-up taking place then was also expensive. The vast sums of additional interest paid on the debt could even have resulted, it can be argued, in an increase in tax rates by the time all was said and done, including later legislation to reduce the deficit. Thus, the ultimate impact of the 1981 cut on receipts depends upon whether one believes that these payments eventually came out of lower expenditures or higher taxes—or, most likely, both. Up front, they were still expensive.

An Uneven Effect among Individuals

The individual rate reductions did not offset inflation evenhandedly. At the time of the Reagan tax reductions, the Treasury's computer models indicated that inflation increased individual taxes proportionately for most income brackets. For the vast middle-class majority, therefore, a proportionate rate reduction in 1981 was appropriate, at least if the goal was to offset bracket creep due to inflation. However, inflation's impact was very different for two groups: high-income and low-income taxpayers.

For a person at the very highest tax rate, inflation normally cannot raise the marginal tax rate.[9] Someone facing the top rate of 70 percent could not pay more than a 70 percent marginal tax rate no matter how much taxable income increased with inflation. Even before 1981, high-income individuals often avoided a top tax rate of 70 percent through a special provision of the tax code that limited the tax rate on earnings, or income from labor, to a maximum of 50 percent. (For many persons, an interaction among provisions resulted in a higher marginal rate than 50 percent.) For taxpayers able to invoke that provision, therefore, the 1981 reduction of the top rate from 70 percent to 50 percent provided few additional benefits. But for high-income persons with capital income, the lower rate was more generous. The 20 percent drop also effectively reduced the top rate paid on capital gains from 28 percent to

20 percent, since 60 percent of reported gains could be excluded from taxation both before and after the 1981 legislation.

The 1981 act offset bracket creep the least at the bottom of the income distribution. If a taxpayer moved from paying no income tax to paying $200 simply because inflation eroded the value of personal exemptions and standard deductions, a 23 percent reduction in all tax rates compensated for only $46 of the total increase. Thus, the 23 percent rate reduction was not big enough to keep inflation from driving more people into the tax system between 1981 and 1984. Only a 100 percent offset would have kept them out of the system. Another way of saying this is that personal exemptions and the standard deduction were not indexed for inflation, so a smaller share of income was subject to tax at a zero rate. Following supply-side concerns that items like the personal exemption did not have much effect on incentives, the Reagan tax cut emphasized lowering tax rates and not worrying about such issues as the decline in the real value of the exemption.

In many ways, the neglect of the working poor in 1981 merely continued the trend of the late 1970s by allowing inflation to drop the real-income ceiling above which income is taxed. At the same time, inflation continued to force households with dependents to bear an increasing share of the total tax burden since larger households made the most use of personal exemptions available to taxpayers and dependents.

The Business Tax Cuts: Revolution or Parody of the Past?

Both supporters and opponents of the Economic Recovery Tax Act of 1981 liked to claim that the business tax changes represented revolutionary departures from the past. Supporters would tout, and opponents would protest, the extent and size of the new deductions. Here again, though, both sides' assertions were exaggerated. In many ways, the 1981 act would come to repeat, even parody, the past.

Exaggerated Effects

The 1981 cost-recovery provisions were hardly unique. Taxes on depreciable capital had already been reduced three times during the postwar period. Proponents of the business cuts, especially supply-side economists, were especially fond of comparing the 1981 measures with the tax cuts and investment incentives that President Kennedy had popularized. Favoring depreciable assets had become a standard mechanism for reducing taxes on capital, especially as inflation accelerated or the government became enamored with the need to foster growth through the tax code. President Reagan's accelerated cost-recovery system (ACRS) and 10-5-3 proposals in many ways carried to a logical conclusion the precedents set in prior Democratic and Republican administrations. After all, if past depreciation accelerations and investment credits had been worthwhile, then why not enact yet another investment incentive and let effective tax rates on some investments drop to zero or below?

Although the costs of the 1981 business tax program were high, under some lenses that high cost was misleading. Acceleration of depreciation allowances had an exaggerated effect on revenues in the first few years. In other words, tax reductions due to the speed-up of deductions into the first years of an asset's life would be partly offset by the absence of such deductions in the later years of its life. Moreover, the acceleration of inflation justified some speed-up, though explicit inflation adjustments would have achieved this result more directly and avoided overcompensation for inflation when inflation rates fell. By the same token, the cost of the 1981 act would have been much larger had not some cost-recovery provisions been pared back through legislation in 1982 through 1984.

Despite the costs of the Reagan-era cuts, as a simple mathematical matter the investment tax credit reduced tax rates on most assets by far more than the allowance of accelerated depreciation. This distinction would prove crucial later in the decade, when an elimination of the investment credit, not a change in depreciation allowances, would provide the most important revenue generator for financing cuts in corporate tax rates.

Perverse Effects

While the novelty of the ACRS depreciation schedules was exaggerated by both its proponents and opponents, the new law did have some perverse economic effects that eventually could not be ignored. The 1981 business tax cuts contained the seeds of their own destruction. Since the president's tax package was never reworked following his election with equity, efficiency, or compensation for inflation in mind, the final formula was simplistic and the depreciation benefits were shared unequally among holders of different forms of capital, thus distorting investment patterns.

Why? First, when combined with the investment credit, the new cost-recovery schedules resulted in effective tax rates on new purchases of certain types of equipment that were often near zero and, in some cases, quite negative—even before taking borrowing into account (see Auerbach 1983). That is, the combination of an investment tax credit of 10 percent, plus the ability to write equipment costs within 5 years, yielded allowances so generous that they were often mathematically equivalent to not taxing investment income at all. When these assets were purchased with borrowed dollars, the effective tax rate often fell below zero and became a tax shelter for income from other sources.[10]

Second, like past tax preferences, ACRS put all the benefits up front. The investment credit and the new accelerated deductions would be received in the first year, or first few years, of owning an asset. Since deductions and credits could be used only against other income or income tax, new businesses or businesses with current losses found themselves at a severe competitive disadvantage with respect to new investment. Almost none of them had enough income to take advantage of such generous up-front deductions and credits. On balance, the law favored old established businesses over new ventures that often face other start-up costs.

Third, under the formula for providing depreciation allowances, different forms of capital received very different treatment. The new ACRS system especially favored long-lived equipment. Yet the common 5-year "tax life" for writing off costs did not correspond with the actual operational lives of assets. Why should an asset built to last 20 years and one designed to last 7 years both be written off over the same 5-year period? One calculation showed that returns from equipment on average would be taxed at an 11 percent rate (although the rate varied widely by type of equipment), structures at a 38 percent rate, and inventories at a 58 percent rate.[11] These types of unreasonable disparities meant that the return from equity investments in different assets would be taxed at different rates.

For such equipment as computers, the tax-depreciation schedule was not generous at all—it did not even allow real economic depreciation. For plants and structures, which never received an investment credit, acceleration of benefits in 1981 were also less than for most equipment. For returns on inventory investments, there was no direct benefit from tax preferences for depreciable assets. This failure to provide benefits more evenhandedly was to prove crucial later in the decade, when those industries and companies that had been left behind in 1981 joined a business coalition to support tax reform.

The Tax Shelter Bonanza

By the late 1970s, the growth in the tax shelter market had left some promoters uncertain how much further they could go. While most shelter dollars were put into oil, gas, and commercial real estate, investment in movies, alternative energy sources, rehabilitated structures—basically anything that lawyers could argue qualified for one type of incentive, quick write-off, or overvaluation leading to excess deductions—attracted capital, too. The Treasury and the IRS had already tried with limited success to keep the most egregious shelters from expanding, but each year their threat and need for legislative action became greater.

Here, then, came a tax shelter bonanza. In 1981, Congress and the president defied, or simply denied, the threat of expanding shelters and moved essentially to promote them. Thanks to zero or negative tax rates and the availability of up-front deductions to offset current tax liability, the feasible supply of tax shelter investments was greatly expanded. Further, the tax act compounded a rapidly growing problem for the U.S. economy at a time of high inflation by encouraging leveraged purchases of assets at the very time when changes in inflation or interest rates made such schemes riskier. Sometimes the examples were highly visible: windmill "farms" in the desert where acres of land would be covered with small windmills generating electric power, usually at far greater cost than that produced by other utilities, or "see-through" buildings where one wall of an old building would be propped up so new construction incorporating that wall qualified for "rehabilitation" credits. Sometimes gyrations in markets, such as commodities, were responses to tax shelter demands. The savings and loan fiasco and the bank failures of the late 1980s were also partly driven by tax-related attempts to build more and more commercial real estate on a sheltered basis, even in saturated markets.

This problem involved more than inequity in the tax system. Investment in unproductive assets added to economic stagnation. As an example, take a piece of equipment for which excessive tax preferences were granted. If the purchase wasn't financed by borrowing, tax preferences were equal to about 28 percent of the asset's cost, roughly equivalent to reducing tax rates on an equity-financed investment to zero. In a world of, say, 10 percent inflation and 14 percent interest rates, however, a leveraged purchase could produce a rate of return of negative 9 percent and still make money for the taxpayer (table 5.1) (Steuerle 1985b, 104).[12]

Shelters also proliferated at the corporate level. New lease arrangements created under the 1981 act allowed corporations to sell negative

Table 5.1 *Example of Profits from an Unproductive Investment*

Income or expense	Return (as a percentage of asset value)
Real income from asset	− 9.0 percent
Interest paid	− 14.0 percent
Inflationary increase in value of asset	+ 10.0 percent
Tax reduction on interest paid	+ 6.4 percent
Tax reduction on real losses	+ 4.1 percent
Tax preferences	+ 2.8 percent
Net profit to owner	+ 0.3 percent

Source: Author's calculations.

tax liability they could not use themselves. Under so-called "safe-harbor" leases (which were soon rescinded by Congress), other corporations could buy tax benefits by taking only minimal ownership of another company's assets and then "leasing" the assets back to the user and true owner.[13] The purchasers of these negative tax liabilities paid little net tax.

By the mid-1980s, tax shelters were beginning to swamp the IRS. In 1985, over one-eighth of all technical tax examiners were assigned to the tax shelter program, and that fraction would grow. Meanwhile, the early Reagan administration attempted to shrink the IRS, only to reverse its position later for both revenue and administrative reasons. Indeed, by the end of the 1980s, the number of IRS employees reached an all-time high—the upshot of a concerted effort to avoid other legislated increases in taxes to meet budget deficits.

Even though the tax shelter craze of the early 1980s gets laid at the door of the 1981 tax act, the underlying trend was in effect well before 1981. Yet, tax arbitrage was enhanced enough in 1981 that it gave impetus to tax reform later in the decade. How?

First, the 1981 tax breaks were enacted in a way that made a mockery of traditional tax principles. Abandoning all subtlety and artifice, Congress and the president granted special favors openly and just as openly tried to create zero, or negative, effective tax rates economy-wide without regard to the efficiency and equity concerns that derived from providing very different tax rates for different types of assets. If they had wanted simply to favor saving, or convert the income tax to a consumption tax, there were ways to do this without creating so many distortions. But that would have required significant other changes, such as limiting interest deductions or counting borrowing as negative saving that could be taxable absent any investment. This harder route was not taken, and many taxpayers began to believe that government favored not so much new saving, but the purchases of shelters with existing saving. Fear of disputes with the IRS dissipated. Elected officials seemed to claim, at least temporarily, that what was good for the tax shelter market was good for the country.

Second, throughout the 1970s and 1980s, lawyers, brokers, and other tax experts had honed their skills and were now poised to take advantage of nuances and new tax breaks in the tax code, some of which had been around since the 1960s. Once the investment tax credit could be combined with increases in interest deductions far in excess of the real interest rate, the race was on. Shelter promoters and taxpayers moved up a learning curve at an accelerating rate, while the computer revolution made it easier to craft and sell shelters. The arithmetic behind tax preferences was easier to figure out than ever before, and the transaction time and costs shrank to nothing, even for international transactions.

Third, the amount of debt available to finance leveraged purchases of tax-preferred assets continually increased in both absolute terms and relative to the economy's size. The increased use of debt can also be traced partly to taxpayers who effectively lent money to themselves by, for instance, keeping their mortgages higher so they could add to their individual retirement accounts (IRAs) (Steuerle 1990b).

It Didn't Add Up

There were early warnings that some officials would try to play games with the numbers to hide the impact of the 1981 legislation on the budget. When Reagan's tax and fiscal program was presented to the Treasury to get its estimates, the news was bad. Combined with the rest of the package, particularly the increase in defense expenditures, tax cuts would lead to very high out-year deficits.

Interestingly, Office of Management and Budget (OMB) Director David Stockman, Domestic Adviser Martin Anderson, and later Council of Economic Advisers Chair Martin Feldstein indicated that the administration was counting on, among other things, higher inflation to reduce the cost of their program. Higher inflation (at least until indexing was fully implemented) would raise individual tax rates, offsetting some of the cost of the legislated reduction. A corollary, however, is that this portion of the deficit risk could simply have been eliminated had the Treasury been allowed to replace some of the rate cut with actual indexing.[14]

Here it is also important to note how executive branch projections are made. The Office of Tax Analysis (OTA) in the Treasury Department estimates revenues by making assumptions about GNP, inflation, interest rates, labor market participation, and so forth, assuming the president's proposals become law. At the same time, agencies and departments handling spending play a similar role—with the exception that these agencies must submit their numbers to the OMB to be added together. OMB then compares its aggregate total with the revenue total from the Treasury Department and makes deficit projections.

In this elaborate exercise, he who calls the macroeconomic assumptions calls the tune. OMB, along with the Council of Economic Advisers and the Office of Economic Policy in the Treasury (the "Troika") put forward a set of economic assumptions, and the OTA then provides estimates of revenues produced under those assumptions. What happens when the first set of revenue estimates are not politically attractive? Democratic and Republican administrations alike ask the Treasury if they can't do better given these economic assumptions. Time and again though, the reply has been a steadfast "No," and OTA manages to operate above the political fray, although not without hearing occasional accusations that it is not a team player.[15]

Such situations mean that politicians go elsewhere looking for numbers more to their liking. OTA does not control economic assumptions, and OMB is free to change them with the consent of the chairman of the Council of Economic Advisers and the assistant secretary of the Treasury for economic policy. Often, adjustments do get made. Assumed inflation rates might be raised to yield revenues in excess of the increased costs of expenditure programs. More likely, the estimate of real growth in the economy will be increased to raise projected revenues. At another level, corporate profits might be assumed to rise faster than individuals' income. If profits are taxed at a higher rate than individual income, then revenues go up even if assumptions about real growth in the economy do not change.

The process still creates problems for the budgeters with political briefs. Often, multiple targets for real growth, deficits, inflation, and other parameters are mutually inconsistent once politicized analysts rearrange them. Changing one economic assumption often moves one target in the "right" political direction, but another in the "wrong" direction (e.g., showing progress against inflation might reduce revenues). Multiple scenarios are then proposed. Eventually, the sobering reality sets in that not all political targets can be met, and last-minute compromises attempt to minimize the political damage. In his book, David Stockman (1986), director of OMB in 1981, revealed some of the wrangling over economic assumptions in 1981 and the final acceptance of a "Rosy Scenario" (a euphemism applied ever since to rosy economic assumptions unlikely to be met).

In fairness, most members of the executive branch do not play this game, and for many years during the 1980s, estimates were made honestly and were proven quite accurate by events. Moreover, even in 1981, the efforts of OTA and the other agencies insured that estimates would be consistent, even if based upon rosy economic assumptions outside of their control.[16] Even so, the 1981 fiasco hurt the executive branch's credibility for years.

Can such debacles be avoided? Clearly, presidents probably do not fully understand the budget process, especially when they first come to office. However, they should not be absolved from ultimate responsibility. If a president ever said that he or she wanted the best set of economic assumptions possible and did not want them tailored to fit other political goals, the problem would largely go away. The process could also be changed by setting economic assumptions through other means or in other settings— for instance, requiring the major economic assumptions to be determined permanently before the rest of the budget process begins.

Consistency and Accuracy of Numbers

Poor and fungible economic projections have lives of their own, but short-term political gains are quickly overturned. In one of Ronald Reagan's most famous speeches—his address to the nation on February 5, 1981— he argued that "prior to World War II, taxes were such that on the average we only had to work just a little over one month each year to pay our total federal, state, and local tax bill. Today we have to work four months to pay that bill." In fact, total taxes as a percentage of GNP had approximately doubled, not quadrupled, during that period—from about 14 percent of GNP in the period from 1937 to 1939 to a little less than 27 percent between 1978 and 1980 (see appendix table A.1).

When the White House speechwriters first sent this speech to the Treasury's Tax Policy office for verification, staff responded that the numbers were wrong. This process was repeated, with the same response from the Treasury. Perhaps the numbers were the president's own or perhaps were translated from some unreliable source and no one had the courage to tell him the figures were wrong. Finally, one request was sent through the Office of Economic Policy, which verified the numbers' correctness. When staff were asked how they could possibly accept this deception, they responded: "Well, the president didn't exactly say how long before World War II!"

The speechwriters' cavalier attitude toward accuracy and their lack of professionalism represent more than just an interesting anecdote. Tax policymaking is a microcosm for policymaking in general and has broad implications for the public's attitude toward government.[17] Here it meant that truthful claims would become so jumbled with distorted claims that important information and ideas would be lost. When information is misleading, contradictions almost inevitably emerge. Before long, such contradictions did appear. In 1982, Congress and the president would agree to pass a major bill that in many ways countermanded some of the putative accomplishments of 1981.

The Demise of Easy Financing and the Maturing of Entitlements

The debate over the budgetary impact of the 1981 act cannot be understood as simply a change in tax regimes. In the past, packages the size of the 1981 cuts—even packages much larger—could be adopted and the budget would be expected to move into surplus later. Yet by the 1980s all of the post–World War II sources of easy financing for expenditure or tax changes were declining in importance.

What had changed? First, the national debt had already declined significantly relative to GDP. Thus, any fall in that ratio simply due to inflation (and thus making nominal deficits easier to finance) was likely to be smaller. Additionally, modest increases in the inflation rate—and the accompanying inflation tax they involved—had been abandoned by the late 1970s as useful tools of fiscal or monetary policy.

Second, as total defense expenditures declined in importance relative to GNP, cutting the defense budget became a less important source of revenue to fund domestic expenditures. By the late 1970s and early 1980s, both presidents Carter and Reagan actually proposed increases in the defense budget's share of national output.

Third, bracket creep in the individual income tax was reduced greatly through indexation for inflation, passed in 1981 for implementation after 1984. The eventual enactment of indexation had become almost inevitable by the late 1970s.

Fourth, though given little attention in 1981, the five-decade expansion of Social Security tax rates was ending. The 1980s did see another regular increase of 3 percentage points per decade in combined employer-employee Social Security tax rates, but it was the last rate increase in that century. For the first time in the lives of most Americans, no such increase would be expected in the coming decade, if ever.

Eliminating all four of these sources profoundly affected the politics of tax and expenditure policy. Even though changes in priorities had always required trade-offs, those sources of funds that paid for new priorities in the past had become increasingly unavailable. As that era drew to a close in the late 1970s, policymaking institutions within the executive branch and Congress were caught short. They were not yet ready for the changes about to be forced upon them. When President Carter asked the Department of Health and Human Services for a deficit-neutral welfare reform bill, for instance, he was rebuffed both by Congress and his own appointees, who argued that reform had to involve significant increases in outlays and in the deficit.

In the 1980s, President Reagan supported new priorities: reducing taxes and increasing defense expenditures. Whether or not they agreed with those priorities, voters or their representatives would almost inevitably give a newly elected president some room to maneuver and present new demands. The size of these changes, moreover, was not extraordinarily large relative to some laws passed in the easy financing period.

Even apart from the end of easy financing, policymakers had become increasingly adept at enacting legislation that allowed programs to grow on their own (without any current legislation) and at using up any potential fiscal slack long before it materialized. Expansion by formula, such as in the Social Security program, was sometimes a key.[18] Formulas were set so that benefits would rise over time even if no new related legislation passed. A related phenomenon was the growth of "entitlement" programs that could be cut only through legislation, unlike discretionary programs that require annual appropriations legislation simply to be maintained. Entitlements were supposedly derived from a "social contract" to pay future benefits on the basis of a formula fixed in the past. Allen Schick

(1990, 123–26) similarly points to "sticky expenditures"—entitlements, obligated bonds, and long-term commitments that respond only weakly to contraction policies.

The political tendency to commit funds not yet available was hardly confined to legislation promising additional spending in future years. Each method for maintaining or increasing funding for direct-expenditure programs had a parallel on the tax side. Many tax subsidies or expenditures, for instance, might be labeled as tax entitlements rather than discretionary-tax expenditures. Preferences, such as those for owner-occupied housing or employer-provided health insurance, expanded along with growth in related expenditures. Except for provisions that had to be extended every few years, policymakers rarely determined the level of tax preference or subsidy on a current or discretionary basis. In a sense, appropriations for 1985 or 1989 were set by legislation enacted as long ago as 1935 or 1954. Once an exclusion or deduction was granted for an activity, its cost would often expand with the private spending on the related activity.

The movement toward 3- and 5-year (eventually 10-year) budgeting helped formalize how Congress appropriates away any positive difference between revenues and expenditures in future years. Under multiyear budgeting, programs could no longer be designed with only first-year costs in mind. At the same time, multiyear budgeting gave Congress information on exactly how much spending might take place or how much revenue might be raised. Thus, Congress often went into the hole after restrictions on spending expired. For instance, the size of a tax expenditure might be limited for five years, then be allowed to rise significantly, raising costs apace. In this negative spiral, Congress gradually eliminated fiscal slack in future years and, by the same token, hamstrung itself.

The 1981 tax reductions were in many ways an extremist parody of previous tax reform efforts, especially the Kennedy round of tax reduction. Investment incentives proliferated and drove many tax rates to zero or below. Depreciation became so accelerated that the term "depreciation"—implying an actual measure of income loss due to change in value—was replaced by "cost recovery." Base broadening to remove special preferences that reduced the tax base was abandoned—not just early on, as in the Kennedy round—but completely.

Most of all, the change in underlying budget conditions was set in the law, and Congress in 1981 effectively removed the fiscal slack that the next congresses would need to enact their own laws and set their own priorities. This was the biggest mistake of all. Whether or not the tax cut of the early 1960s represented good macroeconomic policy, the availability of future automatic sources of funds kept the cut from permanently increasing the deficit. The 1981 cut, on the other hand, was enacted in an era when it would be vastly harder to harvest future revenues that hadn't yet been committed.

Throughout much of the post–World War II era up to 1982, concern with macroeconomic fiscal issues made it easier for policymakers to skirt or postpone hard choices and decisions. Macroeconomic fiscal policy was continually demanded to spur the economy and was consistently interpreted by politicians as a justification to reduce taxes, regardless of whether the underlying apologetics were Keynesian or supply-side in orientation. Such issues as fairness, efficiency, and administration were disdained as microeconomic, institutional, and structural issues worthy of less or even no attention.[19] After all, it was argued, spurring additional growth through changing one simple variable—whether lower average tax rates to spur demand or lower marginal tax rates to spur supply— would swamp all these other mundane issues. Unfortunately, this upside-down view implies that tax policy mainly exists to serve as a macroeconomic policy tool rather than as a means to finance government fairly and efficiently. Of course, macroeconomic policy cannot be the dominant purpose of tax policy. One can hardly imagine, for instance, a government collecting taxes merely so it can reduce them later. It collects them ultimately to pay for government, while recognizing that their timing and distribution have consequences as well.

The stage was now set for another swing in policymaking—a long series of budget policies centered almost entirely on deficit reduction and a temporary end of the reign of macroeconomic fiscal policy.

NOTES

1. The mathematics of the proposal were that rates would be reduced each year to 90 percent of their previous level. Hence, taxes would be reduced to $.9 \times .9 \times .9$, or 72.9 percent of their original level. The proposed reduction in taxes was actually 27.1 percent (100 percent minus 72.9 percent), not 30 percent.

2. A fascinating aspect of the California law is how it now discriminates against new homeowners, including migrants from other states. They are not protected against the tax increases, thus leading to different taxes on individuals who own similarly valued property in the same locality.

3. In comparing notes as to why they favored reform, Senator Bradley (D-NJ) stated, "Mr. President, you came to this [tax reform] because you were an actor who paid at the 90 percent rate; that's why you want a lower rate" (Birnbaum and Murray 1987, 26).

4. The exemption might move some taxpayers into lower brackets. In the example, a taxpayer with $15,200 of income would move down to the 20 percent bracket if the exemption were raised from $5,000 to $5,300.

5. In the Treasury Department, the Office of Tax Analysis (OTA) forms the economic arm of the Office of Tax Policy, which is in charge of the administration's tax policy efforts. The OTA estimates the receipts of the U.S. government and the revenue costs of tax proposals, prepares tax studies for both Republican and Democratic administrations, and develops models and data files in order to examine the impact of tax changes. The OTA also performs economic analyses of proposals. Those who wanted it to show low costs for favored proposals often misunderstood the Office's insistence that the integrity of the cost estimation function be maintained.

6. Shelters would be encouraged further by the maintenance of higher tax rates, which increase the value of the deductions.

7. The net reduction in tax is actually about 23 percent rather than 25 percent. Taxpayers' liabilities were reduced, first to 95 percent of their original level, then to 90 percent of the new level, and then to 90 percent of the previous level. Thus, excluding other economic changes such as inflation, their taxpayers' burdens ended up at 77 percent of their original level.

8. These calculations do not even include the additional $10 billion in tax reduction that would have taken place with indexing for real growth over and above inflation.

9. Inflation can raise the average tax rate by pushing a larger share of income into the higher marginal tax rate brackets.

10. Tax preferences may lead to no higher return for individuals buying the preferred assets, as before-tax rates of return fall for the preferred assets or rise for nonpreferred ones. Steuerle (1985b) deals with the unlikelihood that such a full equilibrium can be attained, largely because many capital income taxes are based upon discretionary realizations.

11. See table 7.1 under the column, "old law."

12. The calculation assumes that tax preferences (credits and accelerated depreciation) are designed to provide a tax break that is available regardless of actual inflation, interest rates, and return from the asset. Tax preferences here are assumed to offset a tax rate of 46 percent (the corporate rate in 1981) times a 6 percent real rate of return, or 2.8 percent. Then the taxpayer can make a net profit if the real rate of return from the asset (in the example, a negative 9 percent) and the after-tax interest payments (14 percent $\times$ [1 − 0.46]) are offset by the tax preferences, plus the additional tax write-off on the real losses (0.46 times the negative 9 percent), plus the inflationary increase in the value of the asset.

13. If the government wants to provide incentives for certain equipment purchases, a strong economic argument can be made to apply that incentive equally to corporations with and without tax liability. Nonetheless, the appearance of corporations buying and selling tax liabilities called into question the fairness of the underlying tax structure.

14. It is not clear how much importance Stockman attached to the point at the time. His recollections can be found in Feldstein (1994, 226), Feldstein's found in Feldstein

(1994, 48–49), while Anderson's were taken from personal conversations with the author. Note also that the lower rates of inflation were one consequence of the recession that also lowered expected revenues through lower real economic growth; so some blamed the recession in general for the deficits.

15. Technical review will always be performed, but it almost never results in change of any significance. Indeed, the change is as likely to go in one direction as the other.

16. A secondary debate was whether the Treasury's Office of Tax Analysis adequately took into account so-called "feedback" effects from growth in the economy that derived from tax reductions. As it turns out, OTA did nothing more than prevent double counting and force the presentation of consistent numbers. The "Troika" had to make projections of substantial economic growth under the president's plan in order to show small deficits in future budgets. The feedback effect, therefore, was already in the numbers by being built into the economic assumptions. By assuming that growth would be 4 percent per year with enactment of the president's program rather than, say, 3 percent, additional receipts of tens of billions of dollars for the government were projected. Misleading attacks on OTA were to last throughout the 1980s and were printed repeatedly in such places as the editorial pages of *The Wall Street Journal*. One attack associated OTA and CBO with the Kremlin. The strange irony was that OTA never had control of these "feedback" effects, whereby lower taxes led to economic growth that, in turn, led to higher tax collections. It merely had control of the machinery to make revenue estimates consistent with assumptions on the state of the economy. Supply-siders and others who wanted to show feedback effects simply needed to present to the public two sets of economic assumptions—one with the policy they favored and one without. Revenue, as well as expenditure effects, would have followed.

17. Lessons are often ignored. The flare-up in 2003 over inaccurate information put forward by President George W. Bush and by Prime Minister Tony Blair about weapons of mass destruction in Iraq could be traced, in part, to a similar lack of professional standards applied to speechwriting and the related process of fact-checking. The error keeps repeating itself until the process is reformed.

18. Social Security presents a classic example. The benefits paid to each generation of workers were purposely designed to be increased over time by a formula that adjusted payments to growth in wages. Barring the complications of demographic cycles and changes in rates of inflation, wages usually grow as fast as the economy—thus, so do benefits. Through such devices, Social Security's level of existing benefits relative to the economy usually represented a minimum bound that would be made available in absence of legislation. New legislation could increase benefits as a share of national income, but decreasing those benefits was argued to go against a social contract by "cutting" (growing) benefits.

19. The fault lay not just with the politicians. Many academic researchers fail to get involved in detailed structural issues, partly because they are ignorant of the many details of tax and expenditure law and often cannot incorporate such details into their simple models of the economy. In a deceptive way, issues become defined as unimportant because they are absent from researchers' economic models.

6

Prelude to Major Reform: 1982 to 1984

Don't tax you, don't tax me, tax the man behind the tree.
—Senator Russell Long, D-Louisiana

The Reagan administration invested great effort in its 1981 proposals and claimed great success. Its core successes, however, were reducing tax rates, accelerating depreciation allowances, and increasing defense expenditures. Despite the rhetoric from both sides of the aisle, neither Congress nor the administration initially reduced other expenditures more than modestly, and most cuts were in subsidies to state and local governments. Moreover, the bidding war on the tax bill had added many extra and costly provisions. By the time the president signed the bill, almost all parties and much of the public knew that more had been bitten off than could be paid for.

As David Stockman writes, "After November 1981, the administration locked the door on its disastrous fiscal policy jail cell and threw away the key. The President would not let go of his tax cut . . . The nation's huge fiscal imbalance was never addressed or corrected; it just festered and grew" (1986, 13). Stockman admitted that, by 1982, he knew the Reagan Revolution was impossible and turned his attention to reducing the "national fiscal disaster."

Since the new administration had succeeded in getting many of its early policies enacted, it naturally hesitated to put forward additional proposals that might expose some of the weaknesses of what had just passed

Congress. In this sense, the Reagan administration acted little different from most administrations. Still, the president's policy proposals had come mainly out of campaign promises, and the executive branch had yet to develop a major initiative. The legislative process, however, abhors a vacuum, and the next three years were to witness a shift in the direction of tax policy and in the source of new initiatives. Once again, tax policy would dominate the agenda, but in an unexpected way: the enactment of three major tax increases in consecutive years was a precursor to the most significant income tax reform in the nation's history. Indeed, legislative peacetime tax increases were almost unheard of after World War II.[1]

The president and the White House rarely took the lead in working out the details of initiatives during those three years. Instead, real responsibility rested with the Republican Senate and with a commission designed to deal with the possibility that the Social Security program might not have enough funds to meet its obligations. Here Republican Senators Robert Dole (Kansas) and Peter Domenici (New Mexico) played a special role in their leadership positions in the Senate Finance Committee, the Senate Budget Committee, and, later, the Office of the Majority Leader.[2] Within the administration, political forces were more split: some proclaimed the need for further tax cuts and others worked to reduce the deficit. The administration waffled in its role. It did not want to take responsibility for any tax increases, but some deficit hawks were willing to increase taxes. The president's public position was that he opposed all taxes, though he eventually accepted many increases.

The Tax Increases Begin: 1982

Less than two months after the victories and celebrations of 1981, work was already afoot in the Senate Finance Committee, the Joint Committee on Taxation, the Treasury's Office of Tax Policy, and the Office of Management and Budget (OMB) to find ways to reduce the looming federal deficit. In mid-1981, as had become the annual custom, both the administration and the Congressional Budget Office (CBO) produced new estimates of a "mid-session" budget review. By late August, the deficit debate was renewed. On September 10, 1981, CBO officials testified before Congress that $80 billion deficits (2.6 percent of the gross domestic product [GDP]) loomed for 1982 and that expenditure cuts of $100 billion (3.3 percent of GDP) would be needed to balance the budget by 1984 (Berry and Dewar 1981). These CBO assumptions proved optimistic. Even before a recession hit in late 1981 and made matters worse, both Congress and the administration began to admit that the budget imbalance needed to be corrected.[3]

On September 24, 1981, the administration came out with a fall initiative to cut the deficit further, mainly through entitlement cuts, across-the-board cuts, and even some paring of defense appropriations. Measures also included about $22 billion in tax increases over slightly more than two years. The proposals were never called "tax increases," but rather "revisions in the tax code to curtail certain tax abuses and enhance tax revenues" (OMB 1981). Senate Republicans, in particular Domenici, along with other members of the Senate Budget Committee, also began looking for ways to reduce the deficit and prepared legislation calling for tax increases of $60 to $80 billion over the next three years, along with numerous expenditure reductions (Edsall 1981; Tate 1981).

This congressional initiative stalled mainly over disputes about the size of the tax increase. At one point, President Reagan declared that he had "no plans for increasing taxes in any way," only to be contradicted by his press spokesman, who indicated that the president still planned to ask Congress for $22 billion of tax increases (Bacon 1981). Those Senate Republicans who had put themselves on the firing line for suggesting tax increases were especially upset with the lack of administration support.

Still, by early 1982, the president's budget contained proposals—many first introduced in the fall of 1981—for increasing tax revenues by over $20 billion per year, or more than half of 1 percent of GDP. These proposals included improved tax enforcement and revisions centered on business income, including a minimum tax for corporations and disallowance of some deductions taken before contracts were completed and payments to contractors were made. Almost all of the proposals were revenue raising rather than revenue losing.

The Initiative Switches to Congress

Since there was no strong presidential push behind these proposals, the public and press barely noticed them. Nonetheless, these proposals did signal some willingness on the administration's part to tackle the upcoming deficits. It fell to Congress, therefore, to take up the deficit-reduction gauntlet. In particular, Robert Dole, then chairman of the Senate Finance Committee, began the arduous task of grafting together a package of proposals that he could get through the Senate. He received technical assistance from the increasingly important congressional staff of the Senate Finance Committee and the Joint Committee on Taxation and, within the administration, by the Treasury Department's Office of Management and Budget and the Office of Tax Policy. From this brain trust came the Tax Equity and Fiscal Responsibility Act of 1982 (TEFRA).

TEFRA's base included some of the president's proposals. But it went much further. The act emphasized compliance and collection procedures through expanded information reporting and increased penalties. For instance, it was estimated that only 60 percent of reportable capital gains appeared on individual income tax returns. Taxpayers were either negligent or noncompliant on the rest. TEFRA gave the Treasury permission to require brokers to report customers' gross receipts from selling capital assets. Withholding taxes on interest and dividends was also enacted, but later retracted. Life insurance company taxation was partially reformed. The act increased excise taxes and employment taxes for unemployment insurance. Other reforms related to leasing and Medicare coverage of federal employees were also enacted.

A Reversal of Some 1981 Tax Cuts

TEFRA also began reversing some of the actions taken in 1981. While the 1981 tax act had allowed higher-income individuals greater opportunity to take deductions for deposits to individual retirement accounts, TEFRA restricted the benefits available to them from other pension plans. The 1982 act also reduced the tax benefits from investment. First, the value of investment tax credits was reduced slightly.[4] Second, TEFRA repealed generous depreciation allowances that were scheduled to become even more generous in 1985 and 1986. Those additional allowances would have cost more than $18 billion by 1987 (Joint Committee on Taxation 1982).[5]

Another slight reversal from the 1981 rhetoric turned up in the Highway Revenue Act of 1982. An increase in excise taxes on gasoline allowed the Department of Transportation to finance further work on the nation's highway and transit systems. Fiercely opposed at first to any mention of a tax increase (Stockman 1986, 139), President Reagan later allowed that some tax increases—for instance, highway taxes that might also be considered user fees—as well as increases in government expenditures could be enacted. The reality of running government programs intruded once again on those who wanted a tax policy process that ran in a vacuum and behaved as though taxes weren't part of the rest of the budget.

A Focus on Revenues

TEFRA 1982 turned out to be only the first of many bills in the 1980s that reduced the deficit by increasing taxes more than by reducing or reforming expenditures. In part, this tax-and-spend approach was due to the nature of the budget process. The tax changes were often permanent, whereas expenditure cuts frequently rested on nothing more than promises to cut programs back in future years. In addition, many expenditure programs were still "off the table"—defense, which the president hoped to expand, and entitlements such as Social Security, which was funded by formulas and didn't have to be voted on from year to year.

Perhaps the most important reversal came from the president himself. Earlier in 1981, President Reagan reacted strongly against David Stockman's attempt to cut back on expenditures hidden in the tax code, even though cutbacks in tax expenditures can be shown to serve the same conservative purpose as direct spending cuts. In signing the 1982 bill, the president had begun accepting the first stabs at "enhancing revenues," eliminating tax loopholes and unintended benefits, favoring compliance measures, and curtailing tax abuse. This was a direct turnaround from his 1979 claim that the term "tax expenditures" was "the new name government has for the share of our earnings it allows us to keep" (see Brownlee and Steuerle 2003, 158).

Of course, this was neither the first nor the last turnaround on taxes for the president. When campaigning for governor of California, he had spoken out against a state withholding tax and indicated that his feet were set in cement. Later, in 1971, he called an emergency session of the legislature and proposed withholding to deal with a budget crisis. At a press conference, a big noise was suddenly heard, and Reagan, ever the actor, quipped that the sound was the cement breaking around his feet. The press corps later sent him a pair of his own shoes set in cement, which Reagan proudly displayed in his governor's office (Smith et al. 1980).

Social Security Reform: 1983

Social Security reform loomed large in 1983. From the beginning, many in the Reagan administration viewed Social Security as an overweight portion of the budget. Some considered disability payments too high; others thought spouses' and students' benefits too generous or unnecessary, and others viewed early retirement as an unaffordable option. Social Security had also matured, and benefit increases more and more became subsidies to the middle class and the middle-aged rather than baseline security for an older, poorer, population. Moreover, monies in the system went out about as fast as they came in. Because they were not saved (as in the case of private pensions), many believed that the Social Security system reduced total saving and investment in the economy. However, early attempts in 1981 to try to cut benefits created a storm and failed miserably (Stockman 1986, 181–93). Demagoguery was quite common on Social Security, and many considered programs for the elderly untouchable—the "third rail" of politics.

Part of the categorical failure, however, stemmed from bad planning and organization. During 1981, the administration held internal meetings on Social Security reform with political officials from the White House, the Department of Health and Human Services, and the Social Security Administration.[6] On hand were many new political appointees with strong but sometimes unseasoned views on what was wrong with the system. The newcomers so distrusted the entire civil service that they prevented many of the executive branch's most talented analysts, even top guns at the Social Security Administration, from attending these meetings. The controversy that eventually enveloped some proposals reflected bad planning and poor design as much as the difficulty and sacredness of the Social Security issue.

Meanwhile, the broader Social Security issue continued to dog the administration. Increasingly, projections began to show that Social Security probably would not have enough funds to pay out benefits during the mid-1980s. In the September 1981 fall budget program, the president proposed establishing a bipartisan task force to develop a "permanent solution to the problems facing the Social Security system" by January 1983. This political compromise created a commission headed by Alan Greenspan. Once again, responsibility for studying the problem fell outside of the executive branch.

The Commission Tackles the Problem

The threat of no more benefit checks eventually forced both the administration and Congress to seek compromise. At a variety of times, still, it appeared that the Commission could come to no solution whatsoever. In the end, however, both political parties came to accept the commission's recommendations, which were put forward in tentative form when Senators Dole and Daniel Patrick Moynihan (D-NY) decided to try to reach some bipartisan consensus. Moynihan's recollection was, "If you really want to do these things, they are not that hard." He boasted, "It took us three years to decide to fix [Social Security]. But when we did, it took Bob Dole, Jim Baker, Barber Conable, David Stockman, Dick Darman, and me exactly twelve days . . . to do it" (Darman 1996, 116). Even then, the Commission's recommendations were lacking in detail, and much was accomplished in the back rooms by the various tax-writing committee staffs and the Joint Committee on Taxation, who, along with Treasury staff, filled in the blanks.[7] The net effect of the enacted bill (known as the Social Security Amendments of 1983) was substantial. It would, for instance, increase Social Security revenues over expenditures by $31.0 billion in fiscal year 1989 (OMB 1988, 4-4). A principal short-run change was to put tax-rate increases already scheduled for 1990 into effect in the early 1980s. Even so, the 1983 legislation contained no permanent increase in tax rates. Employer and employee Social Security tax rates for 1990 and beyond were set at the same level as that scheduled under the 1977 Carter administration reforms.

The Social Security Amendments of 1983 achieved other reforms. First, they required new federal civilian employees and employees of nonprofit organizations to join the Social Security system and to receive the same tax treatment as most other employees. Second, self-employed individuals would now pay roughly the same total tax rate as employees. Perhaps the most important tax reform was that Social Security benefits long exempt from taxation became partially taxable for higher-income beneficiaries. By the 1990s, these other tax changes were to increase revenues by almost $24 billion on an annual basis, or about 0.4 percent of GDP (OMB 1988, 4-4). However, it was the gradual rise in the normal retirement age from 65 to 67 that most affected future recipients, especially the baby boom generation.

The new legislation accelerated the tax-rate increases scheduled under the 1977 Social Security Amendments. Between 1980 and 1990, the combined employer-employee tax rate rose from 12.26 percent to 15.3 percent of wages. This rate increase increased revenues by more than $70 billion annually for 1990 and beyond. When the other tax amendments of 1983 were added to the scheduled increase, Social Security taxes rose by over $85 billion per year.

A new trend? On the contrary, the 1980s were almost identical to the four decades before. Once again, tax rates rose by about 3 percentage points, and other structural reforms were launched to make the system solvent. The 1983 Social Security Amendments repeated the pattern of the major tax bill of 1982 in relying more upon tax increases (including reductions in tax expenditures) than direct-expenditure decreases to reduce deficits (table 6.1).[8] It is easy, of course, to complain that the 1983 amendments were inadequate to deal with the long-term problems of Social Security. They were. But one striking difference between the 1983 legislation and the debate over Social Security around the turn of the century was that politicians acted in the former case and did not in the latter. Benefits, retirement age, and taxes were not so sacrosanct in 1983.

Table 6.1 *Estimated Changes in Social Security Receipts and Benefit Payments Resulting from the 1983 Social Security Amendments*

	Total 1983–1989 ($ billions)	Total long-range cost effects (percentage of payroll)
Tax (and coverage[a]) changes	39.4	0.03
Accelerate tax rate increases on wages and salaries	18.5	0.19
Increase tax rate on self-employed	21.8	0.38
Cover new federal workers and all nonprofit employees	4.2	0.06
Prevent termination of state and local employees and accelerate collection of state and local taxes	26.6	0.61
Tax up to half of benefits for high-income employees		
Subtotal for tax changes	110.5	1.27
Benefit changes		
Raise normal retirement age to age 67	—	0.71
Delay benefit increases by 6 months	39.4	0.30
Other benefit changes	−1.4	−0.22
Subtotal for benefit changes	38.0	0.79
Total[b]	148.5	2.06

Source: U.S. House of Representatives, Committee on Ways and Means (1990, 28–29).

Note: Social Security here includes Old Age and Survivors Insurance (OASI) and Disability Insurance.

a. Coverage changes primarily raise tax collections, although there are also some benefit increases.

b. Excludes changes in general fund transfers for military service credit and reimbursement from general fund for unnegotiated checks (total = $17.7 billion for 1983–1989 and 0.03 percent of payroll for long-range costs).

Another interesting lesson is that the retirement-age increases that began after 2000 have gone on with almost no protest or even press notice, in some ways contradicting the turn-of-the-century assessment that increases in the retirement age are political dynamite.

More Tax Increases and Deficit Reduction: 1984

In 1984, the administration's submitted budget again included net tax increases. One proposed novelty for the 1985 fiscal year was to cap tax benefits for employer-provided health benefits—a reform not only of tax policy, but of health policy. The president, who once had rejected a similar proposal because he viewed it as a tax increase, now considered it unfair that a wage earner without certain benefits should pay substantially higher taxes than one with income in the form of such employee benefits as health insurance.

A modest attack on tax shelters also climbed onto the president's agenda. This lead from an OMB document tells the story: "The administration proposes a number of changes that will curtail transactions that generate unintended tax benefits or form the basis for tax shelter schemes" (OMB 1984, 4-10). In other words, though increasing taxes might not be acceptable, increasing tax revenue by eliminating "unintended tax benefits" and "tax shelters" was allowable. While the 1984 proposals only hinted at a moderate counterattack, tax shelters had gotten so out of hand that no one with political principles of any kind could ignore them by this point.

More detailed structural reform was also part of the 1984 package. Front and center was an effort to change how life insurance companies' income would be measured and taxed—one of many attempts in the 1980s to reform the taxation of financial institutions. By this time, too, the growth in the use of tax-exempt bonds for private purposes had become so great that curtailment was inevitable. The administration's proposals in response were modest: restrictions on tax-exempt leasing and state and local governments' use of nontaxable bonds to finance private industrial development.

The Budget Deficit Reality Sets In

Some effort to bring the budget under control was a necessity. In the contemporary period with its multiyear budgets, most administrations show the deficit coming under control at some point within their fore-casted budget window.[9] By the beginning of 1984, of course, many of the projected costs of the 1981 tax act had been incurred, but the shortfall in revenues created by the recession of 1981 to 1982 had deepened the deficit. In addition, Martin Feldstein, then chairman of the Council of Economic Advisers, pushed the administration to use realistic economic assumptions and to abandon its unfaithful mistress of budget projec-tions, "Rosy Scenario." Chairman Feldstein also worked with David Stockman and others to get the administration to propose a contingency tax plan under which a surcharge would be assessed if the budget deficit exceeded 2.5 percent of GNP.[10]

Despite these budgetary pressures, the administration gave little sup-port in public to these tax proposals, especially the contingency tax plan. Excluding the contingency plan, the other proposals would increase net revenue by only a few billion dollars (a tiny portion of the budget deficit), and even those gains would be offset by proposals for tuition tax credits and tax breaks for businesses set up in low-income areas desig-nated as "enterprise zones."

Congress entered this leadership vacuum with a vengeance. Once again led by Senator Dole, Congress eventually proffered dozens of tax changes under the Deficit Reduction Act of 1984 (DEFRA). Partly fol-lowing the format of TEFRA 1982, Congress tried to improve tax com-pliance by extending information reporting to such items as state and local tax refunds. Excise taxes on distilled spirits and other items were increased, numerous corporate transactions and sales of assets were made taxable, contributions and benefits under pension plans were fur-ther limited, and tax-exempt leasing was further restricted. The aggre-gate volume of some private activity bonds sold by state and local governments (e.g., certain industrial development and student loan bonds) was capped or limited.

Various tax shelters again came under fire. So-called "tax straddles," for instance, had become too popular for the legislature to ignore any-more. This shelter allowed taxpayers to buy and sell rights to future com-modities in a way that created equal gains and losses—like flipping a coin and betting on both heads and tails. The taxpayer would then take losses on whichever "leg" of the straddle generated a loss, use that loss to offset other taxable capital gains, and then defer recognition of the "leg" with a gain to future years. DEFRA 1984 also placed some controls on the growing market for fictitious or "on-paper only" shelters that had no real investment or significant risk behind them.

By fiscal year 1990, DEFRA raised $31 billion or 0.5 percent of GDP on an annual basis. While the revenue yield was not quite as large as TEFRA was in 1982, in many ways DEFRA went beyond the earlier act. DEFRA relied more on tax base reform and less on changes in tax compliance or the elimination of provisions enacted in 1981. Like the 1982 and 1983 bills, the emphasis was more on taxes than on expenditures. Tax expenditures remained politically easier to reform than many types of direct expenditures.

Lessons from the Period

As a whole, the period from 1982 to 1984 represented a historical turnaround in postwar tax policy. All in all, tax acts passed during these years had raised over $108 billion—or nearly 2 percent of GDP—by fiscal year 1990. Other than excise taxes, very few changes were increases in tax rates. Most were expansions of the tax base, improvements in tax compliance, and retrenchments of 1981 provisions.

Even with all these tax changes, however, the nation's fiscal house remained in disarray. Costly defense build-ups continued, and by 1984 the 1981 individual tax rate cuts had been fully phased in. The projected economic growth rates from 1981, moreover, had never materialized, and the nation was only in the second year of recovering from a deep recession. Deficits were large, and many of the 1982 and 1984 reforms were proving inadequate. All of this signaled the dawn of a long and tortuous period of deficit reduction that would last until the end of the 1990s.

As a consequence of leadership on taxes moving from the White House to Congress in the period from 1982 to 1984, momentum in the executive branch for reforming expenditure and tax programs dissipated. Even in the 1984 campaign, the administration seemed content to simply defend the actions it took in 1981. Consultants to the administration suggested that its domestic agenda was bare.[11]

The Formation of Liberal-Conservative Coalitions

Even before the end of 1984, several events signaled a need for major tax reform. For example, state and local governments increasingly used the federal exclusion from taxing interest on state and local bonds as an excuse to lend at below-market rates, even for private purposes—thus usurping the private lending market. Congressional attempts to stem this practice in 1980, 1982, and 1984 had proven ineffective. Increasingly, investment followed bureaucratic rules and flowed through networks of state and local government decisionmakers. As another example, installment sales—selling an asset but deferring taxes on capital gains by recognizing the gains in installments over time—were used to reduce current taxes. Many financial institutions became more important in the economy, but paid little federal tax on their income.

These medium-size problems might have been ignored longer or attacked through a more modest bill, perhaps on the order of the tax bills of 1982 or 1984, but for two major problems. First was the proliferation of tax shelters and tax arbitrage opportunities that had to be contained, and second was the increasing taxation of the poor and of families with dependents. The two distinctive liberal-conservative coalitions that eventually united behind tax reform developed largely in response to these issues.

Addressing Tax Shelters while Lowering Tax Rates

One major hemorrhage of the tax system demanded attention far beyond the measures enacted in 1982 and 1984. Tax shelters and tax arbitrage were deterring growth, reducing public confidence in government, turning the civic exercise of filing tax returns into a prolonged headache, and decimating the ability of the Internal Revenue Service (IRS) to administer the tax laws.[12] Often misled by advertising, many of the purchasers turned out to be middle-income savers sacrificing much higher yields in favor of only moderate tax saving. Even students with little tax liability were investing in shelters, many centered on leveraged purchases of real estate or oil and gas. The system of financial intermediation was supposed to help direct saving toward optimal economic investment, but few people were looking any longer for the investment with the highest economic return. They wanted the tax breaks! Along the way, billions in savings were being cast to shelter promoters and organizers, and many individuals lost money on their investments.

It was in the large market for publicly offered shelters, often advertised directly on the financial pages of newspapers, that the problem came into the spotlight. Available information on partnership activity began to support reformers' concerns. Between 1965 and 1982, the number of partnerships reporting net losses grew from 229,000 to 723,000, while the number of partners in all partnerships grew from 2.7 million to 9.8 million. Net "losses" reported in oil and gas partnerships grew from $128 million to $13.2 billion, and in real estate from $619 million to $23 billion. Together, oil and gas and real estate partnerships accounted for about 60 percent of all losses reported on partnerships. And the growth rate in sheltering was phenomenal. New public offerings of partnerships grew from $38 billion in 1979 to $64 billion by 1982 (Nelson 1985, 58–59).

Corporations also sheltered their income from tax, often through direct purchase of equipment that was leased to other companies. General Electric was an often-cited example because it aggressively pursued this course and reduced its tax liability to zero. For instance, General Electric would buy depreciable assets with generous cost-recovery provisions and investment credits, then lease them to companies that might be less profitable and unable to take full advantage of the incentives. Without compunction, many of these corporations with low tax liability could correctly claim that many tax benefits were passed on to consumers or other companies through lower prices or reduced lease rates. However, the appearance of large and profitable corporations paying no tax at all was a public relations disaster.[13] Whatever the economic justifications for low taxes on corporations, tax shelters were an unseemly way to get there.

Of course, simply going after tax shelters alone was not enough to fire up a coalition to attack the status quo. However, the quest to level tax shelters became one more thing that spurred the formation of this first liberal-conservative coalition.

In several respects, the core of this coalition had been around for years. Economists trained in traditional public finance principles had been taught how the unequal treatment of various sources of income led to inefficient patterns of investment and consumption. The literature on this subject stretches back to the birth of the income tax.[14] The basis for broad-based taxation and traditional tax reform had been popularized in economics books and texts by scholars ranging from Henry Simons (1938) at the University of Chicago to Richard Musgrave (1959) of Harvard University to Office of Tax Analysis alumni Joseph Pechman (1983) and Richard Goode (1976), who published their work at the Brookings Institution.

Eliminating individual and corporate income tax shelters while lowering tax rates gradually became a trade-off that many conservatives and liberals found palatable. Under this banner, the coalition for tax reform would eventually prove potent. Even opponents of reform could not comfortably argue for higher tax rates to support a growing tax shelter industry that let many wealthy individuals and corporations go tax free.[15]

The Turnaround on Taxation of the Poor and Families

Growth in income taxes paid by the working poor and households with dependents was the accidental by-product of a multidecade decline in the relative and real value of the personal exemption (see chapter 3). This decline increased taxes most for those who most needed the money. Thus, single heads of households and joint-return-filing couples with dependents had borne much greater increases in taxes in the postwar era than had other households.

Almost by accident, the media latched onto policy analysis revealing the extent of the rise in family taxes.[16] The *Wall Street Journal, Forbes,* and the *Washington Times,* among others, ran the story, and *USA Today* gave it the banner front-page headline. This publicity helped galvanize liberal and conservative politicians in both political parties. Quoting this research, for instance, Senator Moynihan argued strongly to increase the personal exemption in a book on the family and, later, on the floor of the Senate (Congressional Record 1986; Moynihan 1986). Representative Jack Kemp (R-NY) incorporated substantial increases in the personal exemption in his tax reform proposals. Perhaps most important, Bruce Chapman, who became director of planning and evaluation in the White House office, raised the issue with the president and claimed that without the research "there never would have been a presidential decision to double the personal exemption."[17] Thanks to Chapman, the president took a stand in favor of substantially increasing the personal exemption. Meanwhile, social conservatives, including some of the religious right, discovered tax policy.

This proposal quickly became the Reagan administration's principal initiative to help the "family."[18] Family tax policy was on the agenda and would be there for years to come. The concern for the poor and for the family combined to inspire the formation of the second major liberal-conservative coalition that later would prove crucial to tax reform. Between 1982 and 1984, however, the coalition had nowhere to go because it had no way to pay for the changes it embraced.

The Debate Expands

The growing problems of the tax system catalyzed the development of widely varied tax proposals in the early 1980s. The proposals diverged on many points but raised the level of the tax reform debate and opened more political room for initiating a tax reform that would succeed.

Consumption Taxes and Flat Taxes

Many proposals went beyond traditional income tax reform. By the late 1970s and early 1980s, numerous economists had revived interest in consumption or expenditure taxes as replacements for income taxes (see chapter 2). The Treasury's 1986 tax reform study, Blueprints for Tax Reform, offered both income and consumption tax models as superior to current law. Although some consider consumption taxes to be the antithesis of income taxes, in fact a comprehensive consumption tax in many cases would work similarly to a comprehensive income tax.

Both taxes move toward uniformity of treatment, but in different ways. The comprehensive income tax ideally treats all income the same regardless of where it comes from or how it is spent. The comprehensive consumption tax, on the other hand, ideally treats all income spent for consumption the same, regardless of source or use. Thus, consumption tax advocates sought many of the same efficiency goals favored by comprehensive income tax enthusiasts, such as neutrality in the types of assets that might be purchased, but placed more emphasis on efficiency in the choice between saving (or consumption tomorrow) and consumption today, and less on the choice of work versus leisure.

One set of proposals receiving increased attention during the Reagan administration centered on a consumption tax with two rates: a zero rate and a "flat" positive marginal tax rate. Whether applied to income or consumption, this type of proposal is as old as economics itself. Indeed, Adam Smith proposed a proportional tax on income on the grounds of fairness. The application of progressive rates to the income tax—that is, average tax rates rising with income—had been a bone of contention since the enactment of an income tax in this country.

The new "flat tax" advocates had more in mind than eliminating multiple rates. They also objected to the various exclusions, deductions, and credits in the income tax. Their goal was also that of traditional income tax reform in broadening the base to get the rate as low as possible. In addition, they could simplify the tax system by both eliminating special provisions and applying a single tax rate. The flat rate would allow banks and other payers effectively to pay on behalf of individual taxpayers. For instance, if every individual receiving bank interest owes exactly 15 percent, the bank could pay the exact amount of tax without sending statements to individuals, and individuals would not need to report this income on their tax returns.

Almost all "flat tax" proposals at that time combined consumption taxation with flat rate taxation (see, for instance, Hall and Rabushka 1983). Of course, it would have been possible to have a flat *income* tax rate as well, but it was generally not in the political mix, except as an abstract academic idea.[19]

Both flat rate taxes, with and without the consumption tax base, and consumption taxes, with and without the flat rate, have many merits and problems that are not examined here.[20] But even those outlined above were enough to keep the tax debate just below the boiling point.

Bradley-Gephardt, Kemp-Kasten, and Other Congressional Proposals

Between 1982 and 1984, congressionally developed proposals also began to receive attention. Senator Bill Bradley (D-NJ), with Representative Richard Gephardt (D-MO) as a cosponsor, put forward the most important of these, known simply as "Bradley-Gephardt." Unlike most congressional bills, it was both detailed and grounded in technical realism.

Bradley's public leadership on tax reform had been well recognized, and for two unrelated technical reasons his proposal received more attention than others. First, the proposal resurrected the notion of a comprehensive income tax with a progressive rate structure. Second, Bradley engaged experts and staff who could stitch together a proposal without too many hidden barbs. These technical experts helped especially in ensuring that the proposal would not increase the deficit during this time of fiscal stringency.[21] The analyses of the Joint Committee on Taxation gave the senator accurate revenue estimates and distributional tables, thus eliminating the problems other proposals faced when oversimplified promises ignored budgetary realities.

The Bradley-Gephardt proposal was followed by a slew of congressional bills favoring tax reform, including the so-called "Kemp-Kasten," "Roth-Moore," "Nickles-Siljander," and "DeConcini-Shelby" bills. Of these other bills, Kemp-Kasten was to command the most attention for several reasons. By putting such supply-side advocates as Jack Kemp behind base broadening, a portion of the Republican Party would favor traditional income tax reform. A significant portion of all bills, moreover, contained identical elements, making it easier to create a coalition in favor of tax changes that lowered tax rates. Finally, Jack Kemp was a Republican who would run for president and who sought a leadership role in the Republican Party, and the White House did not want to oppose him publicly.

Some Common Themes

Perhaps the only theme truly common to all tax proposals of this period was the exchange of lower rates for a broader base—a traditional theme, but one applied more consistently to labor income and uses of income than to taxes on capital. A lesser consensus was obtained on other issues. Tax shelter and tax arbitrage problems had not yet been solved, yet lower tax rates would make even dubious deductions less valuable. Some consumption tax proposals and congressional proposals, however, would have expanded rather than contracted the shelter market. In all of the proposals with progressive rates, and in some of the flat-rate tax proposals, there were efforts to reduce taxes on the poor and for larger families with dependents.

The Beginning of the Tax Reform Process—Almost

Amid this swirl of activity, in his January 1984 State of the Union address, President Reagan asked the Treasury Department to prepare "a plan for action to simplify the entire tax code" and to present specific recommendations to him by December 1984. Notice the nuances. Not even a proposal was required, simply a "plan for action," whatever that was. The recommendations were to be made to him, not necessarily to the public, and were not to be released until after the 1984 election. Not exactly a mandate for major reform!

Using hindsight, many of the actors in tax reform claimed to have a strong idea of just what was to develop.[22] At the time, however, the only sure thing was that the administration did not want a tax reform debate during the election.

Lack of Direction

The president's cautious statement gave little basis on which to proceed. In 1984, even the meaning of "reform" was contentious. The administration was still strongly defending its 1981 tax cuts while signing legislation in 1982 and 1984 that contradicted some of the 1981 effort. Many wanted to deepen the 1981 cuts. The flat-tax debate continued apace, and some felt that its time had finally arrived. Several members of the administration, such as OMB's David Stockman, were trying to maintain congressional focus on deficit reduction.

Opposition to a broad-based income tax on capital income included many high-level administration officials, especially some political appointees within the Treasury's Office of Economic Policy, who identified themselves as "supply-side" economists. They knew that the investment credit, plus rapid depreciation, had already reduced the effective tax rate on many types of equipment to almost zero even before borrowing was taken into account. Many of them sought to maintain or even enlarge this negative tax rate, sometimes by "expensing" all capital purchases—writing off costs immediately rather than more gradually. Still others, such as Martin Feldstein, then chairman of the Council of Economic Advisers, were willing to keep an investment credit and vastly accelerated depreciation allowances even if they had to be supported with higher corporate rates. One argument here was that investment subsidies favored new capital, and high corporate rates collected taxes from returns to capital that already existed. Of course, the logic of this argument can be used to favor ever-higher tax rates and investment credits.[23]

A Plan

In March 1984, I returned to the Treasury Department from a sabbatical year of studying capital income taxation and other issues at the Brookings Institution. The role as economic coordinator of the tax reform work fell into my lap. Moreover, the charge to study reform came with no instructions on what tax reform was to entail.[24]

As noted, a temporary stalemate resulted from the debate in 1984, so some questioned whether the request for a study should be taken seriously. Several weeks after the president's address, the project had not really gotten off the ground. Sensing the many reasons for a void, I decided to put a plan of action on the table and proposed developing a comprehensive list of more than 20 major "modules" to be studied. These modules centered on such issues as itemized deductions, employee benefits, low-income exemptions and deductions, depreciation and investment credits, energy and minerals taxation, and international tax matters.

The modules were taken to the Secretary of Treasury one at a time, starting with non-capital income issues.[25] A gradual approach would help us get around one major source of stalemate—whether to further reduce the tax on capital income or to move toward a consumption tax. This opening salvo would emphasize the common base-broadening theme running through the income tax, consumption tax, and flat tax proposals.

My colleagues and I also decided to set tax rates at the end of the process. This would allow incremental decisionmaking on base-broadening issues and encourage Treasury Secretary Donald Regan not to reject reform proposals before seeing how much rates could be lowered. That tactic proved sound: the secretary's initial acceptance of eliminating some tax preferences for powerful constituencies (such as the middle- and higher-income elderly population) set the stage for accepting many other attempts to broaden the base. It also meant that no particular issue needed to be decided on grounds of progressivity since the system's overall progressivity would be determined later by adjusting the rate schedule. If the secretary decided to eliminate any particular subsidy, later rate adjustments would cancel out the distributional effects of that decision.[26]

At the time of the Treasury study, tax reform's future was uncertain. The 1982 and 1984 experiences led me to coin a "hopper" theory of reform. The more good things that get into the hopper, the more good and the fewer bad things emerge in the legislation when Congress finally decides to act. This homespun theory meant that far more than an academic study was required. We ultimately wrote a "how to" manual on just how changes could be implemented should Congress move toward drafting a bill. The need for such back-up analysis was plain. For example, it was not adequate simply to state that families with equal incomes should be taxed equally. Instead, detailed rules for operating trusts and treating family-member income had to be developed.

Extremely important to the development of the tax reform package was support within the Office of Tax Policy by its three successive assistant secretaries. John E. (Buck) Chapoton had led the fight for base broadening in 1982 and 1984 and convinced the secretary to take on a broader reform effort for the 1984 study. The enthusiasm with which Ron Pearlman took on the task after replacing Chapoton in mid-year allowed the reform effort to be comprehensive and rigorous; Pearlman solidly backed reform principles and worked hard to keep the onslaught of special interests at bay. His replacement, Roger Mentz, also fought for tax reform principles, often behind closed doors, as the Treasury's mandate by then was to work for reform but not to publicly criticize and possibly derail developments in Congress. The deputy assistant secretary in charge of the project, Charles McLure, was brilliant in his analysis and writing of much of the study.

Finally, to make the study as comprehensive as possible, we pulled every observation possible from the staff on ways in which the tax base was incomplete or overstated and every idea on how to fix these problems. Comprehensiveness, of course, meant attacking the small, often overlooked problems.

The second advantage of a comprehensive tax study was political. Comprehensiveness may tend to take more special benefits away from more people, but it has a positive side: the opportunity to convince the public that the reform effort was sincere. Tax reform would be an attack, not on particular groups or individuals, but on inefficient, unfair, but broad-based preferences. Many taxpayers would only be willing to pay the price of tax reform if they believed that they were not being singled out to pay its cost.

The Debut

Although a comprehensive review of the tax code provided direction for the study, other important steps were crucial to its reception and the ensuing debate.

Establishing Principles and Constraints

Step one was setting forth principles and objectives to guide tax reform. The touchstones were fairness, efficiency, the elimination of favoritism toward one form of investment or consumption over another, lower tax rates, fair treatment of families and removal of income tax on the poor, and greater simplicity.

Two constraints on the reform process served these principles. First, a commitment to revenue neutrality meant that revenues would be neither greatly increased nor greatly decreased. Second, distributional neutrality meant that tax burdens among income classes would not shift significantly. Within income classes, on the other hand, reform favored—largely through reductions in tax rates—those who were benefiting least from special provisions. These revenue and distributional neutrality constraints were pursued largely to allow policymakers to concentrate on the tough choices necessary to reduce inequities and promote the efficient allocation of resources and not get diverted back to the never-ending fights on size of government and amount of progressivity.

Collecting and Analyzing Data

Another formidable task remained. Vast quantities of data needed to be assembled and analyzed.[27]

Early on it became clear that constructing distributional tables required fixing a thorny problem related to tax shelters. By limiting shelters, the tax base's top tier could be expanded. But most tax shelter losses were from partnerships or other unincorporated business, and claiming these losses lowered the taxpayer's adjusted gross income and "expanded income," the traditional measures used to classify taxpayers. Often, this accounting trick placed tax shelter owners in low- or middle-income brackets, where by rights they didn't belong. For instance, someone with $500,000 of wages would buy into a shelter that gave off $495,000 of fake losses, so the shelter buyer would end up with a reported net "poverty level" income of $5,000. It was necessary to make sure that negative statements of taxable income from these shelters were not used to misclassify these owners within economic-income classes. We achieved this result primarily by imputing some level of economic income to individuals owning different assets and not allowing shelter ownership to, say, reduce a doctor's earnings of $200,000 toward a total income of $0.

Picking through the Options

The Treasury's proposals were more thorough, more developed, and more related to what IRS could administer than the congressional proposals that had developed by that time. Policymakers and congressional staff were not remiss. Rather, the executive branch is far more able to muster the needed personnel and expertise to develop major reform packages when many overlapping details are involved.

The congressional plans had many limitations, some of which were being worked out while the Treasury study was being developed. First, the plans were not comprehensive. None of the reforms dealt with abuses derived from entertainment deductions or deductions for "seminars" on cruise ships. Income shifting through children was ignored. Nor did these proposals touch on such complicated issues as multiperiod production (whereby deductions are taken before income is realized); deductions by banks carrying tax-exempt bonds; the taxation of life insurance, property insurance, and casualty insurance companies; international tax issues; the windfall profits tax; tax penalties; and many other provisions. (For a detailed comparison of proposals, see U.S. Department of the Treasury 1984, 169–83.)

Second, some of the proposals entailed revenue losses and often gave far more away at the top of the income distribution than to other tiers of taxpayers. The Kemp-Kasten proposal was a case in point. The giveaways in this proposal were so great for some capital income items that a significant deficit increase would have resulted. The Bradley-Gephardt proposal was much more forthright in meeting revenue and distributional constraints, though it too was far from comprehensive.

Staying on Course

Initial principles, constraints, data development, and comprehensiveness all helped determine the direction of the tax reform process. The goal of rate reduction, combined with the constraints of revenue neutrality and distributional neutrality, prevented the process from deviating too far from its original path. Here are a few examples of how these constraints played out:

- *Setting Aside the Consumption Tax Debate.* Although advocates of consumption taxes and of expensing for capital equipment opposed many features of tax reform, they never came up with viable alternatives, largely because such proposals would involve significant reductions in the tax base. In a revenue-neutral proposal, tax rates would have to rise to accommodate the loss in revenues from not taxing capital income. Of course, tax arbitrage opportunities were so intense at the time that, ignoring issues of how the transition would take place, the net cost might eventually have been fairly moderate.[28] In any case, many consumption tax advocates were not willing to bite the political bullet and treat borrowing and lending consistently (e.g., if net interest was to be made nontaxable, then interest deductions would not be allowed). This would have constrained some of the revenue loss from any switchover at the time.

- *Abandonment of Investment Policy through the Tax Code.* A major difficulty with the investment credit adopted in the early 1960s and the cost-recovery allowances in the Economic Recovery Tax Act of 1981 was that the same subsidy was applied to almost all equipment no matter how fast it actually depreciated. This one-size-fits-all subsidy system created incentives to buy one type of equipment as opposed to another for tax rather than economic reasons—a terrible idea from the standpoint of industrial efficiency. Once the principles of equity and efficiency were adopted in tax reform, depreciating very different assets at the same rate was hard to justify, and a schedule more related to how long the asset would actually be used (its asset-life) had to be developed.

- *Abandonment of Simplistic Supply-Side Objectives.* Absent base broadening, reducing tax burdens on the poor is nearly impossible in a revenue-neutral bill without increasing average marginal tax rates. In turn, these higher rates dampen incentives (a concern to supply-siders) and, in effect, tax capital income at a higher rate (a concern to those who want to lower the cost of capital). Two ways out of this dilemma are to reduce expenditures or, in the case of capital, to shift even more of the tax burden to labor. Another alternative is to broaden the tax base but, in practice, the funds provided by base broadening can almost always be used to reduce the cost of capital more if those funds are not spent on low-income individuals. In fairness, not all supply-siders opposed reducing taxes on low-income individuals. This group, like many others unfairly associated with a single narrow goal, was quite split. That said, the tax-reform objectives on the table in 1984 clearly contradicted the tenets of supply-side extremists whose theories require taxing the first dollars of income the most—hence, taxing low-income people more if that allows greater reductions in top rates and in the tax on capital income.

The stage was now set for full-fledged reform. Political and economic forces had come into alignment, and a process for engineering major tax reform had been established. The ball, so hard to shove up the hill, was now starting to roll down the other side. In the end, no one could stop it.

NOTES

1. In 1985, John Witte noted that up until the early 1980s, "the only legislated peacetime tax increases in U.S. history have been the Revenue Act of 1932, a slight one-year increase later in the 1930s, and a relatively modest and mostly administrative increase in 1982" (Witte 1985, 249).

2. Senator Dole was chairman of the Senate Finance Committee from 1981 to 1985, Senate Majority Leader from 1985 to 1987 and 1995 to 1996, and Senate Minority Leader from 1987 to 1995.

3. Perhaps an even earlier catalyst for action was the public "discovery" of new deficits after CBO released its summer update of the Economic and Budget Outlook in 1981. That document was issued just before the Reagan tax cuts were enacted.

4. The amount of expenditure to be depreciated was adjusted partially for the size of the investment credit. If a taxpayer spent $100 on an asset and received a $10 credit, a new basis adjustment only allowed depreciation on $95 of the asset's value.

5. For discussion of change in the ACRS system of depreciation, see Joint Committee on Taxation (1982, 39–40).

6. I represented the Treasury Department at some of these meetings.

7. For instance, the Commission compromise called for taxing benefits above a certain income level but did not come to terms with the need to phase in that requirement so that earning one additional dollar did not suddenly cause tax liability to rise by hundreds or even thousands of dollars.

8. Expenditure reductions, in fact, were confined almost entirely to a six-month delay in benefit increases and to the gradual phase in, between 2000 and 2022, of a higher normal-retirement age (67). This last adjustment had been long expected, but was still far less than adequate to compensate for cost burdens of greater human longevity. From 1983 to 1989, tax increases provided almost three-fourths, or $110.5 billion, of the $148.5 billion of changes in Social Security receipts and payments (see table 6.1). Over the long term, the tax increases covered almost 62 percent of the total reduction in the Social Security deficit.

9. Of course, the future move toward balance within the budget window may be temporary. For instance, the deficit may be seen to fall as a percent of GDP after 5 or 10 years, but then ignore the impact of the upcoming retirement of baby boomers on expenditures for elderly programs.

10. See Steuerle (1996) and Carasso and Steuerle (2002) where this surtax is discussed in much more depth.

11. Stuart Spencer, a California political consultant, met with key political strategists to map Ronald Reagan's second campaign. As he would later say, "The problem is we've

been talking to everybody at the White House over the past few days and the Reagan administration fired all its bullets very early and very successfully in the first two years . . . The most striking thing I discovered is that they don't have a goddamn thing in the pipeline. They don't have an idea" (Mayer and McManus 1988).

12. To see how far these shelters extended by the mid-1980s, Susan Nelson of the Treasury Department and I initiated some studies with the IRS to see who was investing in these tax shelters.

13. For a discussion of some of the most egregious examples of corporate tax sheltering and how they were publicized, see Birnbaum and Murray (1987, 9–11).

14. For a detailed discussion of the historical development of the American income tax and the role of equity principles, see Witte (1985).

15. Birnbaum and Murray (1987, 186) discuss the formation of this coalition in a related way: "Reform was also achieved because it combined goals that were important to both political parties. Ending loopholes for the privileged had long been the desire of some Democrats. But the 1980s also saw the emergence of a new wing of the Republican party that was crucial to tax reform's success—the supply-siders, whose influence grew dramatically after President Reagan's election and who were passionately committed to lowering tax rates. These activist-conservatives had no deep interest in closing loopholes, but if that was the only way to pay for lower rates, they were willing to go along. By combining with the older Democratic reformers, they created an impressive bipartisan coalition."

16. By happenstance, my research was the original source of this movement. Rudolph Penner (later director of the Congressional Budget Office, but then at the American Enterprise Institute) asked me to write an article on the taxation of households of different sizes, long a neglected topic, as part of a book on taxation of the family. My earlier work on changes in the tax base led to this work on the decline in the value of the personal exemption and the resulting conclusion that worst hit were households with children.

17. Bruce Chapman, letter to the author, July 28, 1985.

18. It is also likely that my research on taxation of the family was accepted because it was published under the auspices of the American Enterprise Institute, where Rudolph Penner, the editor, then resided. Earlier research on the taxation of the poor had not received a similar reception. One of the more unfortunate aspects of policy-related research is that it tends to get labeled as acceptable to conservatives or liberals depending upon which research institute publishes it.

19. As a technical matter, it involves a few major shifts from the consumption tax format; in particular, investment in depreciable capital would be written off over time rather than expenses or written off immediately.

20. For a more elaborate treatment of these issues, see chapter 12 in Steuerle (1985b), Boskin (1996), Aaron and Gale (1996), and Zodrow and Mieszkowski (2002).

21. Credit here goes mainly to Joseph Minarik, then at the Urban Institute, and Randall Weiss and James Wetzler, then at the Joint Committee on Taxation, with Gina Depres leading the senator's own staff efforts.

22. See, for instance, former Secretary of the Treasury Donald Regan's comments in Regan (1988, 202–203) and further discussion in Brownlee and Steuerle (2003, 166–67).

23. One dilemma for those favoring investment incentives was where to stop. For instance, should effective tax rates be allowed to be negative? A consumption tax would

maintain tax rates at zero. Because of tax arbitrage, an investment credit system might maintain a positive tax rate for equity investments and a negative tax rate for investments purchased with borrowed dollars.

24. Former Treasury Secretary Donald Regan once commented that President Reagan never really advised him on how to spend his tenure as secretary: "To this day, I have never had so much as one minute alone with Ronald Reagan! Never has he, or anyone else, sat down to explain to me what is expected of me, what goals he would like to see me accomplish, what results he wants" (Regan 1988, 38–40).

25. The Treasury Department group involved in discussing these modules with the secretary included the assistant secretary for tax policy, John E. (Buck) Chapoton and, later, Ronald Pearlman; the deputy assistant secretary for tax analysis, Charles McLure; the assistant secretary for economic policy, Manuel Johnson; the undersecretary of the Treasury, Beryl Sprinkel; commissioner of the internal revenue, Roscoe Egger; deputy secretary, Tim McNamar; assistant secretary for legislative affairs, Bruce Thompson; assistant secretary for public affairs and public liaison, Alfred Kingon; and Thomas Dawson and Chris Hicks, who worked as close aides to the executive secretary (Birnbaum and Murray 1987).

26. In many ways, this approach was parallel to academic research, which stressed that different types of tax systems should be compared on a revenue and sometimes distributionally neutral basis.

27. The success of this effort was due in large part to the efforts of Susan Nelson of the Office of Tax Analysis, who initiated an effort to insure that the data sets being developed could properly account for many of the changes being proposed.

28. See Gordon and Slemrod (1989) and the update by Gordon, Kalambokidis, and Slemrod (2003).

7

Tax Reform and the Aftermath: 1985 to 1988

Who is the figure behind every great man, the individual who knows his ultimate secrets?
A father confessor? Hell, no, the tax expert.

—Louis Auchincloss, *The Partners*

On October 22, 1986, nearly two years after calling for tax simplification in the 1984 State of the Union address, President Reagan signed the final bill (PL 99-514). Earlier, in November 1984, the Treasury Department had released its blueprint for action. Then, in May 1985, the administration put forward a revised version. In November 1985, the House Ways and Means Committee produced its draft; the Senate Finance Committee approved a separate measure in May 1986. Hammering out the differences through August, a conference committee produced a report that the House voted on and the Senate cleared in September.

Yet each stage of the process was similar: first, certain constituencies or policymakers were appeased by new giveaways, then estimates revealed significant revenue losses because of those giveaways, and, finally, new packages restored some revenues by scrambling to find new "reforms" that could be substituted for the ones abandoned.

Onward to Enactment

Treasury Secretary James Baker—who had traded his White House chief of staff position with Donald Regan—led the team that developed the stage two president's proposals. When the bill went to the House Ways and Means Committee, Chairman Dan Rostenkowski (D-IL) took responsibility; in the Senate Finance Committee, Chairman Robert Packwood (R-OR) played that role. The process was often acrimonious. Most of the giveaways favored higher-income groups and most of the compensating measures affected them, too.

The additional revenue sources that ultimately paid for the giveaways fell mainly into four categories: higher tax rates, double taxation of certain forms of income, new base expansions, and complex backdoor provisions, including a new alternative minimum tax.

- *Higher tax rates* were achieved in several ways. A promised increase from $1,000 to $2,000 in the personal exemption was implemented over time rather than immediately. Some tax rates below the top rate were also raised. A proposed statutory tax rate of 25 percent for many middle-income individuals turned into a 28 percent rate by the time the bill passed, which relieved pressure to broaden the base in middle-income brackets.
- *Double taxation of income* was an especially popular way to amend the reform proposal. Proposed moves away from double taxation of corporate income were curtailed and then abandoned. Indexing of realized capital gains for inflation was eliminated, then replaced in the final bill with full taxation of all nominal gains, even those due to inflation. Proposals to index depreciation allowances were also removed. This full taxation of gains, however, did greatly simplify the tax system, at least temporarily, and removed incentives for many types of arbitrage.[1]
- *New base expansions* were few. Even the revenue pick-up from expanded gains taxation was modest since taxpayers now had the option of realizing fewer gains to avoid the new higher-tax rates on actual realizations. This issue would continue to haunt tax politics after the bill passed, and in later years the provision itself would be abandoned.
- *Complex, backdoor provisions* crept into the bill as it neared its final form. In many cases, these provisions sowed the seeds of policy dilemmas and debates to come. The Senate Finance Committee, for instance, created a fourth rate of 33 percent, and then called it something else—a "phase out of the benefits of the personal exemption and the bottom tax rate." The upshot of this doubletalk was that the 33 percent rate created a so-called "bubble"—marginal

tax rates fell at the highest income levels after rising in bubble fashion at preceding income levels (see figure 3.6).[2] Even more popular were increasingly complex means of imposing minimum taxes and limits on loss write-offs.[3]

- One of these backdoor provisions, a new *individual alternative minimum tax (AMT)*, played an ever-increasing role as the nation moved toward the 21st century. Its complexity increasingly affected taxpayers over time because the exemption levels were not indexed for inflation or real growth in the economy. Under the AMT, as originally adopted in 1986, taxpayers were also required to calculate depreciation and other allowances two ways and then use the less generous of the two. Businesses had to pay tax on the higher of taxable income or income reported on financial returns, even when no special tax preference was involved. This requirement came about in reaction to the populist sentiment that corporations reporting positive financial income should pay tax on that income.[4]

What Did Tax Reform Achieve?

Despite setbacks, the political process only partially derailed the type of tax reform brought forward in the original Treasury study. In general, Baker, Rostenkowski, and Packwood couldn't move far from the ground rules set when reform began. No one wanted to be known for blocking reform once it became clear that a system could be designed to lower rates and eliminate shelters, remove the poor from the tax rolls, help equalize treatment of individuals with equal income, and even coalesce conservative and liberal support. The tax policy process concentrated decisionmaking in the hands of Treasury Secretary Baker and the chairpersons of the tax-writing committees. Thus, at each stage of reform, failure could have been attributed primarily to any one of them, which gave each of them a strong incentive not to fail.[5]

The simple recognition of the basic purpose of a tax system must be listed as one of tax reform's major achievements. As the historian Elliot Brownlee writes, "It can be argued that, as a result of the bipartisan effort, the Tax Reform Act of 1986 advanced a process of restoring to federal taxation the sense of balance sought by the founders of the Republic. The act represented a major step in the elimination of tax-based privilege, while reaffirming the duties of citizenship" (Brownlee 1989, 1620).

The Tax Reform Act of 1986 became one of the most sweeping tax code changes in U.S. history. Certainly, it involved the largest reshuffling of incentives and priorities ever achieved in a roughly revenue-neutral act. The rest of this chapter examines in more detail what was achieved, what was left undone, and what new problems were created.

Progressive Taxation and Incentives for Lower-Income Workers

In the end, tax reform proved mildly progressive, at least at the bottom of the income scale (see table 7.1). It reduced the taxation of the poor and low-income individuals through three changes: (1) increases in the personal exemption from $1,080 in 1986 to $2,000 by 1989 for all taxpayers and their dependents; (2) increases in the standard deduction, which reduced taxable income for all taxpayers who do not itemize or declare interest payments, state and local taxes, or other allowed deductions; and (3) significant expansion, as well as indexing for inflation, of an earned income tax credit (EITC) for low-income workers with children.[6]

Table 7.1 *Changes in 1988 Income Tax Liability under the Tax Reform Act of 1986*

Income class (in thousands of 1986 dollars)	Percentage change in income tax liability 1988	Average income tax rate (percent)	
		Prior law	1986 act
Less than $10	−65.1	1.6	0.5
$10 to $20	−22.3	5.7	4.4
$20 to $30	−9.8	8.3	7.5
$30 to $40	−7.7	9.5	8.7
$40 to $50	−9.1	11.1	10.1
$50 to $75	−1.8	13.3	13.1
$75 to $100	−1.2	15.7	15.6
$100 to $200	−2.2	19.3	18.9
$200 and above	−2.4	22.8	22.3
Total	−6.1	11.8	11.1

Source: Joint Committee on Taxation (1987, 17–18).
Note: These figures do not take into account certain provisions affecting individuals. Thus, total tax reductions are somewhat different from what is indicated in this table.

The placement of "family" issues on the tax agenda would set in motion numerous other EITC and child credit tax relief efforts through the end of the century and beyond. The tax reform drafters also made it easier to enact welfare reform a decade later as welfare checks were being displaced, at least for some, with work-related subsidies. However, the net effect of these changes mainly increased the incentive to work among those not currently working. At higher income levels where the EITC was phased out, the effective marginal rate under the new law was higher than before, and incentives to work were reduced.[7]

As for broadening the tax base, older Americans were gently tapped. The elderly lost their "double" personal exemption and got a less valuable increase in the standard deduction instead. When the continued nontaxability of most Social Security benefits is taken into account, the elderly still paid significantly lower taxes than other taxpayers with equal incomes, but the gap shrunk.

One change—full taxation of unemployment insurance benefits—complemented the tax reductions applied to low-income persons. Under old tax law, low-income unemployed persons received better treatment than low-income workers. Under the new law, the tax burden for low-income persons generally decreased due to the increased EITC and higher level of tax-exempt income, but the unemployed had more incentive to work.[8] Thus, lower (or negative for some EITC recipients) rates of tax on earned income and higher tax rates on unemployment income complemented each other to promote work.

Some comparisons reveal the magnitude of the overall changes in tax treatment of low-income workers. For a married couple with two dependents, the tax threshold excluding EITC was about $7,980 in 1986, but rose to $12,800 by 1988 under the new law. This new tax threshold was placed above the estimated federal poverty threshold of $12,092 for the same year (U.S. Bureau of the Census 1990). If the EITC is factored in, the changes are significant. For instance, the average income tax rate (income taxes, less EITC, divided by income) at the federal poverty level for this type of family dropped from 3.3 percent in 1986 to negative 5.3 percent in 1988.

A Reversal of the Trend to Tax Low-Income Workers

From a historical perspective, the 1986 Tax Reform Act began reversing the trend to raise taxes on low-income workers. Federal income tax rates on a family of four at one-half the median income, for example, were zero until 1960. Inflation and real growth then began to push families at one-half the median income into positive tax brackets, and legislated tax cuts before 1986 weren't big enough to compensate for the tax hikes. By 1985, the average tax rate for this population reached 6.5 percent. Under the 1986 tax act, the average rate initially dropped to about 5 percent, but then rose again to 5.5 percent by 1990. Moreover, the 1986 act triggered a chain of events leading to higher credits for low-income workers in later years.

Put into perspective, tax reform raised the personal exemption to $2,000 by 1989, but at that time it would have taken a personal exemption of almost $7,500 to offset the same relative amount of income as the $600 personal exemption did in 1948.[9] In addition, Social Security tax increases continued almost unabated. For a family of four with taxable earnings from labor equal to one-half the median income, Social Security taxes and federal income taxes together accounted for 5 percent or less of income before 1960. By 1990 these taxes equaled 21 percent of income (figure 3.9). (Of course, benefits also rose over the years, and the distributional effect of taxes should not be considered in isolation.) An important point here is that the lower taxes for low-income workers achieved in 1986 only modestly offset the increasingly higher taxes being paid by that subset of these workers eligible for little or no EITC.

Rewarding Innovation and Productivity

Tax reform significantly improved the allocation of assets and investment within the economy. The government relinquished much of its role in determining which industries and types of business activity should be favored and which penalized. Effective tax rates across assets were made more equal in 1986, and money followed innovation instead of tax shelters. Table 7.2 presents estimates of effective tax rates on new or marginal purchases of assets for various asset types. These calculations take into account both corporate and personal taxes on returns from these assets.[10]

Not shown in the table is another form of reduction in effective tax rates that is important to the economy but difficult to measure using traditional procedures. Investments are made not just in physical assets, but also in research, better management, and human capital. But for tax-

Table 7.2 *Total Effective Tax Rates on Corporate Investment, by Broad Asset Type and by Industry (Tax Reform Act of 1986) (In Percentages)*

	Old law	Treasury[a]	Administration[a]	House	Senate	New law
Total	38	34	30	40	39	41
Asset type						
Equipment and						
structures	29	33	25	38	37	39
Equipment	11	33	24	39	34	38
Structures	38	33	26	37	38	39
Inventories	58	35	44	47	47	48

Source: Jane G. Gravelle (1984, 1986).

Notes: Calculations assume a 4 percent inflation rate and separate marginal tax rates for corporations, interest income, dividend income, and capital gains. Only effective tax rates on corporate investments are shown here, but the effective tax rates include both corporate and personal taxes. Investment is financed one-third by debt.

a. Calculations for Treasury and administration proposals assume that taxation of dividends on existing shares raises overall effective tax rates on capital.

accounting purposes, payments for these intangible forms of capital are difficult to calculate.[11] Closely related to discrimination against dynamic firms was discrimination against new firms and certain older firms that had not been profitable for a number of years. Some established firms with little income were also denied tax benefits if their business generated too little taxable income to allow full use of incentives for marginal investments.[12]

This discrepancy helps explain why some companies in basic industries wanted tax reformers to eliminate the investment tax credit. With a large carryover of unused investment credits from previous years, some industries felt at a competitive disadvantage with respect to new investment. Potential new firms, of course, are always unrepresented in the political process for the simple reason that they don't yet exist.[13]

Investment in More Productive Assets

Because of its positive impact on the economy, restoring the market incentive to invest in productive assets was perhaps the major improvement in the tax bill. At the extreme, it had been profitable to back mediocre or even losing ventures if either the effective tax rate on equity-financed investments was negative or the after-tax real interest rate was negative (see table 5.1). The 1986 tax act took several important steps to reduce the probability that unproductive investment would be profitable after tax adjustments.

First, the investment credit was eliminated. As long as the investor wrote off no more than the real cost, acceleration of depreciation allowances could never result in a negative tax rate on equity investments in depreciable assets. Expensing is equivalent under some conditions to a zero tax rate, so any acceleration less than expensing requires writing off the purchase price over time rather than immediately, making the resulting positive tax rate less valuable than expensing.

The act also lowered the marginal tax rate. At lower marginal rates, the tax consequences of any miscalculation of income are less important. In the case of interest, the failure to index for inflation means that taxpayers get to deduct more than the real interest costs. However, this extra deduction is less valuable at lower tax rates. (During this period, lower inflation rates also lowered the value of the extra deduction due to a high inflation component in interest payments. Both contributed to investment in more productive capital. See figure 7.1.)[14]

Figure 7.1 *Interest Rates Necessary to Prevent Unproductive Investments*

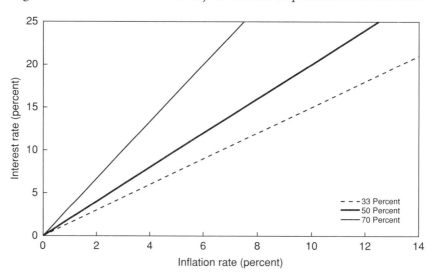

Source: Author's calculations (see note 13 of this chapter).

The 1986 Tax Reform Act significantly reduced the amount of money flowing into shelters that encouraged unproductive investment, just as it reduced other tax arbitrage opportunities by lowering tax rates and by making the effective tax rate positive for more types of equity investments. In addition, the act limited deductions from passive investments[15] and restricted investment interest payments in excess of investment income. These latter approaches, too, stanched the flow of scarce saving dollars into shelter investments. The sales pitches on financial pages for these now-beleaguered tax shelters soon dropped out of sight, and most taxpayers in the end had much simpler financial planning and tax returns simply because they no longer engaged in these shelters.

The lessons for macroeconomic policy were powerful. Economic stagnation ruled when the combination of high inflation, high tax rates, and tax preferences led to profitable investments in unproductive assets (Steuerle 1985b). The monetary and tax policy attack on this combination helped restore economic growth.

Lower Marginal (but Not Average) Tax Rates

As advertised, tax reform did lower the marginal tax rates faced by individuals. Average individual rates also dropped. But, lest we lose perspective here, average corporate rates increased. Marginal rates for both individuals and corporations were still able to fall without major revenue loss largely because the tax base expanded. The drop in rates is shown in figures 3.8 and 3.9.

The distributional tables eventually presented in tax reform tended to exaggerate the extent of tax reduction, since they showed only the effect on individuals. Some considered this a ruse, since the increase in average corporate tax rates partly paid for the reduction in individual rates. Because individuals bear the burden of the corporate tax, tax reform did not lower their taxes on net. The switch from individual to corporate taxes was really more the byproduct of an early Treasury decision to keep the top individual rate and the corporate rate close to each other. Then, too, the switch reflected the simple consequence of a reform more heavily attacking business than individual tax breaks.

The Treasury had argued from the beginning that it was seeking a distributionally neutral tax change, counting all provisions together. Once the individual rates were reduced, however, politicians couldn't stay away from bragging about the tax cut they were providing. All politicians' claims of giving something to the taxpayer should be appraised skeptically.[16]

Reduced Influence of Taxes on Consumer and Producer Choices

Lower marginal tax rates encourage better use of both time and money. The logic is simple: lowering rates reduces taxes' impact on decisions of business managers and individual investors. While the 1986 tax reform eliminated numerous special preferences, deductions, and exclusions, many also survived. At the lower rate of taxation, the value of deductions was calculated at a rate of 33 percent or less for individuals and 34 percent for most corporations instead of such rates as 50 percent (the former top individual rate) or 46 percent (the former rate applying to most corporations). With lower marginal tax rates in effect, taxpayers became more likely to invest directly in equities or savings accounts. Before reform, large potential tax savings from various portfolio strategies subsidized the use of additional financial middlemen for nonproductive transactions. While there is no good estimate of savings lost to these additional transaction costs, the amount was probably substantial. For instance, many tax shelters ultimately used 80 percent or less of the money originally invested to purchase assets, with 20 percent or more going to brokers, salesmen, lawyers, and accountants. As tax savings fell relative to transaction costs after reform, taxpayers became more likely to avoid those additional costs by channeling savings more directly into investments requiring fewer middlemen.

Some Simplification

The 1986 Tax Reform Act simplified financial management in various ways. The reduced influence of taxes on economic decisionmaking made life simpler for the saver and investor, who could now concentrate more on economic issues and less on tax issues.

Among the major simplifications achieved by tax reform was the virtual elimination of trusts for tax-planning purposes. Certain recordkeeping and tax calculations became unnecessary for those no longer eligible for certain deductions. The increase in the standard deduction meant that far fewer taxpayers had to keep the records needed to itemize their tax returns. In addition,

- Fewer individuals needed to keep track of medical expenses;
- Sales tax receipts no longer had to be kept, nor did sales tax deduction calculations need to be made;
- Less recordkeeping was required of those with employee business expenses, the expenses of producing investment income, and other miscellaneous itemized deductions;
- Income averaging, second-earner expenses, political contribution credits, or dividend exclusions no longer had to be calculated; and
- Capital gains became easier to calculate, and the game playing induced by a capital gains preference was largely, if temporarily, eliminated.

Other Gains

Tax reform was so comprehensive in its scope that many improvements are given only scant attention in this book:

- The standard deduction for single heads of households[17] was increased;
- The lower tax rates reduced the inequity between those who could still use deductions and those who could not;
- Preferences for certain (intangible) oil and gas drilling costs and for state and local bonds used to finance private, rather than governmental, activity were limited in the minimum tax;
- Many industry-specific exclusions and deductions were limited or eliminated.
- Tax subsidies for meals and entertainment associated with business were restricted;
- The federal subsidy to all state and local borrowing, not just borrowing for private purposes, was reduced because of the lower tax rates;[18] and
- Other inequities were pared, such as for large prizes or awards, in-kind assistance for services rendered to educational institutions, and a few other types of formerly nontaxable income.

Summarizing the Gains

One measure of tax reform's success can be taken in its impact on tax expenditures. Remember that a basic thrust of tax reform was to eliminate or cut back on expenditures hidden in the tax code so that rates for individuals and corporations would fall and personal exemptions for individuals would increase.

With this in mind, John Witte (1991b), a political science professor at the University of Wisconsin, estimated that of the 72 provisions which tightened tax expenditures, 14 tax expenditures were eventually repealed, a figure approximately equal to the total that had been repealed from 1913 to 1985. Of course, this can be contrasted to the proposals put forward in the original Treasury plan, which advocated repeal of 38 tax expenditures (Witte 1991b).[19] The largest income tax reform in U.S. history still could have been much larger. In another analysis, Thomas Neubig and David Joulfaian (1988) of the Treasury staff examined reform's effect on tax expenditures. Figure 7.2 summarizes their estimates that tax reform produced the equivalent of an annual net reduction of $193 billion in expenditures in the tax code for the year 1988.

Failures of the 1986 Tax Reform Effort

As suggested by Witte, despite the successes, a number of proposals were never actualized. Many inefficient and inequitable differentials in taxation remained, and new problems were also created. These sources of neglect and failure would come to haunt tax policy deliberations not long after the major overhaul of 1986 passed.

Limited Base Broadening for Individuals

A major failure of the tax reform was that the base of taxable income for individuals, while expanded significantly, was still far smaller than it needed to be. As a result, tax rates remained high, as did losses of economic welfare arising from arbitrary distinctions between taxed and untaxed activities.

Undue attention to the top rate had left other tax rates without sufficient reductions. Many middle-class preferences remained. Essentially untouched were most nontaxable employee benefits, nontaxable transfer payments, deductions of state and local taxes, and mortgage interest payments, which together comprise most of the tax benefits granted to individuals.

Figure 7.2 *Total Tax Expenditures before and after Tax Reform (at 1988 Levels of Economic Activity)*

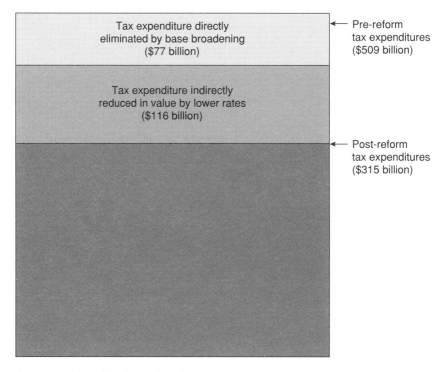

Source: Neubig and Joulfaian (1988).
Note: Details do not add to total due to rounding.

Whether to treat the full taxation of capital gains as base broadening is debatable. In many cases, the failure to account for inflation meant that taxpayers (such as mutual fund owners) would be taxed on more than their real income when inflation increased asset values. Of more relevance here, any increase in tax rates on capital gains was significantly offset by a lower rate of realization. By some estimates, net taxes on capital gains go down when rates increase in certain ranges. Other estimates predict a modest increase, but all conclude that a higher rate means fewer realizations.[20] Thus, even though these estimates are open to debate, the extent of any base broadening of those reporting capital gains is limited because this discretionary tax can be avoided.

Some elements of tax reform are wrongly viewed as base broadening. The so-called phase outs of "the benefits of the bottom brackets" and of the personal exemption, later called the "bubble effect," were simply disguised rate increases.

Lack of Indexing of Capital Income Measures for Inflation

When it drafted the 1986 tax bill, Congress ducked the problems of indexing capital income measures to account for inflation. Accordingly, future changes in the inflation rate continued to play havoc with the effective tax rate applied to various forms of investment income. John Makin and Michael Allison (1986) estimated that inflation indexing in the mid-1980s effectively would have been worth several hundred billion dollars to the economy over time.[21]

Although the failure to index creates significant economic problems, the implementation of indexing is difficult. The calculations, for instance, become quite complex unless financial institutions do them with computers (Halperin and Steuerle 1988). The complexity of indexing was perhaps the major reason for its rejection in tax reform, and lower inflation rates since then have further sidelined the issue.

Other Neglected Issues

However comprehensive the Tax Reform Act of 1986, Congress failed to include many relevant tax issues. First, though the legislation contained some important pension changes—notably to individual retirement accounts, rules regarding 401(k) plans, and the ways to integrate private pension plans with Social Security—pension policy was never examined holistically.

Second, though many scattered international tax issues were raised during tax reform, most enacted final provisions were not based on any thoroughgoing notion or acceptance of how international tax issues should be treated over the long run.

Third, to keep some preferences on the books, Congress quickly abandoned the plan to partially integrate corporate and individual income taxes as the original Treasury proposal suggested.[22] Riddling the new tax system, therefore, were many problems associated with taxing corporate income twice—the encouragement of debt rather than equity financing, the legal problems of distinguishing between dividends and interest; and the discouragement of corporate (as opposed to noncorporate) ownership. Corporate integration would come to the fore again more than once before achieving some legislative success in 2003.

Little or No Decrease in the Cost of Capital

Treasury had proposed a combination of changes that would have reduced the effective tax rate on capital investment—the rate that results when individual and corporate rates are combined and depreciation and other preferences and penalties added in. As tax reform worked its way through the political process, the effective tax rate on returns from capital investment was increased relative to the Treasury plan. This process offset some of the gains from the more neutral taxation of different forms of capital investment. Table 7.2 shows estimates at the time that the 1986 law yielded a higher effective tax rate on capital than the old law.[23]

The effect can be exaggerated. As it turned out, reductions in the rate of inflation over time provided offsetting reductions in the cost of capital or effective tax rate.[24] Whether in the end the rate went up slightly or down slightly—the alternative estimates in figure 3.12 show a slight reduction—less was accomplished than could have been.

Interestingly, a common perception in 1986 was that business had succeeded in arm-twisting Congress to lower effective tax rates on capital, at least relative to the Treasury Department's initial proposals. That perception is wrong. True, some compromises helped certain types of investment escape taxation temporarily. But to get this gain, negotiators acquiesced to an effective tax rate increase on many types of structures and inventories and on the returns to invention and "ideas." The trade-offs generally increased the cost of capital because what had been abandoned (especially indexing) was worth more over time than what was gained (some faster write-offs of depreciation).

While some economic achievements were limited, tax reform would not hugely affect aggregate investment, or consumption—an assumption borne out by economists examining the effects of the 1986 Tax Reform Act some years later (Slemrod 1990). The principal behavioral changes noted were improvements in the allocation of consumption and investment, such as the dramatic decline in the use of tax shelters. Still, total investment and domestic saving increased after tax reform, and economic growth accelerated. This was especially remarkable since economic growth often slows after the economy has expanded for several years, as it had by 1986.

Backdoor Complications and Complexity

Political constraints on direct ways to broaden the tax base meant that more and more of the revenues needed to finance rate reduction would come in through the back door. Congress not only failed to index the measure of capital income for inflation, but also failed to make appropriate adjustments (mainly due to inflation) in the moving expenses and costs of childcare that could be counted toward a deduction or a credit. But Congress also went further and increased taxes in a way that was complicated by design—partly to befuddle opponents, make costs difficult to calculate, and otherwise hide the manipulation of the tax code to achieve political objectives. Even when backdoor approaches are attempted for honorable distributional, equity, or appearance reasons, they often make the tax code more complex.

THE ALTERNATIVE MINIMUM TAX

The new AMT arrived through the back door in unsightly garb. For individuals, the principal items that appeared for taxation were not shelters at all, but rather personal exemptions, miscellaneous itemized deductions, and state and local tax deductions.[25] In effect, personal exemptions—say, for taking care of a dependent—were treated as if they were tax shelters! Even though miscellaneous itemized deductions were subject to abuse, some were quite legitimate, and they had been pared already in the regular tax. And, while state and local taxes might legitimately be considered as payments for services received, reducing or eliminating this deduction did not need to be achieved through the back door nor in such a complex manner. Lesser items were also needlessly complex: a tiny adjustment to normal depreciation allowances might have provided the same revenue gains as the contorted alternative calculation of depreciation allowances under the AMT.

INTEREST PAYMENTS

Various forms of interest payments were also limited in needlessly complex ways in the 1986 reform. Personal interest payments on automobile loans and credit card balances were no longer deductible. On the other hand, mortgage interest was (and is) deductible for up to $1 million in debt on a primary mortgage and $100,000 on a second mortgage, but only for a taxpayer's first and second residences.[26] One effect of this new design was to encourage taxpayers to move from house to house as the primary mortgage on one house was paid off or the house increased in value. One reason for this awkward design, including disparate treatment of different types of interest, was that President Reagan had earlier sworn that the home mortgage deduction would remain untouched.

INTERNATIONAL INCOME

The taxation of international income became extraordinarily complex and the bane of tax accountants. Some complexity resulted from the drive to achieve a revenue target rather than a target based on principles. On the other hand, some complexity was simply unavoidable: attributing costs and income to various affiliates and subsidiaries operating in multiple jurisdictions at different exchange rates is necessarily complicated. The simple lack of a consensus on how to tax and measure the income of multinational companies and their owners also boggled the process.[27] The difficult issue of transfer pricing—how to account for intracompany transfers of know-how and other items—grew in importance over the years as well, although this likely would have occurred to some extent with or without tax reform.

HOW COMPLEXITY ARISES: AN EXAMPLE

The treatment of minors' income illustrates how tax reform increased equity and simplified tax planning but complicated tax filing unnecessarily. To simplify the taxation of trusts, the initial Treasury plan tried to reduce tax-motivated transfers of wealth to children through trust instruments.[28] Reducing these incentives and requiring children who had received sizable financial transfers to pay tax on the income from those assets at the tax rate of the parent (rather than at their own lower rates) would greatly simplify planning and remove many wasteful transactions, even if it might mean a bit more filing complexity for those who continued to transfer such wealth.

Also proposed—and this was vitally important—was that minors be allowed to retain their own personal exemption. In typical cases, then, only capital income in excess of the new personal exemption of $2,000 would be taxed. At an interest rate of 5 percent, for instance, this would require $40,000 or more in assets—an amount likely to be reached only through sizable transfers from parents, guardians, or other taxpayers.

As reform wound through Congress, however, various giveaways in other parts of the tax code resulted in a shortfall of revenues. Some Congressional tax analysts then noted that on pure equity grounds there was little justification for allowing personal exemptions for a dependent twice—once to the head of household or parent, and once to the dependent himself. They then proposed eliminating this second personal exemption and leaving only a small standard deduction.

This approach to taxing trusts significantly increased the complexity of filing tax returns. The additional personal exemption for minors was not fundamentally a matter of equity but of simplicity. The amended rule meant that hundreds of thousands of children with only modest assets would now have to file tax forms. To add to the complexity, some income was to be taxed at the child's rate and some at the parent's rate.

In this classic case, the political system simply accorded too little weight to the value of administrative efficiency and simplification. Those children with moderate amounts of wage income from a summer job needed to file and pay tax at their parents' rate on a few dollars of interest from a small checking or saving account. Without doubt, after 1986 a significant portion of children with income and their parents violated this provision, often without knowing it.

The Aftermath to Tax Reform, 1987–1988

For two years after President Reagan signed the 1986 tax reform package, legislative activity was notably muted. Many tax practitioners, hard-pressed to absorb all the changes, felt that the tax code should be left alone. Some of those who had advocated tax reform, such as Secretary of the Treasury Baker, also feared a rear-guard action against reform and did not want to open up tax reform issues that had just been settled.

In addition, the economy performed remarkably well during the years after tax reform. All the predictions of a reform-driven downturn turned out to be false. Instead, the economy grew at 3.4 percent in 1986 while reform was being anticipated, then at rates of 3.4 percent in 1987 and 4.2 percent in 1988 (Executive Office of the U.S. President 2003, table B-4). As this growth combined with the slow descent of Defense Department spending as a percentage of the gross domestic product (GDP) after its 1986 peak, the deficit declined substantially from $221 billion in FY 1986 to $150 billion in FY 1987 (OMB 1990, A-281). This remarkable drop temporarily spared politicians from tackling the ever-nagging issue of debt and deficit policy.

A strong economic performance, the lack of a crisis, and the desire to "leave the tax code alone" reinforced perhaps the strongest political tendency in 1987 and 1988—to delay major decisionmaking until after the 1988 election. Yet, even in this environment, not all tax legislation could be avoided. Legislation in 1987 and 1988 consisted of modest attempts to reduce the size of the deficit mingled with deficit-neutral attempts to change some social policy.

The Deficit Reduction Act of 1987

In 1987 especially, there initially was little appetite for enacting any major tax legislation after the three years of intense political battle leading up to tax reform. Nonetheless, under the budget rules then in effect (named after Senators Phil Gramm [R-TX], Warren Rudman [R-NH], and Ernest Hollings [D-SC]), the deficit would have to be reduced through legislation, or else the president would be required to sequester funds from most government agencies. The latter course of across-the-board cutbacks was so arbitrary and excluded so many saner options that most observers viewed it as impossible to implement. The political momentum to comply with the rules, moreover, was weak, and Congress could always vote to avoid them.

By late 1987, the economy itself was to puncture this complacency with a nosedive in the stock market. On October 19, the Dow Jones average dropped 508 points in one day to a level of 1739—a drop that followed a decline the previous week of 235 points. On a percentage basis, the one-day drop of 22.6 percent far exceeded the 12.8 percent drop of October 28, 1929 (*Wall Street Journal* 1987). The lingering fear that inaction in 1929 had contributed to the Depression made swift corrective action politically necessary. The monetary authorities immediately added liquidity to financial markets by increasing the money supply and lowering interest rates, while the White House and the Treasury Department moved quickly to insure passage of a deficit-reduction package. The momentum to "do something" in a crisis often is more important than what is done: in this case, a potential downturn was fought not by Keynesian fiscal stimulus, but deficit reduction to remove fears in financial markets that the government budget was out of control!

The resulting Omnibus Reconciliation Act of 1987 was achieved largely through a chaotic bargaining session involving congressional leaders, committee heads, and members of the administration. Despite the political inertia of early 1987, the act turned out to be the largest of those enacted and sustained in the 1987–1989 period, if measured by the amount of revenues involved.

The conferees' main goal in those uncertain times was to minimize political damage by making tax changes that individual taxpayers would scarcely notice. To wit, the only significant items finally passed that affected individuals' income taxes directly were simplification of the mortgage interest limits passed in the 1986 reform and an increase from 80 to 90 percent in the amount of current year's tax liability that individuals must pay during that year (rather than by April 15) to avoid penalties. The latter move, like many taken to reduce the deficit for a short period, had almost no long-run effect on revenues. It simply speeded up payments slightly.

Under the 1987 act, businesses were to bear increased burdens, both financial and transactional. The changes entailed modest reform in a few cases, such as improved reporting of income related to installment sales and to contracts that were not yet completed. Attempts were made to tax various types of corporate transactions, such as conversions of some types of corporations to a special lower-tax status,[29] limits on carry-over losses after an ownership change, and cutbacks in allowable deductions by corporations for dividends paid by other corporations. Closing some loopholes created in the 1986 act also brought in significant revenues.[30]

All in all, the 1987 act raised between $14 billion and $16 billion in each of the fiscal years 1989 through 1992, or about 0.3 percent of GNP in years with deficits of 3.0 to 3.4 percent of GNP. On net, the 1987 act could be considered tax reform insofar as it did broaden the tax base (OMB 1990, 4-4). Also, the deficit decrease achieved through tax increases significantly exceeded any reduced expenditures, following a deficit reduction tradition that marked the 1980s—the tax committees delivered while the expenditure committees did not.

The Election Year of 1988

Action to reduce the deficit all but stopped in the election year of 1988, with one exception. Enactment of the Technical and Miscellaneous Revenue Act of 1988 provided technical corrections to the 1986 reform, some minor simplifications of the 1986 tax reform bill, extensions of expiring provisions, some special interest concessions, and some restrictions on the use of life insurance sold mainly to defer tax on investment income. It also contained a special tax break for those purchasing U.S. savings bonds spent for educational purposes. The last item was advocated by then Vice President George H. W. Bush, but, like many social tax expenditures backed by Republicans, received substantial bipartisan support, including that of Senator Ted Kennedy (D-MA), whose staff was quite active in the legislative drafting.[31]

Social Policy Changes

The future of tax policy was defined by social policy changes with tax implications as much as by tax policy changes with social implications. In 1988, Congress attempted to expand social programs in a pay-as-you-go, or deficit-neutral manner. One such change, the Family Security Act of 1988, raised a small amount of revenues to expand welfare programs by crimping the availability of a dependent-care tax deduction for children age 13 to 15 and by requiring taxpayer identification numbers, first required for dependents age 5 and over in 1986, to be extended to even younger ages. This led to a significant reduction in the number of dependents falsely reported (OMB 1990, 4-6 to 4-7).[32] The revenue gain of this last change was substantial relative to the small administrative change involved. Cutbacks in some other welfare benefits paid for much of the rest of the change, as did mandates that states require a certain percentage of welfare recipients to work—a harbinger of future welfare legislation in the 1990s.

Catastrophic Health Insurance for the Elderly

A much more elaborate attempt to extend social policy was made through the Medicare Catastrophic Coverage Act. In early 1987, the president proposed modestly expanding Medicare benefits.[33] Congress quickly decided to take advantage of this crack in the door by the president and moved to expand Medicare benefits much more extensively. The final act, initially passed in 1988, expanded catastrophic and prescription drug benefits for the elderly by approximately $7 billion in the first year or two and by large multiples of that amount as time progressed. The cost was to be covered in large part by a surtax on the income of the elderly, with rates rising over time from 15 to 40 percent or more of income tax liability.

By 1989, the act was repealed, largely because its design embodied a failed concept of tax policy. The act's history provides important lessons on the future use of the tax code to back up social policy changes. In enacting catastrophic health care legislation for the elderly and disabled, Congress pursued worthwhile objectives without devoting adequate attention to their financing and administrative costs.

The act's rapid repeal also illustrated elderly constituents' continued power. In a furor, some of them attacked the car of House Ways and Means Chairman Dan Rostenkowski with signs such as, "Seniors for Repeal of the Catastrophic Act." One elderly woman threw herself on the car's hood. (*Chicago Tribune* 1989). Though Rostenkowski escaped on foot, any inclination toward making the current elderly population pay for additional benefits—at least in the short run—was thwarted.

Two related errors proved fatal. First, Congress had lost sight of what had become "ordinary" medical expenses. Second, collecting an additional premium or surtax for the Medicare system through the income tax system would have tied both systems into knots and created fundamental administrative problems. The first error led to the second by forcing Congress to try to find some means of paying for what were more ordinary expenses.

The real lesson from the 1988 experience is that there is no substitute for getting things right the first time. In the case of catastrophic care, the financing should have been given weight at least equal to the benefit side from the beginning. Congress cannot continually impose new administrative complexities on taxpayers and the IRS simply to achieve a relatively minor benefits-redistribution goal. Grafting a monthly benefit system onto an annual collection (income tax) system also made little sense.

In the end, perhaps the 1988 Medicare legislation simply filled a void—giving Congress something to do in an election year when it was clear that the Reagan era was ending and most presidential candidates, whether Republican and Democratic, were promising or at least implying that they would have a softer touch when it came to social issues. Indeed, under the next president, George H. W. Bush, domestic spending increased significantly, but despite his initial intentions, tax increases were not left off the table.

NOTES

1. The indexing of various items each has a different type of complexity associated with it. See Halperin and Steuerle (1988).

2. This debate, too, carried forward to later years. Amendments were made in 1990 in the structure of the top rate, but once again Congress attempted to impose those rate increases through the back door.

3. The means by which the Joint Committee performed distributional analysis also supported the political tendency to deal with some issues through the back door—through increases in minimum taxes and limitations on write-offs of "passive" losses and interest payments. When limits were imposed on the extent to which business losses could be taken or when minimum taxes were imposed, the Joint Committee imputed these increases in taxes almost entirely to high-income individuals. While this method mainly attacked shelters, it also drew under its wings a number of business owners who were not high income.

4. Citizens for Tax Justice, a labor-backed, Washington-based organization, had significant influence here through the publication of tables relating tax liability to financial income. Tax Analysts had performed similar calculations over the years.

5. The eventual support and sometimes conversion of each is chronicled well in Birnbaum and Murray (1987) and Conlan, Wrightson, and Beam. (1990).

6. When fully phased in, the expansion and the indexing together raised the maximum credit (from $550 in 1986 to $874 in 1988), while the credit did not phase out completely until income exceeded $18,576 (IRS 1988, 145).

7. For further discussion of issues surrounding the EITC, see Steuerle and Wilson (1987); Steuerle (1990c); Hoffman and Seidman (1990); Dickert, Houser, and Scholz (1995); and *National Journal* (2000). The EITC also has income effects: increases in income that could lead to decreases in labor supply for those receiving the credit. In any comprehensive bill one also needs to examine the income (and substitution) effects throughout the income distribution. Thus, increases in income for EITC recipients are paid for by decreases in income and higher tax rates for other taxpayers in a revenue-neutral bill.

8. Many unemployed are married to employed workers, and most are not unemployed for the entire calendar year. Hence, the drop in earnings due to temporary unemployment may increase the probability of receiving an EITC for part-year work or work by a spouse.

9. Increases in the standard deduction offset only a part of the decline in the personal (taxpayer and dependent) exemption, mainly for smaller households that did not make much use of the dependent exemption.

10. The marginal rates used are effectively averaged across individuals by weighting each taxpayer relative to the amount of interest, dividends, or capital gains received. Different marginal rates are used for capital gains, interest, dividends, and so forth. A constant debt/equity ratio for corporate investments is also assumed. For further details, see Gravelle (1984, 1986).

11. Charles R. Hulten and James W. Robertson (1984) found that high-technology industries within manufacturing experienced higher average effective tax rates during the 1970s than other manufacturing industries. Note that limits on loss write-offs arise

in part because the tax system is based in realizations, so that losses can be realized even while gains are deferred. For further discussion, see Auerbach (1988) and Kaplow (1994). Hulten and Robertson also treat the case where there would be no limit on use of incentives, even by firms owing no tax.

12. In some cases, this limitation could be offset through carry-back of current-year tax losses and credits to offset income and taxes in previous years.

13. Here is an example of how discrimination among assets worked under the old law. At a zero inflation rate, an asset generates output valued at about 31 percent of the initial price of the asset over a two and a half years if it depreciates at 10 percent per year and yields about a 4 percent real return over and above depreciation. Yet under old law, tax deductions and credits could offset income equal to 80 percent of purchase price over the same period. Since the income from the asset is less than half of the allowed offsets, only the established firm with existing flows of taxable income could make immediate full use of the deductions and credits. The new law reduced some of the disparities between new and established firms. After passage, deductions in the first two and a half years only offset income up to 56 percent of the purchase price. Thus, while discrimination against new business was not eliminated, it was lessened considerably.

14. It is apparent that negative after-tax interest rates can induce investment in unproductive capital. When borrowing takes place, the investor must receive a return from the investment itself that is greater than or equal to the after-tax interest rate. If the after-tax real interest rate is positive and real, then the after-tax return from the investment itself (calculated without regard to the borrowing) must be higher than the effective interest rate, hence also positive in real terms. Otherwise, the borrower-investor will not earn enough to pay the after-tax interest rate. However, when the after-tax interest rate is negative in real terms, the investor may profit personally from investment in an unproductive asset, that is, one with a negative real rate of return. While it is true that investors should still invest in those assets with the highest rates of return, different assets have different amounts of risk. With a negative after-tax interest rate, investment in assets with little perceived or actual risk may become competitive on a risk-adjusted basis. For instance, if commodities are expected without much risk to increase in price with inflation, some saving may be diverted to the wasteful storage of commodities. The corporate manager may also be induced to invest in fairly riskless assets that almost surely would not have been purchased if the after-tax interest rate were positive.

15. An investment is "passive" if the taxpayer does not materially participate in the conduct of the activity. Limited partnerships are presumed to be passive, as are most rental activities. Most activities in which the taxpayer provides substantial services are not defined as passive.

16. Of course, if the paring of tax expenditures were to be accounted for as a reduction in expenditures, then in a sense average rates of tax did fall and were paid for by the reduction in the expenditures.

17. This approval was based partly on my earlier research showing how different family groups had been affected over time.

18. "Changes in the 1980s, and especially in the Tax Reform Act of 1986, have reduced the size of the federal subsidy to state and local borrowing, but improved the relative allocation of benefits to those governments rather than to high-income investors" (Break 1991, 527).

19. Also, according to Witte (1991b, 11), "Treasury I called for the outright elimination of 38 of the approximately 105 tax expenditures on which we have long-term data. To put this in context, in the prior history of the income tax we had only eliminated 13 tax expenditures, once permanently enacted."

20. The debate on the relationship between tax rates and capital gains realizations has not been settled. See Auten and Clotfelter (1982); Feldstein, Slemrod, and Yitzhaki (1980); Lindsey (1988); Minarik (1984); and Office of Tax Analysis (1985). The debate is explained well and in an unbiased fashion in Auten and Cordes (1991).

21. Their estimates actually compare the new tax law with the original Treasury Department proposal, but relate much of the gain in welfare—an economist's way of measuring inefficiency—to the indexing provisions of the former proposal. At 4 percent inflation, the present value of welfare gains in 1973 dollars is $131 billion for the new tax law and $393 billion for the Treasury proposal. At 7 percent inflation, the corresponding numbers are $63 billion and $505 billion. As inflation increases from 4 to 7 percent, most of the relative gains are due to inflation indexing under the Treasury proposal.

22. A corporate deduction, rising eventually to 50 percent of dividends paid out of previously taxed earnings, was proposed in Treasury I. Treasury II (the president's proposal) lowered the proposed deduction to 10 percent. The Ways and Means Committee phased in this lower 10 percent deduction over 10 years, and the Senate Finance Committee abandoned integration completely. The Treasury would put forward another study of integration in 1992, and yet another version would pass in 2003 after being proposed by President George W. Bush.

23. Another table, reflecting the view that a lower tax rate on dividends has no effect on total tax rates on capital income, was calculated by Yolanda Henderson and can be found in Steuerle (1992a, 151). The "new" view that dividends do not matter is that once income has already been taxed in the firm, paying the tax on dividends is a toll charge that ultimately must be paid. However, this table shows essentially the same change in effective tax rates by the time that tax reform was over.

24. The calculations are also sensitive to the way that one assumes that investors project future inflation rates. Table 7.1 was produced mainly to show differentials among bills and types of assets at that point in time; for that purpose, differences across time were less important. Figure 3.12 focuses more on differences across time and uses slightly different assumptions about expected inflation, derived more from a consistent survey than from a weighted average of past inflation rates.

25. Even the much simpler alternative minimum tax in prior law was prone to much error and resulted in understatement of tax on at least 32.6 percent of affected returns (IRS 1985, table 10).

26. Mortgage interest on these homes, however, is not deductible on mortgage debt amounts above the original purchase price of the residences plus the cost of major improvements. A proposed but later defeated exception was to allow the excess mortgage if debt was incurred for educational or medical purposes. Technically, secondary mortgage interest is not deductible at all against the alternative minimum tax unless the money is used to make capital improvements.

27. The common practice—where corporate income was taxed on the basis of the source while interest, dividends, and other payments were taxed on the basis of residence of the recipient—has a long history that is embodied in both law and tax

treaties, although it results in inconsistent treatment of income from equity versus income from debt.

28.   Here I was fortunate to be able to work with Victor Thuronyi, one of the most important contributors to the early tax reform work of the Treasury and the person who led much of the effort to reform the taxation of minors. We had concluded that this was the best way to reduce wasteful tax planning through trusts.

29.   Subchapter "C" corporations pay corporate tax; those organized as subchapter "S" corporations are treated more like partnerships.

30.   These included estate tax deductions for sales of employer stock to an employee stock ownership plan (ESOP), a requirement that certain publicly traded partnerships be treated like corporations, and limitations on the use of net operating loss carry-forwards (NOLs) following ownership change of a loss corporation.

31.   Background information on the hearings on this subject can be found at Joint Committee on Taxation (1988).

32.   Required reporting of taxpayer identification numbers for dependents age 5 or over was first required in the Tax Reform Act of 1986 (Public Law 99-514, Title XV, subtitle C, section 1524).

33.   According to some participants, the proposed expansion was partly a response to "Iran-gate." The administration was seeking some proposal to move attention away from the selling of arms to Iran and the misallocation of those funds to the Nicaraguan rebels. An expansion of benefits, proposed by then Secretary of Health and Human Services Otis Bowen, was suddenly chosen to provide the necessary vehicle. Whether true or not, the proposal filled a vacuum in domestic policy suggestions coming out of the White House.

8

Bush I: "No New Taxes?" 1989 to 1992

We do not have, and never had, and could not have a "voluntary" tax system.
—Donald C. Alexander, former commissioner of the Internal Revenue Service

T he first year under a new president is often considered a honeymoon period with a high probability for legislative success. Yet when the new president succeeds a popular two-term maverick, the ante is high. George H. W. Bush tried to be more Reagan-like than Reagan himself, and campaigned on a pledge of "no new taxes." Though catchy, the pledge handicapped President Bush from pushing hard for deficit reduction during 1989. The Congress, in turn, was in no mood to attempt much by itself, and a stalemate existed between Republicans and Democrats.

Initial Inaction on the Deficit

Both the executive and legislative branches of government essentially agreed to defer decisionmaking on the deficit in the primary vehicle for action, the Omnibus Budget Reconciliation Act of 1989. The act did increase taxes about $3 billion to $5 billion per year (or less than one-tenth of 1 percent of the gross domestic product [GDP]), mainly through corporate transaction changes and some small excise and social insurance tax increases (OMB 1990, A-50 to A-51). Some corporate payments were speeded up by the new legislation, and the generous give-away for employee stock ownership plans (ESOPs) was cut back. The corporate minimum tax calculation was simplified somewhat.[1]

At year's end, skepticism reigned. Years of budget games had left a sour taste in all participants' mouths. Many in Washington believed that most tax and expenditure changes within the deficit agreement were "smoke and mirrors" or, at best, temporary speed-ups in revenues or slowdowns in expenditures. After three years of nominal deficit-reduction activity, policymakers faced greatly exacerbated problems by 1990. The failure to stick with deficit reduction during the prosperous late 1980s slowed the march toward low deficits. Yet the deficit had fallen from a peak of 4.9 percent of GDP in fiscal year 1983 to about 4.3 percent in fiscal years 1984 to 1986, and to 3.1 and 2.4 percent, respectively, in 1987 and 1989 (Executive Office of the U.S. President 2003, tables B-1 and B-82). Since 1981 tax cuts were still being implemented in 1984, this progress was significant. However, a historically long recession-free period was ending.

A Turn Back to Deficit Cutting

By early 1990, the deficit began widening once again relative to the size of the economy. The final figure for fiscal year 1990 was 3.0 percent of GDP, while for fiscal year 1991 the estimated deficit rose closer to 3.6 percent. A federal bailout due to the wholesale failure of the savings and loans industry only exacerbated these increases. On the heels of the higher-than-normal economic growth rates of 1987 and 1988 came subnormal growth rates as 1990 approached. By mid-1990, a recession hit. Lower growth rates, in turn, translated into decreased revenues and increased outlays for social safety-net programs.

To the credit of both the president and Congress, an agreement was reached to try to reduce the deficit by $500 billion over five years. Work toward compromise began not long after President Bush finally abandoned his "no new taxes" campaign pledge. President Bush also intimated that he would accept further sizable cuts in defense expenditures as a percentage of GDP, which in most years since World War II had been the primary way to either pay for domestic policy expansion or reduce the deficit. Democratic leaders quickly backed him, including Dan Rostenkowski, chairman of the Ways and Means Committee, as did many Senate Republicans. Many House Republicans were more reluctant, and a House revolt led by Newt Gingrich led to temporary defeat in October 1990.

Measured simply in terms of reducing the deficit, the budget summit between the executive branch and the Congress must be labeled a success. The scheduled rise in U.S. debt relative to national income could not continue forever, and the summit led to annual deficit reductions of 1 to 2 percent of GDP. Both Congressional Budget Office and Office of Management and Budget figures initially projected that deficits would decline relative to the size of the economy—though not for the first couple of years.[2]

Those initial projections were optimistic because, as is usual in budget agreements, it was assumed that no new emergencies would arise. But by mid-1991, OMB would raise five-year deficit estimates by over $200 billion to cover guarantees of bank and savings and loan deposits and the now-established fact of recession (OMB 1991, 1). Even if intermediate-term deficits would eventually shrink, longer-term problems, especially financing for Medicare and Social Security in future decades, stubbornly remained.[3] In effect, the day of reckoning for longer-term budgetary problems was simply delayed, even though most of the deficit reduction was real and the package was one of the largest in peacetime history.

The 1990 agreement also laid down the budget rules—the Budget Enforcement Act—that guided much of budget policy for most of the 1990s. These rules limited various expenditure increases significantly and also required putting tax and entitlement spending on a pay-as-you-go basis. Bills containing increases in entitlements or other mandatory spending or reducing revenues could not be considered by Congress unless accompanied by offsetting entitlement cuts or revenue increases.

A Lack of Guiding Principles

The 1990 budget agreement contained the most important tax or budget policies since the Tax Reform Act of 1986. Like the 1986 act, securing the president's early backing insured enactment. Once he became committed, failure would have reflected badly upon him, as well as upon Democratic leaders who had pushed hard for deficit reduction and derided President Bush for his pledge not to increase taxes. Outside of this common element, the two bills were developed in very different ways.

Except for reducing the deficit by a target of almost $500 billion over five years, no guiding tax principles or expenditure goals accompanied the 1990 budget proposal. There was a call to bargain, but no administration or congressional blueprint for development. Even the $500 billion target was set with no particular ceiling on government's long-term debt or future interest payments. In this vacuum, negotiators embraced the normal political pull to enact the least politically offensive changes possible.

The president separately pushed hard for a capital gains tax cut, but not with the stated purpose of eliminating double taxation of already taxed income or trying to encourage saving in an efficient and equitable way. Thus, those bargaining over an agreement had few guidelines for deciding which taxpayers or expenditure recipients should bear the costs of deficit reduction, and which might receive even more tax breaks along the way.

By way of contrast, the 1986 tax reform had proceeded from principles—in particular, equal treatment of equals and efficiency. These principles made it easier to lay out which tax expenditure programs could be reduced or eliminated. They also limited other changes from being jammed through the tax system. Distributional constraints established early kept the focus trained on the real targets of the 1986 legislation. These constraints helped channel congressional energy into very specific traditional tax reform goals. In 1990, tax changes lacked such momentum and direction.

Not surprisingly, a bargaining process guided by few principles led to surprises and unexpected obstacles. For instance, the Bush administration was taken aback when the Joint Committee on Taxation began to prepare tables of the package's distributional effects. These tables showed that a tentative 1990 agreement would require a greater percentage reduction in after-tax income from lower-income than from higher-income households. Although these tables can be misleading, they nonetheless helped to mobilize opposition, especially among a coalition of Democrats and Republicans who opposed any type of tax increase. Together this coalition temporarily defeated the initial agreement struck by the leaders of both parties.

With no conceptual or political groundwork laid, the choices among tax and expenditure programs seemed more arbitrary than necessary. The amount of an increase in consumption or income taxes normally bore little relation to energy and health policies, government incentives and disincentives, or tax policy principles. And with some exceptions, expenditure program cuts were not based either on simplicity or efficiency.

Sources of Deficit Reduction

Despite these limitations, the Omnibus Budget Reconciliation Act of 1990 (PL 101-508) ranked among the largest and most successful acts in the entire deficit-reduction period of 1982 to 1997. Once again, the tax-writing committees did much of the work. Outside of defense cuts, the final agreement followed the pattern of the deficit-reduction bills of 1982, 1984, and 1987. Excluding interest savings and deficit cuts "promised" in the bill but left for future Congresses to enact, table 8.1 shows that almost 50 percent of total deficit reduction came from taxes, fees, and premiums—that is, higher charges rather than lower outlays or direct expenditures. Cutbacks in gross domestic expenditures, on the other hand, totaled only about 7 to 17 percent of the package. (The principal difference between these calculations and those presented in official budget documents is that here fees and premiums are treated as part of taxes, fees, and premiums, instead of as negative outlays.) Factoring in some expenditure increases, the cuts in domestic expenditures accounted for only 7 percent of the total deficit reduction. Another 10 percent came from attempts to regulate prices and payment levels to service providers, particularly those paid through Medicare and Medicaid.

Strictly speaking, cutbacks in gross domestic expenditures may not have added up to even the small amounts just noted. Many of the increases in user-related taxes and user fees went directly into trust funds (such as those for highways) and not into general revenues. This accounting tactic encouraged Congress to spend these funds later.

Despite limited success in reducing spending directly, the 1990 agreement was generally able to control spending. How? As we shall examine, the 1990 budget rules would eventually slow the growth rate in domestic discretionary expenditures, mainly by constraining new domestic spending proposals. In other words, the 1990 agreement was a precursor to a period of both limited discretionary spending increases and little new entitlement legislation.

When it came to taxes, the 1990 budget act did little to expand the corporate or individual income tax bases. Weary of that route after taking it throughout the 1980s, Congress looked elsewhere for revenues. In

Table 8.1 *1990 OBRA Budget Agreement: Slicing the Pie*
(In billions of dollars)

	Total	Percentage
Taxes, fees, and premiums	181.0	48.9
Net change, income tax base provisions	−15.4	
Income tax base erosion[a] (−27.4)		
Income tax base expansion (12.0)		
Income tax rate increases[b]	40.2	
Employment payroll tax increases	41.5	
IRS enforcement and penalties	11.2	
Excise tax increases, not user-related[c]	42.1	
User-related taxes and fees[d]	61.4	
User-related excise taxes[e] (27.0)		
User fees (19.4)		
Other premiums, contributions for pensions,		
health programs, housing programs (15.0)		
Net cutbacks in gross domestic expenditures	27.2	7.3
Attempts to regulate prices or expenditures	37.4	10.1
Defense cuts[f] (first three years plus estimated		
carryover to fourth and fifth years)	124.8	33.7
Total, current legislation	370.4	100.0
Other		
Promises[f] (mainly fourth- and fifth-year defense		
and domestic cuts)	57.6	
Interest savings	68.5	
Total	496.5	

Source: Author's calculations are based on Congressional Budget Office preliminary estimates of the Deficit Reduction Reconciliation Conference Agreement, October 1990.

Note: OBRA = Omnibus Budget Reconciliation Act.

a. Includes $18.2 billion progressivity offset and $9.1 billion in miscellaneous tax incentives.

b. Includes $11.2 billion personal income tax rate increase, $10.8 billion personal exemption phaseout, and $18.2 billion limit on itemized deductions.

c. Assumes no increase in transportation spending because of new motor fuels taxes.

d. Ignores increases in user-related activities (e.g., new air traffic control) because of new user-related taxes and fees.

e. Assumes that half of motor fuel taxes are put in trust funds and half are treated as general revenues.

f. Example assumes that defense cuts in first three years yield half of saving committed for fourth and fifth years (i.e., half of $115.2 billion), even without major changes, and that the other half represents new "promises" under revised budget procedures.

fact, excluding "progressivity enhancements" for low-income individuals, the bill created new special preferences for oil and gas development and other activities that, collectively, just about offset the revenues picked up from yet another round of tax changes paid by insurance companies, plus a few other minor attempts to broaden the tax base. Although the tax reform dam still held, new holes were chiseled and leaks allowed. Tax legislation throughout the rest of the decade would follow the 1990 abandonment of 1980s-style reforms.

Significant attention was paid to revenues and fees within pay-as-you-go programs and trust-funded programs. Employment payroll taxes were increased by raising the fee to cover unemployment insurance, subjecting a bigger share of wages (up to $125,000) to the Hospital Insurance (HI) share of the Social Security tax, and by expanding Social Security and Medicare tax coverage for some state and local employees. User fees within expenditure programs were increased by over $19 billion; user-related excise taxes (such as those designated for highway and airport trust funds) were increased by $27 billion; and higher premiums for Medicare, pension guarantees in the Pension Benefit Guarantee Corporation, and various financial programs raised about $15 billion.[4]

Many of the excise-tax increases generated only limited controversy. Not so for luxury tax increases for furs, jewelry, private airplanes, expensive cars, and especially boats. Partly because the enactment took place around the time of the economic downturn, the luxury boat industry was already hurting, and it quickly launched a counteroffensive arguing that the tax especially hurt laborers in that industry. While luxury taxes had been prevalent in World War II, most had been abandoned or allowed to dwindle in importance over time, partly because economists generally believe that picking on one item of consumption or another is not efficient, even if the goal is to tax those with high levels of income or consumption. At the time, however, Congress was looking for items that it thought would generate the least opposition.

Family and Children's Issues

Many tax improvements for families and children made the 1990 Budget Act more progressive, but at a cost. All these child-related bells and whistles were relatively uncoordinated, further complicating the taxation of low-income individuals. The legislation imposed most rate increases at the top and granted some further tax breaks to low-income individuals. This victory for low-income advocates was only partly in response to the political debate over the budget package and distributional effects documented in Joint Committee on Taxation tables. The residual momentum needed to launch change also came from both liberals and conservatives who began paying more attention to family and children's issues after the personal exemption doubled and the earned income tax credit (EITC) was expanded in the Tax Reform Act of 1986. After the mid-1980s, "family tax issues" were in the limelight, and both political parties fought over who was most "pro-family."

During the 1988 presidential campaign, candidate George H. W. Bush pushed his own "pro-family" tax agenda by pledging to try to enact a "child credit."[5] This would be only the first of many Republican efforts to enact or increase child credits. President Bush's credit was to apply only to workers with children.[6] Eventually, this proposal was translated into a large addition to the EITC. The president also demanded a supplement for young children, and, as a conservative attempting to focus the help on stay-at-home parents, he further required that those with credits for work-related child care expenses not be eligible for the supplement. Senator Lloyd Bentsen, as Democratic chair of the Senate Finance Committee, added a supplement for low-income workers with children who pay out-of-pocket for health insurance.

Another reason for the president's support, as well as that of other Republicans, is that analysis showed that an increase in the EITC was much more efficient than an increase in the minimum wage to bolster moderate-income families. Minimum-wage increases are spread to secondary workers, including spouses and teenage dependents who are not in low-income families. Moreover, minimum-wage increases can have a negative impact on employment. EITC changes were believed to be better targeted, and this gave some reprieve to Republicans wishing to show that they were not indifferent to the needs of low-income families.

The bill also made clear for the first time that subsidies for low-income individuals would move well beyond tax relief. With the old EITC, "tax" relief was already refundable—available even if in excess of income taxes owed. But some argued that such relief was not really "refundable" if one also took account of Social Security taxes (the Social Security tax rate was 15.3 percent of wages by then and the EITC was equal at most to 15 percent of wages). With the 1990 act, that argument lost its meaning. Now the EITC rate would clearly yield more for low-income taxpayers than income or Social Security taxes would take away. In sum, this milestone made clear that the EITC is an expenditure, not a tax reduction, even though it is administered by the IRS.

Conferees in Congress paid scant heed to the new incentives for cheating encouraged by the enhanced EITC. For the first time, individuals would find it worthwhile to claim earnings from work even when they had none. Congress also ignored the sheer complexity of what they were creating, which would all but force low-income workers to make use of paid tax preparers by giving them tax forms more complex than those of many middle-income taxpayers.

The budget document labeled the EITC changes, along with a few others, as "progressivity offsets" against some of the increases in excise taxes on low- and moderate-income individuals. Near the end of the legislative process, Congress played some games to enhance the appearance of progressivity. Analysis showed that if the EITC were adjusted for household size as originally proposed, those with family income levels just above the federal poverty level would benefit more than those at or below the poverty line. Households with more members looked better off than smaller families in the new distributional tables only because per-person income wasn't counted there (e.g., a family with $12,000 of income looks better off than a single person with $10,000 if family size is not taken into account). Rather than target the money where most needed, Congress scrapped most of the adjustments for family size and increased the basic credit equally for all families.

Bubbles, Bangles, and Beads

Meanwhile, at the top of the income distribution, President Bush's effort to decrease the capital gains tax was rejected, and tax rates for high-income individuals rose almost certainly as a result of direct-rate changes.

Recall that in the compromises leading to the 1986 tax reform, Congress created a "bubble" in the tax-rate schedule. Taxpayers in successively higher income levels paid a tax rate of 15, 28, 33, and 28 percent again on their last dollar earned.[7]

To please the majority, two other proposals were retained or added. First, a "bangle"—itemized deductions would be limited by 3 percent of the extent to which adjusted gross income exceeded $100,000, with some exceptions. For most affected taxpayers, this translated into nothing more than an increase in the marginal tax rate of 0.93 percent.[8]

Next, a "bead"—the value of the personal exemption would be phased out at higher income levels. The conferees decided to further complicate matters by making the phase-out rate dependent on the number of personal exemptions. For a family of four, this translated into an increase in marginal tax rates of 2.13 percent; for a family of two, 1.06 percent.[9]

Legislators prided themselves on their handiwork, however Byzantine. Believing they had met some arbitrary standard to which the public had acquiesced (e.g., a maximum statutory tax rate), Congress delighted in circumventing the declared standard. In certain high-income ranges, the maximum tax rate was now 31 percent, plus 0.93 percent through reduction in itemized deductions, plus some additional percentage for the phase out of the personal exemption (2.13 percent for families of four). The bottom line? This part of the package raised taxes on higher-income individuals by about $40 billion over five years. The ultimate goal of the majority of conferees—to confine income tax increases to a limited few in the upper part of the income distribution—was reached, no matter that the means was abysmally complicated.

The New Budget Rules

Like so many tax policy changes, the 1990 agreement imitated past actions. Congress even returned to the same funding sources tapped in previous years. The act represented yet one more attempt to increase revenues through IRS enforcement, though the amounts claimed were unrealistic. One more attempt was made to rely on Social Security taxes, but the revenues raised were small compared with those provided by the substantial tax increases of the past. Even delaying indexing of individual tax brackets was included in a House version, but later dropped.

In many ways, the collapse of communism triggered the anticipated defense cuts in the bill. More generally, the bill followed the spending of a peace dividend that had prevailed after World War II, with the exception of temporary build-ups during the Korean conflict, the Vietnam War, and the early 1980s.

The 1990 budget agreement, however, did make a fundamental change in budget policy. This policy limited future Congressional actions and provided much of the impetus for reducing the deficit by simply letting revenues grow along with the economy, yet without committing to new tax cuts or expenditures beyond the huge automatic increases in entitlement programs. One related legislative consequence was to stall major tax-reduction or expenditure-increase legislation until near the end of the Clinton administration. Another legislative consequence was the near-guarantee that any major budget legislation after the 1990 agreement would require the participation of the tax-writing committees.

The new "pay-as-you-go" budget rules sorted different programs into different "baskets." All "discretionary" spending was divided among defense, international, or domestic spending, each basket subject to a spending cap. Any increases in spending above specified allocations had to be balanced by at least an equal spending decrease in that same basket. If the basket's spending cap was exceeded, then all programs within that basket had to be cut back through a presidential "sequester." Trade-offs could not be made using budget resources outside the basket; nor could increased spending in one discretionary basket be paid for by decreasing spending in a different basket. These changes greatly limited the power and leeway of expenditure committees. Even after these baskets were combined years later, the committees still couldn't finance changes by increasing revenues except when the rules were set aside.

In 1990, revenues, tax expenditures, and such "mandatory" entitlement programs as Social Security and Medicare (which are mainly under the jurisdiction of the tax-writing committees) were also lumped together in one huge basket. Spending on that basket was capped. Congress could make trade-offs within or between revenues and mandatory programs only if the net effect on the deficit was zero. Broad expenditure or tax reform could be engineered only by going through the tax-writing committees.

The turn toward pay-as-you-go financing also created some pressure for many expenditure committees to increase spending through internal fee and collection mechanisms. This intensified pressure on federal programs to move toward "benefit" financing—that is, raising such fees and premiums as user fees for parks, roads, bridges, and medical care. More broadly, the act entrenched pay-as-you-go financing within the entire congressional budget-making process. For a good part of the coming decade, most program expansions could not even be brought up on the floors of Congress unless a payment mechanism was attached. Some economists, including those who tended to favor benefit taxation, transparency in government, and rules that make clear that there is no "free lunch" in government legislation, would say that the move toward more explicit connection between spending and payment is a good thing.[10]

Extremely important from a macroeconomic policy standpoint, the 1990 act redefined deficit targets. Changes in the deficit *per se* became relatively less important than changes in the deficit due to changes in the current law. As long as the law doesn't change, this logic goes, additional deficit reduction wasn't required during recessions or crises, as it was under the rules applying throughout the latter half of the 1980s. By the same token, further straightjackets were wrapped around discretionary programs, restrictions not placed on the automatic growth in entitlement programs. In effect, the unlevel playing field between discretionary and entitlement spending was tilted even more against discretionary spending.

Other Tax Actions

The 1989–1992 period saw a considerable slowdown from the flurry of tax activity marking the 1980s. One reason for the slowdown was Congress's sheer weariness from the many changes and battles of that earlier period. Another was that many Bush appointees, such as James Baker, who had moved on to become Secretary of State but was still a close adviser of the president on domestic matters, remained committed to the 1986 reforms. A third was the "no new taxes" pledge of the new president, who was loath to contradict himself until the demand for deficit reduction and the need to compromise with a Democratic Congress forced him to act in 1990. Interestingly, taxes had increased many times under President Reagan, who was not held to such a tight standard and perhaps enjoyed residual credibility as a tax-rate cutter from his 1981 pronouncements and successes.

This surface calm notwithstanding, many smaller enactments mostly fell below the radar screen of the public and the press. The tax-writing committees worked ceaselessly. For instance, tax extensions by then had become the order of the day for such high-ticket items as research and development tax credits and targeted jobs credits that expire periodically. Many of these credits resembled expenditures that had to be periodically renewed, and gave advocates plenty to debate as long as they weren't made permanent. Permanency, however, weakens review. One possible compromise would have been to renew such provisions for five years or so, but politics quickly began to dictate shorter extensions. This way, the cost of extending a provision for only one year might be all that was counted as a cost in a bill covering tax changes for five years. This gave many experts trouble even estimating "reasonable future deficits" under differing notions of "current law." Does current law really end or "sunset" various credits or is continual extension the norm?

Another example of the ambiguity in budget-making during this period was the Energy Policy Act of 1992, which provided subsidies sought by energy companies and some environmentalists alike. For example, the alternative energy investment credit was made permanent and some tax preferences for depletion and other costs of independent oil and gas producers and royalty owners were removed from the reach of the alternative minimum tax. Small energy bills like this seldom involved enough money—whether effective in terms of bang-per-buck or not—to affect total energy consumption and production measurably.

Two presidential vetoes in 1992 did reveal the extent to which tax policymaking had become acrimonious. For much of the post-war period, tax bills had been bipartisan and obtained significant support from both parties. In his 1992 State of the Union message, President Bush reported that the economy was faltering and challenged Congress to give him, by March 20, a stimulus bill that included such items as a new investment tax allowance, a credit for first-time home purchases, and a reduction in the capital gains tax rate to 15.4 percent. Congress met the deadline, but gave it a Democratic twist, such as capital gains relief mainly for those below the top tax-rate bracket. The president vetoed the bill without waiting to read the details—marking the first veto of a tax bill since 1943. Ironically, a major reason for the Franklin D. Roosevelt veto was that Congress had extended capital gains treatment to timber harvests; a major reason for the Bush veto was that Congress failed to grant more generous capital gains relief to taxpayers with higher tax rates.

Also in 1992, another bill was vetoed. This bill contained some items desired by the Bush administration (such as extensions of expiring provisions, the establishment of enterprise zones, and repeal of most luxury excises taxes passed in 1990), but then added tax increases manifested as a major reform of the taxation of securities dealers, a denial of deductibility for club dues, and some removal of estate tax cuts. So, after nearly 50 years without a presidential veto on a tax bill, two occurred in one year—perhaps telling examples of the breakdown of bipartisanship in tax legislation.

Unfinished Business

So much attention had been paid to the deficit in the 1980s that it became a handy excuse for dodging other social issues. Although the

1990 act reduced the deficit yet again and put financing for some programs on a better footing, it dealt with only a few of the thousands of spending and tax expenditure programs on the books. Some of the programs that were left alone worked and some did not. The alternative minimum tax (AMT) juggernaut started to build up steam. Created in 1986, its exemption level remained fixed so that incomes driven higher by both real gains and inflation moved more and more people into its clutches. No politician openly embraced this insidious bracket creep, but no Democrat or Republican wanted to pay the cost of fixing it. "Not just yet" started to become the rallying cry of AMT reform.

It is the combination of expenditure and tax programs that makes the federal government effective or ineffective. The cost of the expenditure programs, less the revenues collected through the tax programs, equals the budget deficit—the "dissaving" of the U.S. government. Financing this dissaving by floating government bonds is simply one more governmental program. Fixing this bond-based financing program was hardly considered a panacea for society's other ailments: it could not clean up the environment, better educate our children, increase our inventiveness, reduce the crime rate, improve health coverage, or adapt our defense policy to 21st century demands.

Despite all these microeconomic concerns, the years from 1989 through 1992 saw successes that cannot be ignored. The Cold War ended and the Iraqi invasion of Kuwait was quashed. The 1990 budget agreement was the most notable domestic achievement, though the political costs were high. Despite careful political attention to limiting who was affected, some losers had to be identified directly, and President Bush essentially had to renege on his campaign promise to stop new taxes. Whether this turnaround cost President Bush a close election in 1992, or the short 1990 recession did him in, his son would later draw some political lessons from his father's experience. But first we must turn to President Clinton, who ended up using the tools of the 1990 agreement to become a true budget hawk.

NOTES

1. There was also an extension of what has been labeled "completed contract" reform, which largely related to the time period in which payments made under contracts would be made taxable.

2. Assuming compliance with the discretionary spending caps in the 1990 Budget Enforcement Act, federal debt as a percentage of GNP was projected at the time to rise from 44.6 percent of GNP in 1990 to 49.7 percent by fiscal year 1993, then fall to 45 percent by fiscal year 1996 (Congressional Budget Office 1991, 98). Getting the budget under control still had a way to go.

3. The conferees had available information showing that under typical assumptions, the Old Age and Survivors and Disability Insurance (OASDI) program in Social Security was expected to continue accumulation in the Trust Fund until peaking in 2014. After that, it would draw down a large accumulated trust fund, which at the time was projected to last until 2043. After 2043, OASDI would have to increase payroll taxes, cut benefits, or be subsidized by general revenues to avoid bankruptcy. Medicare Hospital Insurance (Part A) was expected to exhaust its trust fund as soon as 2003. See Board of Trustees of the Federal Old-Age and Survivors Insurance and Disability Insurance Trust Funds (1990) and Board of Trustees of the Federal Hospital Insurance and Federal Supplementary Medical Insurance Trust Fund (1990). There were modest changes in Social Security taxes in 1990—mainly in the tax base for Hospital Insurance—but these affected the calculations only slightly, with bankruptcy for Hospital Insurance to come later in the same decade. Later reports altered the projected dates of exhaustion. See the annual reports from various years for more information.

4. Closely related to the movement toward pay-as-you-go programs was the enactment of significant reform of governmental credit systems. In many cases, the reform was to charge the private sector for the value of the government insurance provided. In addition, budget accounting rules were to require greater up-front recognition of the real cost of these guarantees down the road. Charging taxpayers directly for services and for the value of government guarantees had already achieved some momentum in the 1980s, but this was the first budget bill to give these efforts such prominence relative to changes in the income tax. Again, this was the type of action that would be favored by those who like benefit taxation.

5. The campaign promise was partly an attempt to offer an alternative to Democratic Candidate Michael Dukakis's support of bills to provide monies directly to states to establish day care programs for young children.

6. The credit was to be made available only to workers, but "worker" was not defined in the campaign. Still at the Treasury Department in early 1989, I deliberately interpreted the "work" requirement to imply a phase-in schedule identical to the one in the earned income tax credit, in the hope that for administrative simplicity the two might be combined. As the process evolved, that is exactly what happened.

7. The suspect 33 percent bubble between the two 28 percent brackets grew out of an attempt to proclaim a top marginal rate of 28 percent while actually imposing a higher rate by phasing out the personal exemption and the benefits received by those in the 15 percent bracket. At one point the conferees for the 1990 budget agreement agreed to get rid of the bubble. Speaker Dick Gephardt angled for a deal of a top rate of 33 percent and a reduction of the capital gains tax rate to 20 percent, but the Senate Majority Leader Mitchell would not agree. In the end, rather than raise the last or top rate to 33 percent, they combined the 33 percent rate and the 28 percent rates into a single top rate of 31 percent. Because of the amount of income in the 28 percent bracket, the change actually raised revenues.

8. The calculation is as follows: an additional dollar of income reduces itemized deductions by 3 cents. At a tax rate of 31 percent, this provision increases taxes by 0.93 cents for each additional dollar of income. The tax rate, however, applies to adjusted gross income rather than taxable income—that is, income after deductions.

9. For a joint return with income between $150,000 and $272,500, personal exemptions were phased out at a rate of 2 percent for each $2,500 by which the taxpayers' income exceeded the threshold amount. In effect, assuming a personal exemption of $132,150 in 1991, additional income produces an increase in taxable income of $(0.02 \times \$132,150) / \$2,500$ for each exemption. For four exemptions and a taxpayer in the 31 percent tax bracket, net tax burden increases by: $4 \times [(0.02 \times \$2,150) / \$2,500] \times 0.3$, or 0.0213.

10. Economists from the so-called "public choice" school would almost certainly find themselves in that camp. Some in this school believe that government employees and elected officials have an incentive to always expand government and that, to control this "leviathan," rules and often constitutional limitations must be put in place. However, one does not have to belong to that school to favor a balanced approach to expenditure and tax legislation that forces taxpayers to recognize that they must pay for government actions one way or the other.

9

Clinton and the New Democrats: 1993 to 1996

As a cop, the IRS has to balance customer service and law enforcement . . . The agency's motto could be: "We're your friend. But if you push that friendship too hard, we'll ruin your life and throw you in jail."

—Chris Bergin, *Tax Analysts*

Bill Clinton campaigned as a new Democrat and successfully played to voter concern over the recent recession and the state of the economy—and the general perception that President Bush was doing little about it. The Democratic Leadership Council claims that the modern "Third Way" approach to governing began with Clinton's 1992 campaign.[1] Regardless of labels, that the former left now favored a moderate government somewhere between left and right became the implied message. Clinton would later declare, as a corollary, that "the era of big government is over."

Political metaphors, however, do not make policy. Candidate (and later president) Clinton floated many proposals, attempting to appease almost every constituency through government. There was no personal pain that he didn't feel, some quipsters would say. His initial campaign promise to cut taxes for the middle class was soon dropped or at least deferred, although he did follow through with threats to increase taxes for upper-income taxpayers. That campaign political promises cannot always be fulfilled because of budgetary constraints is hardly a new issue—witness President George H. W. Bush's reversal on taxes a few years earlier. But two deputy assistant secretaries for tax analysis during the Clinton years argue forcefully that the administration, particularly Robert Rubin, chair of the National Economic Council (1993–1995) and later Treasury Secretary (1995–1999), continually demanded adherence at least to the budget and deficit-reduction goals that began in the campaign.[2] It was one of these fiscal campaign pledges for another $500 billion deficit-reduction package that essentially put the middle-class tax cut on the back burner.

Clinton's strategy as a campaigner and as president was to respond positively to almost all constituencies. There was little the Republicans wanted that Clinton did not claim that he wanted, too, at least in some general way. This approach clearly had an impact on the government's ability to develop simple and efficient tax policy. By the same token, Clinton was able to stick to many of his budget goals by making these proposals modest in size, often adding more to tax and budget complexity than to revenue or deficit drains.

Besides the goal of lower budget deficits or even surpluses, there were two other areas where Clinton's approach to policy was fairly consistent. As a new Democrat, he also favored both free trade and further help for the poor—but not in the form of traditional welfare *per se*. Free trade proposals had only modest direct impact on tax policy, but aid to the poor, like deficit busting, would profoundly influence its development.

Early Action on the Deficit

President Clinton, in his quest to be a different type of Democrat, wanted to show he would do "something" about the economy, and budget policy became his best vehicle. His administration decided early on to bear down mainly on the deficit. Several reasons led him to defer dealing with other promises. Big reforms of health and welfare couldn't be designed overnight. Having watched how President Bush was hurt by his inaction during the economic downturn in 1990–1991, Clinton understood the political perils of ignoring the economy. Lurking in the background was another reason for deficit-cutting—the baby boomers' inexorable march toward retirement and the lack of societal saving for that day.

Perhaps most important, Democrats had been chastising and blaming Republican presidents Reagan and Bush for deficits ever since the tax cuts in 1981. Although the origins of the deficit were far more complicated, particularly the persistent growth of entitlement spending, the

Democrats set themselves up to deliver on deficit reduction, with a special focus on using taxes to achieve that goal.

Finally, significant deficits still existed, and path dependency—or at least resorting to familiar ways of dealing with the deficit, whether adequate for the long-term or not—was to act as a major determinant of tax policy development. By now, Congress had ample experience with big deficit-reduction packages, particularly from 1982, 1984, 1987, and 1990, so this newest venture was in keeping with its practice of enacting a significant deficit-reduction bill about every three years.

With that said, it was still fairly unique for a president to begin the first year of his first term by taking something away from people. In the Easy Financing era, Kennedy, Johnson, and Nixon sought tax cuts and spending increases early on. Carter started off with a moderate tax cut, while Reagan and later, George W. Bush, initiated their presidencies with big ones. Even George H. W. Bush waited a year before engaging in significant deficit reduction. In terms of political strategy, a contrast between Clinton and his predecessor raises the interesting question of whether, if a political price has to be paid to garner some control over the budget, it might be best to pay it as early as possible.

The Omnibus Budget Reconciliation Act of 1993

Despite some striking differences in approach to the deficit between the former Bush and the first Clinton administrations, the new president's first budget enactment was remarkably similar to the 1990 agreement negotiated by Bush. When all was said and done, the Omnibus Budget Reconciliation Act of 1993 reduced deficits by just about the same amount in nominal dollars as had the 1990 act. Congress in both years aimed to reduce the deficit by $500 billion over five years, and despite some game-playing in both acts through such devices as temporary changes that would "sunset" after five years, most of the deficit reduction was real. When calculated in inflation-adjusted dollars, or as a percentage of GDP, the 1993 act was smaller than the 1990 act.

As president-elect Clinton prepared to take office in January 1993, his transition team was busy sculpting the theory that would come to be called "Clintonomics"—which eventually would come to mean higher standards of living through deficit reduction. Treasury Secretary Lloyd Bentsen and National Economic Council Chairman Robert Rubin reasoned that the performance of the stock and bond markets was in part governed by the collective opinions of financial analysts. Impressing these analysts with a sacrifice-oriented, deficit-reduction plan might help to lower interest rates and thereby lift the country and the markets out of their malaise (Waldman 2000, 40). The short-term danger from a Keynesian perspective, of course, was that a deficit-reduction strategy could also sink the country back into recession and bite into the 8 million new jobs the president had promised in his campaign (Woodward 1994, 83–85). Of course, long-term deficit reduction was increasingly being viewed as positive for saving and growth, and even short-term negative effects could be called into question.[3]

Rubin, later Clinton's Treasury Secretary, recalls a crucial pre-inaugural meeting on January 7. On the way in, chief political adviser George Stephanopoulos indicated to Rubin that if Clinton decided on a significant deficit-reduction target, he couldn't follow through on his middle-class tax cut and various domestic proposals. At the meeting, the president-elect responded to the data he was given on the deficit, and made the decision then and there. Deficit reduction, Clinton said, had become the "threshold" issue. It was what the country needed "to get the economy back on track" (Rubin and Weisberg 2004, 119).

However it happened, the president chose deficit reduction over his campaign promise of a tax cut—the promise of halving the deficit in four years collided with middle-class relief. Health care reform, an "end to welfare as we know it," and other campaign initiatives would also have to wait. Further, a successful deficit-reduction effort could make such ambitious undertakings more affordable down the road.

Eventually, even the title of the Clinton-supported budget act was the same as that enacted under President Bush, except for one digit. On the expenditure side, the Omnibus Budget Reconciliation Acts of 1990 and 1993 tried to rein in health spending through additional controls, particularly on Medicare payouts. And both bills continued reducing defense expenditures as a percentage of GDP, now under the banner of a peace dividend at the Cold War's end.

On the tax side, elected officials tried to dodge political fallout in both bills by restricting the number of taxpayers impacted by tax increases. Democrats were more willing to achieve this goal through higher tax rates on those at the top of the income distribution—though those were the same people hit by some of the Bush tax bill changes.

If Bush could raise the top rate from 28 to 31 percent (with some reduction for those facing the 33 percent bracket bubble), Clinton could increase it further to 39.6 percent, counting a "surcharge" of one-tenth over and above a new 36 percent rate. The corporate rate (for income over $10 million) would also be raised in 1993 by 1 percentage point—from 34 to 35 percent.

Under President George H. W. Bush, the Social Security Medicare or Hospital Insurance tax base was decoupled for the first time from the rate applying to the old age and disability portions (OASDI) of Social Security, which had been set at $53,400 (indexed for inflation). If that Hospital Insurance cap for the tax base could be raised to $125,000 in 1990, it could be eliminated altogether by 1993.

Excises (such as those for motor fuels) were also increased modestly again. The 1993 motor fuels tax increase, however, was a substitute for a far more ambitious Clinton proposal to impose a broad-based energy tax. Congress rejected the energy tax, and even the motor fuels tax increase raised some consternation since the money would not be earmarked, as in a pure benefit tax, toward more spending on highways or items used by those paying the tax. The politically disastrous 1990 tax on such luxury goods as furs and boats was shelved. The luxury boat industry succeeded in its highly successful campaign, complaining that this tax on the relatively wealthy would wipe out middle-class jobs in the boatmaking industry.

Although not much attention was paid to base broadening, some preferences were pared. Business meals and entertainment deductions were cut back, partly on the grounds that someone was benefiting from the additional consumption even if it was the client of the business who never recognized the value of this in-kind income. The possessions tax credit, a special tax break that applied mainly to Puerto Rico, was reduced and redirected more at trying to increase employment there.

The 1993 act also expanded the maximum taxable portion of Social Security benefits from 50 to 85 percent. While most seniors were still exempt from the tax, over time their numbers dwindled since the threshold ($44,000 for joint returns and $34,000 for single returns) for starting to pay the 85 percent rate was not indexed for inflation or income growth. This move, including the lack of indexing, mirrored the cutbacks of after-tax benefits set forth in the 1983 Social Security amendments and challenged once again the notion that Social Security was the untouchable third rail of politics. That said, budget rules created the unusual requirement that the extra revenues raised not be placed in the Social Security trust fund. The Hospital Insurance trust fund was chosen as the recipient, partly because it was facing solvency problems.[4]

The legislation also insured that tax rates under the alternative minimum tax (AMT) would move with the statutory rates—basically maintaining higher AMT tax collections by preserving the differential between normal and AMT rates. Revenues from the unpopular and unwieldy AMT were simply too hard for Congress to pass up. This action would help insure that the AMT stayed on course to dominate tax policy increasingly in future years. In the arcane calculus of the AMT, lock stepping the two rates insured that raising the higher regular or statutory tax rate generally would not reduce the number of AMT filers. (Recall that taxpayers subject to the AMT calculate their taxes in two ways and pay the higher of the two resulting sums.) In effect, the AMT would continue to expand just as under old law—a problem left for future leaders to solve.

Like the 1990 act before it, the 1993 act expanded the earned income tax credit (EITC) yet again. While Republicans in 1990 had accepted an EITC expansion in lieu of increases in the minimum wage, 1993 expansions were undergirded by the argument that the credit should be adjusted for household size. Thus, households with two or more children would receive more help than a one-child household for whom no increase was provided. Another argument was that some compensation should be provided to low-income households for the excise tax increases.

The net effect in 1993 was to give more to low-income families, leave the middle class more or less untouched, and zap the rich. According to the tax historian Elliot Brownlee (1996, 137), "Clinton stressed the point that tax increases enacted by Congress on families who earned more than $200,000 would raise 80 percent of the new tax revenues imposed." The Clinton administration also stressed that, except for the gas tax, the tax increases affected only the top 2 percent of income recipients. Yet polls showed that close to 50 percent of the public thought the 1993 act increased their taxes, a continual source of frustration and puzzlement to Clinton political appointees who thought they had targeted their tax increases to the rich.[5] Robert Rubin (2003, 153) put some of the blame for the Democratic losses in the 1994 election "debacle" to the "mischaracterization of our deficit reduction as tax increase on the middle class, which proved extremely hard to shake."

Further girding tax-based "family" policy, the 1993 act extended a modest EITC to single workers earning $9,000 or less, apparently to give single persons and absent fathers in the group a stake in the wage subsidy. However, the expansion was modest, partly because of the expense and partly because of the potential for large marriage penalties.

Throughout this dance of legislation, Clinton did not pursue broad-based tax reform in the mold of 1986. In fact, the president "favored the traditional politics of offering tax benefits to specific interests, groups, and classes, rather than a base-broadening strategy" (Brownlee 1996, 138–39). Lloyd Bentsen, Clinton's first Treasury secretary, was no fan of broadening the tax bases; nor was the president's National Economic Council about to forgo use of special provisions in the tax code to promote its domestic agenda if it couldn't make headway by increasing direct expenditures.

Claiming Credit for the 1993 Changes

Although easy to exaggerate, political backlash of the sort that always trails attempts to cut spending or raise taxes dogged Clinton and his congressional allies after passage of the 1993 act. In this instance, the lack of major new or increased tax benefits for the middle class made the matters worse. A number of elected officials lost re-election bids in 1994 because they sided with the tax-raising president. One notable example was Congresswoman Marjorie Margolies-Mezvinsky of Pennsylvania, who had been elected for only one term and was persuaded to cast the deciding vote for the president's 1993 tax bill in the House. Meanwhile, the anti-tax Republicans gained ground with the claim that Clinton had passed the largest peacetime tax increase in history. Of course, they were counting only nominal dollars and ignoring its size relative to the economy. The voter response was perhaps a rebuke of big government (see also the discussion below about the failed health reform initiative).

As time progressed, the economy expanded while deficits fell. President Clinton increasingly claimed credit for these economic developments, his mettle now tested as a new Democrat. The realignment of the political parties on matters of budget discipline was now complete. Democrats fully accepted the mantle of fiscal conservatism in practice as well as in word—a shift that had started in 1981 with their objections to the Reagan tax cuts. (Given their approach to large entitlements, of course, one can question whether they were fiscal conservatives for the long-term.) By the end of his eight years, in fact, success in reducing the deficit would be listed by many Clinton stalwarts as the primary measure of his administration's success. Ironically, even though President George

H. W. Bush had actually presided over a larger deficit-reduction package, he never tried to claim similar credit.

The Clinton administration was also accorded most of the public credit for increases in the EITC in the 1990s, even though the EITC reforms enacted on Bush's watch were more generous than Clinton's. But Bush and his colleagues made less fanfare of them. The reluctance of some Republicans to claim credit was further enhanced by a technical point: some of the EITC increases signed into law by President Bush were not available or fully phased in until the Clinton years.[6] When the EITC came under increasing congressional assault by Republican members of Congress, such as Ways and Means Chairman Bill Archer, the Clinton administration would try to counter by citing the bipartisan support in the past for the EITC, including that of both George H. W. Bush and Ronald Reagan.

The Health Reform Debacle

After passage of the 1993 Budget Reconciliation Act, the Clinton administration increased its efforts on the largest and most important domestic reform initiative it would launch during its first term—health reform. Tax policy figured centrally in Clinton's health policy reform initiative, and the initiative exemplified the entanglement of tax and social policy. Ira Magaziner, Clinton's health care policy adviser, anticipated that health reform would entail a substantial tax increase, even over the objections of then Ways and Means Chairman Dan Rostenkowski. Magaziner initially proposed adopting a national value-added tax to raise $60 to $80 billion. Apparently, Treasury Secretary Bentsen partially supported the plan—as he had earlier proposed a BTU tax on energy consumption—because he felt it opened the way to a broader value-added tax. However, once the prospect of middle-class voter backlash set in, the administration proposed only modest direct financing of health care reform—a 75-cents-per-pack tax increase on cigarettes and a 1 percent income tax surcharge on large businesses that failed to join the proposed pools of insurance buyers. Some in the administration thought much higher direct taxes would be necessary to pay for reform (Brownlee 1996, 138).

Postmortems on the Clinton health care proposal abound. Many conservatives believe the Clinton reform failed because a massive health care bureaucracy with controls emanating from Washington was as politically unpalatable as the tax increases the administration abandoned. Many liberals trace its failure to the doorsteps of special interests—especially in the burgeoning health care field.[7] Critics also derided Congress for catering to both health care providers and consumers.[8] Fearing political repercussions, the administration began promising something for everyone—the uninsured or inadequately insured, those needing portable health insurance, the elderly, large businesses that might already be insuring their employees, small business, and so on. Somehow all these pipers had to be paid.

Some might also claim that the attempt to legitimately pay for the change—as opposed to the traditional postwar tradition of paying for major change through increases in the deficit—derailed health reform. But that critique belies why tax reform succeeded in 1986. Perhaps it is better to say that that the movement from an Easy Financing era to one where budgetary discipline tended to require pay-as-you-go financing translated into tough sledding for any major new initiative. It may also be the case that the two divergent objectives of achieving health coverage for all and reducing the growth of health costs were difficult to pull together in a way that could appeal to the public.

Though the probability of success was low, health reform also failed because of a badly organized political process and a fatally flawed design (see, for instance, Skocpol 1995). The health reform proposal percolated within the confines of the White House, where political considerations kept trumping fiscal realities. In effect, the new fiscal constraints were not heeded early enough in the health reform process. The ever-rising influence of health costs on the budget simply had to be addressed—and the public convinced of the necessity for action—before any health reform achieving the more populist notion of universal coverage could succeed.

Health and Taxes

Tax policy permeates health policy both on the financing and subsidy side. The largest tax subsidy in the tax code, as measured by revenues foregone, is the exclusion from taxation of health insurance benefits provided through employers. If losses on federal and state income taxes and Social Security taxes are included, this tax benefit cost more than $100 billion per year in lost revenues by the early 1990s and is projected to rise to over $200 billion by the middle of the first decade of the 21st century (Burman et al. 2003).[9] Most major health reform proposals affecting the nonelderly aim to modify or replace this provision for two reasons: it is inefficient because it encourages excess costs, and it is inequitable because benefits rise significantly as one becomes richer. The Clinton health care proposal sought to indirectly redirect those forgone revenues to finance some of the proposed changes.

Major health reform required reassessing many other taxes and tax breaks—from the tax exclusion noted above to the amount of Medicare taxes and other taxes required to fund government health care for the elderly. These would have to be integrated or, short of that, the financing and operation of any new government system for the nonelderly and another for the elderly (Medicare) would have to be coordinated. By the early 1990s, government health care spending at all levels averaged over $5,000 per family, so the unsustainable growth in government health costs was compounding on a very large base already.

In this political and budgetary milieu, employer mandates and cost controls emerged triumphant in the ill-fated health care proposal. The administration had boxed itself in. Congress, however, balked at cost controls and even mainstream business, such as the Business Roundtable, balked at some aspects of the employer mandates. Since the administration hoped that large employers already providing health insurance to their workforce would buy into a mandate, their reaction was a blow. After all, the already insured were constantly cross-subsidizing the uninsured who did not cover their share of hospital and other costs. Employers, however, feared the government controls that would follow. Even attempts to buy out business with subsidies for retiree health costs were not adequate to win them over.

A major debate over these mandates was how to account for them in the government budget—should they be viewed as a tax or simply treated as regulations that didn't flow through the budget. After long and rancorous wrangling, and despite intense lobbying from the White House, the Congressional Budget Office determined that the mandate as it was designed would be counted as a government receipt (Reischauer 1994).[10] Thus, those who looked at government receipts as equivalent to taxes and a measure of government's size would conclude that health reform had significantly increased the government's interference in the economy. For many, this decision was a sign that health reform was in its dying days.

Finally, the health care reform process may have lost support by giving too little attention to principles as opposed to goals such as "greater health insurance coverage." For instance, while the administration indicated that it wanted a progressive proposal, the final plan design was not progressive. The employer mandate proposed would have applied in large measure to low- and moderate-income employees since employees indirectly bear the costs (in lower wages) of employer mandates. Employees with access to charitable care or welfare would have ended up paying more and having less after-tax income if they had to bear the full cost of their insurance while forfeiting free services to boot.[11]

The proposal also abandoned the principle of equal justice or equal treatment of equals. By subsidizing only the uninsured, the proposed plan effectively gave a preference to a person with $30,000 of income and no insurance over someone with $30,000 of income who already bought insurance. To make matters worse, different types of employer subsidies were proposed on the basis of employer size or the average wage of the employer group, but not employee income. The Treasury's Tax Policy Office fought for a more rational approach that recognized issues of horizontal equity, but lost because of revenue concerns. As proposed, two employees with equal incomes could receive very different subsidies.

One major lesson is clear: major expenditure reform in areas like health care are as much matters of tax and revenue policy as anything else, and these matters cannot be secondary.

The Contract with America: 1995–1996

Both houses of Congress were taken over by the Republican Party in the 1994 mid-term elections, at least partly an expression of discontent over the 1993 tax increases and the failed health reform effort. Winning the House of Representatives for the first time since 1952, many Republicans ran on a platform outlined in a new "Contract with America"—a political and legislative strategy crafted largely by new House Speaker Newt Gingrich of Georgia. The "contract" featured many non-tax provisions, including term limits on elected officials and removal of some Congressional perks. Its tax provisions centered mainly on "family tax policy" and on relief for the taxation of capital. Promises were made to grant tax credits for adoption expenses, home care for the elderly, and other provisions mainly for children. Also high on the social priority list was marriage tax relief. Meanwhile, capital gains relief was to be extended, cost-recovery allowances expanded to eliminate the taxation of new capital, and fewer estates taxed. Under the contract, the offer to expense or write off the costs of physical capital assets would have been extended even to those who borrowed and did not save at all—posing the potential tax shelter problems of the early to mid-1980s.

The Contract with America was full of many ideas that would eventually be enacted into law, but the two years immediately following its introduction were largely a stalemate when it came to taxes. Numerous battles ensued between the Democratic president and the Republican Congress—largely over tax cutting. When the president and the Congress could not strike a compromise on the fiscal 1996 budget, the government shut down. Congress could not muster a two-thirds majority to override the president, and the president would veto, or threaten to veto, the budget bills that Congress did concoct. Meanwhile, in absence of a budget resolution, Congress refused to increase the debt ceiling to allow the Treasury to sell debt to finance the deficits government was running. Even the traditional trick of a continuing resolution—allowing the government to temporarily continue operating as usual in absence of a budget—was sent forward with riders and amendments that the president said he could not accept.

Eventually, a modest shutdown became unavoidable. Nonessential government workers were sent home, and a few functions ceased, including the operation of national parks—to the ire of vacationers. Direr actions, such as the suspension of Social Security payments, were dodged. The Treasury played a variety of games to narrowly avoid a default on debt because it feared a meltdown of financial markets.

Eventually, a public outcry led to compromises that allowed government to operate. President Clinton pinned much of the blame for the shutdown on the Republican Congress. Bolstering his claim was Speaker Gingrich's stance that he didn't care if the government were shut down because nobody would miss it. On the other hand, Bob Dole, the leader of Republicans in the Senate, worked strongly behind the scenes to prevent things from being pushed over the brink.

Modest Tax Action in 1995 and 1996

Despite this budget stalemate and brief government shutdown, the legislative process stuck fairly tightly to the 1990 pay-as-you-go budget rules, as extended in 1993 and beyond. Of course, the budget rules did not stop the newly Republican Congress from aggressively pursuing significant tax proposals.

In January 1995, House Speaker Newt Gingrich and Bill Archer (R-TX), who had replaced Rostenkowski as House Ways and Means Committee

Chairman, proposed an array of tax cuts for middle- and upper-income families following closely upon the "Contract with America." Under the American Dream Restoration Act, the authors proposed a $500 per child tax credit for families earning up to $200,000, "marriage penalty" relief through a new income tax credit for two-earner married couples, and tax-free contributions to "American Dream" savings accounts (similar to IRAs) that could be used for certain housing, educational, and medical expenses, as well as retirement savings. Additionally, under the Job Creation and Wage Enhancement Act, Gingrich and Archer proposed to halve the tax rates on capital gains, index gains for inflation, and allow the deductibility of losses on the sale of principal residences.

Despite the substantial scale of the proposed cuts, the Contract with America made no attempt at base broadening or broader tax reform, whether in the form of an income or consumption tax. Enough lawmakers voiced warning over the deficit size and voted down—at least temporarily—the tax proposals in the Contract with America (Brownlee 1996, 140–41).[12] Reacting to the Republican takeover, the Clinton administration also proposed its own version of a child credit and an expansion of IRA accounts, and added a deduction for tuition (U.S. Department of the Treasury 1995). In addition, Clinton proposed a tax credit large enough to pay for the first two years of college at most community colleges. The Clinton political strategy after the 1994 elections generally followed this push for major new expenditures and entitlements. The president would do it through the tax system so he could argue he was for tax cuts, too, while claiming budget responsibility by limiting costs to below what the Republicans proposed. In general, tax policy principles such as horizontal equity and efficiency did not come into play, partly because equal-costing rate reductions (often the most equitable and efficient way to cut taxes and distribute the benefits) appeared small when divided up across the population. Small rate cuts also could not generate the same type of publicity as "new" programs.

Clinton supporters also argued that Republican tax cuts would be unfair. Rubin and Weisberg (2004, 162) note that Speaker Gingrich helped the administration win the public battle in 1996 by planning to "to cut Medicare by $270 billion and reduce taxes by a similar amount, in a way that primarily favored the affluent . . . an issue with special political force." We have already noted that most tax cuts in a social welfare state are likely to cut back on net redistribution once expenditures are viewed along with taxes; here pieces of the Gingrich plan made that type of connection obvious and politically exploitable.

During 1995 and 1996, Republicans floated many broad tax reforms, but all to little consequence. Such proposals took the form of a national sales tax or a flat tax (Brownlee 1996, 142–150). In general, the flat taxes being proposed were consumption taxes, not income taxes—equivalent technically to a value-added tax (using what is called the subtraction method) with a wage deduction. Senator Richard Lugar (R-IN) and Representative Archer proposed a national sales tax with a single rate of 16 percent on everything except food and medical expenses with the goal of "eliminating the IRS" and the income tax. Also resurrected were versions of a 1980s flat-tax proposal that would apply a single rate of consumption tax to both individuals and corporations (Hall and Rabushka 1983).

Although the broad reform proposals were largely ignored, many of the smaller proposals pushed by both the president and the Republicans were later to pass (demonstrating, once again, the "hopper" theory that what gets put in the hopper often eventually comes out). Even at the end of Clinton's first term, some tax measures, significantly less expansive, managed to get around the stalemate. One bill worthy of note was called the Taxpayer Bill of Rights 2. Although much of this bill reduced or amended penalties and interest applied to various types of activities, it also established the Office of the Taxpayer Advocate. Since then, the Taxpayer Advocate has increasingly served as an intermediary between the public and the IRS in some controversies, and independently advocated for a simpler tax code.

Throughout the 1990s, tax legislation, appropriations, and internal decisionmaking were changing the IRS. In particular, after it grew to handle deficit-reduction measures in the 1980s, the IRS was cut back, although the paring accelerated in the second Clinton term. Meanwhile, a very large portion of the staff covering criminal activities moved to drug and other enforcement only loosely related to taxes rather than simply going after tax cheats.[13]

The largest tax bill at the end of Clinton's first term was the Small Business Job Protection Act of 1996, which gave small businesses and savers numerous benefits, including an increase in the amount of assets that could be "expensed"—deducted immediately rather than depreciated. For other assets, the depreciation lives were reduced, making deductions available sooner. Some pension changes were enacted. In particular, an individual retirement account deduction was allowed for spouses who did not work.

In keeping with the spirit of the budget resolutions, these changes were "paid for by other budget offsets." Some special employee or pension benefits—a $5,000 exclusion for employees' death benefits and the averaging of lump-sum distribution over five years to fend off large, one-year increases in marginal tax rates—were repealed. The biggest revenue offset was a cutback in the availability of "possessions" tax credits—credits of special value to companies that do business in Puerto Rico and other U.S. possessions. On balance, from 1995 to 2006, revenues increased by $5 billion (Joint Committee on Taxation 1996, 414).

Finally, one part of this small business act was devoted to trying to improve compliance or reduce availability of the EITC to unintended recipients. For instance, certain losses could not be deducted from adjusted gross income (AGI) under the EITC, moving some individuals out of EITC income ranges.[14] Improving EITC compliance was increasingly being identified as a goal of Congress, and this was only one of many initiatives to follow.

Welfare Reform in 1996

Once again, social policy was never far from the tax policy agenda. The Personal Responsibility and Work Opportunity Reconciliation Act of 1996 (PRWORA) created the Temporary Assistance for Needy Families (TANF) block grant, replacing the Aid to Families with Dependent Children (AFDC) (Gallagher et al. 1998). It turned over to states much responsibility for administering welfare.

The enactment of a welfare-reform measure broke a trend. The Clinton administration had been largely either unsuccessful or uninterested in systematic program reform. Health reform failed, the proliferation of special tax provisions stymied tax reform base broadening, Social Security reform never got off the ground, and most policy changes were muddled by compromise. Although perhaps the norm, this type of policymaking heightens tax complexity and often leads to incongruity among measures—whether through higher hidden tax rates, unintended marriage penalties, difficulty in filing and planning, or other problems.

Welfare reform was more systematic, although it was hardly simple and was highly contentious. Indeed, several of the administration's top welfare policy officials resigned in frustration or protest just before or just after the bill was signed.[15] But President Clinton was in a bind. He had promised welfare reform as part of his 1992 campaign but still had not been able to fashion a plan. Now, four years later, a very activist Republican House of Representatives felt that it knew something about the subject, too, and would take President Clinton at his word that he was willing to "end welfare as we know it." By ending the entitlement to cash assistance, the 1996 welfare act became landmark. This reform also significantly contributed to a new federalism by expanding states' flexibility to structure their own programs (although significant movement in this direction had already occurred through waivers granted by the Department of Health and Human Services).

However, the federal TANF payments were fixed in a block grant formula tied to (generally higher) 1994 spending levels; as a result of its fixed nature, the cost of any expansion of the welfare program would have to be borne almost entirely by the states. To get the maximum federal amount, states had to reduce caseloads over time. For their share of money, states also had to meet maintenance-of-effort requirements, but generally they were required to spend less than they had been spending in recent years. The extra federal money up front was part of a deal with the governors; much was channeled into such assistance as child care benefits. These benefits were not integrated with the more universal dependent care credit in the tax code available to those with positive income tax liabilities. Thus, to get many child care benefits, recipients either had to sign up at the welfare office or have enough income to pay income tax. Many families fell into the fissures between these two approaches.

Key to understanding welfare reform is the evolution of the EITC. Under welfare reform, total funds available to low-income individuals didn't change much, at least from a historical perspective. Though the new welfare program set time limits on welfare receipt and penalized states that didn't get larger percentages of beneficiaries to meet work requirements, the block grants were still equal to or greater than federal AFDC entitlement spending. But, by 1996, the monetary value of the EITC had far exceeded that of AFDC or TANF (see figure 3.4). In many ways, the availability of an increasingly generous EITC made it easier to push people off the welfare roles and into the work force.

After welfare reform, the labor force participation rates of former AFDC recipients and, in particular, low-income women with children, grew significantly. These changes can be traced to welfare reform, state efforts, the expanding economy, or to the EITC. Regardless of which causes were most important, clearly the rewards for working—especially in the stronger economy—had expanded greatly relative to the benefits of not working (see, for instance, Michalopolous and Berlin 2001).

Continued Deficit Reduction

Whatever else might be said about tax legislation between 1993 and 1996, deficits continued to drop. What was legislated (in particular, the 1993 budget agreement) became less significant than what was not legislated. Neither political party could enact many new expensive programs, whether tax cuts or new health or other expenditure benefits. After 1994, power was balanced, albeit because of the irreconcilable agendas of the new Republican House and the Democratic president.

Meanwhile, the economy was picking up steam, and the first hints of the revenues available from a so-called "new" economy—led by technology advances and a stock market bubble—appeared before the 1996 presidential campaign. This virtuous cycle of more revenues and fiscal restraint in new legislation would be reinforced as the economic expansion gathered momentum and revenues grew with growth in capital gains and stock options.

The long period from 1982 to the late 1990s, when budget policy was driven mainly by concern over deficit reduction, was about to end, at least temporarily. But not before debate erupted over what to do with a surplus—an economic debate unfamiliar to many young and middle-age voters who had never witnessed a surplus.

NOTES

1. The Democratic Leadership Council (DLC) asserts, "Starting with Bill Clinton's presidential campaign in 1992, Third Way thinking is shaping progressive politics throughout the world. Inspired by the example of Clinton and the new Democrats, Tony Blair in Britain led a revitalized New Labour party back to power in 1997. The victory of Gerhard Shroeder and the Social Democrats in Germany the next year confirmed the revival of center left parties." See the DLC website. Actually, the term "Third Way" has a much longer history, often referring to various middle-way approaches, as between laissez-faire capitalism and socialism.

2. Personal notes to author.

3. Among the many issues involved are the reactions of monetary policy and the extent to which short-term deficit reduction is necessary to convince financial markets of

the seriousness of the effort. Finally, if a budget is to be balanced over a long cycle, then deficit reduction is often best achieved as an economic expansion makes headway. See, for instance, Blanchard (1985) on deficits and time horizons.

4. Alan Cohen, then at the Treasury Department, is credited with suggesting this allocation as a means of staying within the budget rules.

5. Note to author from Eric Toder, deputy assistant secretary of the Treasury for tax analysis under President Clinton.

6. I personally would go to conferences where increases in EITC benefits post-1992 would all be credited to Clinton with nary a mention of the Bush increases.

7. Health reform also showed the growing power of interests to influence public perception. Commercials showing "Harry and Louise" having to give up some existing health insurance they liked, as well as diagrams showing an extraordinary labyrinth of new proposed health bureaucracy, were deemed highly effective in turning the public against the plan.

8. In recent history, no complex systematic reform has ever been designed in the White House, mainly because it seldom has the knowledge and capability to deal with all the policy and administrative issues involved. The emphasis on personal loyalty, moreover, often keeps crucial information off the table. Meanwhile, designers of plans become wedded to their own logic, so that when the White House takes on the role of initial designer, it cannot easily take on the role of objective critic of its own design. That would be especially true this time, since the First Lady was supposedly in charge.

Meanwhile, in Congress, the organizational problem is as bad, if not worse. If the debate is over the size of a single parameter, such as a tax rate, members might not reach the most efficient or equitable solution, but they can find one that is workable and manageable mainly because they usually are taking a given structure and tweaking it here or there. However, if too many committees and individual power brokers try to redesign a basic structure with many interlocking parts, they often make decisions that are contradictory and unsustainable. Given a strong proposal—that is, a workable base from which to build—the congressional staff can be put to better use in modifying, not merely taking apart, a reform effort.

9. The tax expenditure budget only counts the loss of federal income tax due to the tax subsidy (see OMB 2003, 104). This estimate shows that tax expenditures on the exclusion of employer contributions for medical insurance premiums and medical care will grow to $145 billion by 2006. However, there is also substantial loss to Social Security tax collections and to state income tax collections that are not even counted in the federal budget.

10. Whether revenues should be counted as taxes is another matter. Robert Reischauer, head of CBO at the time, claimed, "the T word has not crossed my lips" (Tax Analysts' Calendar 1997).

11. At minimum wage levels, of course, the employee could not bear the cost in the form of lower wages. This may also have contributed to employer opposition. Here the effect can be considered similar to a minimum wage increase. (See Holahan et al. 1994.)

12. See also Pollack (1996), chapter 5, for more detail on the Republican proposals as laid out under the "Contract with America."

13. After an initial increase in the IRS workforce between 1982 and 1993, there was a significant decline in IRS personnel. Particularly between 1996 and 2000, enforcement and

processing personnel were reduced by about a third while taxpayer service personnel more than doubled in number during that same time. By virtually every measure (both inputs and outputs), IRS enforcement of the tax laws outside of computer-generated document matching programs has been in decline for many years, but particularly starting about the mid-1990s to the beginning of the new century. (See Plumley and Steuerle 2002.)

14. If a household's AGI was $20,000 without the losses, but $10,000 once losses were counted, the taxpayer would essentially lose eligibility for the EITC because the $20,000 income level was too high to be eligible for any credit (though the $10,000 level was not).

15. Peter Edelman, Wendell Primus, and Mary Jo Bane were assistant or deputy assistant secretaries of the Department of Health and Human Services.

10

The New Economy?
1997 to 2000

The avoidance of tax may be lawful, but it is not yet a virtue.

—Lord Denning

In the 1996 presidential campaign, both Republican candidate Bob Dole and Democratic President Bill Clinton accused each other of having presided over the "largest tax increase" in the peacetime history of the nation. Dole applied the appellation to Clinton's 1993 tax increases; Clinton applied it to the tax increases in 1982, when Dole chaired the Senate Finance Committee. Neither would take credit for what had been one of the major legislative feats of their careers—pulling a large deficit-reduction package out of a reluctant Congress. Though both packages contained unpopular tax components, those components were still modest relative to the overall level of tax collections. But it was campaign time—time to promise more, not to acknowledge how government's past or future costs must be covered by taxes.

Voters reminded President Clinton of his 1992 presidential campaign promises for tax cuts. He renewed those promises, asserting that the deficit had taken precedence in his first term. With his second White House victory, he finally turned to those old promises, in part to prevent congressional Republicans from controlling the agenda. After all, Republicans would hand him some form of tax cut, and he wanted to be able to shape it—not just take it.

By 1997, the economy was on a roll. The last recession had hit seven years before, in the middle of President George H. W. Bush's term in office. Meanwhile, asset valuations were beginning to skyrocket. The decline in real estate values from the early 1980s to the mid-1990s ended and real estate took off and joined a longer-term stock market spurt. One consequence was a danger sign: total household net worth (largely driven by stock and real estate together) relative to gross domestic product (GDP) was starting to exceed its all-time high (see figure 10.1). But in 1997, few knew how to take the new economy's measure, so the rising euphoria was still tempered by a last ounce of skepticism. True, technology stocks seemed touched by Midas, but no large real wage gains had registered yet, and deficits remained, ending up at 1.4 percent of GDP for fiscal 1996 (CBO 1997, 18).

The Taxpayer Relief Act of 1997

With voters sending mixed messages and scant evidence explaining the new economy—or even whether it was new—contradictions riddled budgetary politics. As a consequence, Congress and the president reached

Figure 10.1 *Net Household Worth as a Percentage of GDP, 1945–2003*

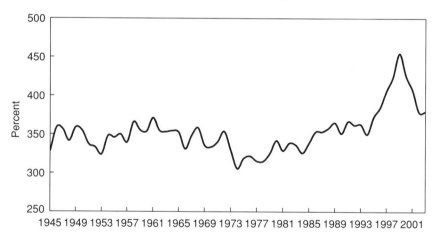

Source: U.S. Federal Reserve, Flow of Funds Data, http://www.federalreserve.gov/releases/Z1/Current/data.htm, table B.100, line 43 and BEA data on GDP.
Note: Year 2003 net household worth was estimated by the author based on the first three quarters of 2003.

a clumsy compromise to provide deficit-increasing tax relief and overall deficit reduction at the same time. A stated goal would be to balance the budget, which meant that the expenditure reductions had to be significantly larger than the tax reduction.

Those expenditure cuts would once again take the form of caps on discretionary spending. As a result, from fiscal year 1997 to fiscal year 1999, discretionary defense spending fell from 3.3 to 3.0 percent of GDP and domestic discretionary spending from 3.1 to 3.0 percent. These reductions were smaller than those of the first Clinton administration (in fiscal year 1993, the comparable starting figures were 4.5 percent of GDP for defense and 3.4 percent for domestic discretionary spending). Most gains on the nondiscretionary side of the budget were to come from further constraints on the growth in Medicare cost. These expenditure reductions turned out to be temporary, with turnarounds or reversals in all major categories—defense, other discretionary spending, and Medicare.

At the time, however, the expenditure cuts paved the way for the first significant tax cuts since 1981. Although far less dramatic than the tax cuts in 1981 (and those to come in 2001), cuts under the Taxpayer Relief Act of 1997 totaled some $28 billion per year by the time most were phased in. By fiscal year 2000, the net cost was about 0.3 percent of GDP; for the 10 years after passage, the total cost was about $300 billion (JCT 1997, 545).

The Child Credit

A new child tax credit—at $500 per child by 1999—stood out as the biggest ticket item in the new tax relief bill, accounting for more than 60 percent of the 10-year cost (JCT 1997, 512). The credit was not indexed for inflation, so its relative value would decline over time absent new legislation. Promised by the Republicans as part of their "Contract with America," the Democrats had reason to favor a credit as well. A credit for children would be fairly progressive compared with the dependent exemption since the credit's value did not rise with income.[1] As proposed and adopted, in fact, the credit was not extended at all to higher-income families.[2]

The credit finally enacted was "nonrefundable"—that is, taxpayers who owed no income tax could not receive it. The small exception was for larger families—a fairly complicated exception that would play out more fully when debate over expanding the credit reemerged in 2001.[3]

A child credit became a new feature in the U.S. tax scheme. Some of its origins can be traced to a refundable $1,000 tax credit proposed to the National Commission on Children in 1990 as a partial alternative to cash assistance and as a way to counteract disincentives to work and marry (Juffras and Steuerle 1991).[4] The Commission, along with its chair, Democratic Senator Jay Rockefeller (D-WV) had backed this provision with gusto (National Commission on Children 1991.)

The child credit also can be contrasted with three primary provisions aimed at families with children. While a credit reduces taxes paid, the non-refundable dependent exemption (or personal exemption for dependents) reduces taxable income. The earned income tax credit (EITC), in turn, also reaches low- to moderate-income families only if they have some earnings from work or self-employment, but it is refundable for low-income families and phases out for middle-income families. It had already been expanded significantly in 1986, 1990, and 1993, which provided part of the political motivation for doing something "new" like a child credit rather than simply expanding the EITC once again. Finally, the child credit can be contrasted with the nonrefundable child care tax credit available to offset some workers' child care expenses.

This new child credit cannot be defined strictly in tax terms. The credit can also be compared with the grants used on the expenditure side of the budget in such programs as cash assistance and food stamps. These expenditure programs phase out as the beneficiary's income rises, creating systems that penalize work and saving. The child credit, as of 2004, typically is not available until a certain income level is attained and, at the same time, phases out much more slowly and is more broadly available for the middle class. Recall that the higher burden placed on families with children motivated the mid-1980s family tax reform efforts. That extra burden, in substantial part, was a middle-class issue that was addressed through the credit. The child tax credit was also designed to phase *in* as income rises and the expenditure programs and earned income tax credits are phasing *out*. Thus, the child tax credit potentially helps reduce the work disincentives and palliates the marriage penalties that arise from these other programs.

Any refundable portion of an EITC or child credit is counted in the federal budget as a direct expenditure, not as a tax cut. The arbitrary parsing out of pieces of each program into tax-reduction and direct expenditure "baskets" may be appropriate from an accounting point of view, but it also demonstrates just how inseparable tax and expenditure policy are.

Social Policy and New Tax Subsidies for Education

The second biggest item in the bill provided for various tax benefits related to education—both credits proposed by President Clinton and savings incentives suggested by Republicans. Either a HOPE or lifetime learning credit would offset a modest amount of educational expense for families at all but the highest income levels. The first was modeled partly on the Georgia HOPE scholarship and gave allusion to President Clinton's claim that he was the man from Hope, Georgia, although he really wasn't from there. The basic idea, though complicated, allowed that a HOPE credit could equal $1,500 per student for the first two years of college, while a lesser lifetime learning credit could be spread over more than two years. Other education boosts came from an income-tested deduction for some student-loan interest; allowable withdrawals from individual retirement accounts (IRAs) without penalty if used for undergraduate post-secondary, vocational, or graduate education expenses; the expansion of state-sponsored prepaid tuition and state savings plans, and a new deduction on deposits to education IRAs (even though the "R" in "IRA" stands for retirement).

The broader education establishment considered these various provisions a mixed blessing. The proposals were not designed to meet any particular target such as helping the neediest students or increasing enrollment in higher education. On the other hand, it *was* additional money, so few educational lobbyists opposed the measures. Many of the new tax credit benefits would be available to those attending junior colleges—generally, a group passed over as most direct aid flowed to those attending costlier and more prestigious colleges. Indeed, according to Waldman (2000, 179), the Taxpayer Relief Act used the tax code to create a *de facto* entitlement that would pay for nearly all community college tuition—"the biggest single investment in college education since the G. I. Bill." Still, many low-income persons with no tax liability could not make use of the credit.

Needless to say, educational aid was already a complicated thicket, and this act only added to the underbrush. Even deciding which educational subsidy to take was not easy, and these new measures made it harder for parents, students, and educational establishments to sort through the many options. As one of Clinton's later Treasury deputy assistant secretaries, Len Burman (1997), summed up the Taxpayer Relief Act, "Even with all of these new incentives, one is missing: the 'Hope to learn how to do your taxes' credit.' "

Like so many other items proposed in the 1990s, these credits served a purpose far removed from the principles that inform education policy or tax policy. The administration wanted to propose tax provisions that would be somehow "better" than the rate reductions proposed by many Republicans in Congress. "Better" here meant more visible (and, hence, more politically marketable as something new) to the public, as well as lower in cost and more progressive. Whether the credits embodied such principles as equal treatment of equals or efficiency (e.g., in providing educational assistance) was not a primary consideration.

The Republicans and Democrats had united under the banner of smaller government and budget rhetoric. In effect, the political logic was fairly straightforward: tax expenditure increases and tax cuts in general were deemed acceptable; direct expenditure increases were not, and the latter were harder to get through the budget process in any case (see Toder 1998, 2000). Congress would put forward a tax bill no matter what. For the administration, the trick was to tuck expenditures and subsidies into the tax system, as well as to make proposals that might have more populist appeal than simple rate reduction. A $500 educational credit sounds better than a tax-rate reduction from 25 percent to 23 percent. The administration also emphasized social expenditures in lieu of the House Republicans' pitch for business or investment tax breaks. And, finally, Clinton's team argued that their approach would cost less than the tax cuts of their political adversaries.

Provisions for Savers and Investors

Along with sizable social expenditures, the 1997 legislation embraced other tax relief. For instance, the act raised the ceiling on the estate tax from $625,000 in 1998 to $1 million in 2006. At the same time, modest relief was provided by removing a complex calculation for depreciation under the corporate alternative minimum tax (AMT), thereby simplifying and aligning this tax calculation with the regular income tax. Also, the research tax credit and work opportunity tax credits were extended once more.

Taxes can become mind-numbingly complex. Consider capital gains policy as an example. Those who favor capital gains relief often point to (1) the double taxation of income already taxed as corporate income and then retained within a firm, creating an increase in stock value on which capital gains are taxed again; (2) the extent to which capital gains merely represent inflation; and (3) limited revenue loss since individuals realize more gains when tax rates go down. Those opposed point to (1) the heavy concentration of capital gains among the richest taxpayers; (2) the extent to which capital gains tax rates for the rich are often even lower than the rates on wages paid by middle-income taxpayers; (3) transactional complexity of capital gains relief provisions; and (4) the tax shelter opportunities created by capital gains relief, especially when people borrow to buy stock.[5]

In 1997, Congress essentially gave up on reconciling these arguments and translating them into a coherent tax bill. Instead, it lowered capital gains by imposing six new tax rates that, when combined with existing taxes on capital gains, left 12 rates to sort through (7.5, 8, 10, 14, 15, 18, 20, 25, 28, 31, 36, and 39.6) (Burman 1997). Which rate applied depended on the taxpayer's normal tax rate, the sale year of the assets, and the asset holding time before being sold. A special rate and even more complex rules apply to real estate, where account must be made of an asset's depreciation for tax purposes.

The act also provided generous allowances for IRA deposits. One new break especially deserves note. Congress created a Roth IRA with much more generous income limitations than regular IRAs, so many people without regular IRAs could choose the Roth IRA preference instead. In part, this meant abandoning the policy that IRAs only benefited the middle class and those in higher-income classes not already covered by an employer-provided plan. For tax year 2003, for instance, a regular IRA allows a single or joint filer to deduct the full value of contributions made, provided their adjusted gross income falls below $32,000 or $52,000, respectively; for Roth IRA filers, a phase-out doesn't begin until $95,000 or $150,000, respectively.

A Roth IRA allows no deduction up front, so a taxpayer putting money into a Roth IRA rather than a regular IRA pays more tax to the government initially. The advantage to the taxpayer? All interest and all withdrawals are tax-free forever. Thus, a teenager putting aside money today in a Roth IRA and eventually bequeathing it to her children could skip tax on all capital income on that IRA for more than three-quarters of a century.

The Roth IRA became especially appealing in the politically charged budget process because in the first few years this tax break was counted as a tax increase! Despite very large long-term cost, estimators indicated that revenues initially rose when individuals put deposits into a Roth IRA rather than taking deductions for deposits to a regular IRA. Then, to top it off, Congress offered to let individuals switch money already in regular IRAs into Roth IRAs and pay a tax up front which, of course, the tax-payers believed would more than pay for itself with tax saving later. This rollover provision was especially inimical to good budget policy since, for the most part, there wasn't much additional saving at stake.[6]

Generally speaking, tax-cutting legislation is backed up by revenue estimates only over the first 3, 5, or 10 years. Yet losses from Roth IRAs will stretch out over many decades. In a more typical retirement plan, the government recognizes up front many of the losses associated with the provision, but down the road gets revenues back as individuals spend down their retirement accounts.[7] Roth IRAs, therefore, are about as back-loaded as tax provisions can get, and their impact on the budget won't fully be felt for a long time. About the time that the nation's retirement and health systems for the elderly are placing strains on the nonelderly, many elderly individuals will escape paying tax on income from their Roth IRAs. As we shall see, following its usual path of copying and expanding recent achievements, Congress would make this only the first of many Roth-like proposals for back-loading the cost of retirement and saving incentives.

Other Tax Changes

Excise taxes on airplane tickets were extended but also changed in the 1997 tax legislation. A major battle ensued among the airlines over charging excise taxes on a per-passenger basis versus per-dollar-of-ticket value (which favored lower-cost airlines). The new compromise based the charges on both price and number of flight segments.

Finally, to Congress's credit, the 1997 bill did contain some tax simplifications. Examples include eliminating some filing requirements for charitable gifts over $10,000 and simplifying the audit procedure for partnerships. Another simplification forgave capital gains tax (for up to $500,000 of gains for couples) on sales of most owner-occupied homes. The old law was found to discourage people from downsizing at retirement; the capital gains tax on home sales was full of enforcement problems, and home-owning taxpayers almost never have the data to calculate correctly the gains they have made on their homes.[8] Most of the simplification provisions were restricted to uncontroversial provisions and had minor revenue impact.

IRS Restructuring

As in his first term, President Clinton signed most major tax legislation in the first year after the election. However, congressional tax-writing committees were far from idle in the succeeding years of his second term.

One resounding debate over the IRS was heightened in 1997 and solidified into legislation in 1998. This followed several years of complaints mounted against the IRS, its antiquated computer system, and the too-often erroneous advice tendered to taxpayers who called for help. The debate went from red to white hot as Congress began dealing with constituent complaints about the extent to which IRS harassed taxpayers. The Senate Finance Committee held four days of hearings, after first combing the country for cases of significant abuse (IRS 1998).

While some IRS workers apparently did abuse their positions, the hearings later proved to be more bark than bite. With IRS staff numbers hovering around 100,000 per year, the countrywide search for sensational examples turned up very few clear-cut cases of ineptitude or abuse. Close analysis by the General Accounting Office released many months after the hearing indicated that almost none of the cases trotted out at the hearing involved abuse and that proof of significant IRS wrongdoing was simply not evident (Donmoyer 2000).

One common complaint voiced at the hearings concerned IRS seizures of assets, which are quite rare. A primary example involves taxpayers who fail to pay taxes owed and do not turn over the taxes withheld on the earnings of workers in the business, thus stealing from other taxpayers' accounts as well as cheating the government. The Senate Finance Committee also examined a raid that had not even been organized by the IRS; rather, a local enforcement agency dealing with non-tax issues had launched it.

Whatever the merits of their anecdotal findings, the increased attention to the IRS prompted a major restructuring of the organization. This overhaul came about not only through legislation, but also through administrative efforts. For the first time, the head of a major information technology corporation, rather than a lawyer or accountant, was appointed Commissioner of Internal Revenue in the hope of moving the Service fully into the computer age. Charles O. Rossotti came to the IRS from American Management Systems, where he had been chairman of the board.

In the Internal Revenue Service Restructuring and Reform Act of 1998, numerous protections were added, some penalties and interest were abated, some limits on audits were established, more disclosures to taxpayers were required, and, perhaps most important, organization structure and management were revamped over the succeeding months and years (JCT 1998, 16–29; Price Waterhouse Coopers 1998). A new IRS Oversight Board oversaw the agency in its administration of the laws, the Taxpayers' Advocate Office was given greater independence, and the IRS geographic administrative units gave way to operating units serving particular groups of taxpayers such as small businesses.

Despite this partially successful reform of IRS, many defects and problems remain. First, even after numerous efforts and all the best intentions over the succeeding years, the IRS still has not succeeded in modernizing much of its information systems. This can be traced in part to the lack of resources put into hiring good computer people for years prior to the reform. In one of the most complex agencies in the world, there must be highly trained people internally who can figure out what to buy.[9] Second, the agency is still not equipped to monitor, analyze, or gather adequate data on charitable deductions, housing tax credits, enterprise zones, health subsidies, research credits, energy production incentives, or the many hundreds of other programs it administers. No one knows who benefits from many programs, their administrative costs, the number of filing errors in each, and so forth. In this information vacuum, programs are more difficult to run well, congressional program objectives are harder to meet, and policymakers lack the research they need to improve the programs over time. While the IRS may never be equipped to do the full policy analysis of these programs that the public deserves, at least it still needs to have people assigned to ensure that data is collected and the various programs are monitored sufficiently.

The agency became much less aggressive about auditing returns after Congress's public attack. Code section 1203 of the Restructuring and Reform Act of 1998 law listed ten categories of misconduct—often called "deadly sins" by IRS personnel—for which an IRS employee could be fired. From the time of the hearings up to 2002, audit rates plummeted, and so especially did levies, liens, and seizures in cases where IRS personnel feared that action could hurt their careers (Murphy and Higer 2002;

Plumley and Steuerle 2002).[10] A huge backlog developed in efforts to collect known tax debts and the concerned tax community began to fear that IRS enforcement—particularly on such hard-to-detect items as self-employment income—was practically nil (Burman 2003).[11] So by 2003, Congress reversed its position, pressing the IRS to bump up its audit rate—albeit only with a 3 percent budget increase. The fear by then was that cheating was expanding as taxpayers realized the likelihood of detection was low.

Some caution is called for, however, in interpreting the declining "audit" rates. The IRS still computer-matches paper documents prepared by payers, such as banks, with the income declared by taxpayers.[12] Contacts with taxpayers plummeted mainly where such information matching was not possible, as with charitable contributions, business income, and self-employed independent contractors.

In sum, the IRS reorganization improved the agency's technology, gave taxpayers additional layers of protection, and removed some inefficiency of its divisions. But the IRS is still incapable of analyzing or even reporting on many of the policy programs it administers, its information system is still inadequate, its lines of responsibility are still confused, and its audit and collection functions function must be restored and strengthened.

Trade and International Issues

In a world increasingly global and dependent upon trade, international issues have naturally come to the face of tax debates. Those discussed here are "perennials" that take on new urgency in the early 21st century as the globalization of production and markets accelerates.

Subsidies for Exports

In the FSC (Foreign Sales Corporation) Repeal and Extraterritorial Income Exclusion Act of 2000, Congress attempted to tackle one part of the exceedingly complex issue of how to tax the foreign income of U.S. companies. Knotty complexities arise with this issue because different tax regimes prevail in different countries, and tax rates and tax bases differ. Income and sales are often taxed both in country of origin and country of receipt, and laws and treaties both try to limit the double tax and to assure that the home country collects some. The United States generally grants a tax credit for foreign taxes on income earned abroad, while income earned by a foreign company from foreign operations is subject to U.S. tax mainly when dividends are paid to U.S. individuals. Many other countries use a "territorial" system in which the corporate tax on income earned abroad is determined mainly by the country where the income is earned.

Eligible foreign sales corporations, many of which are owned by a U.S. company but located outside the United States, exist to secure partial exemption from income tax for sales profits made abroad. The production itself is usually done (sourced) in the United States and the FSC is usually just a paper conduit. The World Trade Organization (WTO) Dispute Settlement Panel found that the FSC provisions were a prohibited export subsidy, in violation of U.S. treaties with foreign countries. Generally, corporate income taxation is taxed at the country of "source"—i.e., where the production takes place—and, by the treaty, is not supposed to be assessed at a lower rate on profits from goods produced for export than for goods produced for domestic consumption. On the other hand, consumption taxes are not based on where the product is produced but where it is consumed. Accordingly, the treaty allows rebates of any withheld consumption tax such as a value-added tax on exported items.

Politicians from both U.S. political parties have often argued that they wanted to grant some type of tax relief to companies producing for export the same way that European countries rebate value-added taxes (VAT). These politicians also argue that they want to keep production at home, so they want to forgive domestic producers from tax on goods produced for export the same way they would defer or forgive tax on these companies if they simply located their plants abroad and then deferred or avoided U.S. tax. The WTO position, however, backs a treaty regime long pushed by the United States that tries to keep companies neutral as to whether they produce for export or not.

Notably, the FSC provisions replaced a 1971 Domestic International Sales Corporation (DISC) subsidy that also was declared illegal. Accordingly, in 2000, Congress repealed this FSC subsidy but then substituted a new Exclusion for Extraterritorial Income. In short order, U.S. trading partners opposed it as an illegal export subsidy, thus rekindling the dispute first ignited in 1971. Congress continually struggles with how to deal with this issue, and corporations constantly remain split over how to allocate these types of subsidies.

There are no easy answers here. Direct export subsidies will continue to be declared illegal. An imperfect answer to this problem is to keep government as lean as possible so that tax rates are low. If subsidies must be provided, to meet treaty obligations they probably have to be done in a way that is even-handed—that is, given to all companies whether for export or not. Even by early 2004, Congress had failed to find a replacement for its subsidy scheme, toying with direct subsidies such as lower tax rates for "industrial" corporations only.

Tax Shelters and Foreign Income

Foreign tax shelters also came under scrutiny in the late 1990s (see chapter 3). The legality of seeking tax havens in foreign companies and subsidiaries became increasingly contentious, and efforts by the Treasury and the IRS to get better reporting from accounting, law, and other professional firms—an effort which stretched into the next administration—were often stymied by opponents who claimed that such reporting would be burdensome and difficult. An earlier dispute in 1994 and 1995 had dealt with the number of Americans becoming expatriates to avoid capital gains income tax and estate tax on income earned or wealth accumulated in the United States in previous years. Here, too, for the most part, the administration was able to do little to tax these persons upon expatriation. Some opponents seemed to base their arguments on the notion that all taxes were bad, so any way of avoiding them, even if it was on the border of what was legal, was probably all right. In this environment, shelters and use of tax havens continued to grow.

Social Security Surpluses and Savings Accounts

By 1998, the federal government, for the first time in decades, was beginning to project budget surpluses under current laws. Clinton's 1998 State of the Union address was intended partly to persuade the electorate that, despite the projected bounty, the country ought to stay the course of fiscal discipline begun in 1993 (Waldman 2000). Congressional Republicans warned that they would seek to return any surpluses as tax relief, boasting that "it would be gone before it arrived." After six years of budget discipline, both parties were ready to open government's coffers to constituencies' demands. They had already wriggled out from under the pay-as-you-go budget rules (which had been largely enforced since 1990) when in 1997 they passed a large transportation bill that the president felt compelled to sign.

The budget bulge began building. Ever-larger surpluses were projected. Meanwhile, reduction in federal debt lowered interest payments, and the compound effect sparked further positive projections. By the end of the 1990s, the debate would extend to what to do if the federal debt was entirely paid off—for instance, what types of assets the monetary authorities might have to buy and sell when they wanted to change the money supply if there weren't enough federal bonds to do the job. Forecasts got rosier still as the economy strengthened. The nation would move toward its longest peacetime expansion ever without a recession, and people saw the value of their wealth soar. Technology and Internet stocks by now were booming and new theories held that such stocks should be valued on their growth in sales even when there were no profits to show. Increasingly sweeping generalizations about the "new" economy and what it all meant colored the debate on taxes and spending.

Some of the forces behind the budget surpluses were entirely predictable. Most baby boomers were still working, and the largely retired baby bust population of the Depression and World War II was too small to swell the ranks of the elderly. But, other budget boosters were unexpected as well. Wage growth was higher than anticipated, while the stock market boom prompted extraordinarily high levels of capital gains realizations relative to the size of the economy. Stock options were also being realized. Moreover, at least initially, the Medicare constraints enacted in 1997 were holding down costs better than projected.

An often-contradictory debate sprang up over what to do with these unexpected surpluses. Within the divided government, many Republicans eschewed more spending; many Democrats abhorred more tax cuts. A major contest arose over who was more likely to "save the Social Security surplus." In Washington-speak, this meant avoiding a deficit apart from any savings taking place in the Social Security trust fund. Historically, government saving in Social Security was more than offset by government dissaving or deficits in the rest of the budget—leaving a net deficit even as unfunded promises to future retirees built up. Most Social Security taxes had not been saved in its trust funds throughout most of the program's history but instead were spent immediately to pay for benefits. Nonetheless, for the brief period from enactment of the 1983 amendments (see chapter 6) to the peak of the baby boomer retirement (about 2018), Social Security will take in slightly more in taxes than it will pay out each year (Social Security and Medicare Boards of Trustees 2003).

In this confusing debate, neither party ever made clear what a policy of "saving the Social Security surplus" would mean once the program started running huge deficits. But that didn't stop both Republicans and Democrats from competing over who could do it better. Initially, the goal meant running a positive non–Social Security budget surplus (that is, a unified budget surplus in excess of the Social Security surplus) at some point down the road—say, in 10 years. But as the budget numbers began looking rosier and rosier, running these types of surpluses right off the bat became a possibility so long as no significant tax cuts or major expenditures were enacted in 1999 or 2000. The administration and some House and Senate members also began billing Medicare surpluses as funds that should be "saved" as well.[13]

Both the Treasury and the White House toyed with ideas of Social Security reform. However, the attention to President Clinton's impeachment basically derailed any attempt at major reform. The president's national economic adviser, Gene Sperling, indicated that this was one of the real disappointments of Clinton's second term.[14] Nonetheless, one net result of partisan fights was greater budget stringency. A government divided proved to be a more fiscally prudent government, at least as measured by deficits (see Liebman, Elmendorf, and Wilcox 2002).

Individual Accounts and USA Accounts

No serious discussion of Social Security can avoid the growing debate by century's end over whether to establish accounts in which government taxes (particularly Social Security taxes) would be treated as if they are deposits in individual retirement accounts similar to IRAs or 401(k) plans.[15] This issue's implications for tax policy are enormous since the fundamental ways that taxes are used to meet retirement needs would change if these accounts are ever adopted.

For almost seven decades, federal tax policy has supported two retirement pillars. First is a Social Security system largely financed on a pay-as-you-go basis, with the Social Security taxes of some individuals paying for benefits to others. Second is a voluntary private system subsidized by tax policy, which favors saving for retirement over other forms of saving—usually by allowing deferral of tax on any earnings or compensation deposited to a pension or retirement accounts, as well as for the income earned on those deposits. This income is taxable only when withdrawn. In this tradition, pensions are favored by delay of taxation, but the system provides no grants or similar direct subsidies. The Roth-type savings accounts discussed earlier differ in excluding (rather than deferring) capital earnings from tax, but likewise do not rely on grant-like subsidies.

By the late 1990s, a number of analysts had begun to consider whether Social Security taxes should be deposited directly in "individual accounts," as was being done increasingly in other countries around the world. Although the issue needn't be so partisan, advocates from some think tanks such as the Cato Institute and from some parts of the financial services industry decided to make individual accounts—and a simultaneous attack on traditional Social Security—into more of a crusade. But some from other think tanks and labor venues began a counter-crusade, holding that traditional Social Security is almost sacrosanct. Loathe to tap Social Security funds, President Clinton proposed instead in early 1999 that a more modest sum be put in "USA accounts" financed out of general revenues.

Political implications aside, individual account and USA account proposals have many common elements. Either would establish a pillar that is a hybrid of the existing two pillars. Mandated taxes still have to be used (whether income or Social Security taxes), but are deposited into accounts for individuals. In many cases, the individual has to do nothing—the tax money is deposited on his or her behalf—but in others the individual may have to provide some matching money.

One distinction is worth noting. USA accounts were dressed up as an income tax credit, rather than an expenditure credit. President Clinton had not relinquished his use of the income tax code to try to deliver his programs.

Proponents of these two types of accounts disagree about whether to use non–Social Security money for financing or to redirect Social Security taxes to the accounts. Under the second approach, other Social Security benefits are usually pared eventually to help deal with the loss of Social Security revenue, but the first faces a similar budget requirement that the money must come from somewhere. Both approaches at the time remained vague on what expenditures would be cut or what other taxes increased. Another issue is whether deposits to these accounts should be made disproportionately higher for moderate-income individuals than for better-off taxpayers; both political parties have now bought into this idea at some level or another. (A commission formed by the succeeding Republican president, George W. Bush, would have had subsidies to the accounts higher as a percentage of earnings for taxpayers whose income was lower.)

Although rhetoric in the individual account debate has often been highly charged, the amounts of money involved total only one-tenth or so of promised expenditures for elderly programs. In fact, focus on this issue so skewed the debate on the elderly budget that it was difficult to address many other serious issues, such as Social Security anti-poverty effectiveness and possible discrimination against single heads of households (Steuerle and Favreault 2003). The point for tax policy is that mandated saving accounts are a very different and new way of using tax dollars to subsidize retirement—one that has been already adopted by many countries around the world and one that would come up again in future Social Security reform debates.

The Community Renewal Tax Relief Act of 2000

The Community Renewal Tax Relief Act of 2000, signed into law by President Clinton on December 21, 2000 (after the election of his successor) deserves attention as a prime example of how tax policy is used to try to serve communities.

Ever since the advent of enterprise zones in the 1980s, policymakers have looked for types of market-based initiatives designed to spur growth by granting special favors to particular places or regions. Although such programs were initially conceived as help for poor communities, the requirement to appease lawmakers resulted in the establishment of communities in almost every state. In the Clinton administration, "empowerment zones," "renewal communities," and "new markets" partially replaced enterprise zones. Empowerment zones were first authorized in the 1993 and 1997 tax acts. The 1997 act cost $32 billion over ten years, with costs rising to $5 billion by 2009.

The 2000 community renewal act designated 40 areas to be "renewal" communities. They would receive wage credits, extra deductions for purchases of depreciable assets, and a zero percent capital gain tax rate for qualifying assets. Nine new "empowerment" zones were created. New tax credits were allowed for qualified equity investments in low-income communities through the acquisition of stock or a partnership interest in a selected community development entity (CDE). The bill allowed states to float more private-activity bonds and increased the amount of low-income housing tax credits that states could issue.

As in the case of earlier enterprise zones, the subsidies were a potpourri, and their impacts were hard to track. The General Accounting Office was assigned to make assessments in 2004, 2007, and 2010. As noted, IRS for the most part simply does not gather much data on such programs, making it exceedingly hard to know how much of this $30 billion is misappropriated, much less what proportion goes to lawyers, bureaucrats, and other intermediaries. Indeed, there are very large questions as to how much benefit inures at all to the targeted communities, particularly their poorer constituents.[16] For instance, the new markets tax credits go even further than some of the capital gains relief and wage credits available through other tax breaks. Apparently trying to mimic the low-income housing tax credits, they provide for a significant share of the up-front cost (perhaps 25 percent) of an investment.

We do know this: any time tax subsidies are allowed for something done on one side of a street or community boundary and not another, issues of efficiency and equity will arise. However, such geographically based subsidies as those in the 2000 act may catalyze a community to deal with its problems (see Steuerle 1992b). But equity is not served when particular geographic regions are favored over more broadly available wage subsidies aimed at the poor, wherever they may live. The few studies that have been done on enterprise, empowerment, renewal, and new markets zones and communities call into question their effectiveness (see for instance, Papke 1993 and 2000).

Century's End

It is hard to discern defining principles or rules behind tax policy over the second Clinton term. The divided government rarely evoked such tax policy principles as efficiency, equal justice, or simplicity. The domestic policy focus was on deficit reduction, and the administration dictated almost no large domestic initiatives, especially after the failure of health reform in Clinton's first term and the 1994 Republican takeover of the House of Representatives. For President Clinton, deficit reduction was valuable in its own right, and it was his way of fighting tax cuts he considered unjust or unaffordable. He fought off big tax cuts with the veto.

Where Clinton accepted tax cuts, they often had more redistribution from rich to poor than most across-the-board alternatives. Clinton also favored smaller cuts if they were a way of creating new programs that had middle-class appeal, such as educational subsidies. Perhaps the most interesting new development of these sanguine "new economy" years was the evolving debate on alternative ways to subsidize private pensions through different types of tax breaks or mandated saving that went into individual accounts.

Clinton proposed in his final budget (fiscal year 2001) to provide $33 billion of AMT relief over 10 years to appease the "soccer moms," as well as the swing voters who came out in force in the 1994 election to return congressional power to the Republicans (OMB 2002, 410). His proposals would have allowed the use of personal exemptions and the standard deduction in the AMT—effectively treating them the same way as in the regular tax rather than the way tax shelters are treated in the AMT.[17] Len Burman, then deputy assistant secretary for tax analysis at the Treasury, recalls how "nobody disputed the facts that the AMT was horrible tax policy and that it was going to affect millions of taxpayers in a few years. But the Treasury/White House position for a long time was that it mostly affected higher-income people and was therefore a Republican problem."[18] Swayed by stories about the AMT impact, Clinton agreed to Treasury's request for the budget item, accepting the advice of Secretary Lawrence Summers over Gene Sperling, his White House national economic adviser. Of course, the budget was only half serious: no one expected the Republican Congress to back the president's proposals in an election year. On the other hand, Treasury proposals do tend to revive over time.

By the end of the Clinton presidency, Congress had tasted modest tax cutting and wanted more. Temporary surpluses put that goal within reach and the way was paved for the next president to take those surpluses and spend them on his own priorities—which would turn out to be major tax cuts but without fixes to items like the AMT.

NOTES

1. One must be careful to distinguish the political from the economic argument. Ignoring differences in family size, it is possible to design a credit with a rate schedule that would exactly match an exemption with another rate schedule. An equal-cost credit is only more progressive than an exemption if the rate schedule is assumed to be fixed.

2. For more on the re-emergence of tax expenditures as a tool of social policy, see Howard (2002).

3. For families with three or more children, the act allowed the credit to offset not just income tax, but the employee share of FICA or Social Security and Medicare payroll taxes minus earned income tax credit. In a sense, then, for some taxpayers the credit was refundable up to the amount of Social Security tax paid. Interpreted differently, one might argue that the credit was nonrefundable if the income and Social Security tax

were considered together. The provision required a lot of calculation, however, to get a small amount of money to a few people.

4. We had proposed this credit to the Commission partly as a way of reducing taxes for lower-income workers and partly as relief from the types of work and marriage disincentives in welfare.

5. For details on many other issues surrounding capital gains, see Burman (1999).

6. Technically, the additional tax paid up front could represent additional saving since the after-tax value of the account down the road was enhanced.

7. During parts of 2002 and 2003, Michael Boskin, former chair of the Council of Economic Advisors under President George H. W. Bush emphasized that there was a large stock of taxes due the government under the traditional IRAs and pension plans (Boskin 2003). He stressed that this might help pay for the deficit. Later critiques (see, for instance, Auerbach et al. 2003) noted among other things that much of this revenue was already accounted for in estimates of deficit, and that there were no surprises. Then Boskin admitted a large error in his calculations that treated inconsistently money coming into and going out of pension plans.

8. The proposal followed upon some research by Leonard Burman, Sally Wallace, and David Weiner (1997).

9. The IRS for years was unable even to hire computer science majors because its pay was so low and its systems so antiquated that working there became a dead-end career move for the highly talented (see Steuerle 1986c.)

10. The "10 deadly sins" in the IRS Restructuring and Reform Act of 1998 had related unintended consequences such as low output and collection rates.

11. At the time of the Senate finance hearings, IRS levies were at 14 per million of population, seizures at close to 4 per million and liens were about 2 per million. Just two years later, these numbers dropped to about 2 levies and 1 lien per million and practically no seizures (see Plumley and Steuerle 2002.)

12. Typical reports include 1099 forms used for interest, dividends, or payments from pension plans.

13. The Medicare surplus was much more tenuous than even the Social Security surplus. First, expenditures in Part A of Medicare (Hospital Insurance) are scheduled to exceed taxes and other income excluding interest even sooner. Moreover, a large share of Medicare is in Part B (Supplemental Medical Insurance), which is mainly financed out of general revenues anyway. See Social Security and Medicare Boards of Trustees (2003).

14. Comments to author.

15. To access papers and reports on the subject, see the Retirement Project page on the Urban Institute web site: www.urban.org/retirement.

16. Congress passed the New Market Tax Credit (NMTC) legislation as part of the Community Renewal Tax Relief Act of 2000 in December 2000 with the intent of generating $15 billion in new private sector equity investments for for-profit, "community development entities" that serve low-income urban and rural communities.

17. The long-term cost continued to grow; since more and more taxpayers became subject to the AMT over time in absence of the provision, the number who got relief from the provision also rose.

18. Personal statement to author.

11

Bush II and Compassionate Supply-Side Conservatism

In the time of the Emperor Vespasian, the government provided urinals in the streets of Rome, and charged a fee for their use . . . His son asked the emperor whether the additional receipts should be considered a tax increase or a reduction in government expenditures. To this the emperor made his famous reply . . . 'Non Olet' . . . [or] 'It doesn't smell' . . . [or] 'It's all money, and it doesn't matter which side of the ledger you put it on.'

—Herbert Stein

The beginning of the 21st century holds many parallels to the beginning of the 20th. The economic progress evidenced in new medical wonders, cell phones, and ever-faster Internet connections rivaled the mechanical and energy revolutions a century earlier. Each made it plain that a "new economy" was displacing the old. And, during presidential elections at both junctures, euphoria prevailed.

Good times in the new millennium invited the belief that predicted federal budget surpluses could be spent even before they arrived. Neither major candidate running in 2000 had suggested that anything much must be foregone today to make the nation or world a little better tomorrow. Rather, promises abounded, whether it was an immediate tax cut or continually rising shares of national income spent on Social Security retirement and enhanced Medicare benefits—with costs, either way, to be covered by the next generation of taxpayers. Taking a leaf from his opponent's projection of himself as a new Democrat, George W. Bush suggested that he was a new type of conservative, a compassionate conservative who favored expanded spending on Medicare and educa-tion, along with sizable tax cuts. As few can forget, his contest with Al Gore ended in a dead heat; until the Supreme Court passed judgment on the validity of recounting contested ballots, the winner could not be named.

The Two Santa Claus Policy: Tax Cuts and Spending Increases

For many Republicans, George W. Bush's victory signaled a chance to return to the halcyon days of Ronald Reagan, at least on the tax front. Supply-side economics was back in the saddle, though not to the extent its critics contended. Reductions in tax rates largely defined the domes-tic debate in 1981 and again dominated—both in rhetoric and dollars—the new president's domestic policy for, not just his first year, but his first term. At least in terms of dollars, even the new homeland security initiative took a distant back seat. According to Bush's first Secretary of the Treasury, Paul O'Neill, budget-concerned people like himself and the chairman of the Federal Reserve Board, Alan Greenspan, fought a losing battle, with the latter asserting that without somehow insuring that debt targets could be met, "that tax cut is irresponsible fiscal policy" (Suskind 2003, 162).[1] In remarkable replication of the 1981 tax cuts, the White House depended upon economic predictions that were not sustained and, more importantly, prevented the Treasury from putting forward any type of redesign that could have avoided the severe increase in deficits that followed.

Several of the administration's early tax cuts were phased in over time. One reason for phasing in tax cuts was not publicly stated; it traces back to the growing budgetary problem sketched in the past few chap-ters. Budget politics in Washington had become like a game of "chicken." One side played the game by building expenditure increases far into the future. Opponents of bigger government—the "other side"—often felt trapped, not wanting to incur the public's wrath by reneging on promises or failing to approve any spending increases. They, too, began to make more promises, but now on the tax-cutting side.

The game transcends partisanship. The learned instinct of both par-ties, given existing budget rules and a public addicted to politicians' promises, was to get what you can while you can. Not to overstate the case, but it had become clear that the winners in budgetary politics were those who promised easy gratification now but left financing to future policymakers. In one sense, this was nothing new: politicians have always fought over how to appease the public through increased spending or reduced taxes. However, the fight over prescribing today the use of most *future* revenues marked a new phase.

In 2001, the temporary budget surplus appeared to delay the time of collision, offering politicians an opportunity to drive even faster in this game of chicken and schedule even more long-term giveaways. For opponents of big government, tax cuts built into the future might even avoid collision if they could successfully squeeze expenditure programs the same way that built-in expenditure growth could strangle tax cuts. As we have seen, one might argue that the tax cuts of 1981 exacerbated the budget shortfalls of the 1980s and 1990s, and eventually precipitated some cutbacks in discretionary spending, along with temporary reductions in Medicare growth. For the near term, however, the administration decided not to fight that battle and attempted new giveaways on the expenditure side, including new benefits for farmers and a very large increase in health benefits for senior citizens. But what about the effect of reduced surpluses or, as soon would become apparent, higher deficits? O'Neill quotes Vice President Dick Cheney as arguing in late 2002 that "Reagan proved deficits don't matter" (Suskind 2003, 291), but the context of that statement seems to have been in backing yet further tax cuts rather than higher expenditures, per se.[2]

The 2001 Tax Cuts: An Emphasis on Tax Rates

For now it was clearly the tax cutters' turn. The primary economic initiative advanced by President Bush was a tax cut weighted heavily toward reducing tax rates. Naturally, bells and whistles were added, but the administration succeeded in constraining Congress so that the final bill still primarily contained rate reductions. The Economic Growth and Tax Relief Reconciliation Act of 2001 cut average rates for taxpayers at all income levels, and cut marginal rates for about 62 percent of taxpayers.[3] Though rarely portrayed that way, marriage penalty relief and the elimination of the estate tax were essentially selective rate reductions. Dropping the "first" or "bottom" rate from 15 to 10 percent for lower-middle income taxpayers also reduced the effective marginal tax rate that applied to people moving into the regular tax system after paying no taxes, easing this potentially painful transition. Many workers at this earning level also saw their earned income tax credit (EITC) drop by 21 cents for every additional dollar they earned, which was one reason for concern with this marginal tax rate.

Going by the book—in this case, the public finance literature—reductions in tax rates are usually more efficient than most other approaches to tax reduction. President Bush's economic advisers bought into this logic, contending that cuts in tax rates create greater parity among taxpayers with equal incomes than do new special deductions, credits, or preferences, which are basically new expenditures administered by the tax authorities instead of direct-spending agencies. Moreover, with lower rates, remaining deductions or exclusions are worth less, and the tax system as a whole distorts individuals' choices less. Of course, whether rates are really cut over the long haul will depend upon whether the tax cut is eventually financed with tax increases or expenditure cuts. Dodging the all-important budget issue by initially emphasizing rate cuts over larger preferences, Bush's tax cutters were more in line with traditional tax principles such as efficiency and horizontal equity than were Clinton's tax cutters. However, in its reluctance to propose any base broadening—and in its willingness to favor new preferences in other tax bills—the Bush administration showed itself to be quite similar to the Clinton administration.

Progressivity and the Integration of Taxes with Spending

The tax cuts enacted as part of the Economic Growth and Tax Relief Reconciliation Act of 2001 should have made it clear that it is increasingly hard to treat taxes and expenditures as separate components in a tax bill. Consider the debate in 2001 over the cut's progressivity.

Unlike the 1981 Reagan tax cut, the Bush administration proposal (excluding for the moment the estate tax and the alternative minimum tax) gave a significantly larger percentage tax cut to those at the bottom than at the top. In the 1970s, such a proposal would have been considered reasonable by usual standards. Recall that bracket creep was often proportional to current taxes for those in the broad middle-income bracket, so a proportional cut roughly compensates in those classes. The complication, of course, is that cutting taxes permanently means something has to give on the expenditure side. From this broader budgetary perspective, few tax cuts are likely to be progressive in the sense of leading to more redistribution. Thus, consider a cut in a regressive tax like Social Security—regressive by the rate standard—that taxes the poor at a higher rate than the rich. The poor may still be worse off after the cut if they eventually lose more in expenditures in absolute dollars than they gain in tax cuts.

Under a more consistent measure of progressivity, therefore, most attempts to shrink the modern welfare state reduce net redistribution (ignoring effects related to efficiency and growth).[4] After all, expenditures are much more evenly split in dollar terms (sometimes even aimed only at low-income households) than are taxes. For those always wanting more redistribution, it sometimes matters not a jot whether government has become bloated, a society wants to move away from communism or socialism, excess revenues flood in unexpectedly, inefficiency rises exponentially as government grows, or slimming down government enhances overall economic growth. Tax cuts will generally be opposed if the redistribution is the sole criterion by which to judge policy.

When the 2001 tax cuts are compared with previous tax increases, the progressivity debate can be seen to play out in different ways. To minimize political fallout, most modern statutory tax increases (e.g., 1990 and 1993) have tended to hit only a few people, usually at the top of the income scale. When tax cuts, such as those in 2001, reduce taxes for a much broader spectrum of households, including those who faced little or no tax increase in previous years, the net effect over time may well be a more progressive system. Of course, the calculation of net change in progressivity over time involves much more than legislative increases and decreases in the income tax, and must include such factors as bracket creep in the individual and alternative minimum taxes. Partly as a consequence of the overall dynamic, over most of the postwar period, there was little net change in the progressivity of the tax system as a whole (see figure 3.7). When calculations are made for the middle of the first decade of the 21st century, my guess is that the same result is likely to apply—with exceptions at the very bottom and top of the income distribution, as discussed below.

A significant part of the 2001 progressivity debate centered on how to help those at the bottom of the income scale. Partly because tax cuts in 1986, 1990, and 1993 took so many lower-income people off the income tax rolls, the only way to give them some share of benefits in 2001 was through expenditures. By making the child credit partially refundable, that is precisely what the 2001 bill ultimately accomplished.

President Bush had proposed increasing the child credit from $500 to $1,000 only for those who pay taxes, but the final bill was amended so that the credit would be phased in for those with incomes above $10,000, whether they paid taxes or not. The budget counts the refundable portion of credits (EITC and child credit) as expenditures even though the IRS will administer them. In short, the distributional fight over progressivity in 2001 could not be resolved within the tax system alone. Both sides of the budget had to be aligned.[5]

Table 11.1 shows the distributional impact of the 2001 and 2003 income tax cuts, counting the expenditure increases in the child credit, when fully phased in (the 2003 cut mainly phased in the 2001 rate cuts faster, so it is easiest to show the distributional effect of both bills together). For tax years 2003 and 2010, the reduction in effective tax rate (and the corresponding percentage change in after-tax income) is fairly significant for all brackets at about the 30th percentile of the income distribution. Below that, where tax rates are already significantly negative (counting the EITC and child credit expenditures), the reduction in effective tax rate is less dramatic. For the lower half of the income distribution, it is the change in the child credit that provides the greatest impact.

Aligning tax and expenditure programs is also required when determining the appropriate combined marginal tax rate schedule. Figure 11.1 shows marginal tax rates for a married couple with two children in 2010 under prior tax law (before the 2001 legislation passed) and under the new law.[6] The figure counts rates from both the regular income tax and the EITC. At about $20,000 of income, the marginal rate formerly jumped up toward 36 percent. This combined marginal rate derives from a 21 percent tax rate for those whose EITC was being reduced because of higher income, plus the 15 percent marginal tax rate applied to the lowest-income tax bracket. By making the child credit partially refundable, phasing out the EITC at a higher-starting point for married filers, and creating a 10 percent bracket, the final bill lowered marginal tax rates for many of these taxpayers nearer the bottom of the income scale. Once again, the net change for lower-income individuals was addressed primarily in the expenditure portion of the bill (through refundable credits).[7]

This particular approach to enhancing the progressivity of the 2001 cut evolved from debates over how to reduce fairly high work disincentives and marriage penalties among those generally with too low an income to owe income tax[8] (see Bull et al. 1999; Ellwood and Liebman

Table 11.1 *Distribution of Income Tax Change under the 2001 and 2003 Tax Cuts*

| | Effective income tax rates[b] | | | | | |
| | 2003 | | | 2010 | | |
Income percentile[a]	Pre-2001 tax cuts	Post-2003 tax cuts	Difference (Post–Pre)	Pre-2001 tax cuts	Post-2003 tax cuts	Difference (Post–Pre)
0–10	-0.3	-0.7	-0.5	-0.2	-0.2	0.0
10–20	-9.4	-9.5	-0.2	-10.3	-10.4	-0.1
20–30	-6.7	-7.4	-0.8	-7.3	-8.2	-0.9
30–40	-1.1	-3.3	-2.1	-0.8	-3.2	-2.4
40–50	3.8	1.4	-2.4	4.7	2.3	-2.4
50–60	7.2	4.9	-2.2	8.1	6.3	-1.8
60–70	8.9	6.8	-2.1	10.0	8.4	-1.6
70–80	10.1	8.1	-2.0	11.4	9.9	-1.5
80–90	11.8	9.2	-2.5	13.6	12.1	-1.5
90–100	21.1	18.2	-2.8	22.4	20.8	-1.7
All	13.7	11.2	-2.5	15.4	13.7	-1.7
Addendum						
90–95	14.4	11.6	-2.8	16.0	15.0	-1.0
95–99	18.6	16.2	-2.5	20.5	20.0	-0.5
Top 1 percent	28.1	24.8	-3.2	28.6	25.4	-3.2

Source: Urban-Brookings Tax Policy Center Microsimulation Model (version 0503-1).

Note: Years are calendar tax years. 2001 tax cuts = Economic Growth and Tax Relief Reconciliation Act of 2001; 2003 tax cuts = Jobs and Growth Tax Relief Reconciliation Act of 2003.

a. Income concept is adjusted gross income plus the employer share of payroll tax. Tax units with negative income are excluded from the lowest decile but are included in the totals.

b. Net of refundable credits (earned income tax credit and refundable child tax credit).

Figure 11.1 *Marginal Rates for Married Couple with Two Children in 2010: Prior Law versus 2001 Tax Cut*

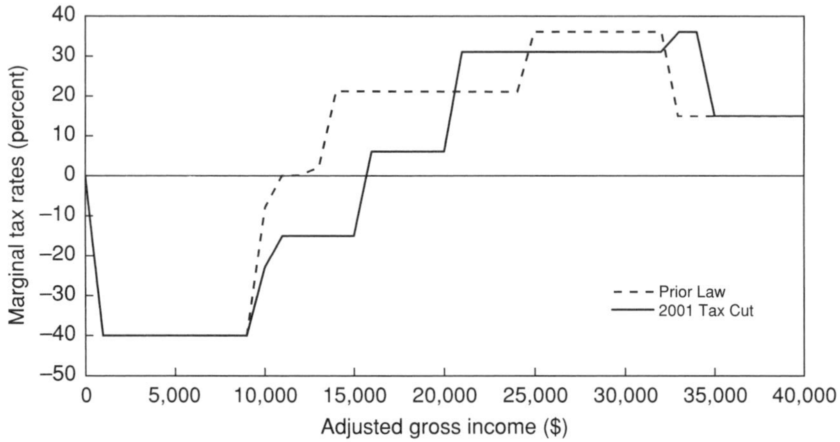

Source: Sammartino, Steuerle, and Carasso (2001).

2000; Feenberg and Rosen 1995; Rosen 1987; Sammartino, Steuerle, and Carasso 2001; Sawhill and Thomas 2001). With significant growth in low-income relief in recent years, more than one-third of households now pay no net income tax. The only way in a tax bill to allocate some share of a cut to them or to deal with their marginal tax rates, work disincentives, and marriage penalties is through adjustments to refundable credits.

Of course, further coordination across programs would be better. As noted, adjusting refundable credits is really an expenditure, not a tax, fix.[9] Because of both precedent and jurisdictional boundaries among committees of Congress and executive branch departments, however, refundable credits are the only types of expenditures that are coordinated to any extent with taxes.

Estate Taxes and the Alternative Minimum Tax

Two changes in the 2001 legislation on the one hand mitigated, and on the other hand, enhanced, the statutory income tax rate reductions for higher-income taxpayers. First, the 2001 act substantially increased the number of taxpayers subject to paying the alternative minimum tax

(AMT). The Act failed to lower AMT rates even though statutory tax rates were reduced, thus limiting the extent of any net tax cut. For instance, if a household formerly had a regular tax liability of $20,000 and an alternative AMT liability of $19,000, a reduction in the regular tax liability to $18,000 still left the household paying $19,000 by throwing the taxpayer "onto" the AMT.

As figure 11.2 shows, the AMT offset to the 2001 rate reductions hit hardest those taxpayers with $100,000 to $200,000 or $200,000 to $500,000 of income. The very top group is almost immune from the AMT mainly because their statutory tax rates are high enough to keep them on the regular tax ladder. Table 11.2 shows the remarkable number of taxpayers, including nearly all middle-income families with children, who will be paying the AMT by 2005 and by 2010 as a result of the 2001 legislation (and its extension in 2003) if the AMT is not repealed or properly indexed for inflation.

Although the near wealthy get a much lower tax break, on net, because of the AMT, a second change tends to further reduce the taxes that would be owed by the wealthiest taxpayers—the phase-out of the estate tax. This change concentrates tax reduction in the highest income group—much more so than most previous tax cuts, including those of Ronald Reagan. If the effects of this change were also calculated in the distributional tables, almost half of all the tax cuts would go to the very highest-income groups.

Figure 11.2 *The Effect of the AMT on the 2001–2003 Tax Cuts in 2010*

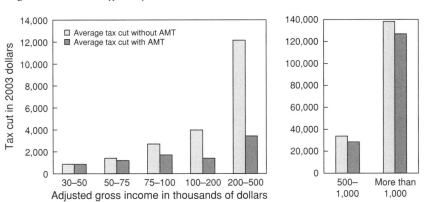

Source: The Urban-Brookings Tax Policy Center Microsimulation Model.

Table 11.2 *AMT Projections for 2005 and 2010*

| | AMT participation rate (percent)[a] | | | |
| | Current law[b] | | Pre-EGTRRA law | |
Characteristic	2005	2010	2005	2010
Tax filers by AGI (thousands of 2002 dollars)				
Less than 30	0.0	0.2	0.1	0.2
30–50	1.5	6.9	1.7	5.0
50–75	9.5	36.6	8.9	19.7
75–100	27.4	72.9	15.6	27.0
100–200	54.3	92.0	15.4	32.2
200–500	83.5	96.2	28.9	48.3
500–1,000	27.4	49.3	12.6	12.2
1,000 and more	18.7	24.1	12.6	12.1
Tax filers by number of children[c]				
0	3.7	15.4	1.1	2.8
1	11.3	29.1	3.0	11.3
2	26.4	44.4	12.5	32.9
3 or more	35.4	50.9	33.0	50.6
Tax Filers by Filing Status				
Single	1.1	2.4	0.5	1.0
Married filing joint	20.9	53.5	9.4	21.7
Head of household	4.0	9.2	3.0	6.9
Married filing separate	18.4	47.1	11.5	19.2
Middle class family, two or more children[d]	65.3	97.2	46.4	84.4

Source: Urban-Brookings Tax Policy Center Microsimulation Model.

Notes: AGI = adjusted gross income; AMT = Alternative Minimum Tax; EGTRRA = Economic Growth and Tax Relief Reconciliation Act of 2001.

a. Includes returns with AMT liability on Form 6251 and those with lost credits.

b. Includes the Job Creation and Worker Assistance Act of 2002 and the Jobs and Growth Tax Relief Reconciliation Act of 2003.

c. Number of children is defined as number of exemptions taken for children living at home.

d. Refers to married joint filers with two or more children and AGI between $75,000 and $100,000.

The phase-out of the estate tax has divided America's wealthiest income classes. Bill Gates, Sr., the father of one of the world's wealthiest people, spoke for thousands of other wealthy individuals who signed onto a petition to oppose the estate tax's repeal. He argued that that the super-rich have an obligation to share their large gains with other members of society. On the other side were such economic titans as heirs to the Gallo wine and Mars candy fortunes (Gates and Collins 2002a; Weisman 2003). One prominent pro-repeal family, the Blethens, who own the *Seattle Times,* rallied more than 75 newspapers across the nation to run "death tax" ads (www.deathtax.com was created and is run by the *Seattle Times*). Pollsters working for the anti-estate tax crowd bragged that labeling the estate tax the "death" tax worked wonders on swaying fence sitters to their views. Note, however, the wealthy are not taxed on their estates except to the extent they make transfers to their family or other persons. After all, with a charitable deduction, they can still largely influence society, and government gets nothing if estates are left to charity.

Poll data reveal some interesting aspects of the wealthy class's political leanings. Compared with the past, by 2000, a much larger percentage of that class no longer identified themselves as Republican, abandoning a longstanding political stronghold (Brooks 2000; Connelly 2000; Starobin 1998). One reason may be that income tax rate reductions had already reduced their stake in further tax cuts. Then, too, newer wealth has accrued in such fields as technology, health, entertainment, and law, where well-heeled professionals tend to be more positive about the role of government.

This novel political realignment notwithstanding, the 2001 tax cuts gave only moderate cuts to the near wealthy relative to the wealthy. For the former, increases in the AMT offset most of their tax cuts. The poor and lower-middle class won some benefits, and the very rich got a sizable share of the cuts, especially if the estate tax elimination is made permanent.

Terrorism, Economic Slowdown, and Revenue Shortfall

The collapse of the World Trade Center towers remains the most enduring image of 2001—an act of inexplicable terrorism. Prior to the attack, various economic projections indicated that, even with passage of a tax bill, the nation's budget would still run surpluses for a while—at least until far more baby boomers retired. President Bush had claimed that his 2001 tax cut would use up only a portion of the surplus, still leaving enough aside to bank the temporary Social Security surplus and to meet unforeseen contingencies.[10] Not long afterward, those very optimistic surplus projections had to be abandoned. A modest economic slowdown combined with a slump in stock prices to produce an unprecedented fall in revenues.

The terrorism threat and the economic slowdown gave Congress and the president excuses to throw budgetary caution to the wind. The pay-as-you-go budget rules, which had survived in tattered form since 1990, were now essentially shoved aside in almost all legislation. On the expenditure side, spending rose to meet new needs, real and perceived. Generous farm subsidies and defense increases totally unrelated to forestalling terrorism passed handily, and some social spending bills got expensive boosts, too. One Congressional Budget Office study indicated that the fiscal 2003 deficit alone increased by about $70 billion thanks to discretionary spending.[11] The administration wanted to show it was still concerned about the economy. And tax cuts were its vehicle, once again, even though the cumulative shortfall in revenues was starting to balloon.

The end result was the Job Creation and Worker Assistance Act of 2002. The act provided for additional temporary unemployment assistance, extended tax relief to New York City in the wake of the terrorist attack, and, once again, renewed some expiring provisions. Among these were the "Work Opportunity" tax credit, the "Welfare to Work" tax credit, and a deduction for clean-fuel vehicles. In terms of its revenue impact, however, a special depreciation allowance for purchases of certain property, mainly equipment, topped the heap (Joint Committee on Taxation 2002b).

Accelerated Depreciation or "Partial Expensing" of Asset Purchases

Eager to provide an economic stimulus, both Republicans and Democrats supported an immediate deduction or expensing option for some portion of physical capital expenses.[12] This super-acceleration of depreciation allowances proved popular on both sides of the aisle because it immediately provided more money to businesses than it eventually cost the U.S. Treasury.

Getting deductions up front is equivalent to a reduction in effective tax rates, since it is like getting a zero-interest loan from government on taxes otherwise due.[13] It also has a sizable impact on cash flow to the firm. Take a very simple example of an asset costing $1,000 that is normally written off over five years. With an up-front 30 percent write-off of costs, the first-year deduction is allowed to rise to $440 instead of $200. Payback is soon required, however, and more deductions for a particular investment today mean fewer deductions tomorrow. Perhaps the easiest way to think about the incentive is that while the loan is interest free, it still must be repaid to the Treasury coffers. Thus, while the firm deducts $240 extra in the first year, it deducts $240 less in following years ($96 of which falls in the second year).[14]

Many advocate the practice of accelerating depreciation allowances as a way of reducing taxes on capital income. In particular, some consumption tax advocates embrace any precedent for expensing or moving toward 100 percent write-offs of cost the first year, since this is one step toward transforming the income tax to a consumption tax. But those who like to pump money into the economy temporarily to stimulate growth may be happiest of all: the cash infusion they get is large relative to the amount of eventual revenue loss. In effect, supply-siders ("lower effective marginal tax rates"), consumption tax advocates ("expensing investment"), and the Keynesians ("getting more money sloshing around") all found reasons to support the temporary partial expensing of physical capital investment.

Unfortunately, none of these camps paid much attention to the problems that will plague the payback period. Encouraging firms to move capital investment into the qualifying period, for instance, can easily slow down capital investment once the qualifying period ends. Moreover, if a temporary incentive lasts three years, the acceleration of investment into the qualifying period is more likely to occur later in the period. For this reason, the incentive to shift investment into that three-year window could be more powerful than any incentive to increase it, but the shift then could cause a slowdown after the third year. Agreeing to live with a paring of incentives ahead of time could be dangerous if it coincides with a continuing or new economic slowdown.

Still another problem is that the next time there is an apparent slowdown in the economy, business may slow down investment more quickly since it might anticipate that a new incentive will be provided. Thus, just in terms of expectations, the precedent may have future costs.

The classic argument against discretionary fiscal policy is that Congress waits too long to provide incentives. It can't get the timing right. With accelerated depreciation, there is not only a lag of several months between discovery of a downturn and congressional action to start the incentive, but Congress sets the timing for ending the incentive years in advance of any knowledge of what state the economy may be in when it ends. So both removing and activating incentives exacerbate the timing problem.

Two additional costs of this type of incentive bear mention. First, the incentive tends to help established businesses more than new businesses, which generally do not have enough in the way of taxable income to use the extra deductions. Thus, the method serves as a potential threat to innovation. Note that in 1986, tax reformers argued that rate cuts were preferable to old-style accelerated depreciation because the latter favors established firms with taxable income from old investments over new firms and because new temporary allowances add to tax accounting complexity.

The Extraordinary Additional Revenue Shortfall

Between January 2001 and November 2003, the Congressional Budget Office's revenue projection for fiscal year 2003 dropped by about $450 billion, or from 20.8 to 16.6 percent[15]. In one fell swoop, revenues as a percentage of gross domestic product fell from an all-time high to the lowest level they had been since 1959. Yet the new tax laws, with some provisions still to be implemented, accounted for only about one-third of the initial fall-off. Nor was the economic slowdown to take full blame. The CBO projections indicated that the decline in economic growth forced receipts down by $144 billion. Meanwhile capital gains realizations fell precipitously (capital gains distributions from mutual funds alone dropped by about 80 percent) and—due to fewer stock options, less incentive pay, and so forth—the income distribution became more equal.

The total revenue drop was extraordinary by any stretch of the imagination. Of this, about 1 percentage point was due to the drop in GDP itself (if average rates had stayed constant) and the rest due to the drop in average rates. Meanwhile, state and local revenues plummeted as well. The total drop in the government's deficit actually exceeded the total drop in national output! This was a level of stimulus, as measured by change in government cash flow, that defied any historical standard and would be almost impossible to repeat in any downturn for the near future. And there was more to come.

Still More Stimulus in 2003

In mid-2002, the economy picked up steam again, only to slow modestly late in the year and in the first part of 2003. More important, however, was the failure of the unemployment rate to fall, and the employment rate to rise faster, along with the recovery in economic growth. Correctly or not, blame for the former President Bush's political defeat was laid on his lack of a strong domestic policy to combat the 1990 recession. Paying heed to this sentiment, the administration of the younger Bush was determined to not take this slowdown sitting down—even though it was becoming clearer that the economy was already back on at least a modest growth path. Further, a U.S. invasion of Iraq in 2003 complicated both the political and economic picture.

For the third year in a row, the domestic agenda was topped by a tax cut emphasizing lower rates and reduced capital costs. First, the administration proposed accelerating some tax cuts enacted in 2001—in particular, the rate reductions and child credit. Its biggest new initiative was relief from the double taxation of corporate income: income that was taxed once at the corporate level would no longer be subject again to tax when paid out as dividends and capital gains. A third set of initiatives was designed to simplify some complex retirement plan and saving provisions, but soon expanded to dramatically increase opportunities to put away money in individual and retirement accounts. These tax-simplification proposals soon morphed into something resembling a consumption tax on the individual receipt side, but not the deduction side, by allowing almost all saving to receive the treatment formerly confined mainly to tax-favored retirement accounts.[16] However, interest deductions—and huge arbitrage opportunities—would still be allowed (Steuerle 2003d). Most of these savings proposals were ignored in 2003, but some were put into other bills for later consideration or resubmitted in various forms in the next year's budget.

After the war in Iraq, there were new calls for humanitarian assistance and money to restore order and help the Iraqi economy recover, while debate fomented over how the United States would engage the new international order. These costs added to the deficit. Although the economy shifted out of recession, the budget offices continued to show a downward slide in revenues during the first part of 2003. Partly because of the deteriorating budget, some Senate Republicans balked at the cost of the administration's proposed tax cut and joined with Democrats to draft a more affordable package.

In the end, the Jobs and Growth Tax Relief Reconciliation Act of 2003 adopted the following provisions, with a variety of expiration dates to hold down cost. The dates, along with the often-high cost of extension to 2013, are shown in parentheses (Gale and Orszag 2003a):

- Increased child tax credit (2004, $56.9 billion)
- Expanded 10 percent bracket (2004, $46.4 billion)
- Tax breaks for married couples (2004, $26.5 billion)

- Temporary increase in the alternate minimum tax exemption (2004, $244.5 billion)
- More favorable depreciation rules for small business (2005, $12.5 billion)
- Expanded (50 percent write-off) depreciation for corporations (2004, $170.5 billion)
- Lower dividends and capital gains tax rates (2008, $164.9 billion)

Like so many congressional actions, this act copied or repeated what had been done in other recent legislation. Much of the cost in 2003 and 2004 derived largely from accelerating into that year the various rate reductions, child credits, and tax breaks for married couples already scheduled in 2001. At the same time, reform of the alternative minimum tax was deferred, but some temporary alleviation was provided through an increase in the exemption level.

Despite accelerating most of the 2001 tax cuts, Congress refused to accelerate the increased expenditure associated with that (refundable) portion of the child credit that would go to those paying no tax.[17] This led to considerable debate, once again, over progressivity. Interaction between the 2001 and 2003 tax acts also fueled the progressivity debate. By 2003, most of the 2001 cuts that affected low- and middle-income taxpayers had already been phased in. Hence, when the 2003 act accelerated the remainder of the income tax cuts, they were concentrated more on higher-income taxpayers. Of course, in the long run, acceleration of changes makes little difference on distributional estimates. Table 11.1 shows the combined effect of the 2001 and 2003 tax cuts in 2010 by income class.

Congress and the president also used the 2003 act to expand the temporary investment relief provided in the 2002 legislation (Joint Committee on Taxation 2003b). Taxpayers were allowed to write off ever-larger minimum amounts of investment (up to $100,000),[18] and all businesses were now allowed to expense or write off 50 percent of capital investments (even more than the 30 percent allowed under the 2002 legislation). First-year deductions for five-year equipment rose from $240 under normal law and $440 under temporary allowances in the 2002 legislation to $600. Representative Bill Thomas of California, chair of the House Ways and Means Committee, stated that unlike other provisions of this act, this acceleration was clearly meant to be temporary in nature. However, to get money into the economy prior to an election year, Congress effectively scheduled a slowdown for 2005 when the depreciation allowances would end. This acceleration further favored established businesses that have profits already and can make use of the additional tax allowances.

As noted, the new aspect of the 2003 legislation offered relief from the individual taxation of dividends and capital gains. The president had proposed to extend individual relief only for corporate income that had already been taxed once at the corporate level. This back-door attack on tax shelters would have caused some significant accounting changes, but would have been consistent with notions of equity, as well as efficiency. After all, the greatest gains from lowering tax rates—at least from a supply-side perspective—comes from reducing the highest rates of tax. Hence, according to this theory, revenues spent on reducing double taxes improve general welfare much more than do removing taxes on individuals whose income was never subject to double taxation. However, this approach was considered too complex and eventually abandoned.

Instead, capital gains and dividends were taxed at a maximum rate of 15 percent (5 percent for some moderate-income individuals). Since capital gains had been already taxed at a maximum rate of 20 percent before the 2003 legislation, most of the revenue loss applies to dividends.[19] Clearly, some of the revenue loss went toward reducing a double tax on income. Where no corporate tax was paid, however, the bill guaranteed that some capital income would never be subject to more than a 15 percent rate and then only when realized as dividends or capital gains.

The long-term direction for tax policy remained largely unanswered. The plethora of sunsets in the legislation guaranteed future arguments over what should be extended. Indeed, simply extending the provisions of the 2001 and 2003 acts from 2010 to 2013 would more than double the 2004–2013 cost of the tax bills (Concord Coalition 2003; Gale and Orszag 2003a).[20] Not only do the sunsets leave businesses and individuals in doubt as to how to plan their affairs, but they make it extremely difficult for budget analysts at places like the Congressional Budget Office to project the government's fiscal position under current law.[21] What is current law under these circumstances?

Size of the Tax Cuts: A Historical Comparison

Figure 11.3 shows taxes as a percentage of GDP with and without extensions of the 2001 to 2003 tax cuts.[22] The 2001 cut, as finally enacted,

Figure 11.3 *Revenues If 2004 Tax Law Remains Constant*

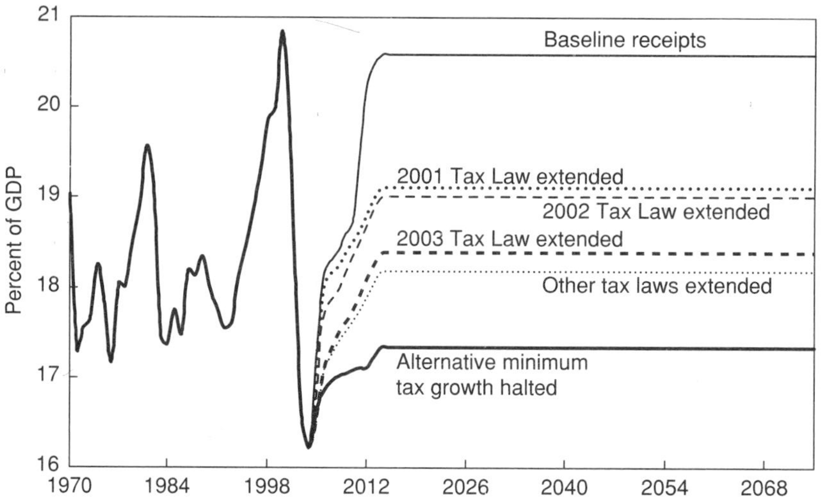

Source: C. Eugene Steuerle, Adam Carasso, and Meghan Bishop, The Urban Institute, 2003. Authors' calculations are based on data from Gale and Orszag (2003a).

turned out to be a bit smaller than what the president had initially pro-posed, but the 2002 and 2003 cuts increased the amounts sizably.

The traditional way of making sense out of the long-term change in direction is to look at costs in a distant year (when the provisions in ques-tion are fully implemented) as a percentage of GDP. Examining the cuts this way is hard because Congress scheduled most breaks to be eliminated after 2010 or 2013, enacted some changes for only a few years, and failed to index the child tax credit or the exemption level in the AMT for infla-tion. Still, roughly speaking, a fully implemented bill like the 2001 legisla-tion would eventually cost about 1.5 percent of GDP per year; the 2002 legislation, about 0.2 percent of GDP; the 2003 legislation, about 0.5 per-cent of GDP; other extensions such as the research and development credit, about 0.2 percent of GDP; and a fix in the AMT (assuming those tax increases were not sought) anywhere from 0.5 to 1.0 percent of GDP. Thus, the total cost can add up to 3.0 percent of GDP or more depending on what is extended and what is not.[23]

How does this figure compare with tax increases and decreases histor-ically? The biggest increases of the 20th century helped finance World

War II and the Korean conflict, while the biggest decreases came in their wake. Since then, total federal revenues as a percentage of GDP have remained remarkably constant. The Reagan tax cut of 1981—often evoked by both proponents and opponents of the Bush cut—would have been about 6 percentage points of GDP, if fully implemented. Thus, relative to the economy, the initial Reagan cut was more than twice as big as the initial Bush tax cut. But, if one adds up all of the tax cuts in Bush's first term, takes into account likely changes in the AMT, and compares them with the tax cuts and increases of Reagan's first term, the two are much more in line.[24]

Besides asking how much a cut will cost over its lifetime, comparing new cuts with the preceding years' tax changes also yields perspective. The Reagan tax cuts were about the same size as the effective tax hikes in the years preceding the cuts. Much of these hikes can be traced back to the substantial bracket creep in the late 1970s, when annual inflation rates sometimes exceeded 10 percent. The increases in marginal tax rates during this earlier inflationary period were especially large for families at about twice the median income (see figures 3.8 and 3.9).

Revenues as a percentage of GDP also rose prior to the 2001 tax cut. One governing factor was the 1993 tax act, but even more important were large increases in realizations of capital gains and stock options due to the stock market bubble. Also, many upper-middle-income and richer families—especially two-earner couples in which both spouses had higher-than-average wages—moved into higher brackets. And finally, average tax rates rose in the years prior to 2001 because of the continuing trend, starting back in the late 1970s, toward unequal distribution of income. For these and other reasons, average tax rates—especially if state and local taxes are counted—rose to a peacetime apex (see chapter 3).

The year 2001 was an unusual year when it came to taxes. At first the Bush cuts appeared to simply reduce the highest peacetime average tax rate (for all receipts) ever achieved, largely due to the tax increases of the late 1990s. However, capital gains realizations and taxes paid by higher-income taxpayers fell tremendously in 2002. In that sense, the tax increases of the late 1990s may have been temporary, as opposed to the increases of the late 1970s, which would have been permanent absent legislation.[25] In any case, by 2004, the country witnessed the lowest level of receipts as a percentage of GDP since 1950—due to an economic slump, as well as the tax cuts themselves. Income taxes, corporate plus individual, reached the lowest level since 1942, but that calculation ignores other taxes, particularly the Social Security tax.

In sum, from a longer-term perspective, the 2001 Bush tax cut, by itself, did not drastically cut tax collections, which remained close to the narrow range of average tax rates typical of the post–World War II period. However, when the 2001 to 2003 tax cuts are added together and extended permanently, the AMT growth halted, and other provisions like the research and development tax credit extended, these tax cuts add up to be as high as 3 percent of GDP and put total tax collections near its lowest point since the end of World War II. Still, receipts as a percentage of GDP have never varied widely over that period, and even the Bush administration by 2004 was suggesting in its budget that some revenue growth would be allowed. From yet another perspective, President Bush has also been the first president in the modern era to preside simultaneously over significant cuts in taxes, defense increases, and domestic policy expansions, and as of the beginning of 2004 he had vetoed virtually no legislation—in contrast to more than 2,500 for his predecessors (Galemore 2003).[26] Whether the cuts were too large given budget obligations, and whether the numbers really added up to a viable long-term budget, are issues that therefore must be weighed along with trends in expenditures and entitlement growth.

The 2003 Medicare Act

Compassionate conservatism came back to the fore in late 2003 with the passage of a bill establishing drug benefits as a part of Medicare. The 10-year cost of the bill was initially listed as $395 billion, but that number was soon raised even though many benefits would not start for several years. The cost in the second ten years was expected to be closer to $1 trillion. Perhaps a better measure of cost is the prediction of annual cost of $75 billion for 2013 alone, rising to $190 billion by 2023 (Holtz-Eakin and Lemieux 2003, 3). Democrats didn't complain so much about the cost but worried that the benefit was too small. But, of course, neither political party indicated how they would pay for the benefit.

In addition to its long-term pressure on budget and taxes, the bill also had a significant side effect. The Joint Committee on Taxation (2003a) estimated that taxes would increase by $4.6 billion in 2013 alone simply because some employers would drop tax-favored health coverage for retirees once the government starts providing drug insurance. Additionally, Congress adopted an employer subsidy aimed at stemming the loss, but budget scorekeepers viewed it as less than fully effective. The employer subsidy itself was designed in a way that violated principles of tax policy, such as efficiency and equity. It was made nontaxable—thus adding to its subsidy value, but only for employers with sufficient taxable income. In effect, the subsidy discriminated against nonprofit organizations, governments, and nonprofit corporations by providing them less subsidy for maintaining retiree coverage.

A less-noticed part of the bill also put into place a new income-based premium on high-income Medicare recipients beginning in 2007. Recalling the last time (1988) that it had tried to impose an extra fee or tax on Medicare recipients (see chapter 7), Congress this time significantly delayed the date of implementation and made the tax conditional upon signing up for part B of Medicare (mainly covering the cost of doctors and tests) (Gould 2003). As opposed to having IRS collect the money, Congress also decided to let the IRS furnish the information on income to Medicare, who would then take the extra fee out of Social Security checks (as an addition to what is now deducted as a flat premium for getting part B coverage). Over a long period of time, this provision is meant to push a number of higher-income elderly into buying their insurance in the private market, which might make them cost conscious—but raising the issue of whether the healthier would be the ones to opt out of Medicare. Whether any of this can be administrated in a reasonable fashion remains to be seen.

Among the more controversial provisions was a new health savings account (HSA) for those under age 65. The accounts have little to do with Medicare. Taxpayers or their employers are allowed to deposit tax-free the deductible on a high-deductible health insurance plan—up to $2,600 for singles and up to $5,150 for families—into one of these accounts. These consumers must also purchase a catastrophic health insurance policy. The money in the accounts may be withdrawn tax-free, both now and in the future, to pay for other health costs not covered by insurance. Unused balances accrue interest in the account, tax-free. The extra savings incentive, of course, favors higher-income taxpayers over those with less income and in lower tax brackets. After age 65, the accounts may be used as a kind of IRA. Withdrawals for nonmedical expenditures are taxed as income, but not subject to the penalty that applies to such withdrawals at younger ages.

The policy argument behind HSAs, as well as some of their related predecessors, such as medical savings accounts (MSAs), is that people who pay directly for some of their health care costs are more cost-conscious than those whose care is covered by insurance. Therefore, HSAs encourage a more efficient market and drive down costs. HSAs convey similar tax benefits for health expenses as employer-provided insurance. (Actually, HSAs provide more benefits because of the preference also given to savings in HSAs.)

But, among the controversies generated are whether HSAs will mainly favor high-income people looking for another tax break for their saving (regardless of health concerns), whether HSA availability will discourage middle- and upper-income individuals from demanding employer-provided health insurance, and whether healthy and wealthy employees will demand high-deductible policies, which will drive up premiums on more comprehensive insurance, ultimately threatening its viability. Since a $5,000 deductible is tantamount to no insurance for people with lower incomes, these individuals might decide to go without insurance, and national insurance coverage rates—already alarmingly low—could decline further (Burman and Blumberg 2003). A contrary argument is that employers, especially small ones or ones not now offering insurance, might find this an attractive way to provide help for employees to buy at least a modest-cost catastrophic insurance policy. Moreover, by making people more cost-conscious, the new system might constrain cost growth and thus reduce the number of uninsured as well.

The simple fact is that no one likes any way of dealing with costs—either imposing it on individuals, using intermediaries like health maintenance organizations (HMOs), or further ratcheting up government controls on prices and quantities, as is done partially under Medicare. HSAs are one more patch, this time leaning toward the first approach. But like so much of what government does in health care, in 2003 it tried once again to buy its way out of the problem by spending even more on people, thus only aggravating the budget situation.

Toward the Future

The combination of deficit concerns and demands on the nation's health and retirement systems will likely once again be the dominant force influencing tax policy throughout the first part of the 21st century. Other forces, including the demands of the international order, are also likely to be powerful, if far less predictable. If we have learned one thing for certain, it is that tax policy is the handmaiden of budget policy. For both federal and state officials, whether Republican or Democrat, a brief holiday from fiscal discipline was declared from about 1997 to 2004, when unexpected surpluses, a recession, and a terrorist attack made tax cuts or expenditure increases politically irresistible. This spending and tax-cutting legislative splurge will be short—a mere few years compared with the two-decade long Easy Finance Era from the end of the Korean conflict to the mid- to late 1970s. For the most part, the new splurge had already ended by 2003 at the state level, where legislators enacted tax increases, avoided tax decreases, and constrained spending growth (Jenny 2003). Those elected at the federal level, however, were still trying to make it through the 2004 election. The retirement of the baby boomers will force many tough choices, likely to be reflected in legislation over many years, while the worldwide aging of societies will change economies in unpredictable ways. Elected officials more than ever will have to worry about how to pay for their promises, which now extend further into the future and pledge to support larger portions of the population through government coffers than at any time in the nation's history.

The squeeze between higher retirement and health spending and lower levels of tax revenues, therefore, will dominate tax and budget policy for years to come. My own calculations show that maintaining the tax and expenditure promises as of 2004, while balancing the budget, will leave nothing for any domestic policy other than retirement and health by 2012. Since such a scenario is impossible, it means either cutbacks in retirement and health program growth, higher levels of revenues, or likely both. Figure 11.4, therefore, is less a trajectory of future spending and revenues than a representation of the level of unsustainable expectations, even in the short run, that government officials had set up by 2004.

Like any tale ending in the present, this chronology must end without climax.[27] One sure expectation is that tomorrow will bring the unexpected. In the final chapter, I will turn to some of the implications of this tale of an ever whirling and contradictory tax policy, where both left and right agree mainly on one thing: using the tax code to try to change the behavior of people and control the direction of government.

Figure 11.4 *The Current Budget Squeeze*

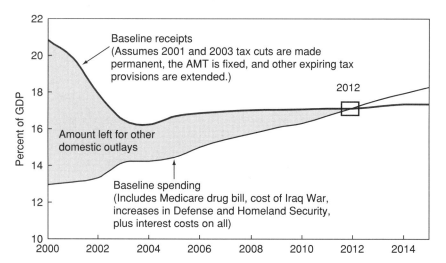

Source: Eugene Steuerle, Adam Carasso, and Meghan Bishop, The Urban Institute, 2003. Authors' calculations based on data from CBO; the U.S. Budget FY 2004; and the 2003 OASDI, HI, and SMI Trustees Reports.

NOTES

1. The mechanism being discussed was a "trigger"—not an easy mechanism to design.

2. I doubt seriously that the vice president believed that any and all deficits do not matter, but the statement seems to discount the possibility that the costs of higher deficits could lead to bigger, not smaller, government, as bills became due. More generally, it is doubtful that even extreme supply-siders believe that deficits "don't matter" when they are caused by higher expenditures. Jude Wanniski, who proclaims himself as the "primary political theoretician" in the supply-side camp, had begun arguing for what he called a "two Santa Claus" policy as early as 1974. However, it is not clear that he thought both Santa Clauses (tax cuts and expenditure increases) would show up at the same time. He felt that tax cuts would provide the economic growth to make the deficit less onerous.

3. See Kiefer et al. (2002). Major reasons that not all taxpayers saw their marginal rates cut were that many remained in the 15 percent bracket and that others remained at the same marginal tax rate under the AMT.

4. For greater discussion of these issues, see Steuerle (2002a) and Steuerle (2003a).

5. What made this particular compromise possible was that the tax-writing committees of Congress have jurisdiction over these particular spending programs (the refundable portions of credits).

6. This is the same rate that applied under the 2003 legislation, which merely accelerated the point at which the lower rates applied.

7. See Burman, Maag, and Rohaly (2002) for the details of how the 2001 tax cuts affected families with children.

8. The final act included a provision that was close to an option first put forward by Sawhill and Thomas (2001).

9. The compromise in the 2001 legislation allowed some refundability starting at $10,000—close to the level of income where the EITC was fully phased in. The administration itself had proposed increases in child credits and a new 10 percent tax bracket so that positive income tax rates would not be faced generally below about $32,000. At this income level, the EITC would have fully phased out (i.e., its 21 percent phase-out rate would not then combine with the lowest tax rate in the income tax rate schedule). In general, the 2001 legislation did tend to lower marginal tax rates and reduce marriage penalties for many low-income individuals, although they were raised for others.

10. From 2002–2011, the tax relief was estimated to comprise only 29 percent of the baseline surplus. See OMB (2001, 499).

11. These figures have been updated from Steuerle (2003b). Author's calculations based on data from the Congressional Budget Office's "The Budget and Economic Outlook: An Update (August 2003)."

12. This subsection is taken largely from Steuerle (2002b).

13. In some economic models, an immediate 30 percent write-off of capital expenses is equivalent to a reduction in the effective rate of tax on that capital of about 22 percent, from approximately 35 percentage points to 27.4 percent. The calculation is provided by Alan Auerbach (note to author).

14. Without any special expensing provision, the law allowed year-to-year write-offs for "five-year" equipment of 20, 32, 19.2, 11.52, 11.52, and 5.76 percent. With 30 percent expensing, the write-offs change to 44, 22.4, 13.44, 8.064, 8.064, and 4.032 percent. With 50 percent expensing (made available in 2003), the write-offs become 60, 16, 9.6, 5.76, 5.76, and 2.88 percent. Six years of deductions are required for five-year equipment because the equipment is assumed to be put into commission at mid-year.

15. Portions of this section are taken from Steuerle (2002f).

16. The proposals also would convert new forms of saving into Roth-like vehicles where there was no up-front deduction (hence, saving on near-term budgetary costs), but no taxation of income from capital in the accounts.

17. The refundable portion was already being phased in at 10 percent. Congress refused to accelerate to 2003 the 15 percent rate at which refundability was eventually allowed.

18. The special exemption also phased out at $400,000 rather than $200,000 of income.

19. Also, some capital gains rate reductions lead to increases in capital gains realizations, thus reducing the revenue impact. This was especially true for temporary reductions in tax rates.

20. The Concord Coalition bases its estimates mainly upon Gale and Orszag (2003a).

21. Economic modelers also are left in a quandary as to defining what is permanent and temporary tax policy.

22. Portions of this section and the two succeeding sections are taken from Steuerle (2001a).

23. The calculations are the authors based upon various data reported at www. taxpolicycenter.org. See also Gale and Orszag (2003b) and Orszag, Kogan, and Greenstein (2003).

24. But it's not quite that simple. The Reagan individual tax rate brackets were not indexed for years before 1985, so there was some bracket creep between 1981 and 1984. Also, in 1982, Congress passed a bill that halted implementation of some of the long-term changes built into the Reagan tax cut, and in 1983 and 1984 it also increased taxes. In the case of the Bush tax cuts, just the opposite happened: more tax cuts were enacted in 2002 and in 2003. Then again, the Bush tax cuts still are not permanent. A final verdict on which president presided over the larger set of tax cuts may never be possible.

25. Once one moves up in brackets because of inflation, one generally doesn't move down. But tax increases due to unusually high levels of stock valuation relative to GDP are likely to be temporary.

26. Galemore (2003) lists 37 for Clinton, 44 for George H. W. Bush, 78 for Reagan, 31 for Carter, and so on. The last president with no vetoes was James Garfield.

27. Continuing developments can be followed at www.taxpolicycenter.org, a joint center run by the Urban Institute and the Brookings Institution.

12

Who Won?

We don't pay taxes. Only the little people pay taxes.
—Leona Helmsley, wife and heir to a real estate tycoon

Whether "good" tax policy has won out over time is worth closer examination in this final chapter. The history outlined in this book makes it possible to reflect broadly on the success or failure of various tax theories or advocacy groups in influencing policy developments, and to look at how competing tax theories have combined to produce contemporary tax policy.[1] This chapter does not promote some particular school of thought or set of policy choices, even though the public, through its representatives, must directly or indirectly make such choices. Based on what this history reveals about the extraordinary and continual demands that legislators and the public place on the tax system, I conclude that the primary tax reform agenda is not centered on enacting some pure form of taxation. Instead, the more fundamental issue for tax policy—and the budget policy that constrains it—is how to evolve with shifting needs and democratic sentiments. This chapter, therefore, examines some of the steps necessary to develop a "good" policy process that is broadly based upon principles to the neglect of none and leaves adequate flexibility for future voters to respond to the needs of their own time. But first, here is a brief recap of the overarching tax policy trends of the past half-century.

The 1950s—Codification of the Modern Income Tax System

The adoption of the Internal Revenue Code of 1954 codified or recodified many practices, regulations, and laws that had evolved previously, including many of the major exclusions from tax that had never formally been approved by legislation. Progressives and traditional tax reformers exerted strong influence during this period by making the World War II build-up in taxes more permanent. Business interests and those promoting capital attained a moderate acceleration of depreciation allowances, while the corporate tax rate was kept well below the top individual rate. But bigger government seemed here to stay: taxes were reduced only moderately relative to wartime increases. After the Korean conflict, average federal tax rates never fell nor rose much relative to gross domestic product—a story that remains true even today. Meanwhile, in backing Social Security tax rate (and benefit) increases, President Eisenhower added a Republican imprimatur to that system, and, indeed, for at least the next couple of decades, the political parties competed over who could next propose another benefit increase for the elderly.

The 1960s—Macroeconomic Issues to the Fore

President Kennedy was the first president effectively to advocate the use of tax policy primarily for non-revenue purposes—a step that would have repercussions ever after. Although British economist John Maynard Keynes had pushed for a more activist fiscal policy in the 1930s, it took three decades before a macroeconomic rationale (that is, temporarily higher deficits to spur demand, lowered cost of capital to spur new investments) would drive U.S. tax legislation. While Keynesian theory technically touted expenditure increases to stimulate demand, U.S. macroeconomic policy centered largely on the tax code and, in particular, on rate cuts and investment credits.

As a matter of budget policy, it didn't matter greatly whether the Keynesians were right to claim that the Kennedy round of tax cuts would generate additional growth. Even subnormal growth would have been sufficient to wipe out temporary deficits eventually, as revenues increased relative to fixed expenditure levels. At the time, most government expenditures were discretionary. Only later would non-discretionary retirement and health programs come to both dominate federal expenditures and grow without new legislation faster than the economy or revenues; even higher economic growth, normally a cure for budget deficits, only made retirement and health programs grow more rapidly. During the Kennedy round of tax cutting, congressional leaders gave the administration a choice between promoting traditional tax policy principles, such as equity and efficiency, and cutting taxes to spur the economy—but not both. It chose tax cuts.

The 1970s—Coping with Stagflation

Escalating inflation and slower economic growth began to dampen enthusiasm for Keynesian policy. The combination of high tax and inflation rates helped prompt misdirection of investment resources toward less productive capital and to stagflation. Tax policy adjustments were varied. As inflation drove up average and marginal tax rates, legislated tax cuts came in ever-greater profusion, but couldn't keep up with tax increases due to inflation. In fact, the decade's most significant tax changes—the steep increase in marginal tax rates on individual income for upper-middle classes and the large percentage increases in local and state real estate taxes—were not legislated directly. Both were driven by high inflation—in the former case, leading to significant bracket creep and, in the latter, to higher property values partly because of huge tax-arbitrage opportunities for property secured by borrowing.[2] In terms of macroeconomic policy, economists and government officials increasingly began to turn toward monetary policy, although it wasn't until the end of the decade that Paul Volcker, as chair of the Board of Governors of the Federal Reserve System, began to reign in ever-rising inflation.

The 1980s—Tax Reform and Lower Rates

The Tax Reform Act of 1986 stands out as the most significant traditional tax reform in the history of the income tax—by one measure, over $200 billion of tax expenditures annually were exchanged for lower rates. But much more than an acceptance of traditional reform principles was at play: President Reagan's opposition to high tax rates also influenced the reform. The acceptance of business tax reform with lower rates and fewer investment incentives in many ways reflected the movement from an economy based on physical capital to one in which human capital, technology, and information were dominant. From 1982 to 1987, the income tax went through more base broadening and traditional tax reform than at any other time in its history.

The tax revolt against higher real estate and income taxes (largely due to 1970s inflation) had played itself out at the state level mostly in the late 1970s and at the federal level with the so-called Reagan Revolution. In 1981, President Reagan lowered tax rates by 23 percent and further accelerated cost recovery for depreciable assets. The 1981 act also retained an investment credit as the primary tax incentive for physical capital investment. Outside of the tax cuts in 1981 and the roughly revenue-neutral Tax Reform Act of 1986, almost all significant tax changes for the rest of the decade—indeed, until well into the 1990s—were driven by budget demands to raise revenue.

The 1990s—Backseat to Budget and Expenditure Policy

This period is one of the hardest to characterize. Almost all of the battles of the previous decades—over high tax rates, progressivity, capital gains taxation, the use of the tax code for macroeconomic and non-revenue purposes—were reengaged. Politically, the arguments became shriller even though voter apathy reigned. How to eliminate the deficit defined tax policy debates for most of the decade, until the question of what to do with the surplus was raised at the decade's end. Thus, the decade is bracketed by deficit-reduction and surplus-reduction efforts.

In the early 1990s, statutory tax rate increases fell primarily upon the top earners in the income distribution. Then, in the mid-1990s, top earners saw their share of tax payments grow along with their significant gains in income, capital gains, and stock options. At the same time, social spending and expenditure policy were implemented more and more through the tax code—symbolized, for example, by the growth in earned income tax and child credits.

The Early 2000s—Domestic Policy as Defined by Tax Cuts

This period started out with tax-rate cuts as the primary domestic policy initiative of President Bush and Congress. At first, tax cuts were suggested as a way to spend what appeared to be a potentially large surplus.

Later, as the surplus evaporated and the deficit rose significantly, tax cuts were sold as a stimulus. The emphasis was clearly on supply-side considerations, with individual rate reductions and reduced taxes on capital income accounting for 60 to 100 percent of revenue losses legislated in 2001 through 2003. The 2001 act focused on cuts in the top rates—the very rates that had seen tax increases in the 1990s—but, more broadly, the act reduced tax rates on most earners across the income spectrum. Tax cuts remained the primary domestic policy response to almost everything, even after a terrorist attack, wars in Afghanistan and Iraq, a recession, a temporary stock market plunge, a dramatic fall in revenues, and predictions of large deficits stretching far into the future. The period was also the first, at least in the contemporary era, to witness significant tax cuts, defense spending increases, and domestic spending increases all at the same time.

Although it is still too early to see through the haze of the first decade of the 21st century, some trends can be perceived. Family policy increasingly became the focus of groups attempting to reform the tax code, with refundable child credits as the latest manifestation of their success. Some shuffling sounds—Treasury studies, press attention, public outrage— perhaps indicate movement toward broadening the tax base, simplifying tax policy, attenuating the growth in the alternative minimum tax (AMT), increasing compliance, and going after the latest wave of tax shelters. Exacerbating the deficit has been the combination of tax cuts with new spending initiatives for farm support, defense, homeland security, drug benefits, and many other items. But that combination inevitably portends greater future pressure on all parts of the budget, including revenues.

The Tenacity of Tenuous Tax Theories

Figuring out whether good tax policy transpired over these past decades depends on how you define "good tax policy." Do you adhere to the arguments of those who want to use the tax code for revenue raising, economic, or social policy purposes? Do you accept the traditional arguments for a broad base and low rate? Do you favor income taxes over consumption taxes or some blend of the two? Do you limit the use of the tax code to conduct expenditure policy? Do you tend to be Keynesian, supply-side, pro-capital, or none of the above? Or do you simply want lower taxes on capital gains and estates no matter what? Each of these camps has won some battles and lost some. None has really laid down its sword in defeat, and each reasserts itself whenever tax policy climbs back on the agenda.

Traditional Tax Reformers

The legislative heyday of traditional tax reformers was from 1982 to 1987, when both broad-based tax reform and some budget bills attempted to tax different sources of income or consumption more equally, and to treat those with equal incomes similarly. Some traditional tax reformers seem to maintain hope that the type of large-scale reform that occurred in 1986 can and will occur intermittently. Many of the principles these reformers favor—efficiency, equal justice or equal treatment of equals, and simplicity—should hold regardless of the size of government, the progressivity of the tax system, the level of capital taxation, or the extent of macroeconomic fiscal policy employed.

Traditional tax reformers don't easily fit in a conservative or a liberal camp. In the past, their favored type of reform was often associated with progressives. Yet some of their strongest adherents were economists such as Henry C. Simons at the University of Chicago, whose economics department has often been viewed as conservative. While this traditional approach has always had some sway, lately it has had to operate mainly in the background. For the Clinton administration, reducing the budget deficit or enhancing progressivity almost always carried more weight than traditional tax principles such as equal justice or efficiency.[3] For the George W. Bush administration, lower rates were the main goal.

Still, almost all major tax bills, even those that provide tax breaks to special interest groups, contain many provisions aimed at creating equal justice, reducing disparities in taxation, and simplifying taxes. Thus, even when the net change in any particular bill could be considered anti-reform, traditional tax principles keep rearing their heads. When special preferences prevail, issues such as equal justice can't be avoided entirely. For example, when one type of energy production is favored, usually all producers of that type are subsidized in an equal way that still encourages the most efficient producer among them.

Tax Expenditure Theorists

All modern presidents have used the tax code to enact new subsidies, whether for business or social policy. These subsidies could have been designed as direct expenditures, as they essentially served the same purpose: a cash bonus for the taxpayer. But then they would have been "counted" as larger government through higher outlays rather than smaller government through lower taxes. Some opponents of tax expenditures would say that even exceptions for medical expenses or charitable contributions are inconsistent with a pure tax system. However, few people today accept such a pure version of tax-expenditure theory.

Tax reform in 1986 successfully replaced many tax expenditures with lower rates, but mainly with respect to business incentives. Since 1986, the number of tax expenditures has grown, especially in the arena of social and middle-class entitlements (see figure 3.3). The full impact of ever-expanding tax breaks has been attenuated by lower rates, a situation that has still made the "expenditure cost" of many of these breaks less than they otherwise would have been.

Certainly, winners from the proliferation of tax breaks and expenditures include special interests—rich, middle-class, and poor alike—who got their special provisions enacted along with other changes. The crafting of large bills allows each member to put in one or two items to favor campaign contributors or home constituencies—a less-than-pretty aspect of democracy hardly confined to tax legislation alone.

Consumption Tax Theorists

Consumption tax theorists usually adhere to traditional tax principles, but would tax equally those with equal consumption rather than those with equal incomes. Many are quite willing to preserve progressivity in the tax system as a whole (Bradford 1984, 1996a, b; McCaffery 2003; Shaviro forthcoming). Perhaps their strongest argument is that, among equal earners, it is unfair to tax more those who save more—since savers pay the extra tax on their income from saving. This raises the question of what to do with those who do not consume all their income and wealth during a lifetime. Some economists would accept an inheritance or estate tax as a means of taxing equally those with equal lifetime incomes or endowments, even though they would tax only consumption while the individual is alive.[4]

Consumption tax advocates and theorists of all types face large hurdles. Some of them especially do not like the ways that the current income tax system favors owner-occupied housing over other forms of capital investment.[5] Attacking tax breaks for owner-occupied housing, however, does not resonate well with the public. Politically, it is difficult to change the treatment of debt—either by denying deductions for interest payments or counting borrowing as a taxable event—as consumption tax theory requires. Further, a pure consumption tax would remove incentives for pension saving so as to treat the return from all types of saving the same way. But does it make sense to remove retirement plan incentives in an economy where a large proportion of the population already saves little for retirement? Although some, such as the anti-tax lobbyist Grover Norquist, argue that recent tax breaks for capital income move toward a consumption tax, others suggest just the opposite: since borrowing is still favored, these special tax breaks reward game playing more than saving.

Another major hurdle for consumption tax advocates is created by all the back-door income taxes derived from the phase-out of such benefits as the earned income tax credit (EITC), food stamps, and college aid. If these programs continue to base eligibility on income, then the nation still effectively has taxes on income and the need to have in place most or all of the reporting systems that attribute income to individuals. Simply switching from an income to a consumption tax while maintaining all these extra income tax "systems" would reinforce the awkward result already prevalent to some extent in current law—a combined tax and expenditure system that tends to reward saving by those who are relatively well-off but to penalize saving by those with low or moderate income.

One compromise between consumption and income taxation would be to displace some of the income tax with a base level of consumption tax.[6] A version of this approach was suggested by the Treasury Department under the administration of President George H. W. Bush. Some tax economists and lawyers (Graetz 1997) suggest adopting a value-added tax (VAT) for the vast majority of the population, with a moderate income tax rate of, say, 20 to 25 percent for those with incomes above $75,000 or $100,000.[7] This compromise would deliver most people from the complicated world of income taxes and remove any tax on their capital income. However, two additional issues arise with this compromise. One is whether it would be worthwhile administratively to graft yet another tax system, such as a VAT, onto the income and Social Security systems. Another is whether the compromise would hold, or whether income taxes would slowly expand to apply to more and more taxpayers (for instance, if real bracket creep is allowed to pull more of them back into the income tax system).

The Keynesians

This activist group reached its heyday in the 1960s. Still, even in the 1970s, Keynesians wielded significant influence, and both Republicans and Democrats pushed for tax cuts to stimulate the economy. In 1981 and 2001, however, presidents pushed tax cuts without much regard for the economic cycle—although, in both cases, a succeeding recession allowed them to claim excellent (almost Keynesian, although they would never use the word) timing for their tax cuts. By the same token, in the deficit reduction period from about 1982 to near the end of the 1990s, tax increases were pushed without much regard for economic cycles. Furthermore, the large deficits projected for the first part of the 21st century may also deter counter-cyclical revenue cuts in times of economic slowdown.

Still, the Keynesians continue to reassert themselves, especially when growth slows or turns negative. Pushed in 2003 to do some "dynamic scoring"—showing how lower rates might lead to greater economic growth through supply-side effects—the Congressional Budget Office and the Joint Committee on Taxation released the results of several models, whose researchers felt compelled by the evidence to include some Keynesian demand effects, at least in the short run. (Even when abandoned in the United States, Keynesian policy is pushed abroad. The Clinton and George H. W. Bush administrations, for instance, often jaw-boned Japan to deal with its economic slowdown by lowering taxes and pumping more money into the economy.[8]) Nor have only its adherents pursued Keynesian policy. President George W. Bush's administration argued many times that its early 2001, 2002, and 2003 tax cuts were fortuitously timed to fight the recession that began later in 2001 and to boost otherwise inadequate growth.[9] The 2001 tax cut even included an early one-time rebate of taxes that added considerably to tax return filing errors (IRS 2002)—a move that had nothing to do with changes in incentives but a lot to do with typical Keynesian pump priming. Similarly, in 2003 taxes were cut to spur the economy.

Counter-cyclical fiscal policy—larger deficits when the economy slows and smaller deficits when it grows faster—reigns even without new or activist tax legislation. One reason for this is that current government is so large that fiscal responses, such as significantly lower taxes in economic downturns, occur automatically and without legislation (government was much smaller when Keynes originally pushed for more discretionary action). With monetary policy reacting quickly in the short run, automatic fiscal stabilizers doing their work, and discretionary and automatic expenditure policy also meeting new needs, discretionary Keynesian tax policy—even when applied—is often one of the lesser players at the table. Meanwhile, downturns have been less severe in recent decades, so less response is required.

Even so, the push for more discretionary stimulus is unending. One telling sign of the extent to which the stimulus argument has become politicized and oversimplified is that seldom, if ever, do advocates estimate what is supposed to be the right amount of stimulus needed well ahead of an economic downturn or the appropriate deficit level under alternative circumstances.[10] The argument for more stimuli in 2002 and 2003, when deficit increases were already larger than the falloff in GDP, exemplifies attempts to shoot without a target (of course, in part this was the Keynesian stimulus argument backing up a supply-side agenda). Nor do many political advocates make improving the automatic side of the system a priority, even though doing so would answer numerous criticisms of fiscal policy, such as Congress's inability to make discretionary changes fast enough and balance the response over the economic cycle. Thus, much of Keynesian advocacy is more political than economic—an attempt to "do something" when there is a downturn. That political need is not likely to go away.

Supply-Side Theorists

Like some Keynesians who never found an economic condition that more tax cuts couldn't help, some supply-side theorists never found a year in which a lowered tax rate couldn't boost the supply of capital and labor—never mind the untoward effect on the deficit and government's absorption of private saving. Many supply-siders emphasize the top rate of taxation, and here they clearly won many major battles. The top income tax rate dropped from 90 percent in the years after World War II to 70 percent under President Kennedy, to between 28 and 33 percent under President Reagan, then back toward 40 percent under President Clinton, and down again to 35 percent under President George W. Bush.

If high marginal tax rates are a priority for supply-siders, then one wonders why their intensity doesn't shift more from the top income group. In particular, those with very low earnings continue to face very high marginal tax rates of up to 100 percent or more as their food stamps, Medicaid, child care, earned income tax credits, and housing allowances are phased out. High penalty rates also apply to some who get educational aid. The 2001 tax legislation did adjust marginal rates at some low-income levels, but only in the income tax system and not in the expenditure and welfare systems.

Although it cannot be proven, supply-siders' extraordinary emphasis on the very top rate of tax paid by the highest-income taxpayers—and not on the high rate paid by other taxpayers—derives as much from politics as economics. Quite simply, some of the rich fight hard for tax relief and finance research organizations and interest groups with friendly views toward lowering their taxes. Enhancing that push, politicians and the public intuitively grasp what it means to lower the top rate from, say, 50 to 40 percent, but find it more difficult to focus on a drop in an intermediate rate—from 25 to 20 percent, for example—much less focus on multiple calculations of how phasing out various benefits creates a very high effective tax rate on additional income. Supply-siders generally agree with tax expenditure theorists in opposing preferences in the tax code, except when it comes to capital income. Since many of these are favored by their tax-rate-cut allies—both middle-class conservatives and social conservatives—the supply-siders have been less successful in opposing these preferences.

Capital Formation Reformers

Capital formation reformers have won their share of battles. From the 1950s through the early 1980s, they pushed for and got various accelerations of depreciation allowances established, along with the enactment of an investment tax credit in the early 1960s. Then in the 1986 tax reform, these investment incentives were essentially abandoned in exchange for lower tax rates without much change in the cost of capital. Capital formation advocates also won some of the battles associated with inflation over its up-and-down cycle. When inflation increased in the 1950s through 1970s, capital incentives were offered, partly to offset inflation's pernicious effect on the value of depreciation allowances. With little fanfare, declines in the inflation rate during the last two decades of the 20th century increased the value of many depreciation allowances, thus lowering the cost of capital without legislation (Gravelle 2004). Capital formation reformers also succeeded at the beginning of the 21st century in temporarily obtaining an allowance to write off (rather than depreciate) 30 percent (in 2002 legislation) and 50 percent (in 2003 legislation) of the up-front cost of capital purchases.

Arguably, depreciation rates are higher now in a tech-based economy, and established allowances don't keep pace with the change. That leaves some debates over depreciation open. At the same time, few lobbying for more accelerated allowances are willing to turn consistently to more scientific measures of actual depreciation. As in many other cases examined here, political goals of capital interests advocates are not always aligned with the economic theories they tout when convenient. Fearing that some assets could turn out to be too favorably treated relative to others, they prefer that information on how long depreciable assets remain in service and whether allowed depreciation matches economic decline in value not be developed systematically for all assets.[11]

Many capital formation advocates align themselves with consumption tax reformers, focusing on expensing—or immediately writing off—purchases of physical capital rather than depreciating them over time. But if these advocates ignore the problem of interest deductions, they end up offering large tax breaks to those who ultimately save little because they simultaneously acquire assets and debt. As noted, with a true consumption tax, borrowing often adds to the tax base, or interest deductions are not allowed.

Capital Gains Advocates

Capital gains advocates want to pay reduced taxes when capital assets are sold. A major measure of their success is that, by 2003, capital gains tax rates were as low as they had been for over 50 years. The full taxation of capital gains, enacted as one of the compromises of the Tax Reform Act of 1986, did not last long. But the realization of gains is often a portfolio choice to sell one asset and buy another: more realizations of gains when capital gains rates are reduced proves little about whether more saving or work occurs when statutory rates are lowered. Think of the taxation of capital gains as a toll charge. With lower tax rates, more individuals are willing to pay the toll to diversify their portfolios. In fact, relief on capital gains already accrued helps make spending that income cheaper than continued saving![12]

The issue of capital gains taxation is one of the most vexing in all of tax theory (Burman 1999). In the aggregate over several decades, capital gains approximately equal the sum of gains due to inflationary increases in the value of all assets plus increases in the value of corporate stock due to retained earnings already subjected to corporate tax (Halperin and

Steuerle 1988). Hence, in aggregate, it may not be necessary to tax individuals' capital gains taxation to tax capital income.

Aggregate analysis of total capital gains in the economy does not tell the full story. Most capital gains recognized upon sales of assets, and most of the benefits of capital gains tax breaks, go to those with very high incomes—that is, the winners in the economic system. The losers, on the other hand, rarely get to deduct the full value of their losses, whether due to inflation or other causes. Yet another complication is that interest deductions are allowed for money borrowed to buy or hold onto assets—often yielding a negative tax rate when the interest is deducted at a high rate and the gains taxed at a lower rate.

Those with substantial capital gains from successful investments want more than a reprieve from double taxation of inflation or corporate earnings already taxed. Ironically, President George W. Bush's proposal in 2003 to remove the double tax on either dividends or capital gains if the income was already taxed at the corporate level would have removed some of the justification for a capital gains preference. Congress, however, extended dividend and capital gains relief even to income never taxed at the corporate level.

Some people recognize little or no gains despite substantial accruals during their life. With elimination of the estate tax, many highly successful people will pay a zero rate of tax on income accrued until death and only a 15 percent rate on that share of gains realized during life. Even that rate is effectively lower than 15 percent since often gains have accrued for years while the tax on those gains has been deferred without interest. In the end, corporate taxes, not individual taxes, have been the major source of taxation of the capital income for most of the nation's richest people. Corporate taxes, too, have been falling in importance over time.

The Progressives

Those who view the tax code as a social policy tool have been a sustained force going back more than a century. Early on, they fought for a fairly progressive income tax and for the removal of tariffs. Since then, no major tax bill has passed without some debate about its progressivity. Even Andrew Mellon, secretary of the Treasury and architect of large income tax rate cuts after World War I, favored progressive taxes (Brownlee 2004; Thorndike 2003).

As historians note, progressivity means different things in different periods. And, as discussed throughout this book, progressivity is usually measured inconsistently in public discussions of government policy. Often, "progressive" taxation means that the average tax rate goes up with income. For expenditures, progressivity is usually measured by whether poorer people get higher absolute benefits. If progressivity is defined as redistribution from richer to poorer members of society, however, then both taxes and expenditures determine progressivity over time regardless of the distribution of rates or absolute benefits in any one program at a time.

As noted, the top statutory rates of income tax have generally fallen since World War II. Is that evidence that progressives have lost the battle? Not really. Congressional Budget Office analysis does not show much change in overall progressivity, as measured by effective or average tax rates, from the late 1970s through the end of the 20th century (see figure 3.7). Those in the middle and higher parts of the income distribution have witnessed only modest changes in their effective tax rates. Meanwhile, the rate on the bottom quintile has dropped substantially to a negative number, if the EITC is counted.

Tax legislation has emphasized cuts over increases in recent decades, but legislation doesn't tell the whole story. Tax increases in 1990 and 1993 were concentrated at the top—and concentrated there much more than were the tax decreases in 2001 and 2003. Consider, more generally, a tax increase followed by a tax cut.[13] The more political side of the progressive movement often argues that the increase shouldn't include any additional tax on the poor and that a larger percentage tax increase should apply at the top, while the cut should give lower- and middle-income classes tax cuts at least a proportionate increase in after-tax income as the rich—which, for those who pay no taxes at all, requires additional expenditures. If such cuts and increases were to take place continually, the net result would be an ever-more-progressive tax system (counting refundable credits). Indeed, additional money was given to the poor in the tax increases of 1990 and 1993, and the tax cut of 2001. In sum, the progressives didn't win all of these battles, especially over the distribution of tax cuts, but when cuts and increases are considered together with automatic changes in the system (such as bracket creep), they won enough battles to keep the overall federal tax system at about the same level of progressivity throughout most of the post-1980 period.

As for the future, assessment of changes in progressivity is further complicated by the temporary reduction in 2003 on the dividends and capital gains tax, which is still concentrated near the top of the income distribution. Offsetting some of these gains might be a shift of investment to the corporate sector, where it is more likely to bear corporate tax. Further confusion comes from uncertainty about whether the temporary investment incentives in 2002 and 2003 for capital purchases will be repeated in future years. The very rich have had significant cuts through reductions in estate taxes, corporate taxes, and capital gains taxes, and, unlike the near-rich, are less subject to bracket creep or the AMT. But many of their tax cuts are precarious or temporary.

Within the tax system, advocates for the poor have actually done quite well. Thanks to increases in the EITC and refundable child credits, tax rates for the lowest-income working families with children have fallen quite significantly. The refundable EITC and child credit make tax rates quite negative for some low-income working families. Of course, most of these credits are expenditures and the right way to measure progressivity would be to measure changes in taxes and all expenditures together. No part of the government produces such statistics, although it is fairly clear that social expenditures to the middle class have expanded significantly over most of the postwar period, largely but not solely due to retirees.

New Challenges and Old

This chapter began by noting that process reform, not adherence to one principle or approach to the exclusion of others, is especially needed at this point in the nation's history. What shouldn't, and in many ways can't, continue is the way tax and budget policy has been made recently. Since 1986, principles have played only a modest role in the crafting of tax legislation. Both the legislative and the executive branch continually put forward internally inconsistent choices, trying in vain to please all constituencies. Our government institutions risk losing their credibility and effectiveness as the traditional principles of equal justice, efficiency, and simplification are neglected in the blind pursuit of political needs and singular priorities, however worthy. Helped along by pollsters skilled at making private greed appear like public need, even the White House, Treasury, and tax-writing committees have increasingly used the tax code to serve special interests instead of the common good.

If the tax policy process stands in need of an overhaul, the budget process requires a whole new vehicle. It simply is too engaged today in giving away the future—before that future has arrived. Health and retirement policies set in motion decades ago leave little money today for discretionary programs that benefit working families and children or meet other societal needs. Tax provisions like Roth IRAs increasingly try to remove further discretion decades into the future. No wonder the public feels that it has such little control over its government: elected officials retired or long dead have determined most of the ways that tax dollars are spent today.

The Retreat from Tax Principles

Bills today are introduced, and often enacted, through a process of almost random reactions to pressures from interest groups and lobbyists. The problem is not that such efforts have no redeeming value. Along with money for campaigns, lobbyists proffer expertise that, however biased, may also be essential to understanding the needs of particular groups and constituents. Lobbyists obtain access by representing powers that legislators cannot ignore and also by mastering the knotty path of tax legislation—one reason those former members of Congress, former congressional and Treasury tax experts, and even former presidential candidates sometimes join lobbyists' ranks. The problem, of course, is that the modern tax policy process gives lobbyists so much heed that disinterested parties—including nonpartisan staffs at places like the Treasury, the Joint Committee on Taxation, the Congressional Budget Office, and the General Accounting Office—often cannot be heard amidst the din created. Sometimes these staffs are so muzzled that their knowledge and information are denied to the public so as not to politically offend somebody somewhere.

Adding further to this retreat from principle, the tax code is now riddled with social and individual expenditures, which often promote the inequitable treatment of equals, distort investment and consumption choices, and boost administrative and enforcement costs for taxpayers or the Internal Revenue Service (IRS). The earliest attacks on using the tax code for subsidies and expenditures came largely from progressives concerned about businesses' tax preferences and the distribution of the tax burden. Then, in 1986, when the choice of lower rates was finally offered in exchange for removing or reducing various tax breaks, many conservatives happily and temporarily joined the ranks of those advocating "base broadening" to achieve lower rates. Today, the budget for tax subsidies and expenditures consists in no small part of middle-class entitlements for individuals (see figure 3.3) that neither progressives nor conservatives are eager to eliminate.

In this milieu, most tax programs—whether subsidies for education, health, pensions, the poor, enterprise zones, commerce, housing, charity, political campaigns, or anything else—are treated *ad hoc,* not as components of a larger policy mosaic. Even a well-considered program based on a good idea can be inefficient or unfair in practice if its details and implementation are not carefully weighed or evaluated. This is part of a broader institutional problem, discussed below.

Among the most slighted principles in recent years is simplification. Joel Slemrod of the University of Michigan estimates that the resources spent on income tax filing alone are equal to about $130 billion a year—about 10 percent of the total income from tax collections. Even these estimates, probably the best available, do not fully account for the true cost of filing to the taxpayer, including the cost of frustration when time is wasted.

This is not an argument for removing every program and subsidy from the tax code. Occasionally, taxes can be used successfully for macroeconomic and social purposes. Some programs, like wage subsidies where reporting wages for tax purposes is essential, might be more easily administered by the IRS than by another agency. However, there is little excuse for the inequities, inefficiencies, and complexities associated with the alternative minimum tax (AMT),[14] layers upon layers of capital gains taxation rates, dozens of complicated retirement and saving subsidies (see appendix table A.5), multiple child credits and allowances, contradictory energy and environmental subsidies, multiple uncoordinated and undirected educational subsidies, and the crazy quilt of sunset clauses applied to tax provisions, to mention only a few. Things have simply gotten out of hand as both major political parties have essentially abandoned traditional tax reform principles.

The Modern Budget Dynamic: Spend It First

Improving tax policy requires minding the budget. Often, budget issues trump tax issues. After all, taxes exist to finance government activity. Yet the lack of budgetary discretion given to elected officials is making governing and legislating much harder. The evidence is overwhelming and reflected in the shrinking share of the budget that is discretionary and subject to annual appropriations.

The name of the game in Washington and most state capitals today is to spend money before somebody else does. Lawmakers don't limit themselves to the money currently in hand. Whatever economic growth might provide for years or decades to come is now fair game. Thus, retirement and health programs are now scheduled to absorb almost all future revenue growth, and if the economy grows faster, then they automatically grow faster also, so as to maintain their grip on a rising share of all resources. Rather than get the budget under control, tax-cutters have joined advocates of program expansion in this dangerous game of pre-spending. Rather than retract untenable promises already made, elected officials compete to make even more unsustainable promises.

Hard as it is to prove, spending ahead in this way has become the most glaring economic problem with federal tax, spending, and budget policy. And there is no end in sight. The implicit inefficiency is obvious when almost all of the population's future needs are assigned priority before most are even known. This practice is equivalent to dictating to our children a list of what they can and cannot consume for decades to come. Thus, we treat future voters as if they are adolescents who cannot be trusted to make wise decisions for themselves, who won't have the sense to vote for the increases in Social Security benefits or for cuts in income taxes we think they need.

Some dismiss this concern. For instance, advocates of maintaining built-in growth in Social Security benefits contend that we can always change the law later, and the tax-cut advocates point out that lawmakers can always raise taxes again. To be sure, some aspects of current law will be overturned, but that chancy prospect is no basis for making expensive promises that might not be fulfilled. Nor is it fair to many people who count on the promised program benefits or tax breaks.

The bottom line is that so much pre-spending on one side and scheduling of future tax cuts on the other takes democracy away from its citizens even as it puts the budget on a collision course. Why let that happen? Why not let tomorrow's voter decide whether taxes should be cut or spending increased tomorrow?

Strengthening Governmental Processes and Institutions

Neither of these two major fiscal problems—the lack of principled tax policy development and the long-range budgetary quagmire—is going to evaporate without dedicated champions. At the same time, waiting for a selfless Congress won't fix the tax policy and budget processes. It requires, first and foremost, an agreement by a large and influential group of elected officials to take action, backed up by strengthened institutions and rules of process. Neither is sufficient by itself. The way to tax reform in 1986 was paved by an agreement between major figures in both parties that something had to be done, along with reform proposals modeled, at least at first, by Treasury and Joint Committee on Taxation staff who were allowed to proceed on the basis of principles. The wrenching march toward smaller deficits from the mid-1980s to late 1990s, in turn, was made possible by bipartisan agreement that something must be done, backed up by modestly successful pay-as-you-go budget rules.

While there is no single way to create a climate that will support traditional tax and budget principles, there are ways to strengthen the governmental institutions and processes responsible for taxation and the budget, so they are prepared for reform opportunities when they arise:

- The *IRS,* first admitting that it does a very poor job at examining the effectiveness of the tax programs and policies it administers, should strengthen its tracking and accountability procedures. For almost every program and subsidy it is called upon to administer, the agency should assemble data and perform studies on compliance, the distribution of program benefits, and at least minimal measures of effectiveness, such as who gets what. Unfortunately, even after its touted modernization around the turn of the last century, the agency still does not profile the beneficiaries of a multitude of tax breaks, ranging from charitable contributions of appreciated property to enterprise and empowerment zones.[15]
- The *Treasury,* in turn, has an obligation to furnish the public with information on various tax policy programs, their successes and failures. There was a day when Treasury testimony much more forthrightly listed the problems with any proposal backed by members of Congress, even at the risk of offending them. Somebody has to do the job of representing the public rather than private interests, and it should be the Treasury, especially since most other executive branch departments are organized to try to appease groups associated with the more narrow functions they serve.[16] The Secretary of the Treasury also needs to take a stand that—barring the president's

direct interventions—appointments to the Treasury are his or hers to make, not that of some political appointee in the White House.

- The *Office of Management and Budget (OMB)* must be restored to a preeminent status in the executive branch, with the capability to deal with broad, crosscutting budget issues. Its small and inadequate economics staff must be built up to the size of the Office of Tax Analysis in the Treasury or the Congressional Budget Office. As a more unified whole, it must be able to examine programs for health, pensions, the elderly, community aid, and so forth—cutting across agencies and avoiding arbitrary distinctions between direct expenditure subsidies and tax subsidies. Like the Treasury, OMB should be known for issuing public studies on what works with programs and what does not. These studies must be in addition to those that are put forward to support the presidential agenda.

- The *Ways and Means* and *Senate Finance Committees* must restore and strengthen the tradition of bipartisan, internal meetings and retreats on issues of important national concern. They must also set up internal processes that insure a greater share of time is spent on obtaining input from the researchers and staff, including their own *Joint Committee on Taxation,* who do not represent any particular interests other than the public. They must also give greater weight to rules that require complexity analyses of bills before they are voted upon.

- Finally, the *congressional budget committees* should be empowered to enforce rules that only through future legislation can any program increase in cost beyond some initial short period—say, four years. Sunset clauses, which require a program to end unless extended by further legislation, should be used to actively force periodic reconsideration of programs. They should not be used simply to hide, say, the cost of what is meant to be a 10-year or permanent program by only paying for the first three years. The moderate success of the 1990 budget rules, extended throughout much of that decade, helped balance the budget temporarily, but those rules are inadequate for now because they applied only to growth in spending through new legislation, not to the built-in growth of old legislation. Since entitlements are now more dominant than in the 1990s, the old rules simply do not cover a large enough portion of the budget. New budget rules must be set up that go beyond those adopted in the past and apply to automatic growth in entitlements and tax subsidies, not just discretionary changes in the laws.

The Opportunities

On a note of optimism, I see two major opportunities arising—one in the tax arena and one in the budget arena. The first will come, one hopes, because the American system's roots are still embedded in principles. The second is far more certain; it will be forced by events, sooner or later, since more has been promised for the future than can possibly be delivered. From a fiscal standpoint, September 11 made clear that there must be enough fiscal slack to meet the unexpected costs of crises.

Occasionally, after leaders take a long vacation from any fundamental principle, it is reasserted in law making. On the tax front, the time once again may be ripe to pay some attention to the virtue of simplicity. So much increased complexity is now programmed into the alternative minimum tax (AMT) that a counterreaction could be the horse on which broader reform rides. It may be politically hard to sell AMT simplification by itself when other principles need attention. AMT reform, moreover, would do little or nothing for all low-income and many middle-income taxpayers. But ignoring AMT's perverse effects on tens of millions of taxpayers will be harder still. For that reason, a wide-reaching reform package advanced by the president may be the only way out of this tax dilemma.

The grand budget compromise that must take place is between those who would allow retirement and health programs to continue to grow without bound and those who would continually prescribe tax cuts into the future. Each side has the right to appeal to voters to move government in one direction or the other, but each also has an obligation to deal with the budget disaster foreordained when both occur simultaneously. What will force some action is the need to maintain other programs dealing with education, jobs, community development, the environment, and so on—those programs now discriminated against in the current budget process and slated to all but disappear if current trends continue. The solution is not to seek some exact mixture of entitlement spending and taxes that will please all present and future voters, but to decide these issues by elections over time. Thus, prudence requires that budget rules constrain both existing policy and policymaking.

A Final Note

This book began by noting that tax policy has become a primary tool used by elected officials to change taxpayers' behavior. It ends by pointing out major forces that are changing the policy world's ground rules, often for the worse, and that must be addressed head on. That said, no single conclusion can or should be drawn about the future direction of tax policy.

Tax policy is not monolithic. Rather, it is a labyrinth of programs exerting influence in almost every sphere of life, and it remains inseparable from the broader budget process. Without question, too much is attempted. The tax system is inefficient and, in many respects, inequitable. Should we strive to align the system with the principles that we embrace as a nation and to make taxation easier to understand, comply with, constructively criticize, and improve? Of course. Even if Americans don't categorically agree on an ideal tax policy, our democratic system still allows us to separate the reasonable from the unreasonable and the just from the unjust. And we can contain the demands of special interests when they are excessive if we stop appeasing them at every turn, while boosting the influence of agencies set up to serve the broad public interest.

Our history of failures is also a history of hope. When the U.S. tax system gets truly out of whack, the political system does respond. When high-income taxpayers or profitable corporations were perceived to be dodging tax in the late 1960s, policymakers made attempts over succeeding decades to get them to pay a fairer share. The proliferation of the tax shelters through the 1970s and early 1980s was reined in during 1982 and 1984, then more thoroughly in the Tax Reform Act of 1986. Even the newer types of tax shelters springing up in the late 1990s and early 2000s have come under congressional and Treasury scrutiny recently. When the budget deficits ballooned in the early 1980s, budget and tax bills in the mid-1980s and 1990s gradually brought deficits to a bearable level, however slowly and oblivious to the impending budgetary impacts of the baby boom generation's retirement.

True, many of those problems could have been anticipated and avoided in the first place. Some of the fixes were not well designed—witness the runaway growth and complexity of the AMT over recent years. But the U.S. democratic system is nothing if not resilient, and its adaptive mechanisms still work. Perhaps the story of the U.S. tax policy process is simply part of democracy's broader story: it's prone to waste, bureaucracy, cronyism, and borderline corruption when no wolf is at the door, but it's good at handling emergencies and responding to powerful forces.

Not everyone will agree with this bittersweet conclusion, but one point is clear cut. Tax legislation's day has arrived. With taxes providing most of government's revenues, and with one-quarter to one-third of all subsidies deriving from breaks rather than expenditures, future elected representatives have no choice but to learn the tax policy ropes. Besides, the appetite of Congress and the public for new legislation is insatiable, so we may as well try to channel that energy in a productive direction. A moratorium on new tax provisions requires politicians to assume that yesteryear's elected representatives got it all right in the first place. Fat chance!

No matter how much badly designed tax policies stand as evidence that getting it "right" is difficult, when good policies are enacted and revisions well timed, they remind us that political honesty, tenacity, and integrity can help create a better, more efficient and equitable system. The powerful dynamic of the democratic process remains at play in tax policy no less than in the rest of our civic, political, and economic life. Edmund Burke deserves the last word here: issues of taxation and finance reside at the very heart of debates over liberty and government.

NOTES

1. While the most radical single changes to the tax system seem to occur only during crises (Brownlee 1996; Pollack 1996), the sum of all the incremental changes over the decades can lead to fairly radical change as well. Even unattended changes can make huge differences over time: bracket creep after World War II brought substantial portions of the population into the income tax.

2. The interaction of inflation and taxes led to shifts in relative values of real estate versus stock (Steuerle 1985b).

3. Politics may be a different matter. It seems clear, for instance, that the Clinton administration felt that small rate reductions would not have the same appeal as special tax breaks to various constituencies and that they would be more likely to lose the budget battle by simply offering smaller or more progressive tax rate reductions as an alternative to the larger rate reductions (see Brownlee 1996, 138–39).

4. In many cash flow versions of a consumption tax, it is usually argued that the extraordinary returns to capital would be taxed, but not the ordinary returns.

5. In a number of economic models, this is one of the larger sources of inefficiency arising from the income tax.

6. Among the issues raised in the conversion to a consumption tax are how much various groups might win or lose. In Hassett and Hubbard (2001), the editors suggest

that such a fundamental change would do less damage than previously thought to home prices and stock market valuations, while Douglas Holtz-Eakin in the same volume finds big effects on the housing stock.

7. Graetz was also instrumental, as a deputy assistant secretary, in writing the Treasury study noted here.

8. Japan's interest rate was already so low that there was also a question of whether monetary policy would have any effect on it.

9. For example, the Bush administration's chairman of economic advisers, N. Gregory Mankiw, was quoted as saying, "But I also believe that if you cut taxes, that's going to stimulate consumer spending and bring you back toward full employment" (Maggs 2003).

10. These include the leading economists at major universities. A major exception was Herbert Stein (1969), who addressed issues of balance over the economic cycle with concepts like the full employment budget surplus.

11. The General Explanation of the Tax Reform Act of 1986 states, "The Secretary, through an office established in the Treasury Department is authorized to monitor and analyze experience with all tangible depreciable assets, to prescribe a new class life for any property (other than real property) when appropriate, and to prescribe a class life for any property that does not have a class life" (Joint Committee on Taxation 1987, 103). Lack of cooperation by some industries and lobbying by others led quickly to the elimination of this office established for depreciation analysis.

12. As in so many cases when capital gains issues are involved, issues become complicated by the availability of borrowing, which also makes it possible to consume out of accrued income without ever paying a tax on it.

13. If the tax increase is plus 10 percent of existing tax rates, then the tax decrease would need to be about minus 9 percent of existing tax rates (i.e., 9 percent of rates that are now 110 percent of where they used to be).

14. Nina Olson (2004) lists the AMT as the top problem facing taxpayers in her annual report to Congress.

15. This relief is greater than that provided to cash contributions since the appreciation in the value of the property is forgiven tax altogether, up to certain income limits.

16. One example was the Transportation Department's efforts in the late 1990s and early 2000s to convince state and local governments to take advantage of a tax shelter—essentially involving tricks like selling their subway systems and then leasing them back—even though the Treasury believed this was done in a way that was illegal.

Appendix A

Table A.1 Total Federal, State and Local Tax Receipts, 1929–2002
(Amounts in billions of dollars)

Year	Gross domestic product (GDP)	Federal individual income tax Amount	% of GDP	Social Security and railroad retirement taxes Amount	% of GDP	Federal corporate profits tax Amount	% of GDP	Other federal taxes[a] Amount	% of GDP	State and local taxes[b] Amount	% of GDP	Total tax receipts Amount	% of GDP	State and local income tax receipts Amount	% of GDP	Total individual income tax receipts Amount	% of GDP
1929	103.7	1.20	1.16	0.0	0.00	1.2	1.16	1.3	1.25	6.2	5.98	9.8	9.45	0.1	0.10	1.3	1.25
1930	91.3	1.00	1.10	0.0	0.00	0.7	0.77	1.1	1.20	6.5	7.12	9.2	10.08	0.1	0.11	1.1	1.20
1931	76.6	0.50	0.65	0.0	0.00	0.4	0.52	1.0	1.31	6.3	8.22	8.1	10.57	0.1	0.13	0.6	0.78
1932	58.8	0.30	0.51	0.0	0.00	0.3	0.51	0.8	1.36	6.2	10.54	7.6	12.93	0.1	0.17	0.4	0.68
1933	56.4	0.40	0.71	0.0	0.00	0.5	0.89	1.6	2.84	5.8	10.28	8.2	14.54	0.1	0.18	0.5	0.89
1934	66.0	0.40	0.61	0.0	0.00	0.6	0.91	2.2	3.33	6.0	9.09	9.1	13.79	0.1	0.15	0.5	0.76
1935	73.3	0.60	0.82	0.0	0.00	0.8	1.09	2.3	3.14	6.3	8.59	9.8	13.37	0.1	0.14	0.7	0.95
1936	83.7	0.70	0.84	0.0	0.00	1.3	1.55	2.6	3.11	7.1	8.48	11.3	13.50	0.2	0.24	0.9	1.08
1937	91.9	1.30	1.41	0.8	0.87	1.3	1.41	2.8	3.05	7.9	8.60	13.7	14.91	0.2	0.22	1.5	1.63
1938	86.1	1.20	1.39	0.8	0.93	0.9	1.05	2.5	2.90	8.2	9.52	13.2	15.33	0.2	0.23	1.4	1.63
1939	92.0	0.90	0.98	0.8	0.87	1.3	1.41	2.6	2.83	8.4	9.13	13.6	14.78	0.2	0.22	1.1	1.20
1940	101.3	1.00	0.99	0.8	0.79	2.6	2.57	2.9	2.86	8.6	8.49	15.6	15.40	0.2	0.20	1.2	1.18
1941	126.7	1.60	1.26	1.0	0.79	7.3	5.76	3.8	3.00	9.6	7.58	22.9	18.07	0.3	0.24	1.9	1.50
1942	161.8	4.00	2.47	1.2	0.74	11.1	6.86	4.5	2.78	9.7	6.00	30.0	18.54	0.3	0.19	4.3	2.66
1943	198.4	15.90	8.01	1.4	0.71	13.6	6.85	5.3	2.67	9.9	4.99	45.6	22.98	0.3	0.15	16.2	8.17
1944	219.7	16.80	7.65	1.4	0.64	12.5	5.69	6.5	2.96	10.2	4.64	46.8	21.30	0.4	0.18	17.2	7.83
1945	223.0	18.50	8.30	1.4	0.63	10.2	4.57	7.7	3.45	10.4	4.66	47.5	21.30	0.4	0.18	18.9	8.48
1946	222.3	16.40	7.38	1.8	0.81	8.6	3.87	10.2	4.59	11.4	5.13	47.7	21.46	0.4	0.18	16.8	7.56
1947	244.4	18.80	7.69	2.2	0.90	10.7	4.38	9.5	3.89	13.1	5.36	53.5	21.89	0.5	0.20	19.3	7.90

1948	269.6	18.10	6.71	2.2	0.82	11.8	4.38	9.3	3.45	14.9	5.53	55.4	20.55	0.6	0.22	18.7	6.94
1949	267.7	15.40	5.75	2.2	0.82	9.6	3.59	9.2	3.44	15.8	5.90	51.5	19.24	0.7	0.26	16.1	6.01
1950	294.3	17.40	5.91	3.2	1.09	17.2	5.84	9.5	3.23	17.8	6.05	64.5	21.92	0.8	0.27	18.2	6.18
1951	339.5	25.40	7.48	3.9	1.15	21.7	6.39	10.2	3.00	19.6	5.77	80.1	23.59	0.9	0.27	26.3	7.75
1952	358.6	30.20	8.42	4.4	1.23	18.6	5.19	11.3	3.15	21.0	5.86	84.7	23.62	1.0	0.28	31.2	8.70
1953	379.9	31.30	8.24	4.6	1.21	19.5	5.13	12.0	3.16	22.4	5.90	88.9	23.40	1.0	0.26	32.3	8.50
1954	381.1	28.10	7.37	5.7	1.50	16.9	4.43	10.8	2.83	23.4	6.14	84.0	22.04	1.1	0.29	29.2	7.66
1955	415.2	30.50	7.35	6.5	1.57	21.1	5.08	11.9	2.87	25.6	6.17	94.6	22.78	1.3	0.31	31.8	7.66
1956	438.0	33.90	7.74	7.0	1.60	20.9	4.77	12.9	2.95	28.4	6.48	101.8	23.24	1.6	0.37	35.5	8.11
1957	461.5	36.00	7.80	8.4	1.82	20.4	4.42	13.6	2.95	30.5	6.61	107.5	23.29	1.7	0.37	37.7	8.17
1958	467.9	35.50	7.59	8.5	1.82	18.0	3.85	13.2	2.82	31.9	6.82	105.8	22.61	1.8	0.38	37.3	7.97
1959	507.4	38.50	7.59	10.3	2.03	22.5	4.43	14.4	2.84	35.9	7.08	120.2	23.69	2.2	0.43	40.7	8.02
1960	527.4	41.80	7.93	12.4	2.35	21.4	4.06	15.6	2.96	39.2	7.43	128.6	24.38	2.5	0.47	44.3	8.40
1961	545.7	42.70	7.82	12.7	2.33	21.5	3.94	16.2	2.97	42.2	7.73	133.3	24.43	2.8	0.51	45.5	8.34
1962	586.5	46.50	7.93	13.7	2.34	22.5	3.84	17.6	3.00	45.8	7.81	144.0	24.55	3.2	0.55	49.7	8.47
1963	618.7	49.10	7.94	16.3	2.63	24.6	3.98	18.2	2.94	49.0	7.92	155.0	25.05	3.4	0.55	52.5	8.49
1964	664.4	46.00	6.92	17.1	2.57	26.1	3.93	19.1	2.87	52.9	7.96	158.6	23.87	4.0	0.60	50.0	7.53
1965	720.1	51.10	7.10	18.1	2.51	28.9	4.01	19.2	2.67	57.2	7.94	171.7	23.84	4.4	0.61	55.5	7.71
1966	789.3	58.60	7.42	25.8	3.27	31.4	3.98	18.4	2.33	62.1	7.87	193.3	24.49	5.4	0.68	64.0	8.11
1967	834.1	64.40	7.72	29.1	3.49	30.0	3.60	19.2	2.30	67.0	8.03	206.6	24.77	6.1	0.73	70.5	8.45
1968	911.5	76.40	8.38	32.6	3.58	36.1	3.96	21.0	2.30	76.2	8.36	239.2	26.24	7.8	0.86	84.2	9.24
1969	985.3	91.70	9.31	37.9	3.85	36.1	3.66	22.5	2.28	85.4	8.67	270.0	27.40	9.8	0.99	101.5	10.30
1970	1,039.7	88.90	8.55	39.4	3.79	30.6	2.94	23.3	2.24	94.0	9.04	272.5	26.21	10.9	1.05	99.8	9.60
1971	1,128.6	85.80	7.60	43.6	3.86	33.5	2.97	25.4	2.25	104.8	9.29	288.5	25.56	12.4	1.10	98.2	8.70
1972	1,240.4	102.80	8.29	49.4	3.98	36.6	2.95	26.0	2.10	120.3	9.70	329.7	26.58	17.2	1.39	120.0	9.67
1973	1,385.5	109.60	7.91	64.2	4.63	43.3	3.13	27.2	1.96	132.1	9.53	371.3	26.80	18.9	1.36	128.5	9.27
1974	1,501.0	126.50	8.43	73.3	4.88	45.1	3.00	27.1	1.81	142.4	9.49	409.6	27.29	20.4	1.36	146.9	9.79

(continued)

Table A.1 Continued

Year	Gross domestic product (GDP)	Federal individual income tax Amount	% of GDP	Social Security and railroad retirement taxes Amount	% of GDP	Federal corporate profits tax Amount	% of GDP	Other federal taxes[a] Amount	% of GDP	State and local taxes[b] Amount	% of GDP	Total tax receipts Amount	% of GDP	State and local income tax receipts Amount	% of GDP	Total individual income tax receipts Amount	% of GDP
1975	1,635.2	120.70	7.38	76.7	4.69	43.6	2.67	29.8	1.82	153.7	9.40	419.6	25.66	22.5	1.38	143.2	8.76
1976	1,823.9	141.20	7.74	85.0	4.66	54.6	2.99	30.2	1.66	175.2	9.61	480.6	26.35	26.3	1.44	167.5	9.18
1977	2,031.4	162.20	7.98	94.1	4.63	61.6	3.03	33.6	1.65	195.0	9.60	539.3	26.55	30.4	1.50	192.6	9.48
1978	2,295.9	188.90	8.23	108.8	4.74	71.4	3.11	34.8	1.52	212.1	9.24	610.8	26.60	35.0	1.52	223.9	9.75
1979	2,566.4	224.60	8.75	128.5	5.01	74.4	2.90	35.8	1.39	227.0	8.85	684.8	26.68	38.2	1.49	262.8	10.24
1980	2,795.6	250.00	8.94	141.9	5.08	70.3	2.51	45.4	1.62	244.0	8.73	745.1	26.65	42.6	1.52	292.6	10.47
1981	3,131.3	290.60	9.28	169.9	5.43	65.7	2.10	62.4	1.99	270.2	8.63	851.9	27.21	47.9	1.53	338.5	10.81
1982	3,259.2	295.00	9.05	181.4	5.57	49.0	1.50	54.2	1.66	288.6	8.85	860.7	26.41	51.9	1.59	346.9	10.64
1983	3,534.9	286.20	8.10	193.9	5.49	61.3	1.73	57.2	1.62	318.9	9.02	911.7	25.79	58.3	1.65	344.5	9.75
1984	3,932.7	301.40	7.66	219.5	5.58	75.2	1.91	60.5	1.54	359.7	9.15	1,010.3	25.69	67.5	1.72	368.9	9.38
1985	4,213.0	336.00	7.98	242.5	5.76	76.3	1.81	59.3	1.41	386.1	9.16	1,093.8	25.96	72.1	1.71	408.1	9.69
1986	4,452.9	350.10	7.86	263.9	5.93	83.8	1.88	58.7	1.32	411.7	9.25	1,161.2	26.08	77.4	1.74	427.5	9.60
1987	4,742.5	392.50	8.28	281.3	5.93	103.2	2.18	60.6	1.28	444.8	9.38	1,275.2	26.89	86.0	1.81	478.5	10.09
1988	5,108.3	402.90	7.89	314.6	6.16	111.1	2.17	64.7	1.27	474.9	9.30	1,360.6	26.64	89.8	1.76	492.7	9.65
1989	5,489.1	451.50	8.23	336.6	6.13	117.2	2.14	66.8	1.22	510.3	9.30	1,473.5	26.84	102.6	1.87	554.1	10.09

Year																	
1990	5,803.2	470.20	8.10	363.3	6.26	118.1	2.04	70.1	1.21	538.3	9.28	1,548.4	26.68	107.7	1.86	577.9	9.96
1991	5,986.2	461.30	7.71	380.1	6.35	109.9	1.84	80.1	1.34	565.5	9.45	1,585.9	26.49	112.6	1.88	573.9	9.59
1992	6,318.9	475.30	7.52	398.0	6.30	118.8	1.88	83.3	1.32	602.5	9.53	1,666.6	26.37	119.6	1.89	594.9	9.41
1993	6,642.3	505.40	7.61	414.8	6.24	138.5	2.09	87.8	1.32	640.7	9.65	1,774.3	26.71	126.0	1.90	631.4	9.51
1994	7,054.3	542.50	7.69	441.9	6.26	156.7	2.22	99.9	1.42	678.1	9.61	1,904.0	26.99	133.4	1.89	675.9	9.58
1995	7,400.5	585.60	7.91	465.7	6.29	179.3	2.42	100.9	1.36	708.3	9.57	2,024.9	27.36	142.5	1.93	728.1	9.84
1996	7,813.2	662.90	8.48	490.8	6.28	190.6	2.44	100.8	1.29	739.9	9.47	2,167.5	27.74	152.9	1.96	815.8	10.44
1997	8,318.4	743.90	8.94	524.7	6.31	203.0	2.44	106.7	1.28	778.7	9.36	2,336.4	28.09	167.6	2.01	911.5	10.96
1998	8,781.5	826.40	9.41	561.3	6.39	204.2	2.33	115.3	1.31	820.4	9.34	2,502.4	28.50	182.7	2.08	1,009.1	11.49
1999	9,274.3	894.00	9.64	598.4	6.45	213.0	2.30	121.5	1.31	864.8	9.32	2,662.9	28.71	199.7	2.15	1,093.7	11.79
2000	9,824.6	999.00	10.17	638.7	6.50	223.8	2.28	126.3	1.29	910.4	9.27	2,870.1	29.21	218.1	2.22	1,217.1	12.39
2001	10,082.2	1000.30	9.92	661.4	6.56	170.2	1.69	124.7	1.24	922.0	9.14	2,850.7	28.27	218.7	2.17	1,219.0	12.09
2002	10,446.2	836.40	8.01	685.3	6.56	179.8	1.72	125.1	1.20	933.1	8.93	2,759.7	26.42	200.3	1.92	1,036.7	9.92

Source: Bureau of Economic Analysis, various years (NIPA tables 1.1, 3.2, 3.3, 3.6).

a. Includes federal estate taxes, gift taxes, and custom duties plus employer contributions for federal unemployment tax, railroad unemployment insurance, and federal worker's compensation. Excludes federal nontaxes.

b. Includes all state and local receipts from taxes and licenses. Excludes non-taxes, receipts from contributions to social insurance, and receipts from federal grants-in-aid.

Table A.2 Personal Income Excluded from Adjusted Gross Income (Amounts in billions of dollars)

| | Net nontaxable government transfers | | | | | | Net nontaxable labor-related income | | | | | | | | | Other net differences | | Total net exclusions from AGI | | |
| | OASDI * RR Retirement (a) | | Medicare (b) | | Other nontaxable transfers (c) | | Pension and profit sharing | | Health insurance | | Other labor compensation | | Other statutory exclusions | | | | | | Personal income |
Year	Amount	%PI	Amount	%PI	Amount	%PI	Amount	%PI	Amount	%PI	Amount	%PI	Amount	%PI	Amount	%PI	Amount	%PI	
1948	-0.2	-0.1	0.0	0.0	9.4	4.5	0.7	0.3	0.4	0.2	1.0	0.5	3.3	1.6	12.6	5.96	27.2	12.9	211.1
1952	0.3	0.1	0.0	0.0	9.2	3.3	1.7	0.6	1.1	0.4	1.4	0.5	3.7	1.3	17.6	6.37	35.0	12.7	276.1
1956	2.5	0.7	0.0	0.0	10.3	3.0	2.2	0.7	2.1	0.6	2.0	0.6	4.2	1.2	17.9	5.25	41.2	12.1	340.0
1960	5.5	1.3	0.0	0.0	13.7	3.3	2.6	0.6	3.4	0.8	2.7	0.7	5.2	1.3	28.2	6.84	61.3	14.9	412.7
1964	8.1	1.6	0.0	0.0	16.1	3.1	2.7	0.5	5.2	1.0	3.6	0.7	7.2	1.4	30.7	5.95	73.6	14.3	515.8
1968	11.4	1.6	2.5	0.3	23.9	3.3	3.6	0.5	8.4	1.2	5.6	0.8	13.8	1.9	35.9	5.03	105.2	14.7	714.5
1972	20.5	2.1	4.3	0.4	46.3	4.7	3.0	0.3	16.2	1.6	7.2	0.7	17.6	1.8	53.7	5.41	168.8	17.0	994.3
1976	41.2	2.8	9.7	0.7	85.8	5.8	6.1	0.4	32.0	2.2	11.8	0.8	26.1	1.8	93.5	6.34	306.3	20.8	1475.4
1980	63.0	2.7	20.0	0.9	114.5	4.9	14.0	0.6	61.0	2.6	21.1	0.9	43.6	1.9	155.1	6.67	492.3	21.2	2323.9
1984	79.9	2.4	35.2	1.1	122.2	3.7	-3.6	-0.1	100.3	3.1	24.4	0.7	136.7	4.2	306.4	9.36	801.5	24.5	3274.8
1988	70.8	1.7	44.6	1.0	142.6	3.3	-42.7	-1.0	147.1	3.4	39.8	0.9	120.1	2.8	334.0	7.82	856.3	20.0	4272.1
1992	96.3	1.8	75.5	1.4	219.7	4.1	-80.5	-1.5	228.2	4.2	52.7	1.0	180.5	3.3	509.7	9.46	1282.1	23.8	5390.4
1996	88.5	1.4	119.4	1.8	274.0	4.2	-136.0	-2.1	257.2	3.9	52.3	0.8	273.2	4.2	467.2	7.14	1395.8	21.3	6547.4
2000	51.7	0.6	119.1	1.4	299.6	3.6	-213.1	-2.5	306.4	3.6	51.7	0.6	394.1	4.7	274.7	3.27	1284.2	15.3	8406.6

Source: Bureau of Economic Analysis, *National Income & Product Accounts* tables 3.6, 3.11, 3.12, 3.28, 6.11, 8.14, 8.28; U.S. Department of Commerce, Bureau of Economic Analysis (2003).

Note: AGI = adjusted gross income; OASDI = Old Age, Survivors, and Disability Insurance (Social Security).

Table A.3 *Tax-Exempt Levels of Income by Filing Status and Number of Dependents, 1948–2003*

Year	Per capita personal income	Single		Joint			Head of household	
		Without EITC	With EITC	0 Dependents without EITC[a]	2 Dependents without EITC + CTC	2 Dependents with EITC + CTC	2 Dependents without EITC + CTC	2 Dependents with EITC + CTC
1948	$1,440	$667	$667	$1,333	$2,667	$2,667	$2,000	$2,000
1954	1,818	667	667	1,333	2,667	2,667	2,000	2,000
1960	2,283	667	667	1,333	2,667	2,667	2,000	2,000
1966	3,085	900	900	1,600	3,000	3,000	2,300	2,300
1972	4,736	2,050	2,050	2,800	4,300	4,300	3,550	3,550
1978	8,302	3,200	3,200	5,200	7,200	7,533	5,200	6,930
1981	11,301	3,300	3,300	5,400	7,400	8,634	5,300	7,515
1984	13,853	3,300	3,300	5,400	7,400	8,783	5,300	8,315
1986	15,425	3,560	3,560	5,830	7,990	9,575	5,720	9,063
1988	17,433	4,950	4,950	8,900	12,800	15,110	10,250	13,940
1990	19,614	5,300	5,300	9,550	13,650	16,296	10,900	15,066
1992	21,004	5,900	5,900	10,600	15,200	18,548	12,150	17,217
1994	22,372	6,250	7,179	11,250	16,150	21,098	12,950	18,887
1996	24,299	6,550	7,546	11,800	16,900	23,672	13,550	19,884
1998	26,917	6,950	7,990	12,500	17,900	27,796	14,350	26,319
2000	29,797	7,200	8,274	12,950	18,550	28,684	14,850	27,144
2002	31,039	7,700	9,156	13,850	19,850	33,210	15,900	30,706
2003	31,606	7,800	9,300	15,600	21,700	39,700	16,150	33,379
% Change								
1948–2003	2095	1069	1294	1070	714	1389	708	1569
1948–1981	685	395	395	305	177	224	165	276
1981–1986	36	8	8	8	8	11	8	21
1986–2003	105	119	161	168	172	315	182	268

Sources: Author's calculations, based on data from the U.S. Department of Commerce; the Internal Revenue Service, *Individual Income Tax Returns,* various years; and the *Green Book.*

Note: All figures are in nominal dollars. Prices as measured by the CPI increased by a factor of 7.67 over the 1948–2003 period. Single filers were not eligible for the earned income tax credit (EITC) until tax year 1994. The child tax credit (CTC) was unavailable before tax year 1998. Data for 2003 projected from first three quarters.

a. Joint filers without children are ineligible for CTC and ineligible for the EITC at the tax entry threshold.

Table A.4 *Average and Marginal Combined Federal Income and Employee Social Security and Medicare (FICA) Tax Rates, 1955–2003*

Year	One-half median income			Median income			Twice median income		
	Income ($)	Average income tax rate (%)	Marginal income tax rate (%)	Income ($)	Average income tax rate (%)	Marginal income tax rate (%)	Income ($)	Average income tax rate (%)	Marginal income tax rate (%)
1955	2,460	2.0	2.0	4,919	7.4	20.0	9,838	11.6	22.0
1956	2,660	2.0	2.0	5,319	8.0	20.0	10,638	12.0	22.0
1957	2,744	2.3	2.3	5,488	8.4	20.0	10,976	12.3	22.0
1958	2,843	2.3	2.3	5,685	8.6	20.0	11,370	12.4	22.0
1959	3,035	2.5	2.5	6,070	9.5	20.0	12,140	12.9	22.0
1960	3,148	3.2	23.0	6,295	10.1	20.0	12,590	13.3	22.0
1961	3,219	3.5	23.0	6,437	10.2	20.0	12,874	13.3	22.0
1962	3,378	4.3	23.1	6,756	10.5	20.0	13,512	13.6	26.0
1963	3,569	5.6	23.6	7,138	11.1	20.0	14,276	14.1	26.0
1964	3,744	5.7	19.6	7,488	9.9	18.0	14,976	12.8	23.5
1965	3,900	5.8	17.6	7,800	9.3	17.0	15,600	12.2	22.0
1966	4,171	6.9	18.2	8,341	10.8	19.0	16,682	13.2	22.0
1967	4,497	7.7	19.4	8,994	11.2	19.0	17,988	13.5	22.0
1968	4,917	8.4	19.4	9,834	12.7	20.4	19,668	15.1	26.9
1969	5,312	9.4	19.8	10,623	13.4	20.9	21,246	16.0	27.5
1970	5,583	9.5	19.8	11,165	12.7	19.5	22,330	15.2	25.6
1971	6,088	9.9	20.2	12,176	12.6	19.0	24,352	15.1	28.0

Year									
1972	6,404	9.6	20.2	12,808	12.7	19.0	25,616	15.4	28.0
1973	6,855	10.7	21.9	13,710	14.1	19.0	27,420	16.4	28.0
1974	7,485	10.0[a]	21.9	14,969	14.2[a]	22.0	29,938	16.9[a]	33.0[a]
1975	7,924	10.0[b]	32.9[b]	15,848	14.8	22.0	31,696	17.5	32.0
1976	8,658	10.5	22.9	17,315	15.1	22.0	34,630	18.1	32.0
1977	9,362	9.5	22.9	18,723	15.6	22.0	37,446	19.0	36.0
1978	10,214	10.8	25.1	20,428	16.3	25.0	40,856	20.0	39.0
1979	11,256	11.2	22.1	22,512	17.0	30.1	45,024	20.3	37.0
1980	12,166	12.2	24.1	24,332	17.6	30.1	48,664	21.5	43.0
1981	13,137	13.5	24.4	26,274	18.4	30.4	52,548	22.9	42.5
1982	13,810	13.2	22.7	27,619	17.8	31.7	55,238	21.9	39.0
1983	14,591	13.2	21.7	29,181	17.1	29.7	58,362	20.9	35.0
1984	15,549	13.2	20.7	31,097	17.0	28.7	62,194	20.7	38.0
1985	16,389	13.6	21.1	32,777	17.4	29.1	65,554	21.0	38.0
1986	17,358	13.8	21.2	34,716	17.6	29.2	69,432	21.4	38.0
1987	18,543	12.3	22.2	37,086	16.1	22.2	74,172	20.0	35.0
1988	19,526	12.7	22.5	39,051	16.8	22.5	78,102	19.5	28.0
1989	20,382	12.8	22.5	40,763	16.9	22.5	81,526	19.7	28.0
1990	20,726	12.8	22.7	41,451	17.0	22.7	82,902	19.8	28.0
1991	21,526	12.7	22.7	43,052	17.0	22.7	86,104	20.3	29.5
1992	22,126	12.2[b]	35.8[b]	44,251	16.8	22.7	88,502	20.1	29.5
1993	22,581	12.0[b]	36.6[b]	45,161	16.8	22.7	90,322	20.1	29.5
1994	23,506	11.0[b]	40.3[b]	47,012	16.8	22.7	94,024	20.2	29.5
1995	24,844	11.2[b]	42.9[b]	49,687	16.9	22.7	99,374	20.3	29.5
1996	25,759	10.6[b]	43.7[b]	51,518	17.0	22.7	103,036	20.4	29.5

(continued)

Table A.4 *Continued*

	One-half median income			Median income			Twice median income		
Year	Income ($)	Average income tax rate (%)	Marginal income tax rate (%)	Income ($)	Average income tax rate (%)	Marginal income tax rate (%)	Income ($)	Average income tax rate (%)	Marginal income tax rate (%)
1997	26,675	10.7[b]	43.7[b]	53,350	17.0	22.7	106,700	20.4	29.5
1998	28,031	8.7[bc]	43.7[bc]	56,061	15.6	22.7	112,222	19.9	29.5
1999	29,991	9.8[bc]	43.7[bc]	59,981	15.5	22.7	119,962	20.5	29.5
2000	31,335	10.6[bc]	22.7[bc]	62,670	15.7	22.7	125,340	20.9	34.5
2001	31,639	7.5[a,b,e]	43.7[a,b,e]	63,278	14.4	22.7	126,556	20.3	34.5
2002	32,077	6.4[a,b,f]	43.7[a,b,f]	64,153	14.3	22.7	128,307	19.9	33.5
2003	32,753	3.7[a,b,f]	28.7[a,b,f]	65,507	13.0	22.7	131,013	18.6	31.5

Sources: Allen Lerman, Department of the Treasury Office of Tax Analysts, updated by the Urban-Brookings Tax Policy Center. Median incomes from U.S. Census Bureau, "Current Population Reports, Series P-60," various issues.

Note: Median income is for a four-person family. All calculations are for a married couple and income is assumed to be earned by one spouse. Itemized deductions are assumed to equal 23 percent of income through 1986 and 18 percent of income thereafter.

a. Reflects one-year rebate under PL 94-12, including income related phaseout for the twice-median income family.

b. Includes effects of the earned income tax credit (EITC), assuming two eligible dependents.

c. Includes effects of child tax credit enacted in the Taxpayer Relief Act of 1997.

d. Sample expanded by 28,000 households. If calculated by old method, this would have been $62,228.

e. Includes effects of $600 rebate given as part of EGTRRA.

f. Includes effects of child tax credit expansion as part of EGTRRA

Table A.5 *Marginal Effective Tax Rates on Capital Income,*
1953–2003 (percent)

Year	Corporate firm level	Corporate total	Noncorporate	Owner-occupied	U.S. total
1953	63	70	37	−1	58
1955	51	58	24	−1	44
1957	55	61	27	−1	48
1959	52	58	25	1	45
1961	49	55	22	1	42
1963	41	47	16	1	34
1965	37	42	13	1	29
1967	40	45	17	1	33
1969	52	58	28	5	45
1971	43	50	21	5	38
1973	43	51	21	5	38
1975	51	56	27	11	44
1977	41	49	23	6	40
1979	47	57	29	11	45
1981	37	48	24	12	38
1983	39	46	20	8	34
1985	38	44	20	7	33
1987	35	44	22	4	33
1989	34	43	22	4	33
1991	32	41	22	3	30
1993	33	42	22	2	31
1995	32	42	22	2	31
1997	31	41	23	2	31
1999	30	40	23	2	30
2001	32	41	22	2	30
2003	27	32	18	2	23

Source: Gravelle (2004).

Figure A.1   *Retirement Plan Options under Current Law*

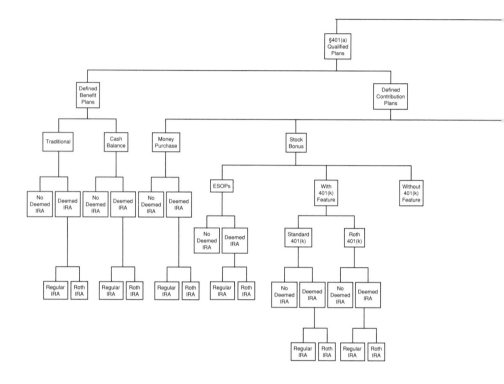

Note: Some provisions not effective until 2006.
Source: Perun and Steuerle (2003).

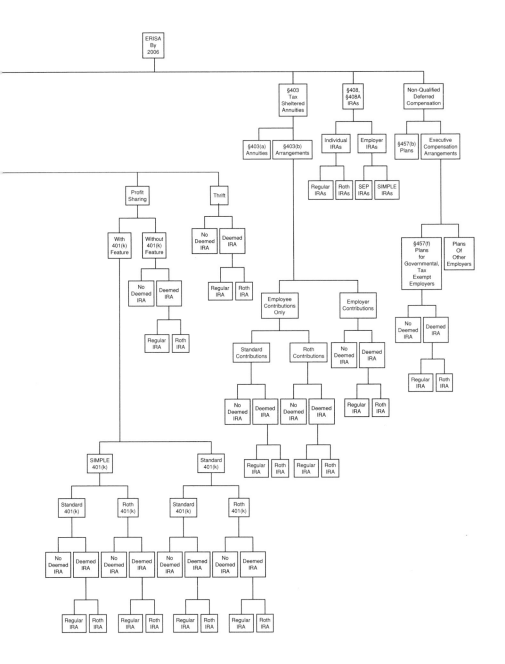

Appendix B
Summary of Major
Tax Legislation, 1981 to 2003

Economic Recovery Tax Act of 1981

- Reduced marginal tax rates 23 percent over three years; reduced maximum rate to 50 percent and maximum capital gains rate to 20 percent; indexed income tax brackets, personal exemption, and standard deduction for inflation beginning in 1985; and provided new deduction for two-earner married couples.
- Replaced facts and circumstances and the asset depreciation range guidelines with accelerated cost recovery system; simplified rules for faster write-off of capital expenditures (most equipment written off over five years, structures over 15 years); and allowed liberalized "safe-harbor" leasing rules.
- Extended eligibility for individual retirement accounts (IRAs) to include active participants in employer pension plans and increased Keogh annual contribution limit to $15,000.
- Permitted unlimited marital deduction; increased estate credit to exempt from tax all estates of $600,000 or less; and reduced maximum estate tax rate from 70 to 50 percent.
- Accelerated corporate estimated tax payments and tightened rules on tax straddles with mark-to-market rule that effectively required accrual accounting of these assets and liabilities at end of year.

Tax Equity and Fiscal Responsibility Act of 1982

- Imposed withholding on interest and dividends; further accelerated corporate estimated tax payments; expanded information reporting; and increased penalties on non-compliance.
- Strengthened individual minimum tax; repealed future acceleration of depreciation allowances; repealed safe-harbor leasing; and tightened completed contract method of accounting rules.
- Increased airport and airway trust fund taxes, cigarette excise taxes, and telephone excise tax.
- Increased unemployment taxes (under the Federal Unemployment Tax Act [FUTA]) by increasing tax rate and wage base; extended hospital insurance (HI) taxes to federal employees.

Highway Revenue Act of 1982

- Increased excise tax on gasoline and diesel fuel from four to nine cents per gallon for five years.

Social Security Amendments of 1983

- Accelerated scheduled increases in payroll tax rate for Old Age, Survivors, and Disability Insurance (OASDI).
- Taxed some Social Security benefits. At most, 50 percent of Social Security benefits are subject to tax if income exceeds $25,000 for a single taxpayer or $32,000 for a joint return.

Interest and Dividends Tax Compliance Act of 1983

- Repealed interest and dividend withholding and replaced with "backup withholding" and expanded information reporting.
- Enacted Caribbean Basin Initiative (CBI) tax benefits.

Railroad Retirement Revenue Act of 1983

- Increased railroad retirement payroll taxes and railroad unemployment insurance taxes.
- Taxed railroad retirement pension plan benefits.

Deficit Reduction Act of 1984

- Increased excise taxes. Increased distilled spirits excise tax and extended telephone excise tax.
- Increased restrictions on leasing. Reduced benefits from tax-exempt leasing and postponed effective data of liberalized finance leasing rules.
- Increased depreciable life of structures from 15 to 18 years.
- Placed state volume limitation on private-purpose tax-exempt bonds.
- Placed time value of money restrictions on accounting rules.
- Repealed net interest exclusion (ERTA provision) before its effective date.
- Reduced long-term capital gains holding period from one year to six months.

Consolidated Omnibus Budget Reconciliation Act of 1985 (COBRA)

- Permanently extended 16 cents per pack cigarette excise tax.
- Enacted new excise tax on smokeless tobacco.
- Increased excise tax on coal production.
- Extended hospital insurance coverage to new state and local government employees.
- Repealed income averaging for former students.

Tax Reform Act of 1986

- Lowered top marginal tax rate to 28 percent; increased standard deduction to $5,000 for married couples; increased personal exemption to $2,000; and increased earned income tax credit (EITC).
- Repealed two-earner deduction, long-term capital gains exclusion, state and local sales tax deduction, income averaging, and exclusion of unemployment benefits. Limited IRA eligibility, consumer interest deduction, deductibility of "passive" losses, medical expenses deductions, deductions for business meals and entertainment, pension contributions, and miscellaneous expense deductions.
- Reduced corporate marginal tax rate to 34 percent and tightened corporate minimum tax.

- Repealed the investment tax credit and lengthened capital-cost recovery periods.
- Further tightened state volume limitations for private purpose tax-exempt bonds.
- Extended research and experimentation credit; initiated new low-income housing tax credit and deductibility of health insurance costs of self-employed individuals.

Omnibus Budget Reconciliation Act of 1986

- Accelerated state and local government deposits of Social Security payroll taxes.
- Accelerated collections of alcohol and tobacco excise taxes.
- Increased substantial underpayment penalty and penalty for failure to comply with deposit requirements.
- Increased customs user fee on value of imported merchandise.

Superfund Amendments and Reauthorization Act of 1986

- Enacted excise tax of 8.2 cents per barrel on domestic crude oil and 11.7 cents per barrel on imported petroleum products.
- Enacted new broad-based tax on all corporations equal to 0.12 percent of alternative minimum taxable income in excess of $2 million.
- Enacted a 0.1 cent per gallon excise tax on gasoline, diesel fuels, and other special motor fuels in order to finance cleanup of wastes from leaking underground petroleum storage tanks.

Continuing Resolution for Fiscal Year 1987

- Increased Internal Revenue Service (IRS) funding for staffing and equipment.
- Established Immigration and Naturalization Service inspection fee.

Omnibus Budget Reconciliation Act of 1987

- Repealed installment sales method of accounting for dealers and vacation pay reserve.
- Tightened completed contract method of accounting.

- Reduced dividends-received deduction for payments among corporations.
- Accelerated corporate estimated tax payments.
- Limited employer deductible contributions to defined benefit pension plans.
- Limited mortgage interest deduction to debt less than $1 million and to home equity loans of less than $100,000.
- Extended telephone excise tax, FUTA tax, 55 percent estate tax rate, and employer Social Security to cover cash tips.
- Increased Internal Revenue Service (IRS) and Bureau of Alcohol, Tobacco, and Firearms (BATF) fees.

Continuing Resolution for Fiscal Year 1988

- Increased IRS funding for more enforcement staff and equipment.

Airport and Airway Trust Fund Extension of 1987

- Extended airport and airway trust excise tax.

The Family Security Act of 1988

- Extended the debt refund offset provision.
- Tightened eligibility for the dependent care credit.
- Required taxpayer identification number for younger children.

Medicare Catastrophic Coverage Act of 1988

- Passed new supplemental premium tax on all persons eligible for Medicare. Set premium rate at 15 percent of individual income tax liability in excess of $150, increasing to 28 percent in 1993. Limited premium to $800 in 1989, rising to $1,050 in 1993, with future premium cap dependent on medical care costs after 1993.

Technical and Miscellaneous Revenue Act of 1988

- Passed technical corrections for the Tax Reform Act of 1986.
- Extended expiring provisions: research and experimentation tax credit and allocation rules; targeted jobs credit; mortgage subsidy bonds; employer-provided educational assistance and group legal services; Federal Savings and Loan Insurance Corporation (FSLIC) relief provisions; and mutual fund expense exclusion.
- Restricted single premium life insurance and special provisions for Alaskan Native Corporations; reformed completed contract accounting rules; and accelerated corporate estimated tax payments.

Financial Institutions' Reform, Recovery, and Enforcement Act of 1989

- Repealed three provisions that had provided tax relief to financially troubled thrift institutions.

Medicare Catastrophic Coverage Repeal Act of 1989

- Eliminated supplemental premium tax for Medicare catastrophic coverage.

Omnibus Budget Reconciliation Act of 1989

- Limited tax deductions and exclusions for employee stock ownership plans.
- Increased fees and excise taxes on air travel, ozone-depleting chemicals, and oil spill liability.
- Repealed completed contract method of accounting.
- Modified the corporate alternative minimum tax (AMT).
- Extended expiring provisions: employer-provided educational assistance; research and experimentation tax credit and allocation rules; and low-income housing credit.

Omnibus Budget Reconciliation Act of 1990

- Imposed a 30 percent excise tax on the dollar amount above $30,000 for autos, $100,000 for boats, $250,000 for airplanes, and $10,000 for furs. Increased motor fuels taxes by 5 cents per gallon. Increased taxes on tobacco and alcoholic beverages by 8 cents per pack of cigarettes, by $1.00 per "proof gallon" of liquor, by 16 cents per six-pack of beer, and by 18 cents per bottle of table wine. Extended Airport and Airway trust fund taxes and increased them by 25 percent. Permanently extended 3 percent excise tax on telephone service.
- Increased top individual income tax rate from 28 to 31 percent and increased the individual alternative minimum tax rate from 21 to 24 percent. Capped the capital gains rate at 28 percent. Reduced the value of high-income itemized deductions by 3 percent times the extent to which adjusted gross income (AGI) exceeds $100,000. Modified a "bubble" in statutory tax rates by temporarily creating the personal exemption phase-out applicable to the range of taxable income between $150,000 and $275,000.
- Raised the cap on taxable wages for Hospital Insurance (Medicare) from $53,400 to $125,000. Extended Social Security taxes to state and local employees without other pension coverage. Imposed a supplemental 0.2 percent unemployment insurance surtax.
- Adjusted EITC benefit levels and phase-in and phase-out rates for family size. Created a low-income credit for the premium costs of health insurance that includes coverage for children.
- Extended expiring provisions: tax credits for research and exploration, low-income housing, business energy, targeted jobs, and orphan drugs; tax exemptions for mortgage revenues and issue bonds; exclusions for employer-provided legal and educational assistance; and 25 percent health insurance deduction for the self-employed. Extended and created new energy-producer tax benefits: extended nonconventional fuels credit and tax incentives for ethanol production; created a new credit for enhanced oil recovery costs; amended percentage depletion; and reduced alternative minimum tax preference treatment of energy items. Created a small-business-oriented credit for accommodations for disabled persons. Modified estate "freeze" rules. Eliminated

appreciation of certain donated property as a minimum tax preference item.

- Adopted miscellaneous revenue raisers. Permitted transfers from "over-funded" pension plans for retiree health; added chemicals subject to ozone-depleting chemicals tax; re-imposed Leaking Underground Storage Tank Trust Fund tax; reduced loss deductions by property and casualty insurance companies; improved IRS ability to obtain information from foreign corporations; increased harbor maintenance tax; and reduced business income tax loopholes.

Tax Extension Act of 1991

- Provided a six-month extension for a number of tax provisions and credits facing expiration: research tax credits; exclusions for employer-provided educational assistance; targeted jobs credits; alternative energy credits; itemized deduction for health insurance costs; drug clinical testing credits; issuance authority for mortgage revenue bonds, certificates, and manufacturing/farm facility construction; and credits for charitable contributions of appreciated tangible property.

Omnibus Budget Reconciliation Act of 1993

- Imposed new higher individual tax rates of 36 and 39.6 percent. Increased tax rates and exemption amounts under the AMT. Permanently extended the itemized deduction limitation and the personal exemption phase-out legislated in Omnibus Budget Reconciliation Act of 1990.
- Increased corporate tax rate to 35 percent on income above $10 million.
- Repealed the cap on the HI tax base—set at $135,000 in 1993—so that the HI tax applies to all income.
- Expanded the taxable portion of Social Security benefits from 50 to 85 percent when modified AGI goes above $44,000 for joint returns and $34,000 for single returns.

- Increased motor fuel taxes by 4.3 cents per gallon (plus extended the current motor fuels tax of 2.5 cents per gallon).
- Reduced business meals and entertainment deduction.
- Extended EITC to single workers with no children earning $9,000 or less.

Taxpayer Bill of Rights 2 of 1996

- Established position of taxpayer advocate within the IRS, replacing taxpayer ombudsman. Gave advocate (appointed by the commissioner) four responsibilities: (1) assist taxpayers in resolving problems with the IRS, (2) identify problem areas where taxpayers have difficulty dealing with the IRS, (3) propose administrative changes within the IRS that might mitigate these problem areas, and (4) identify potential legislative changes that might mitigate these problem areas.
- Required the IRS to notify taxpayers within 30 days if a paid installment agreement is modified or terminated for any reason other than that the collection of the tax is determined to be in jeopardy. Required the IRS to establish procedures for independent administrative review of installment agreements that are modified or terminated.
- Directed the IRS to abate interest penalties against the taxpayer caused by any unreasonable error or delay on the part of IRS management.
- Reexamined joint and several liability for spouses filing joint returns; provided flexibility in moderating collection activities according to level of compliance; and boosted taxpayers' standing relative to the IRS in legal disputes.

Revenue Provisions of the Small Business Job Protection Act of 1996

- Increased the $17,500 of qualified depreciable property allowable for expensing or immediate write-off to $25,000.
- Provided credit applicable to Social Security taxes paid with respect to employee cash tips.

- Included pension simplification provisions allowing contributions to a spousal IRA for a nonworking spouse (thus doubling potential maximum contributions from $2,000 to $4,000 for eligible participants); simplified distributions from small business pension plans; tightened nondiscrimination provisions; eliminated special aggregation rules applying to self-employed individual plans; and reformed miscellaneous state and local pension rules, special job status, or professional individuals.

Revenue Provisions of the Health Insurance and Portability Act of 1996

- Offered IRA-like vehicles for the tax-advantaged accumulation of assets against possible medical expenses for employees covered under an employer-sponsored high deductible plan (e.g., at least a $1,500 deductible). Applied provision to small employers and self-employed individuals, regardless of the size of the entity for which they perform work. Provided that individual contributions to medical savings accounts (MSAs) are deductible (within limits) in determining AGI (i.e., "above the line"); additionally, allowed employer contributions to be excluded from gross income.
- Increased health expense deduction for self-employed.
- Amended treatment of long-term-care services and accelerated death benefits.
- Provided income tax exemption for state-sponsored health organizations covering high-risk individuals.
- Made IRA withdrawals for health care expenses penalty free.
- Adjusted group health plan requirements to ensure greater portability.

Taxpayer Relief Act of 1997

- Introduced a child credit of $500 per child per year.
- Introduced the HOPE and Lifetime Learning nonrefundable education credits. Provided HOPE credit as the maximum of taxable income or $1,500 per student for at most the first two years

of school. Provided Lifetime Learning credit as the maximum of 20 percent of taxable income or $1,000 per taxpayer return (rather than per student), with no limit on the number of years claimed.

- Boosted the estate and gift unified credit beginning in 1998 from $600,000 per person to $1 million by 2006. Also indexed other estate and gift tax parameters, such as the $10,000 annual gift exclusion, to inflation after 1998.
- Reduced capital gains tax rates from 28 and 15 percent to 20 and 10 percent, respectively.
- Extended AGI phaseouts for deductible IRAs; allowed tax-free withdrawals for first-time home purchases; and created new Roth IRAs and education IRAs.
- Repealed the AMT for small businesses (those averaging less than $7.5 million in gross receipts in the prior three years); modified the depreciation adjustment used in the AMT calculation; and repealed the AMT installment method adjustment for farmers.
- Phased-in an increase in the cigarette tax of 30 cents per pack. Extended air transportation excise taxes.

Surface Transportation Revenue Act of 1998

- Extended current taxes on varieties of motor fuels through 2003: 18.3 cents per gallon on gasoline, 24.3 cents per gallon on diesel and kerosene, 13.6 cents per gallon on propane, and 11.9 cents per gallon on liquefied natural gas, among others.

Internal Revenue Service Restructuring and Reform Act of 1998

- Directed the IRS to revise its mission statement to provide greater emphasis on serving the public; replaced three-tiered geographic organization with a structure that features operating units geared around different types of taxpayers and their specialized needs; and created an independent appeals function within the IRS.
- Created board to oversee the administration, management, and conduct of the IRS, ensuring that the organization and operations of the IRS allow it to properly carry out its mission.

- Gave oversight board authority to recommend candidates with strong management backgrounds to the president for appointment to a statutory five-year term (instead of a nonspecific term), with the advice and consent of the Senate. Recognized that the president can still select and remove candidates.
- Amended taxpayer advocate process so that taxpayer advocate is now to be appointed by the secretary of the Treasury; limited the advocate's former and future involvement with the IRS; and provided clearer definitions and limits on the scope of taxpayer assistance orders that the advocate can issue.

Economic Growth and Tax Relief Reconciliation Act of 2001 (EGTRRA)

- When fully-phased in 2006, levied a new 10 percent rate on the first $12,000 of income for a married couple ($10,000 for a single head of household and $6,000 for an individual), with the 15 percent rate to begin thereafter; reduced the 28 percent rate to 25 percent, the 31 percent rate to 28 percent, the 36 percent rate to 33 percent, and the 39.6 percent rate to 35 percent. Repealed the phaseout of the itemized deduction and personal exemption by 2008. Made the 10 percent bracket retroactive, resulting in refund checks of up to $300 for individuals and $600 for couples during the year.
- Doubled the $500 per child tax credit to $1,000 and made it refundable for persons earning above $10,000 to the extent that their Social Security taxes exceed their income tax liability.
- Lowered marriage penalties for couples by making the standard deduction and 15 percent bracket twice the size as for a single taxpayer.
- Provided a credit of 25 percent on expenditures for employer-provided childcare and increased the dependent care and adoption credits.
- Gradually reduced the estate and gift tax rate from 55 to 45 percent by 2007 and raised the effective exemption from $1 million in 2002 to $3.5 million in 2009. Eliminated the estate tax portion entirely in 2010 in lieu of a capital gains tax with high disregard ($3.3 million) for transfers to a surviving spouse.

- Increased IRA annual contribution limits from $2,000 to $5,000 and 401(k) limits from $10,000 to $15,000; allowed individuals age 50 and older to make larger, catch-up contributions; permitted Roth 401(k) accounts beginning in 2006; and established a temporary credit for retirement savings for households earning $50,000 or less.
- Among others, allowed $4,000 maximum deduction of college tuition expenses; allowed tax-free distributions from prepaid college tuition plans, allowed private institutions to offer these, and allowed taxpayers to simultaneously claim HOPE or Lifetime Learning credits in some instances; and eliminated the 60-month limit on student loan interest deduction.

The Job Creation and Worker Assistance Act of 2002

- Allowed additional first year depreciation or expensing equal to 30 percent of the adjusted basis of qualified property.
- Allowed five-year carryback of net operating losses (NOLs). Temporarily extended the NOL carryback period from two to five years for NOLs arising in taxable years ending 2001 and 2002.
- Provided up to 13 weeks of temporary extended unemployment benefits for eligible displaced workers.
- Expanded targeted categories under work opportunity tax credit to include certain employees in New York City; and created a new targeted group for the credit.
- Authorized issuance of $8 billion in tax-exempt private activity bonds for rebuilding the portion of New York City damaged in the attack on September 11, 2001. For New York Liberty Zone, increased the maximum dollar amount that may be deducted.
- Extended the following: AMT relief for individuals; credit for purchase of electric vehicles; Section 45 credit for production of electricity from wind, closed-loop biomass, and poultry litter; work opportunity tax credit for two years; welfare-to-work tax credit for two years; deduction of qualified clean-fuel vehicle property and qualified clean-fuel vehicle refueling property; taxable income limit on percentage depletion for marginal production; authority to issue qualified zone academy bonds; increased carryover payments to Puerto Rico and the Virgin Islands; tax failure to comply

with mental health parity requirements; suspension of reduction of deductions for mutual life insurance companies; Archer MSAs; tax incentives for investments on Indian reservations; modification of exceptions under Subpart F for active financing income; and repeal of dyed-fuel requirements for registered diesel or kerosene terminals.

The Jobs and Growth Tax Relief Reconciliation Act of 2003

- Expanded child tax credit to $1,000 per child for 2003 through 2004, reverting to present law (2001-enacted phase-ins and phase-outs) in 2005; expanded 15 percent tax bracket and standard deduction for joint filers to double the ranges and levels for single filers for 2003 through 2004, reverting to present law in 2005; expanded 10 percent bracket for 2003 through 2004, reverting to present law in 2005; implemented 2006 rate schedule: 10, 15, 25, 28, 33, and 35 percent; and increased individual AMT exemption amount by $4,500 (single filer) and $9,000 (joint filers) for 2003 through 2004.
- Taxed capital gains with a 15 percent rate for most gains and 5 percent rate for gains of moderate income taxpayers for 2003 through 2007; becomes 15 and 0 percent in 2008 and reverts to present law in 2009. Taxed dividends with a 15 and 5 percent rate structure for 2003 through 2007, 15 and 0 percent in 2008, reverting to present law in 2009.
- Increased bonus depreciation or expensing to 50 percent for physical asset purchases for 2003 through 2004, reverting to present law in 2005; and increased section 179 (100 percent) expensing by raising expensible amounts from $25,000 to $100,000 and the phase-out threshold amount from $200,000 to $400,000.
- Provided states $20 billion in fiscal relief for 2003 through 2004.

The Medicare Prescription Drug, Improvement, and Modernization Act of 2003

- Introduced Health Savings Accounts. Allowed taxpayers under age 65 to make tax-free deposits up to the deductible on a high-deductible plan if they also purchase a catastrophic health policy.

- Provided tax exclusions for certain employer subsidies.
- Increased taxes indirectly by reducing employer incentives to retain prescription drug insurance coverage.
- Introduced a new income-related premium for future Medicare, Part B, participants based on IRS records sent to the Social Security Administration.

Sources: U. S. Department of the Treasury, Office of Tax Analysis; Office of Management and Budget, Budget of the United States Government, various fiscal years; Joint Committee on Taxation, various publications.

Acronyms

ACRS	accelerated cost recovery system
AFDC	Aid to Families with Dependent Children
AGI	adjusted gross income
CBO	Congressional Budget Office
CDE	community development entity
CRS	Congressional Research Service
CTC	child tax credit
DEFRA	Deficit Reduction Act of 1984
DISC	domestic international sales corporation
EEC	European Economic Community
EITC	earned income tax credit
EGTRRA	Economic Growth and Tax Relief Reconciliation Act of 2001
ERISA	Employee Retirement Income Security Act of 1974
ERTA	Economic Recovery Tax Act of 1981
ETI	extraterritorial income exclusion
EU	European Union
FSC	foreign sales corporation
GAO	General Accounting Office
GDP	gross domestic product
GNP	gross national product
HI	Hospital Insurance (under Medicare)
HSA	health savings account
IRA	individual retirement account

IRS	Internal Revenue Service
JCT	Joint Committee on Taxation
JGTRRA	Jobs and Growth Tax Relief Reconciliation Act of 2003
MSA	medical savings account
NTJ	*National Tax Journal*
OASDI	Old Age, Survivors, and Disability Insurance (Social Security)
OBRA	Omnibus Budget Reconciliation Act (various years)
OMB	Office of Management and Budget
OTA	Office of Tax Analysis (Treasury)
OTP	Office of Tax Policy (Treasury)
PRWORA	Personal Responsibility and Work Opportunity Reconciliation Act of 1986
TANF	Temporary Assistance for Needy Families
TEFRA	Tax Equity and Fiscal Responsibility Act of 1982
VAT	value-added tax
WTO	World Trade Organization

Glossary

Adjusted gross income (AGI). A measure of an individual taxpayer's net income used in calculating personal income taxes, but before itemized deductions are taken. As a creature of the tax code, the components of the AGI have changed over the years as the tax law has changed.

Airport and Airway Trust Fund. A trust fund established in 1970, financed by aviation excise taxes and dedicated to funding public investments in the air transport system. A substantial portion of the funding for the Federal Aviation Administration (FAA) comes from the trust fund.

Alternative minimum tax (AMT). A supplemental income tax originally intended to ensure that high-income filers do not take undue advantage of tax preferences to reduce or eliminate their tax liability. The primary items of "preference," however, are for state and local tax deductions, personal exemptions, and miscellaneous itemized deductions—not items normally thought of as preferences or shelters. Increasingly, this complicated tax applies to middle-class families, in part because its exemption was not indexed for inflation.

Average effective tax rate. A widely used measure of tax burdens, particularly corporate tax burdens. Basically, it is a ratio of a taxpayer's nominal tax liability to income. The calculation does not deal with the eventual incidence of the tax.

Base broadening. A term applied to efforts to expand the tax base, usually by removing deductions, exclusions, and other preferences that are unrelated to measuring the tax base correctly. A broader base means that an equal level of revenues can be raised with lower tax rates or that more revenues can be raised at the same rates.

Bracket creep. The movement of taxpayers into higher tax brackets with higher tax rates. Under a progressive tax system, individuals are pushed into higher tax brackets as their incomes increase. In the early 1980s, tax rate schedules were indexed for inflation so that general price increases would not cause bracket creep. More recently, some analysts have expressed concern about real income growth causing bracket creep.

Capital cost recovery. Income tax features intended to allow businesses to deduct over time the costs of tangible capital assets that are used to produce income. It is similar to a depreciation allowance, except that "depreciation" usually conveys that the timing of the write-off will be related to change in value over time. (See *depreciation*.)

Capital gains taxation. A tax on increases (or decreases) in the value of assets such as corporate stock, real estate, or a business. Such taxes are usually assessed only when gains are "realized" by sale or exchange. Unrealized gains generally are not taxed on the grounds that it would be difficult to estimate the assets' value, and it could force the liquidation of assets to pay the tax. Taxation upon realization, however, leads to certain distortions and creates opportunities for tax shelters.

Carryover of basis. Transfer of basis value to a person to whom assets are transferred. The basis of an asset equals its cost, with some adjustments for items like depreciation. When an asset is sold, the realized gain equal sales price less basis (e.g., General Motors stock bought for $1,000 and sold for $3,000 has a basis of $1,000 and a gain of $2,000). Capital gains accrued at death are not only forgiven from tax in the decedent's estate, but the heirs get to treat their "basis" in the inherited assets as equal to the value at the death of the decedent (in the example, the heirs gets to treat $3,000 as their basis even though no one ever paid tax on the $2,000 of gains). With carryover of basis, the heirs would be required to keep the original basis of assets left by a decedent ($1,000 in the example). Under current law, beneficiaries of gifts from donors still alive must carry over basis. Also, under legislation passed in 2001, the estate tax is temporarily eliminated and replaced with carryover of basis for people dying in 2010.

Charitable deductions. Deductions allowed for gifts to charity. Since 1917, individual federal taxpayers have been allowed to deduct gifts to charitable and certain other nonprofit organizations. Corporations are also allowed a deduction under a stricter limit. Among other reasons, the deduction was intended to subsidize the activities of private organizations that provide viable alternatives to direct government programs.

Child care credit. A benefit in the form of a credit for child care expenses incurred by some taxpayers deemed to be gainfully employed or students. A separate exclusion is available for some employer-provided child care.

Counter-cyclical policy. Fiscal (or monetary) policy that moves counter to economic cycles, such as tax cuts in a time of recession. Traditionally, fiscal incentives have been associated with the macroeconomic theories of John Maynard Keynes.

Deficit-neutral. A term applied to bills or proposals that neither increase nor decrease the deficit. For instance, a tax increase equal in value to an expenditure increase would be deficit-neutral.

Depreciation. A measurement of the declining value of assets over time because of physical deterioration or obsolescence. In practice, tax depreciation is calculated by a set of deductions, usually over a code-specified "useful life," through which the full cost of an asset can be written off. Accelerated depreciation means a speed-up in deductions so that more can be taken in earlier years.

Distortion. Changes in behavior due to taxes, government benefits, monopolies, and other forces that interfere in the market. Typical tax distortions are changes in the amount of work or saving that would occur because of tax avoidance.

Double taxation of dividends. A controversial feature of the many tax systems that have both corporate and individual income taxes, whereby corporate profits are taxed once at the corporate level and then again when these profits are distributed to shareholders as dividends.

Earned income tax credit (EITC). An income tax credit for low-income workers, originally enacted in 1975, and now one of the largest antipoverty programs in the federal budget. Unlike other tax credits for individuals, the EITC is refundable. (See *refundable.*)

Enterprise zones. Geographically targeted tax, expenditure, and regulatory inducements used by state and local governments since the early 1980s and by the federal government since 1993. While they differ in their specifics, all the programs provide development incentives in an attempt to encourage private investment and increase employment opportunities.

Estate tax. The taxation of large estates at the time of the owner's death. In 2003, the tax applied to the largest 2 percent of estates (those worth at least one million dollars). Special provisions apply to farms and small businesses, and there is a complete exemption or deduction from the estate tax for assets transferring to spouses or charity. The tax is scheduled to be phased out by 2010, but then to be reinstated the following year.

Flat tax. A proposal for fundamental tax reform that would replace the income tax system with a flat-rate tax on businesses and individuals. Most flat tax proposals are designed to be consumption rather than income taxes, and most are really not "flat" because they grant an exemption at least for the first dollars of earnings.

Foreign tax credit. A credit that allows U.S. residents to subtract foreign income taxes paid from the U.S. income tax due on income earned abroad, up to certain limits.

Gramm-Rudman-Hollings law. A law enacted in 1985 that required budget deficits be brought down to specified amounts and the budget be balanced by 1991. If Congress did not enact legislation to do so, automatic spending cuts would be triggered. When it became apparent that the Gramm-Rudman-Hollings law could not achieve its goals, President George H. W. Bush and Congress negotiated major deficit reductions that were protected or reinforced by the rules set out in the Budget Enforcement Act of 1990.

Health savings account (HSA). A special tax-favored account for deposits made to cover present and future health care expenses paid by the individual. Both the health expenditures and interest earned in the account are tax free so long as funds are used to pay for medical expenses. Enacted in 2003 as part of legislation providing drug benefits under Medicare, the tax preference is only available if the individual purchases a health insurance policy with a large deductible.

Highway trust fund. A federal trust fund, created in 1956, that finances highway construction and certain other federal spending on transportation. The fund keeps its revenues and outlays segregated from the rest of the federal budget.

Homeowner preference. Income tax provisions that favor investments in owner-occupied housing. The mortgage-interest deduction and the property-tax deduction are two of the largest measured tax expenditure items. In truth, the real preference is for the non-taxation of the "rental" stream of income available to a homeowner (compare, for instance, a renter having a savings account with a homeowner who puts the saving into a purchasing a home).

Indexation of the tax system. Measures that prevent bracket creep by "indexing" items such as personal exemptions and tax brackets for inflation. For instance, with 5 percent inflation, a personal exemption of $1,000 would be raised to $1,050. More broadly, the term applies to all efforts to adjust measures of income relative to some index, such as reducing capital gains subject to tax by the amount to which those gains are inflationary, rather than real. (See *bracket creep.*)

Low-income housing credit. A federal tax credit designed to encourage the acquisition, construction, and/or rehabilitation of housing for low-income families, and one of the few tax mechanisms for low-income housing support.

Marginal tax rate. The additional tax that would be paid on an additional dollar of income. It is a measure of the effect of the tax system on incentives to work, save, and shelter income from tax. Provisions such as the phase out of tax credits can cause marginal tax rates to differ from statutory tax rates.

Out year. In budget parlance, a future year beyond the period over which budget costs are tallied (in recent years, the out year has been the year following a 5- or 10-year period over which costs are estimated).

Pay-as-you-go rules and caps. Provisions in the 1990 Budget Enforcement Act that replaced Gramm-Rudman-Hollings (see above). Spending subject to appropriation was made subject to a separate series of annual caps. Pay-as-you-go rules covered the rest of the budget: mandatory spending and revenues could not together increase the deficit in any bill when pay-as-you-go rules were enforced. The law was originally designed to preserve the deficit reductions resulting from the bipartisan budget agreement of 1990.

Real income. Income that is not the result of inflation. Real income is usually calculated by subtracting inflationary income (e.g., capital gains due to inflation) from nominal income.

Refundable. Payable to taxpayers (usually as a refund) even if they have no tax liability. Most credits and deductions are not refundable, although they often may be used to offset liability from past or future years, not just the current year. (See *earned income tax credit*.)

Rent-seeking. The search for extraordinary profits or returns due to, for instance, scarcity, monopoly, asymmetry of information, or segmentation of market demand into different price-sensitive categories.

Revenue-neutral. A term applied to tax bills or proposals that pay for themselves over some budget period by having tax increases equal in value to tax decreases. (See *deficit-neutral*.)

Stagflation. The combination of stagnant growth and high inflation, associated in the United States largely with the 1970s.

Standard deduction. An allowance for a minimum amount of deductions that may be taken in lieu of itemizing deductions on a tax return. Typically, taxpayers with small amounts of potential itemized deductions, such as charitable contributions, mortgage interest, or state and local taxes, choose to take the standard deduction instead. In 2001, about two-thirds of returns claimed the standard deduction.

Tax arbitrage. Profiting from the different tax treatment of different assets, firms, or tax regimes in different countries, sometimes when there is no economic reason for the transactions. The most common form of tax arbitrage is borrowing and deducting the interest to buy tax-preferred assets (even when, on a before-tax basis, the arbitrager pays more in interest than he receives in return on the asset).

Tax expenditures. Spending programs channeled through the tax system. The size of the "expenditure" is approximated by different measures of the revenue losses. These tax provisions generally grant special tax relief to encourage certain kinds of behavior by taxpayers or to aid taxpayers in special circumstances. What counts as a tax expenditure is often disputed.

Taxpolicycenter.org. The web site of the Urban-Brookings Tax Policy Center, established to provide nonpartisan analysis of key tax issues.

Tax Policy Center microsimulation model. A microsimulation model developed by the Tax Policy Center and based on data from the IRS Statistics of Income public use files. The model is used to estimate how proposals affect revenue, the distribution of tax burdens, and incentives to work and save. It is very similar to the models used by the Treasury Department, the Joint Committee on Taxation, and the Congressional Budget Office.

Tax shelters. A popular term applied to investments that take advantage of preferences in the tax system; more generally, any arrangements undertaken to minimize taxes. (See *tax arbitrage*).

Value-added tax (VAT). A general tax on all goods and services based on the value each firm adds to a product (rather than, say, gross sales). Although not required, almost all value-added taxes are based upon consumption, not income (e.g., they allow complete write-offs, rather than depreciation, of capital expenses). Designed to raise large amounts of revenue while minimizing a number of economic distortions, it is almost universal among developed countries other than the United States..

Sources: Author; Cordes et al. 1999; and www.taxpolicycenter.org.

References

Aaron, Henry J., and William G. Gale, eds. 1996. *Economic Effects of Fundamental Tax Reform*. Washington, DC: Brookings Institution Press.

ACIR (Advisory Commission on Intergovernmental Relations). 1989. *Changing Public Attitudes on Governments and Taxes*. Washington, DC: ACIR.

Acs, Gregory, and C. Eugene Steuerle. 1996. "The Corporation as a Dispenser of Welfare and Security." In *The American Corporation Today*, edited by Carl Kaysen (369–71). Oxford: Oxford University Press.

Altig, David, Alan J. Auerbach, Laurence J. Kotlikoff, Kent A. Smetters, and Jan Walliser. 2001. "Stimulating Fundamental Tax Reform in the United States." *American Economic Review* 91(3): 574–95.

Auerbach, Alan J. 1983. "Corporate Taxation in the United States," *Brookings Papers on Economic Activity* 1983(2): 1451–1505.

———. 1986. "Incentives and Windfalls in Corporate Tax Reform." In *Technology and Economic Policy*, edited by Ralph Landau and Dale Jorgenson (119–35). Cambridge, MA: Ballinger Press.

———. 1987. "The Tax Reform Act of 1986 and the Cost of Capital." *Journal of Economic Perspectives* 1(1): 73–86.

———. 1988. "Capital Gains Taxation in the United States." *Brookings Papers on Economic Activity 2*: 595–631.

Auerbach, Alan J., and James Poterba. 1988. "Capital Gains Taxation in the United States." *Brookings Papers on Economic Activity* 1988(2): 595–637.

Auerbach, Alan J., William G. Gale, and Peter R. Orszag. 2003. "Reassessing the Fiscal Gap: The Role of Tax-Deferred Saving." *Tax Notes* 95(11): 567–84.

Auten, Gerald E., and Charles T. Clotfelter. 1982. "Permanent versus Transitory Tax Effects and the Realization of Capital Gains." *Quarterly Journal of Economics* 97(4): 613–32.

Auten, Gerald E., and Joseph Cordes. 1991. "Capital Gains Realizations." *Journal of Economic Perspectives* 15(1): 181–92.

Bacon, Kenneth H. 1981. "Taxes to Balance Budget Rejected by President." *The Wall Street Journal.* December 18.

Bakija, John, and Joel Slemrod. 1996. *Taxing Ourselves.* Cambridge: Massachusetts Institute of Technology.

Bartlett, Bruce. 2003. "Supply-Side Economics: 'Voodoo Economics' or Lasting Contribution?" San Diego, CA: Laffer Associates.

Bernheim, B. Douglas. 2002. "Taxation and Savings." In *Handbook of Public Economics,* vol. 3, edited by Alan Auerbach and Martin Feldstein (1173–1249). Toronto, Canada: North-Holland.

Berry, John M., and Helen Dewar. 1981. "Deficit of $80 Billion Looms for 1982, Hill Told." *The Washington Post.* September 11.

Birnbaum, Jeffrey H., and Alan S. Murray. 1987. *Showdown at Gucci Gulch.* New York: Random House.

Blanchard, Olivier. 1985. "Debt, Deficits, and Finite Horizons." *Journal of Political Economy* 93(2): 223–47.

Blank, Rebecca M., and Ron Haskins. 2001. "Welfare Reform: An Agenda for Reauthorization." In *The New World of Welfare*, edited by Rebecca M. Blank and Ron Haskins. Washington, DC: Brookings Institution Press.

Blum, Walter J., and Harry Kalven. 1953. *The Uneasy Case for Progressive Taxation.* Chicago: University of Chicago Press.

Boards of Trustees, Federal Hospital Insurance and Federal Supplementary Medical Insurance Trust Funds. 1990. Annual Report of the Board of Trustees of the Federal Hospital Insurance and Federal Supplementary Medical Insurance Trust Funds. Washington, DC: U.S. Government Printing Office.

Boards of Trustees, Federal Old-Age and Survivors Insurance and Disability Insurance Trust Funds. 1990. Annual Report of the Board of Trustees of the Federal Old-Age and Survivors Insurance and Disability Insurance Trust Funds. Washington, DC: U.S. Government Printing Office.

Boskin, Michael J., ed. 1996. *Frontiers in Tax Reform.* Stanford, CA: Hoover Institution Press.

———. 2003. "Deferred Taxes in Public Finance." Paper presented at The Stanford Institute for Economic Policy Conference on U.S. Budget Policy and Practice, Washington, D.C., May 8.

Boynton, Charles, Paul Robbins, and George Plesko. 1991. "Earnings Management and the Corporate Minimum Tax." Unpublished manuscript.

Bradford, David F. 1996a. "Consumption Taxes: Some Fundamental Transition Issues." In *Frontiers of Tax Reform*, edited by Michael J. Boskin. Stanford, CA: Hoover Institution Press.

———. 1996b. *Fundamental Issues in Consumption Taxation.* Washington, DC: AEI Press.

Bradford, David, and U.S. Treasury staff. 1984. *Blueprints for Tax Reform*, 2d ed. Arlington, VA: Tax Analysts.

Break, George F. 1991. "Major Fiscal Trends in the 1980s and Implications for the 1990s." *Tax Notes* 50(5).

Break, George F., and Joseph A. Pechman. 1975. *Federal Tax Reform: The Impossible Dream?* Washington, DC: The Brookings Institution.

Brooks, David. 2000. "An Emerging Democratic Majority" *The Weekly Standard.* December 18, page 26.

Brownlee, W. Elliot. 1989. "Taxation for a Strong and Virtuous Republic: A Bicentennial Retrospective." *Tax Notes* 45(13): 1620.

———. 1996. *Federal Taxation in America: A Short History.* New York: Woodrow Wilson Centers Press and Cambridge University Press.

———. 2004. *Federal Taxation in America: A Short History,* 2d ed. Cambridge, U.K. and Washington, DC: Cambridge Press and the Wilson Center Press.

Brownlee, W. Elliot, and C. Eugene Steuerle. 2003. "Taxation." In *The Reagan Presidency: Pragmatic Conservatism and Its Legacies,* edited by W. Elliott Brownlee and Hugh Davis Graham. Lawrence: The University Press of Kansas.

Bull, Nicholas, Janet Holtzblatt, James R. Nunn, and Robert Rebelein. 1999. "Defining and Measuring Marriage Penalties and Subsidies." OTA Paper 82. Washington, DC: U.S. Department of the Treasury, Office of Tax Analysis.

Burman, Leonard E. 1997. "Big, Big Postcard." *Tax Notes* 77(October 6): 193–268.

———. 1999. *The Labyrinth of Capital Gains Tax Policy,* Washington, DC: The Brookings Institution.

———. 2002. "Tax Policy from 1990 to 1991." In *American Economic Policy in the 1990s,* edited by Jeffrey A. Frankel and Peter R. Orszag. Cambridge, MA: MIT Press.

———. 2003. "Tax Evasion, IRS Priorities, and EITC Precertification." Statement before the United States House of Representatives Committee on Ways and Means, Subcommittee on Waste, Fraud, and Abuse. July 17.

Burman, Leonard E., and Linda J. Blumberg. 2003. "HSAs Won't Cure Medicare's Ills." Washington, DC: The Urban Institute.

Burman, Leonard E., William Gale, and Jeffrey Rohaly. 2002. "The AMT: Out of Control." Tax Policy Center Issues and Options Policy Brief No. 5. Washington, DC: The Urban Institute.

Burman, Leonard E., William G. Gale, Jeff Rohaly, and Benjamin H. Harris. 2002. "The Individual AMT: Problems and Potential Solutions." Tax Policy Center Discussion Paper No. 5. Washington, DC: The Urban Institute.

Burman, Leonard E., Elaine Maag, and Jeffrey Rohaly. 2002. "The Effect of the 2001 Tax Cut on Low- and Middle-Income Families and Children." Tax Policy Center Discussion Paper. Washington, DC: The Urban Institute.

Burman, Leonard E., Cori Uccello, Laura L. Wheaton, and Deborah Kobes. 2003. "Tax Incentives for Health Insurance." Tax Policy Center Discussion Paper No. 12. Washington, DC: The Urban Institute.

Burman, Leonard E., Sally Wallace, and David Weiner. 1997. "How Capital Gains Taxes Distort Homeowners' Decisions." In *Proceedings of the 89th Annual Conference on Taxation* (355–63). Washington, DC: National Tax Association.

Burtless, Gary, Thomas Corbett, Katharine Porter, Wendell Primus, and Barbara Wolfe. 2000. "An Open Letter on Revising the Official Measure of Poverty to Secretary Donna Shalala of Health and Human Services, Director Jacob Lew of the Office of Management and Budget, and Director Kenneth Prewitt of the U.S. Bureau of the Census." http://www.ssc.wisc.edu/irp/povmeas/povlet.htm. (Accessed November 2003.)

Carasso, Adam, and C. Eugene Steuerle. 2002. "Saying 'I Do' after the 2001 Tax Cuts." Tax Policy Center Issues and Options Policy Brief No. 4. Washington, DC: The Urban Institute.

Cavanaugh, Maureen B. 2003. "Democracy, Equality, and Taxes." *Alabama Law Review* 54(2): 415–81.

CBO. See *Congressional Budget Office.*

Choi, James J., David Laibson, Brigitte C. Madrian, and Andrew Metrick. 2001. "For Better or for Worse: Default Effects and 401(k) Savings Behavior." National Bureau of Economic Research Working Paper No. w8651. Cambridge, MA: National Bureau of Economic Research.

Chapoton, John E. 1982. "Statement of the Honorable John E. Chapoton, Assistant Secretary of the Treasury for Tax Policy, Before the Senate Finance Committee, September 28." Washington, DC: U.S. Department of the Treasury.

Chicago Tribune. 1989. "Insurance Forum Turns Catastrophic for Rostenkowski." August 18.

Cline, Robert, William Fox, Tom Neubig, and Andrew Phillips. 2004. "Total State and Local Business Taxes: A 50-State Study of the Taxes Paid by Business in FY 2003." *Quantitative Economics and Statistics*, Ernst & Young LLP. Prepared for the Council on State Taxation.

Clinton, William J. 1996. State of the Union Address, January 23. Archived at the University of Oklahoma Law Center. http://www.law.ou.edu/hist/state96.html. (Accessed November 2003.)

CNN.com News. 1995. "Budget Talks Fall Through: Republicans Blame White House." November 11. http://www.cnn.com/US/9511/debt_limit/11-10/debt_ceiling/. (Accessed February 25, 2004.)

Cohen, Lee, C. Eugene Steuerle, and Adam Carasso. 2002. "Social Security Redistribution by Education, Race, and Income: How Much and Why." Paper presented at the Third Annual Joint Conference for the Retirement Research Consortium, "Making Hard Choices About Retirement," Washington, D.C., May 17–18.

Concord Coalition, The. 2003. "Sunsets Hide More than Half of the Revenue Loss from Recent Tax Cuts." Washington, DC: The Concord Coalition.

Congressional Budget Office (CBO). 1991. *The Economic and Budget Outlook: Fiscal Years 1992–1996.* Washington, DC: Superintendent of Documents.

———. 1997. *Budget and Economic Outlook.* Washington, DC: Congressional Budget Office. January.

———. 2003. "Effective Tax Rates, 1997–2000." Washington, DC: Congressional Budget Office.

Congressional Record. 1986. "Tax Reform Act of 1986." *Congressional Record* 132(77): S7151.

Conlan, Timothy J., Margaret T. Wrightson, and David R. Beam. 1990. *Taxing Choices: The Politics of Tax Reform.* Washington, DC: The Congressional Quarterly, Inc.

Connelly, Marjorie. 2000. "The Election; Who Voted: A Portrait of American Politics, 1976–2000." *The New York Times.* November 12, sec. 4.

Cordes, Joseph J. 2002. "Corrective Taxes, Charges, and Tradable Permits." In *The Tools of Government: A Guide to the New Governance,* edited by Lester M. Salamon (255–81). New York: Oxford University Press.

Cordes, Joseph J., Robert D. Ebel, and Jane G. Gravelle, eds. 1999. *The Encyclopedia of Taxation and Tax Policy.* Washington, DC: Urban Institute Press.

Darman, Richard. 1996. *Who's in Control? Polar Politics and the Sensible Center.* New York: Simon and Schuster.

Death Tax web site. 2003. "Death Tax." Seattle, WA: *The Seattle Times.* http://deathtax.com/. (Accessed February 25, 2004.)

De Tocqueville, Alexis. 1835. *Democracy in America*. New York: Signet.

Dickert, Stacy, Scott Houser, and John Karl Scholz. 1995. "The Earned Income Tax Credit and Transfer Programs: A Study of Labor Market and Program Participation." In *Tax Policy and the Economy*, edited by James M. Poterba. Cambridge, MA: MIT Press and National Bureau of Economic Research.

Donmoyer, Ryan J. 2000. "Secret GAO Report Is Latest to Discredit Roth's IRS Hearings." *Tax Notes* 87(April): 463.

Edsall, Thomas B. 1981. "GOP Hunts $60 Billion." *The Washington Post*. October 31, sec. 1.

Ellwood, David T., and Jeffrey B. Liebman. 2000. "The Middle Class Parent Penalty: Child Benefits in the U.S. Tax Code." National Bureau of Economic Research Working Paper No. 8031. Cambridge, MA: National Bureau of Economic Research.

Executive Office of the U.S. President. 1963. *President's 1963 Tax Message*. Washington, DC: U.S. Government Printing Office.

―――. 2003. *Economic Report of the President*. Washington, DC: U.S. Government Printing Office.

Feenberg, Daniel, and Harvey Rosen. 1995. "Recent Developments in the Marriage Tax." *National Tax Journal* 48(1): 91–101.

Feldstein, Martin S. 1976. "On the Theory of Tax Reform." *Journal of Public Economics* 6 (July): 77–104.

―――. 1994. "American Economic Policy in the 1980s: A Personal View." In *American Economic Policy in the 1980s*, edited by Martin S. Feldstein. Chicago: The University of Chicago Press.

Feldstein, Martin S., Joel Slemrod, and Shlomo Yitzhaki. 1980. "The Effects of Taxation on the Selling of Corporate Stock and the Realization of Capital Gains." *Quarterly Journal of Economics* 97(4): 777–91.

Field, Thomas. 2003. "Tax Shelters: Have the Ethics Changed?" *Tax Analysts' Daily Tax Highlights and Documents* 71(36): 1559–61.

Fox, John O. 2001. *If Americans Really Understood the Income Tax*. Boulder, CO: Westview Press.

Fullerton, Don, and Diane Lim Rogers. 1993. *Who Bears the Lifetime Tax Burden?* Washington, DC: Brookings Institution Press.

Gale, Bill, and Peter Orszag. 2003a. "Sunsets in the Tax Code." Washington, DC: The Urban Institute and the Brookings Institution.

―――. 2003b. "The Budget Outlook: Baseline and Adjusted Projections." *Tax Notes* 100(12).

Galemore, Gary L. 2003. "Presidential Vetoes: 1789–Present: A Summary Overview." Washington, DC: Congressional Research Service.

Gallagher, Jerome L., Megan Gallagher, Kevin Perese, Susan Schreiber, and Keith Watson. 1998. "One Year after Federal Welfare Reform: A Description of State Temporary Assistance for Needy Families (TANF) Decisions as of October 1997." Washington, DC: The Urban Institute.

Gates Sr., William H., and Chuck Collins. 2002a. "Tax the Wealthy: Why America Needs the Estate Tax." *The American Prospect* 13(11).

―――. 2002b. *Wealth and Our Commonwealth: Why America Should Tax Accumulated Fortunes*. Boston, MA: Beacon Press.

Giannarelli, Linda, and C. Eugene Steuerle. 1995. "The Twice-Poverty Trap: Tax Rates Faced by AFDC Recipients." Washington, DC: The Urban Institute.

Glenn, Heidi. 1997. "The End of 'Big Government' May Mean a Bigger Tax Code." *Tax Notes* 74(6): 708.

Gokhale, Jagadeesh, Laurence J. Kotlikoff, and Alexi Sluchynsky. 2002. "Does It Pay to Work?" NBER Working Paper w9096. Cambridge, MA: National Bureau of Economic Research.

Goode, Richard. 1976. *The Individual Income Tax.* Washington, DC: The Brookings Institution.

Gordon, Roger, and Joel Slemrod. 1989. "Do We Collect Any Revenue from Taxing Capital?" *Tax Policy and the Economy* 2: 89–130.

Gordon, Roger, Laura Kalambokidis, and Joel Slemrod. 2003. "Do We *Now* Collect Any Revenue from Taxing Capital?" Paper presented at the International Seminar in Public Economics conference, University of California at Berkeley, December 7–8.

Gould, James C. 2003. "The Rebirth of an Income-Based Medicare Program." *Tax Notes* 101(12): 1467–70.

Graetz, Michael. 1984. *A Comparative Analysis of Five Tax Proposals: Effects of Business Income Tax Provisions.* Report No. 84-832 E. Washington, DC: Congressional Research Service.

_____. 1986. *Effective Tax Rates in the Major Tax Revision Plans: Updated Tables Including the Senate Finance Committee Proposal.* Report 86-691 E. Washington DC: Congressional Research Service.

———. 1997. *The Decline and Fall of the Income Tax.* New York: W.W. Norton and Company.

Gramlich, Edward M., Hugh Heclo, Demetra Smith Nightingale, and C. Eugene Steuerle. 1998. *The Government We Deserve.* Washington, DC: Urban Institute Press.

Gravelle, Jane. 1984. "A Comparative Analysis of Five Tax Proposals: Effects of Business Income Tax Provisions." Report No. 84-832E. Washington, DC: Congressional Research Service.

———. 1986. "Effective Tax Rates in the Major Tax Revision Plans: Updated Tables Including the Senate Finance Committee Proposal." Report No. 86-961E. Washington, DC: Congressional Research Service.

———. 2003. "The Enron Debacle: Lessons for Tax Policy." Tax Policy Center Discussion Paper No. 6. Washington, DC: The Urban Institute.

———. 2004. "Historical Effective Marginal Tax Rates on Capital Income." Document RS21706. Washington, DC: Congressional Research Service.

Hall, Robert E., and Alvin Rabushka. 1983. *Low Tax, Simple Tax, Flat Tax.* New York: McGraw-Hill.

Halperin, Daniel, and C. Eugene Steuerle. 1988. "Indexing the Tax System for Inflation." In *The Uneasy Compromise: Problems of a Hybrid Income-Consumption Tax,* edited by Henry Aaron, Harvey Galper, and Joseph Pechman. Washington, DC: The Brookings Institution.

Haskel, Barbara. 1987. "Paying for the Welfare State: Creating Political Durability." *Scandinavian Studies* 59: 221–53.

Hassett, Kevin A., and Glenn Hubbard, eds. 2001. *Transition Costs of Fundamental Tax Reform.* Washington, DC: American Enterprise Institute.

Hoffman, Saul, and Laurence S. Seidman. 1990. *The Earned Income Tax Credit: Antipoverty Effectiveness and Labor Market Effects.* Kalamazoo, MI: W.E. Upjohn Institute for Employment Research.

Holahan, John, Colin Winterbottom, and Sheila R. Zedlewski. 1994. "The Distributional Effects of Employer and Individual Health Insurance Mandates." Washington, DC: The Urban Institute.

Holtz-Eakin, Douglas, and Jeff Lemieux. 2003. "The Cost of Medicare: What the Future Holds." Heritage Lectures No. 815. Washington, DC: The Heritage Foundation.

Howard, Christopher. 2002. "Tax Expenditures." In *The Tools of Government: A Guide to the New Governance*, edited by Lester M. Salamon (410–44). New York: Oxford University Press.

Hulten, Charles R., and James W. Robertson. 1984. "The Taxation of High Technology Industries." *National Tax Journal* 37(3): 327–46.

IRS (Internal Revenue Service). 1985. "Taxpayer Compliance Measurement Program for 1982 Returns." Unpublished data.

———. 1988. *1988 Package X*, vol. 1. Washington, DC: Internal Revenue Service.

———. 1998. "IRS Oversight Hearings Day One." IRS News Release, April 28. http://www.senate.gov/~finance/105-301.htm. (Accessed February 24, 2004.)

———. 2002. "More than 1 Million Errors on New Tax Form Line; IRS Urges Caution to Avoid Refund Delays." IRS News Release, February 14. Washington, DC: Internal Revenue Service.

IRS, Statistics on Income Division. Various years. *Individual Income Tax Returns.* Washington DC: Internal Revenue Service.

JCT. See *Joint Committee on Taxation.*

Jenny, Nicholas W. 2003. "2003 Tax and Budget Review." Fiscal Studies Program No. 69. New York: Nelson A. Rockefeller Institute of Government..

Joint Committee on Taxation (JCT). 1975. *Summary of the Tax Reduction Act of 1975.* Washington, DC: U.S. Government Printing Office.

———. 1976. *General Explanation of the Tax Reform Act of 1976.* Washington, DC: U.S. Government Printing Office.

———. 1979. *General Explanation of the Revenue Act of 1978.* Washington, DC: U.S. Government Printing Office.

———. 1981. *General Explanation of the Crude Oil Windfall Profit Tax Act of 1980.* Washington, DC: U.S. Government Printing Office.

———. 1982. *General Explanation of the Revenue Provisions of the Tax Equity and Fiscal Responsibility Act of 1982.* Washington, DC: U.S. Government Printing Office.

———. 1986a. *General Explanation of Tax Legislation Enacted in the 104th Congress.* Washington, DC: U.S. Government Printing Office.

———. 1986b. *Summary of the Conference Agreement on H.R. 3838 (Tax Reform Act of 1986).* Washington, DC: U.S. Government Printing Office.

———. 1987. *General Explanation of the Tax Reform Act of 1986.* Washington, DC: U.S. Government Printing Office.

———. 1988. *Tax Incentives for Education Scheduled for a Hearing before the Committee on Finance on March 15, 1988.* Washington, DC: U.S. Government Printing Office.

———. 1996. *General Explanation of Tax Legislation Enacted in the 104th Congress.* Washington, DC: U.S. Government Printing Office.

———. 1997. *General Explanation of the Tax Legislation Enacted in 1997.* Washington, DC: U.S. Government Printing Office.

———. 1998. *General Explanation of the Tax Legislation Enacted in 1998.* Washington, DC: U.S. Government Printing Office.

———. 2002a. "Background and Present Law Relating to Tax Shelters." Washington, DC: U.S. Government Printing Office.

———. 2002b. *Summary of P.L. 107-147, The "Job Creation and Worker Assistance Act of 2002."* Washington, DC: U.S. Government Printing Office.

———. 2003a. "Estimated Revenue Effect of Certain Provisions Contained in the Conference Agreement for H.R.1, the 'Medicare Prescription Drug, Improvement, and Modernization Act of 2003.'" Washington, DC: U.S. Government Printing Office.

———. 2003b. "Summary of the Conference Agreement on H.R. 2, 'Jobs and Growth Tax Relief Reconciliation Act of 2003.'" Washington, DC: U.S. Government Printing Office.

Jorgenson, Dale W., and Kun-Young Yun. 2001. *Investment Volume 3: Lifting the Burden.* Cambridge, MA: MIT Press.

Juffras, Jason, and C. Eugene Steuerle. 1991. "A $1,000 Tax Credit for Every Child: A Base of Reform for the Nation's Tax, Welfare, and Health Systems." Washington, DC: The Urban Institute.

Kaplow, Louis. 1989. "Horizontal Equity: Measures in Search of a Principle." *National Tax Journal* 42(2): 139–54.

———. 1994. "Taxation and Risk Taking: A General Equilibrium Perspective." *National Tax Journal* 47(4): 789–98.

Keynes, John Maynard. 1936. *General Theory of Employment, Interest, and Money.* Cambridge, U.K.: Macmillan Cambridge University Press.

Kiefer, Donald, Robert Carroll, Janet Holtzblatt, Allen Lerman. 2002. "The Economic Growth and Tax Relief Reconciliation Act of 2001: Overview and Assessment of Effects on Taxpayers." *National Tax Journal* 55(March): 89–117.

Kristol, Irving. 2003a. "The Neoconservative Persuasion." *The Weekly Standard* 8(47): 23–25.

———. 2003b. "Robert Bartley: 1937–2003." *The Weekly Standard* 9(15): 10–11.

Lewis, C. S. 1943. *Mere Christianity.* New York: Macmillan Publishing Company.

Liebman, Jeffrey, Douglas Elmendorf, and David Wilcox. 2002. "Fiscal Policy and Social Security Policy during the 1990s." In *American Economic Policy in the 1990s*, edited by Jeffrey Frankel and Peter Orszag. Cambridge, MA: MIT Press.

Lindsey, Lawrence B. 1988. "Capital Gains Rates, Realizations, and Revenues." In *The Effects of Taxation on Capital Formation*, edited by Martin S. Feldstein. Chicago: University of Chicago Press.

Lutz, Harley L. 1945. *Guideposts to a Free Economy.* New York: McGraw-Hill.

Maggs, John. 2003. "Deconstructing the Deficit." *The National Journal* 35(41): 3122–24.

Makin, John H., and Michael T. Allison. 1986. "Tax Reform 1986: A Fragile Victory." Studies in the Fiscal Policy No. 10. Washington, DC: The American Enterprise Institute.

Manzon, Gil B., and George A. Plesko. 2002. "The Relation between Financial and Tax Reporting Measures of Income." *New York University Tax Law Review* 55(2): 175–214.

Mayer, Jane, and Doyle McManus. 1988. "How the Reagan Myth Was Made." *The Washington Post.* September 18, sec. C.

McCaffery, Edward J. 2003. "Ten Facts about Fundamental Tax Reform." *Tax Notes* 101(12): 1463–66.

McHugh, Richard, Emil Sunley, and C. Eugene Steuerle. 1978. "Who Benefits from Income Averaging?" *National Tax Journal* 31(March): 19–32.

McLure, Charles. 1988. "The 1986 Act: Tax Reform's Finest Hour or Death Throes of the Income Tax?" *National Tax Journal* 41(September): 303–15.

Michalopolous, Charles, and Gordon Berlin. 2001. "Financial Work Incentives for Low-Wage Workers." In *The New World of Welfare*, edited by Rebecca M. Blank and Ron Haskins. Washington, DC: Brookings Institution Press.

Minarik, Joseph J. 1984. "The Effects of Taxation on the Selling of Corporate Stock and the Realization of Capital Gains: Comment." *Quarterly Journal of Economics* 99(1): 93–110.

———. 1987. "How Tax Reform Came About." *Tax Notes* 40(December 26): 1359–73.

Moynihan, Daniel Patrick. 1986. *Family and Nation*. San Diego, CA: Harcourt Brace Jovanovich.

Murphy, Ann, and David Higer. 2002. "The 10 Deadly Sins: A Law with Unintended Consequences." *Tax Notes* 96(6).

Musgrave, Richard A. 1959. *The Theory of Public Finance: A Study in Public Economy*. New York: McGraw-Hill.

National Bureau of Economic Research. 2003. "Business Cycle Expansions and Contractions." http://www.nber.org/cycles/cyclesmain.html. (Accessed November 2003.)

National Commission on Children. 1991. *Beyond Rhetoric: A New American Agenda for Children and Families*. Final Report of the National Commission on Children. Washington, DC: U.S. Government Printing Office.

National Journal. 2000. "Special Issue on the Earned Income Tax Credit: Proceedings of the Joint Center on Poverty Research's Conference on 'The Earned Income Tax Credit: Early Evidence.'" *National Journal* 53(4).

Nelson, Susan. 1985. "Taxes Paid by High-Income Taxpayers and the Growth of Partnerships." *Statistics on Income Bulletin* 5(Fall).

Neubig, Thomas, and David Joulfaian. 1988. "The Tax Expenditure Budget before and after the Tax Reform Act of 1986." Office of Tax Analysis Paper No. 60. Washington, DC: U.S. Department of the Treasury.

Novack, Janet. 2001. "Government by Tax Credit." *Forbes Magazine*. November 26.

Office of Management and Budget (OMB). 1981. *The Budget of the United States, Fiscal Year 1982*. Washington, DC: U.S. Government Printing Office.

———. 1984. *The Budget of the United States, Fiscal Year 1985*. Washington, DC: Superintendent of Documents.

———. 1988. *The Budget of the United States, Fiscal Year 1989*. Washington, DC: Superintendent of Documents.

———. 1990. *The Budget of the United States, Fiscal Year 1991*. Washington, DC: U.S. Government Printing Office.

———. 1991. "Midsession Review of the Budget." Washington, DC: U.S. Government Printing Office.

———. 2001. *The Budget of the United States, Fiscal Year 2002*. Washington, DC: U.S. Government Printing Office.

———. 2002. *The Budget of the United States, Fiscal Year 2003*. Washington, DC: U.S. Government Printing Office.

———. 2003. *The Budget of the United States, Fiscal Year 2004*. Washington, DC: U.S. Government Printing Office.

———. 2004. *The Budget of the United States, Fiscal Year 2005*. Washington, DC: U.S. Government Printing Office.

Office of Tax Analysis, Department of the Treasury. 1985. *Capital Gains Tax Reductions of 1978*. Washington, DC: Superintendent of Documents.

Olson, Nina E. 2004. "National Taxpayer Advocate, Annual Report to the Congress." Washington, DC: Internal Revenue Service.

OMB. See *Office of Management and Budget*.

Orszag, Peter, Richard Kogan, and Robert Greenstein. 2003. "The Administration's Tax Cuts and the Long-Term Budget Outlook." Washington, DC: Center on Budget and Policy Priorities.

Papke, Leslie E. 1993. "What Do We Know about Enterprise Zones?" In *Tax Policy and the Economy*, vol. 7, edited by James M. Poterba (37–72). Cambridge, MA: National Bureau of Economic Research and MIT Press.

———. 2000. "The Indiana Enterprise Zone Revisited: Effects on Capital Investment and Land Values." *Proceedings of the Ninety-Third Annual Conference*. Washington, DC: National Tax Association.

Pechman, Joseph A. 1971. *Federal Tax Policy*, revised edition. New York: W.W. Norton & Company, Inc.

———. 1983. *Federal Tax Policy*. Washington DC: Superintendent of Documents.

———. 1987. *Federal Tax Policy*. Washington DC: Superintendent of Documents.

Perun, Pamela, and C. Eugene Steuerle. 2003. "Reality Testing for Pension Reform." Washington, DC: The Urban Institute.

Peterson, George, Robert Reischauer, C. Eugene Steuerle, and Van Doorn Ooms, eds. 2000. *Vouchers and the Provision of Public Services*. Washington, DC: The Urban Institute Press, The Brookings Institution, and the Committee for Economic Development.

Plumley, Alan, and C. Eugene Steuerle. 2002. "What Should the Ultimate Objective of the Internal Revenue Service Be? A Fresh Look from a Historical Perspective." Paper presented at "The Crisis in Tax Administration," Washington, D.C., November 7–8.

Pollack, Sheldon D. 1996. *The Failure of U.S. Tax Policy*. University Park: The Pennsylvania State University Press.

Price Waterhouse Coopers. 1998. "IRS Restructuring Legislation." Washington Tax Advisory Pamphlet.

Regan, Donald T. 1988. *For the Record: From Wall Street to Washington*. San Diego: Harcourt Brace Jovanovich.

Reischauer, Robert D. 1994. Testimony before the U.S. House of Representatives, Committee on Ways and Means. February 8.

Rojas, Warren. 2003. "Enron Report Reinforces Need for Antishelter Bill, Tax Writers Say." *Tax Notes* 98(8): 1031–34.

Rosen, Harvey S. 1999. *Public Finance*. Boston, MA: Irwin/McGraw Hill.

———. 1987. "The Marriage Tax Is Down but Not Out." *National Tax Journal* 40(4): 567–75.

Rubin, Robert, and Jacob Weisberg. 2004. *In an Uncertain World: Tough Choices from Wall Street to Washington*. New York: Random House.

Ruggles, Patricia. 1990. *Drawing the Line: Alternative Poverty Measures and Their Implications for Public Policy*. Washington, DC: Urban Institute Press.

Sammartino, Frank J., C. Eugene Steuerle, and Adam Carasso. 2001. "Options for Revising the Child Credit." Washington, DC: The Urban Institute.

Sawhill, Isabel, and Adam Thomas. 2001. "A Tax Proposal for Working Families with Children." Welfare Reform and Beyond Brief No. 3. Washington, DC: The Brookings Institution.

Schick, Allen. 1990. *The Capacity to Budget.* Washington, DC: Urban Institute Press.

Schultze, Charles L. 1992. *Memos to the President: A Guide through Macroeconomics for the Busy Policymaker.* Washington, DC: The Brookings Institution.

Shaviro, Daniel N. Forthcoming. "Replacing the Income Tax with a Progressive Income Tax." Draft manuscript.

Simons, Henry. 1938. *Personal Income Taxation: The Definition of Income as a Problem of Fiscal Polity.* Chicago: The University of Chicago Press.

Skocpol, Theda. 1995. "The Rise and Resounding Demise of the Clinton Plan." *Health Affairs* 14(1): 66–85.

Slemrod, Joel. 1990. *Do Taxes Matter: The Impact of the Tax Reform Act of 1986.* Cambridge, MA: MIT Press.

———, ed. 1994. *Tax Progressivity and Income Inequality.* Boston: Cambridge University Press.

Slemrod, Joel, and Jon Bakija. 1996. *Taxing Ourselves: A Citizen's Guide to the Great Debate over Tax Reform.* Cambridge, MA: MIT Press.

Slemrod, Joel, and Marsha Blumenthal. 1993. "The Income Tax Compliance Cost of Big Business." The Office of Tax Policy Research, The University of Michigan, Report to the Tax Foundation.

Smith, Adam. 1904. *An Inquiry into the Nature and Causes of the Wealth of Nations*, edited by Edwin Cannan, vol. 2. London: Cambridge University Press.

Smith, Hedrick, Adam Clymer, Leonard Silk, Robert Lindsey, and Richard Burt. 1980. *Reagan: The Man, The President.* New York: Macmillan Publishing Co.

Social Security and Medicare Boards of Trustees. 2003. "Status of the Social Security and Medicare Programs: A Summary of the 2002 Annual Reports." Washington, DC: Social Security Administration.

Spragens, Janet. 2003. Panel Statement before the IRS Oversight Board on Enforcement Challenges. January 7, 2003.

Starobin, Paul. 1998. "Party Hoppers." *National Journal* 7(6): 276–81.

Stein, Herbert. 1969. *The Fiscal Revolution in America.* Chicago: The University of Chicago Press.

———. 1988. *Presidential Economics,* 2d ed. Washington, DC: The American Enterprise Institute.

———. 1994. *Presidential Economics: The Making of Economic Policy from Roosevelt to Clinton.* Washington, DC: The American Enterprise Institute.

———. 1998. *What I Think: Essays on Economics, Politics, and Life.* Washington, DC: The American Enterprise Institute.

Steuerle, C. Eugene. 1980. "Equity and the Taxation of Wealth Transfers." *Tax Notes* 10(September 8).

———. 1983a. "Building New Wealth by Preserving Old Wealth: Savings and Investment Tax Incentives in the Post War Era." *National Tax Journal* 36(3): 307–19.

———. 1983b. "The Tax Treatment of Households of Different Size." In *Taxing the Family*, edited by Rudolph G. Penner. Washington, DC: American Enterprise Institute.

————. 1985a. "The Prospects for Tax Reform." *National Tax Journal* 38(3): 291–94.

————. 1985b. *Taxes, Loans, and Inflation*. Washington, DC: The Brookings Institution.

————. 1986a. "The Federal Tax Reform Process: Issues and Implications." *National Tax Journal—Proceedings of the Seventy-Ninth Annual Conference*. Washington, DC: National Tax Association.

————. 1986b. "Lessons from the Tax Reform Process." *Tax Notes* 32(1).

————. 1986c. *Who Should Pay for Collecting Taxes? Financing the IRS*. Washington, DC: American Enterprise Institute.

————. 1987a. "Effects on Financial Decision-Making." In *Tax Reform and the U.S. Economy*, edited by Joseph A. Pechman. Washington, DC: The Brookings Institution.

————. 1987b. "The New Tax Law." In *Deficits, Taxes, and Economic Adjustments*, edited by Philip Cagan. Washington, DC: American Enterprise Institute.

————. 1988. "U.S. Tax Reform: Implications for Other Countries." In *World Tax Reform: A Progress Report*, edited by Joseph A. Pechman. Washington, DC: The Brookings Institution.

————. 1990a. "Federal Policy and the Accumulation of Private Debt in the Postwar United States." In *Debt, Taxes, and Corporate Reconstruction*, edited by John B. Shoven and Joel Waldfogel. Washington, DC: The Brookings Institution.

————. 1990b. "Tax Credits for Low-Income Workers with Children." *Journal of Economic Perspectives* 4(Summer): 201–12.

————. 1990c. "Tax Reform: Just How Sweet Was It?" In *The Impact of the Tax Reform Act of 1986: Did it Improve Fairness and Simplicity?* IRS Research Conference Report. Washington, DC: Internal Revenue Service.

————. 1991. "Effects of the Budget Process on Tax Legislation." In *Improving the Tax Legislative Process: A Critical Need*. Washington, DC: The American Tax Policy Institute and the ALI-ABA Committee on Continuing Education.

————. 1992a. "Enterprise Zones." Testimony before the U.S. Senate Committee on Finance. July 3.

————. 1992b. *The Tax Decade*. Washington, DC: Urban Institute Press.

————. 1996. "Financing the American State at the Turn of the Century." In *Funding the Modern American State, 1941–1995: The Rise and Fall of the Era of Easy Finance*, edited by W. Elliott Brownlee. Washington, DC: Woodrow Wilson Center Press and Cambridge University Press.

————. 2001a. "The 2001 Legislation from a Long-Term Perspective." *National Tax Journal* 54(3): 427–32.

————. 2001b. "Valuing Marital Commitment in Our Transfer and Tax Systems." Statement before the Subcommittee on Human Resources, Committee on Ways and Means, May 21. Washington, DC: U.S. House of Representatives.

————. 2002a. "And Equal (Tax) Justice for All." In *Tax Justice: The Ongoing Debate*, edited by Joseph J. Thorndike and Dennis J. Ventry, Jr. (253–84). Washington, DC: Urban Institute Press.

————. 2002b. "Can Policymakers Time the Ending of Macroeconomic Incentives?" *Tax Notes* 95(1, 3, 5): 121–22, 441–42, 789–90.

————. 2002c. "Defining Tax Shelters and Tax Arbitrage." *Tax Notes* 95(8).

————. 2002d. "The Remarkable Constancy in the Income Share of Corporate Capital." *Tax Notes* 96(14): 1905.

———. 2002e. "Some Future Directions for Public Finance." National Tax Association Presidential Address, Orlando, FL, November 14.

———. 2002f. "Some Implications of the Revenue Shortfall." *Tax Notes* 96(10): 1403–4.

———. 2002g. "Tax Policy from 1990 to 2001." In *American Economic Policy in the 1990s*, edited by Jeffrey Frankel and Peter Orszag (139–69). Boston, MA: MIT Press.

———. 2003a. "Can the Progressivity of Tax Changes Be Measured in Isolation?" *Tax Notes* 100(9): 1187–88.

———. 2003b. "Do We Really Need More Stimulus?" *Tax Notes* 98(4): 597–98.

———. 2003c. "The Incredible Shrinking Budget for Working Families and Children." National Budget Issues Brief No. 1. Washington, DC: The Urban Institute.

———. 2003d. "The Latest 'ZITCOM' and My New Tax Shelter Bank." *Tax Notes* 99(5).

Steuerle, C. Eugene, and Melissa Favreault. 2003. "Social Security for Yesterday's Family." Straight Talk on Social Security and Retirement Policy Policy Brief No. 35. Washington, DC: The Urban Institute.

Steuerle, C. Eugene, and Michael Hartzmark. 1981. "Individual Income Taxation, 1947–1979." *National Tax Journal* 34(2).

Steuerle, C. Eugene, and Paul Wilson. 1987. "The Earned Income Tax Credit." *Focus* 10. Madison, WI: University of Wisconsin, Institute for Research on Poverty.

Stockman, David A. 1986. *The Triumph of Politics: How the Regan Revolution Failed*. New York: Harper and Row.

———. 1994. "Summary of Discussion." In *American Economic Policy in the 1980s*, edited by Martin S. Feldstein. Chicago: University of Chicago Press.

Sullivan, Martin B. 1999. "One Shelter at a Time?" *Tax Notes* 85(10).

———. 2002a. "Corporate Tax Revenues: Up, Down, and All Around." *Tax Notes* 94(12).

———. 2002b. "Shelter Disclosure Could Help Economists... and the Economy." *Tax Notes* 96(8).

———. 2003. "Economic Analysis: Is the Corporate Tax Withering Away?" *Tax Notes* 98(February 10): 878.

Surrey, Stanley S., and Paul McDaniel. 1985. *Tax Expenditures*. Cambridge, MA: Harvard University Press.

Suskind, Ron. 2003. *The Price of Loyalty: George W. Bush, the White House, and the Education of Paul O'Neill.* New York: Simon and Schuster.

Tate, Dale. 1981. "Dispute over Tax Increases Stalls Action on 1982 Budget." Congressional Quarterly, November 7.

Tax Analysts Calendar. 1997. Washington, DC: Tax Notes.

Tax Foundation, The. 2003. "State Individual Income Tax Rates as of December 31, 2002" (Table). http://taxfoundation.org/individualincometaxrates01.html. (Accessed November 2003.)

Thorndike, Joseph J. 2003. "Andrew Mellon." *Tax Notes* 99(3).

———. 2004 "The Price of Civilization: Revenue, Reform, and the American Debates over Tax Justice." Washington, DC: The Urban Instititute and the Brookings Institution.

Thorndike, Joseph J., and Dennis J. Ventry, eds. 2002. *Tax Justice: The Ongoing Debate.* Washington, DC: Urban Institute Press.

Toder, Eric J. 1998. "The Changing Composition of Tax Incentives: 1980–1999." *National Tax Association Proceedings, 91st Annual Conference.* Washington, DC: National Tax Association.

———. 2000. "Tax Cuts or Spending: Does It Make a Difference?" *National Tax Journal* 53(1): 361–72.

Toner, Robin. 1995. "Battle over the Budget: The Republicans." *New York Times.* November 16.

U.S. Department of Commerce, Bureau of Economic Analysis. 2003. *Survey of Current Business.* Washington, DC: Superintendent of Documents.

U. S. Department of the Treasury. 1977. "Blueprints for Basic Tax Reform." Washington, DC: U.S. Government Printing Office.

———. 1984. "Tax Reform for Fairness, Simplicity, and Economic Growth." Washington, DC: Department of the Treasury.

———. 1990a. *Financing Health and Long-Term Care: Report to the President and the Congress.* Washington, DC: Superintendent of Documents.

———. 1990b. "Higher Income Taxpayers Pay a Larger Share of Income Taxes." *Treasury News*, November 2. Washington, DC: U.S. Department of the Treasury.

———. 1995. "Clinton Budget Proposes $63 Billion Tax Cut." *Treasury News*, February 6. Washington, DC: U.S. Department of the Treasury.

U.S. House of Representatives, Committee on Ways and Means. 1990. *1990 Green Book.* Washington, DC: U.S. Government Printing Office.

———. 1996. *1996 Green Book.* Washington, DC: U.S. Government Printing Office.

———. 2000. *2000 Green Book.* Washington, DC: U.S. Government Printing Office.

Verdier, James M. 1988. "The President, Congress and Tax Reform: Pattern over Three Decades." *Annals of the American Academy of Political and Social Science* 499(September): 114–23.

Vidal, Gore. 2001. "The Meaning of Timothy McVeigh." *Vanity Fair.* September.

Waldman, Michael. 2000. *POTUS Speaks.* New York: Simon & Schuster.

Wall Street Journal. 1987. October 20.

Weisman, Jonathan. 2003. "Estate Tax Compromise Sought." *The Washington Post.* June 18.

Witte, John F. 1985. *The Politics and Development of the Federal Income Tax.* Madison, WI: University of Wisconsin Press.

———. 1991a. "Congress and Tax Policy: Problems and Reforms in a Historical Context." In *Improving the Tax Legislative Process—A Critical Need.* Washington, DC: American Tax Policy Institute, ALI-ABA Committee on Continuing Education, and the National Tax Association.

———. 1991b. "The 1986 Tax Reform: A New Era in Politics?" *American Politics Quarterly* 19:438–57.

Woodward, Bob. 1994. *The Agenda: Inside the Clinton White House.* New York: Simon & Schuster.

Yin, George. 2001. "Getting Serious about Corporate Tax Shelters: Taking a Lesson from History." *SMU Law Review* 54(209).

———. 2002. "The Problem of Corporate Tax Shelters: Uncertain Dimensions, Unwise Approaches." *Tax Law Review* 55(3): 405–26.

Zodrow, George R., and Peter Mieszkowski, eds. 2002. *United States Tax Reform in the 21st Century.* Cambridge, MA: Cambridge University Press.

About the Author

Eugene Steuerle is a senior fellow at The Urban Institute, codirector of the Urban-Brookings Tax Policy Center, columnist for *Tax Notes*, and the author or editor of 11 books, more than 150 reports and articles, 50 Congressional testimonies or reports, and 600 columns. He serves on the National Committee on Vital and Health Statistics and on advisory panels or boards for the Congressional Budget Office, the General Accounting Office, the Joint Committee on Taxation, the Actuarial Foundation, and the Independent Sector.

Dr. Steuerle has previously served as president of the National Tax Association (2001–2002), chair of the 1999 technical panel advising Social Security on its methods and assumptions, president of the National Economists Club Educational Foundation, deputy assistant secretary of the Treasury for tax analysis (1987–1989), and resident fellow at the American Enterprise Institute. Between 1984 and 1986, he served as economic coordinator and original organizer of the Treasury's tax reform effort.

Index